Voices RISING

Voices RISING

CELEBRATING 20 YEARS OF BLACK LESBIAN, GAY, BISEXUAL & TRANSGENDER WRITING

Edited by
**G. Winston James
and Other Countries**

REDBONE PRESS
WASHINGTON, DC
www.redbonepress.com

Voices Rising: Celebrating 20 Years of Black Lesbian, Gay, Bisexual and Transgender Writing (Other Countries Volume III)

Copyright © 2007 by G. Winston James and Other Countries

Individual selections copyright © by their respective author(s)

Published by:
RedBone Press
P.O. Box 15571
Washington, DC 20003

11 10 09 08 07   10 9 8 7 6 5 4 3 2 1

First edition

Cover photograph copyright © 1997 by G. Winston James
Cover design by D'Mon McNeil
Book design by Eunice Corbin

Permissions acknowledgments begin on page 576
Printed in the United States of America

ISBN-13: 978-0-9786251-3-9
ISBN-10: 0-9786251-3-7
ISSN: 0893-8296

www.redbonepress.com

"Our history is each other. That is our only guide."
—James Baldwin, *Just Above My Head*

contents

preface

Voices Rising marks the twentieth anniversary of Other Countries, a powerful, far-reaching and deliberate legacy of community expression that began when Daniel Garrett invoked James Baldwin's line "Our history is each other" to convene black gay men to a writing workshop on June 14, 1986—the same New York City summer that gave birth to Gay Men of African Descent and Adodi. One of Other Countries' early commitments was to publishing, producing our first volume *Other Countries: Black Gay Voices* in 1988, which won a Coordinating Council on Literary Magazines award, and five years later *Sojourner: Black Gay Voices in the Age of AIDS*, which won the Lambda Literary Award for small presses.

A collection of sixty-five black gay, lesbian, bisexual and transgender voices, *Voices Rising* breaks brand new ground for Other Countries in two exciting ways. This unique anthology is the first co-gender project undertaken by the group, which began as and remains an organization of black gay men. Despite repeated discussion of the idea, and one effort at doing so, black women were never truly included in the Other Countries writing workshop, which over fifteen years functioned as an important "safe space" where black gay and gender-nonconforming men gathered for conversation and kinship, and many learned to write. *Voices Rising* took shape on the borders of that weekly workshop, from a vision that the anthology would include and serve as a bridge among members of the black gay, lesbian, bisexual and transgender communities. The wealth of talent collected here, and the creation and sharing of art itself, are remarkable foundations upon which to build and strengthen community. In a departure from Other Countries' two previous publications, which included visual art, the pages of *Voices Rising* exclusively celebrate the written word and the personal, political and cultural complexity that writing so well represents. We hope that individuals from all corners of our black GLBT community, and the world, will be enriched, challenged and expanded by the breadth and intelligence of the work they find here.

Additionally, our partnership with RedBone Press in publishing this volume represents an important political and practical gesture we wish to underscore. Other Countries chose this strategy over selling the manuscript to a corporate press or continuing our past practice of independently publishing. Our relationship with RedBone Press reflects our recognition of Lisa C. Moore's success in building a production and distribution infrastructure for work like ours, the importance of supporting and strengthening entities that not only produce such work but have the capacity and commitment to keep that work in print and in wide distribution, and the flexibility RedBone Press promised in honoring Other Countries' history and autonomy.

Collaborative cultural products do not arrive in the world bloodlessly, however. We want this preface to reveal some of the complexity of the fifteen-year gestation of this book and, with the genuine grace one employs at a birth, to acknowledge the range of actors and to celebrate the distinct value choices that were part of that messy process.

G(lenroy) Winston James jealously parented the book over ten years of both progress and stagnation, and his editorial craft more than anyone else's is reflected here. We are eager to recognize, without shade or disrespect, both the yearlong co-editorial collaboration of Reginald T. Jackson and a sad and lengthy dispute that left the project's editorial future again in Glenroy's hands alone. We also acknowledge earlier co-editorial players Christopher Adams, Anthony Brown, Geoffrey Freeman and the late Nene Ofuatey-Kodjoe and Adrian Reynolds who, for various reasons and at various points, entered, exited and re-engaged with the project. We salute the book's "midhusbands," a small group of Other Countries "godmothers" who, along with Glenroy, shepherded its final delivery into the world (a fundamentally practical exercise that proved elusive for far too long), and who took responsibility for the business judgment to depart from Other Countries' tradition to date of self-publishing. Mirroring the administrative roles they played in Other Countries' first effort at publishing, Terence Taylor and Cary Alan Johnson took special leadership in the publication process; Colin Robinson, with the help of his organization the New York State Black Gay Network, provided the sometimes questionable 2004-5 planning framework from which the group's leadership emerged; Kevin McGruder's steadfastness and Doug Jones' insights completed this group, along with Len Richardson's early involvement.

The book also embodies some humbling aspects of community economics and organization. Two black gay writers used their personal philanthropy to sustain the work and organization they helped parent, even beyond their deaths. Assotto Saint, a publisher himself (Galiens Press), and Bert Michael Hunter, who edited *Sojourner*, both bequeathed funds to Other Countries that enabled this project. (Special thanks go to Bert's executor John Manzon-Santos who took additional interest in the success of the project.)

Voices Rising's publication also finalizes a process through which Other Countries has reclaimed our identity and functioning, reversing a 1999 decision to cease administrative autonomy and fold our program activities under the umbrella of Gay Men of African Descent. We acknowledge Tokes Osubu's respect for that choice and—what was not an easy decision for a small nonprofit—his agreement to return Other Countries funds to our control. Though the process was, by its nature, not perfect, Tokes and Susan Li honored their promises to us.

Through other fiscal sponsors—including the New York Foundation for the Arts—the Jerome and Stonewall Foundations and NYFA itself made past awards to Other Countries for general support and this publishing project. Those of us involved with *Voices Rising* have done our best to responsibly steward such funds by applying them to this publication. The Publishing Triangle also contributed knowledge and technical support to Other Countries and this project as it developed. And Rien Murray lovingly directed the Black Gay Network planning work.

In these pages are the collected works of literary artists, both known and until now unknown, living and deceased, who recognized the importance of their stories, and the beauty and effectiveness of the written word. Talent, craft and poignancy were the main criteria for inclusion in *Voices Rising*. So it is with a sense of both regret and joy that we admit that there are many other writers and works that could have been included in this volume, and that we have merely sampled from the ever-increasing pool of talented U.S.-based writers. We thank all those who trusted us with their work, continued to do so over the years that the manuscript remained unpublished, and cooperated with us in the final permissions process. We especially acknowledge the heirs and executors of contributors who died while the publication was in process.

Other Countries is a legacy to which many can now lay various and particular claims, as creators, kin, students, witnesses, supporters or heirs, and in which we invite you to seize your own ownership. Created at a powerful historical moment at which feminism, GLBT people of color organizing and HIV intertwined to unhinge closets and untie tongues, and rooted in a re-excavation of the Harlem Renaissance's queerness and the lessons of black feminist expression, Other Countries was catalyzed from the immediate lineage of the Blackheart Collective and Joseph Beam's anthology *In the Life*. For twenty years we have made lasting contributions to public consciousness about desire, community and identity. We have nurtured committed writers and created talented writers out of many who came mainly for connection. We have preserved their work in print; and have taken these words, through both publication and performance, into diverse community and artistic spaces, including gay bars, community centers, elite museums and universities, and public schools. And we have engaged in the often historically unrecognized struggles with organizational infrastructure, process and personality that community artistic processes undergo.

Other Countries' mission to nurture, disseminate and preserve black gay expression is nourished by the soil tilled by such writers as James Baldwin, Joseph Beam, Steven Corbin, Melvin Dixon, Angelina Weld Grimké, Lorraine Hansberry, Craig

Harris, Essex Hemphill, Terri Jewell, June Jordan, Audre Lorde, Alice Dunbar Nelson, Richard Bruce Nugent, Pat Parker, Marlon Riggs, Assotto Saint, Adrian Stanford and Donald Woods, and it is their seeds of creativity and courage that have enabled the voices of today's crop of writers to rise. A milestone marking our two decades of building on that heritage, *Voices Rising: Celebrating 20 Years of Black Lesbian, Gay, Bisexual and Transgender Writing* continues Other Countries' service to black gay writers and the communities to which we belong and in which we work. It celebrates how deeper, fuller, and continually more complex our community's voices grow as they continue, relentlessly, to rise.

—Other Countries, December 2006

introduction

by Dorothy Randall Gray

This is a visitation. A gathering of spirits ancient and new. An earthquake of excellence unparalleled in the history of publication.

It is an answer to a call heard amidst the whispered prayers and loud silences, the righteous clamor of protest and passion, joy, and sorrow and sweet dreams.

It is a resounding reply to Lucy, unearthed from the bowels of Africa and named first woman. Lucy, calling for her sons and daughters to come home, not as separate but equal vessels sailing the middle passage of a literary aesthetic, but as family, brothers and sisters, survivors of the fittest.

This is *Voices Rising*, a homecoming named first reminder of the kindred spirit we share as black lesbian, gay, bisexual and transgendered children of Lucy. *Voices Rising*, a dazzling compilation of the bones beneath the blood, the sinew and fiber of our existence in all of its painful brilliance.

This book comes home celebrating ancestral landscapes of the past, the power of the present, and the poignant promise of the future. It comes adorned with the armor of our love, filling its pages with silk and studs and leather and lace, boot and Birkenstock realities. The arcane archeology of our lives wrapped in poetry and prose.

Voices Rising comes with spirits dancing between its sheets, sitting on shoulders, daring us to carry on, to remember, to write as if we could not breathe without our words. These visceral voices from bygone days lie in wait behind each page. I heard them sing to me of how our lives had crossed, and how they had lived their days.

Essex Hemphill daring to be black and gay and fiercely eloquent in a deep south reading with Sonia Sanchez, Sapphire, and Imamu Baraka. Terri Jewell, weighing her last thoughts before taking her last breath, a colored girl who did more than consider suicide.

Assotto Saint in his Haitian divaness, arranging his own funeral, dictating whom he did and did not want to have reading poetry at his service. Danitra Vance, a neighborhood girl living on Sterling Place while making a living on *Saturday Night Live*. Dellon Wilson, elegant with pride, receiving transfusions of blood and music while serving poetry and dance, culture and commitment.

I also heard the pioneering activism of Ruth Waters, the ferocious colors of Michael Kendall, and the fighting spirit of Maua Yvonnè Flowers losing her fingers before losing her life. I heard the power of Donald Woods, the effervescence of Roy Gonsalves, and the southerness of Trey Johnson. I heard names I don't hear often enough. I stood witness to their passing, to their memorials in Brooklyn and Boston, in the Village and in the vestal regions of the cities that fed them.

And it is all in this book, between these stirring lines and in the splendid souls who had the courage to create them. A fulfillment of our diasporic destiny. A legacy carried forth from our foremothers and forefathers, from the voices of all who could not finish their song.

This is *Voices Rising*, monumental and magnificent. A home for your spirit to dwell in. Hold this history in your hands, listen to its incantations, and let them live inside your heart. Lucy is well pleased.

kumasi
by Eva Yaa Asantewaa

I.
hours late, buses stumbling
into kumasi
bear tourists—groggy
or jittery with hunger

from my window,
i watch a boy's head twist
toward the sound of our buses
laboring through red waves of dust

he cries, *they are coming!*

goats skitter in muddy gutters
like new york pigeons

as from dismal shacks and fruit stands,
children pelt toward us, cheering at

every window holding a tourist
and every tourist expecting
what tourists expect

the smell of palm
seeps into black american cells and
we are married to palm

bounteous,
the soul of the land rises
through green veins

fish, grits, roots,
fingers licked clean—
all smell deep with palm

the ashante chief parks
his mercedes down the road
and lunges around the sacred circle,
beneath scarlet trimmed in gold

as dancers, smeared with white,
swing dark machetes

savoring the feel of flesh,
spirits clothe themselves in bodies,
bumping around, tipsy on blood

II.
i follow the black american chief's
robust daughter into the circle,
watching her back, her hands

pumping from her bosom
to the open air, legs jutting,
braids lashing her cheeks and neck

sticks smack drums with brutal pings.

my arms lengthen beyond their length,
my hips propelled by cowbells, and
i am blind to the self

motion...air on some close
intangible membrane
all i know

a touch...someone guides me to the stands

someone has left me

the black american chief smirks,
inclines to the ear of one of his wives

has he won a bet:
who will be the next tourist
snatched up by a spirit?

"it's all on video," he says with a nod
toward the acolyte bearing a sony,

but i know i will never see the tape.

hips 'n' ass
(dancing through the ages)
by Eva Yaa Asantewaa

This poem is in itself a kind of evolving dance, moving forward and backward and sideways in time and geography, sampling time, overlapping cultures and personal experiences. Nonlinear, a collage of memory and sensation, of color and sound. The experience of one baby in her mother's womb (as her mom listens to Latin and Caribbean music) and of one girl growing into womanhood within the rich diversity of the world. The story of that world itself.

all history lives in the hips
'n' ass
try to tell me that ain't true
here's how we remember
how we move
forward
first time suspended in time and space
time held by the sea and rocking
rocking rocking towards land
mah tilda mah tilda mah tilda not waltzing
mah tilda run venezuela not waltzing the time
not three-quarters time sometime after ten
humid august
summer's here and the time is
morning run venezuela sounds of cowbells clave
oh clave and the clinking
of beer bottles sounding all the way from harlem
or bed-stuy sizzling streets
bus rocking rocking not waltzing
all through the mountains
where coolness waits
and flutes filling sails that sail beyond familiar
langston hughes would say it's as clean
as a summer sun hips rocking

shoulders swaying the sea the sea held me
here's how we remember
how we move forward
vibrations tito puente dizzy calypso sparrow
spilling spilling spilling a rainforest
waterfall no mountain high enough sound
motion and i dance because i'm happy
i dance because i'm free delivered into sun
like any other great green desire green pirouette
electric emerald slide eyes turned inward coast of
salvador do bahia streets of motown ile-ife
heart a calabash spine a royal palm asway
feeling mighty real mighty sparrow
suspended in time and space her eye is *on*
it's on
a taksim tracing the moon
as she spends her silver lavishly
racing shooting stars
a kashlimar
in the beginning
was undulating
serpent flame-breathing dragon
skakti
on her way through and over the rainbow
so why can't i
why can't i
why can't i
try to tell me that ain't true
this is how we remember
how we move
forward

Sojourner:
an abandoned manifest
by Colin Robinson

for Bert Hunter

More than a year ago, I began to sketch what was to be our publishers' preface for *Sojourner: Black Gay Voices in the Age of AIDS*:

> Three metaphors—generation, location, and voice—haunt my reading of Black Gay writing. And tonight, somewhere in a basement in Boupaloupa, MS, a Black boy is bent over in a basement reading James Baldwin by flashlight, far from the sound of my voice.

> *across the globe*
> *the itchy terrain of our earth life*
> *dark continents we*

> *roll condoms on our tongues*
> *in a round of minor*
> *discords and fleeting harmonies*

> *amputees all*
> *severed at the lips*
> *on the virgin kiss*
> *of brotherhood*

In April 1988, ending a labor that had drawn on for a year and a half, the *Other Countries* journal (the poetry section of which opens with these lines from Donald Woods) was born. In the introduction to *that* volume, I celebrated with our readers the birth of this "new manchild," his 50-year genealogy "in the small but growing canon of Black Gay Male literature," and the significance of the name we had chosen for him. Simultaneously claiming our place on the shoulders of our ancestors and acknowledging our journey into territory they had *not* attained, we celebrated on the dedication page the lives of three black gay forebears—James Baldwin, Bruce Nugent and Bayard Rustin—all of whom had died the year before.

Only five years later, there have been just as many black gay male publications since *Other Countries* as before. There have been black gay films and videos. And there have been many, many more black gay deaths... Over 40,000 black gay men have been diagnosed with AIDS, including ten of the men who made *Other Countries* possible, who are dead, and at least four other men who worked on the first volume who are living with or ailing with HIV. It is now the lives of our own generation to which we dedicate *Sojourner*.

When the four-man Other Countries board first contemplated the dedication of this volume, there were only four people on the list of "AIDS dead," whose names the book would remember. We parried our frustration at the slow progress of this project (much like the first) into cynical humor, noting the growing list of dedicatees as we lost men in the Other Countries community to HIV; and we wondered how long the list would be by the time our project was finally accomplished. Our "list of dead people" was more than three times its initial length when *Sojourner* was published—and three more names have been added since. *Sojourner* has been *too* long in coming.

When in 1989 an education director at the Studio Museum in Harlem had the uncertain idea over late-night fried chicken that black gay writers, one of whom he knew, might have *something* to say about AIDS, my response was: "But what else do we write about?" Though it was with some hesitation, we accepted this role of representing AIDS, knowing, however, that it was our legitimacy as the voices of AIDS, not of our sexual identity/culture, that had gained us entry to one of the gatekeeping institutions of black culture.

Acquired Visions: Seeing Ourselves through AIDS was performed as part of the museum's observance of World AIDS Day/A Day without Art. The performance began with a reflection on censorship and silence, a collage of: our videotaped reflections on HIV and writing/Lyle Harris' photography/television news clips/a newspaper story on the NEA's withdrawal of its grant to Artists Space over David Wojnorowicz's exhibit, "Witnesses against our Vanishing"/Assotto Saint's "Remembrance & a Revelation," which begins "I Want to Celebrate those Cocks…"/Brad Johnson's work in the first journal "On Subjugation"; and it ended with the beginning of our list, the unveiling of Names Quilt panels made by Assotto Saint for the first—and then still the only—three men in Other Countries lost to HIV, as we performed Michelle Lanchester's song "Patchwork Quilt": "And I remember your names…"

Other Countries' tradition of presenting our work in performance had begun in black gay bars as fundraisers for the first volume of the publication. The final fundraiser for that volume was held a few days after publication—it was our third time at TRACKS/NY, and we were in deficit. Outside, unscrupulous Other Countries volunteers skirmished with TRACKS bouncers as we handed out flyers (each of which won us a portion of the door's proceeds) at the corner a block away from the club. Inside, Samuel Delany read sections from *The Motion of Light in Water*, reflecting on the role of the HIV epidemic in shaping the future of sexual consciousness and discourse—after we had turned off the dance music at 1 a.m. After Chip was dismissed by the crowd as "Santa Claus," the main attraction of our *Libido Lit 101* performance, porn star Joe Simmons, was heckled to shut up and take off his clothes as he tried to read a poem by Steve Langley (*i am/chocolate candy/a handful of cookies/the goodies you are/forbidden to eat*)—much less eloquently than he fucks. And Assotto Saint, in drag, went one on one with another heckler, reading him as a "queen with no countries," while she (Assotto) "had *Other* Countries to rule over," and for being nothing, whereas Assotto was "published"—and therefore "immortal."

Like *Acquired Visions*, *Sojourner* brings together this naming of the dead with that other enterprise in which Other

Countries is rooted, reflected in Assotto's signification that night at TRACKS and which Donald Woods names so well in the epigraph chosen for *Sojourner*:

> *sit and write down your writing*
> *you can memorize your fingers at a keyboard*
> *you can leave micro bytes of your living*
> *to be deciphered by*
> *people who loved to love you*
> *who hated to hate you and*
> *loved to hate you and hated to love you all*
> *out of fear and no damn choice*

Likewise, at the closing ceremony of the 1992 OutWrite conference in Boston, former Other Countries board member Melvin Dixon hauntingly gave tribute to his own impending passage, noting that he, like others, will be somewhere listening for his name, and reminding us that we must "guard against the erasure of our experience and our lives," that "our voice is our weapon."

Sojourner is as much about "seeing through AIDS" as it is part of the work of "seeing AIDS through"—about the celebration of a community and communal rituals which both structure our failures in the face of HIV and fortify us to transcend this epidemic.

Assotto observes in his introduction to *The Road Before Us* that "In gay black poetry, [HIV] has been primarily dealt with from a third-person narrative rather than a first-person focus," and he makes the case there, as he also has jumping onto a table at the end of The Long Read (a six-hour fundraiser for *Sojourner*) or rushing uninvited to the front of the church at Donald Woods' funeral, that "when we don't show en masse the lives, the faces, and the hearts of AIDS—ours included—we are accepting all the connotations of shame, all the mystification of sin and repentance…"

And as much as I disagree with Assotto, I admire him

profoundly, for as Audre Lorde has taught us so well, it is our *language* (as black gay men living with HIV) which can imagine a future and transcend our current realities.

Sojourner was grounded in a vision, captured in former Other Countries board member Reginald Jackson's image of a boy in the darkness of a basement in Boupaloupa, Mississippi, reading Baldwin by flashlight. It was this Boupaloupa basement that he challenged prospective editors of the volume to reach. And, five years after his older brother's birth, *Sojourner*'s is equally inspired by the "challenge of…leaving something valuable and permanent of our Black Gay lives for our future generations," by the work we must continue of conjuring ourselves—as Other Countries' founder Daniel Garrett, put it so eloquently almost ten years ago:

> …*I begin to grasp the largeness of the work before us, the fact that we are not only creating essays or poems or stories, but the fact that we are creating culture. We are expressing ourselves as a people, and shaping the consciousness of ourselves as a people. We are creating ourselves.*

What are the voices of the age of AIDS we are leaving for the black boy in that Boupaloupa basement as he creates himself? Through writing we must not only remember our dead, but we must seize on that original metaphor of *generation* and continue to recreate ourselves, to generate the living.

I never finished the introduction… I gave up management of the *Sojourner* project and, angry at Eddy over sex and angry at Donald's death, I left the Other Countries board.

Recently, in North Carolina, at a national lesbian/gay conference, I met Terence—a 24-year-old from Detroit who had spent twenty-four hours on a bus to get there, who had heard a tape of me reading my letter to Joe Beam that's in *Sojourner* at another gay conference in California, and who shared with me how important it was to him for Joe Beam, whose words had inspired him immensely, to be made real in my piece.

Now granted Reggie's Boupaloupa boy may never make it to a national conference, but I began to believe again in that vision of the boy in that basement with the batteries running out in that flashlight. And all those voices that had run out were suddenly mysteriously alive in the echoes of that damp, dimly lit, resonant basement.

Charles Angel... Reginald Patterson... Michael Evans... Redvers Jeanmarie... Joseph Beam... Allan Williams... David Frechette... Craig Harris... Rory Buchanan... BJ Carr... Cliff Goodman... Melvin Dixon... Donald Woods... Bruce Neill... Errol Edwards... David Weems... Roy Gonsalves... Rodney Dildy... Sabah as-Sabah... B.Michael Hunter: Perhaps tonight, somewhere in a basement in Mississippi, a young black boy is crouching in a basement reading *Sojourner* by flashlight, far from the sound of your voice.

Originally begun as a draft preface to Sojourner: Black Gay Voices in the Age of AIDS, *this piece was first read in an earlier version on December 10, 1993 at a post-publication reading for the anthology hosted by Gay Men of African Descent at New York City's Lesbian and Gay Community Services Center.*

It is the mission of the Boy Scouts of America to serve others by helping to instill values in young people and, in other ways, to prepare them to make ethical choices over their lifetime in achieving their full potential.

> *Mission Statement of the Boy Scouts of America,*
> *as quoted in Supreme Court of the United States,*
> *Opinion No. 99-699*

The Boy Scouts of America has always reflected the expectations that Scouting families have had for the organization. We do not believe that homosexuals provide a role model consistent with these expectations. Accordingly, we do not allow for the registration of avowed homosexuals as members or leaders of the BSA.

> *Postion Statement (1993) promulgated by the BSA*
> *after James Dale's adult membership was revoked*
> *by Monmouth Council (BSA) in New Jersey,*
> *as quoted in Supreme Court of the United States,*
> *Opinion No. 99-699, June 28, 2000*

Learning to Speak Heterosexual
by Robert E. Penn

It's very quiet except for a cricket, or two, and the crackling fire, which dries the mild autumn air. A lightning bug flies toward the campfire just as Mr. Carpenter lifts another tree trunk with one hand and adds it to the roaring stack. Sparks leap toward the bug but it manages to rise higher, ahead of the flames and certain death.

There are eleven of us around the fire this weekend. We took a vow of silence before leaving the church where we meet: We promised to sit still —no pushing or shoving—on the long bus trip to Mound Builder Camp, and to remain silent throughout tonight and tomorrow. We are being tested for induction into the Order of the Arrow, the famous, elite Boy Scout group. This is different from working on merit badges and ranks.

Before this trip, I read everything I could find about the Order. I like to read and I wanted to be as prepared as I could be. The Order of the Arrow (OA for short) is a core group of Boy Scouts and Explorer Scouts who are in touch with nature. We are trackers in the old-fashioned way—like American Indian braves, African hunters or South Pacific fishermen.

The circle seems too small to hold Mr. Carpenter's campfire. Even the darkest face is bleached by its light and heat. I can see Roy through the flames. I only know him from our Scout troop. He's the only one of us with a mustache so far. We tease him and call it peach fuzz, but I can't wait until I grow one, too.

Lonnie, my next-door neighbor, is the youngest inductee. He's a third of the way around the circle to my left. We used to be together all the time. Now, I can look at him out of the corner of my eye without turning my head.

My buddy, Jimmy, is right next to me. We earned five merit badges together last summer. His dark hands are resting on his knees. Jimmy's not doing anything. He's just there and his veins are popping. Shoot! Jimmy looks strong even when he's sitting around the campfire.

I want to look right at Jimmy and tell him how happy I am that we paddle canoes and row boats together but I promised not to move or speak. I feel safe on the lake with him because I know if I have a fainting spell and can't row, he will get us back to shore, quickly and safely.

The coach from grade school teased me about the one time I fainted. I was running fast, about to dash over the 100-yard line. Then, all of a sudden, my head got hot and the veins in my neck beat faster than a drum. I was really mad that my father had forced me to run. I said, "No," but he pretended not to hear me. I wanted to pull out of the meet, but my parents were there and I had to keep running even though I thought my head was going to blow off. Nothing could stop me now. I wanted to win if I could and then never have to prove anything to anyone ever again; never have to play sports again. But my head floated up and I fell down. I was publicly embarrassed because my father made me go out for sports.

I tried to convince Daddy that I don't need sports. What I want is to make art and study ballet. Daddy doesn't change; he just repeats the same argument, "Boys run track and play ball. Sports make you a man." After each of my athletic failures, he just makes me try another sport.

I can't turn to Jimmy, so I look into Lonnie's eyes instead. I know him very well. He looks beyond me: The message is something about don't look at me 'cause I think I'm going to crack up sitting around this stupid fire in silence. What is this stuff anyway? If Dad hadn't made me come here, you can believe I wouldn't be here. And I answer, transmit to him: If we were at home you could come over and spend the night again. We could bring the small television into my room and watch a scary movie and hold each other tight, then before falling asleep we could play our guessing game. One of us thinks of a section of his body and the other one has to touch him in different places until he gets the right part. I like that. Lonnie cracks a smile at me for a split second then looks down at the fire to keep from laughing.

I look into the flames, too. Lonnie and I have pulled off some major stunts, right in church. No one suspects us because we do everything they ask: we're in the Scouts, the youth choir, Sunday school, junior ushers, everything. Adults see us doing all the "right" things, so they can't imagine us doing anything "bad." They don't want to.

Lonnie and I are also into sneaking under the church stage and messing around with each other's weeny. That's what we used to call it. Now we're almost teenagers. (Well, I am anyway. Lonnie has two more years to go.) We know that it's really a dick, like Dick Tracy. That's what the boys in our junior high call it. Doctor Jenkins calls it a penis. I heard some white kids at summer camp call it a cock. That's what we call what a girl has. Somebody said white boys are like girls, anyway.

Two years ago, Lonnie and I did something very dangerous together. I mean we could have gotten into a lot of trouble, but we didn't get caught. It was my idea. And Lonnie liked my plan. Well, we were going to sing in the children's choir on Children's Day and we were going to stand next to each other among the other tenors. Lonnie was going to stand to my right. So we cut a hole in my right pants pocket and another one in his left pants pocket. We agreed to wear old baggy underwear. On Children's Day, we choir members wore new short, white robes with the church initials embroidered over the heart. The smocks fit very loosely. The sleeves hung like drapes. You could wriggle your arm and the pleats in the sleeve barely moved. During the performance, Lonnie reached into my right pocket and I reached into his left pocket. I held his dick and he held mine. It was exciting to sing in church in front of everyone while playing with your friend's thing. And it felt good, too.

I smile inside as I remember that feeling. My dick is hard now. I pretend to look respectfully down at the ground so that I can make sure no one can see it. I slowly move my hand close to my dick so I can touch it through the fabric. No one can see. It feels so warm when I push it against my thigh. I lose myself inside with my happy daydream and gaze absentmindedly across the fire.

Peach-fuzz Roy smiles at me, his lips wide enough for everyone to see. He looks right into my eyes. His hands are face down in his lap. That boy is up to no good. During summer camp, he skinned a frog ALIVE. Then he went and showed it to everyone, bragging. His feathery mustache reflects the flames, which accentuate his pointy ears. He really looks like a devil now.

Without moving my head, I look to my right just when Mr. Carpenter stands up. He circles the fire, stirring it but not adding any more logs. His silhouette throws a massive shadow on each one of us as he passes. He begins humming something. His voice is a deep and rich bass. My eyes follow him around the fire, in front of and behind the blaze, in shadow and in light. He slows down after one full revolution and moans something primitive and heartfelt.

The fire is almost out. Mr. Carpenter still circles, in slow motion. His voice grows louder, soulful. He is screeching now but still not saying anything I understand, like he's speaking in tongues.

I think I see something moving, a faint outline behind Roy. I must be dreaming. Or maybe I'm just letting Mr. Carpenter scare me. I can't let him do that. OA members show no fear. I won't fear.

An owl hoots.

And out of nowhere, people camouflaged in animal skins, leaves and blankets jump behind each of us inductees. They are synchronized and rehearsed to perfection because before I can see what is happening behind Roy, I feel strong hands pressing my shoulders down hard. My butt is forced into the rough surface of the tree trunk we used for a bench. I freeze. Thank God I don't wet my pants.

Mr. Carpenter stops. Perspiration glistens red and gold on his jet black skin. I want to free myself of the grip that's pushing me into the bark, but I don't dare. Mr. Carpenter speaks in a very serious voice as if he were praying. "Members of the Order of the Arrow represent a long tradition of providers. We are the most fit men. We care for those around us. We hunt, fish, plant and protect. We don't do this for selfish reasons, but for the survival of our loved ones: our parents, sisters and brothers and wives."

Roy erupts in laughter. Mr. Carpenter glares at him and then nods at the mysterious person behind him. The shadow lifts Roy out of the circle. Roy continues laughing, mocking Mr. Carpenter, then he smiles at me and jiggles his zipper. It catches the light of the dancing flames. Roy unzips his pants, bold and taunting, so everyone can see. My dick gets hard. The frog skinner's apparition jerks him away from the campfire. They disappear into the dark.

Roy's laughter crackles back to us through the dark mantle of the forest. Mr. Carpenter ignores it and continues, "Tonight is a time of silence to consider your responsibilities to your family, to this troop, to your church, your neighborhood and to our people. Without them, we have no purpose." Roy's laughter fades, drowned by the desiccated leaves and overpowered by the chirping crickets, hooting owls, buzzing beetles and a lone screeching falcon. He and his warden can no longer be seen or heard.

"Now walk in silence through the woods with your guides, who are already the hunters, pioneers, warriors and providers each of you may become tonight. Consider the importance of your status if you pass this final test for the Order of the Arrow. It is fundamental and essential to the survival and prosperity of our tribe, both physical and spiritual, that you ponder your purpose." Mr. Carpenter stops and stares silently into the last flames of our special campfire. My guide pulls me to my feet. I push my dick down so it doesn't stick out.

I get everything that Mr. Carpenter said except the tribe. Does he mean those of us here, our people, our congregation, or our neighbors? I hope it's just the troop, but I think he's getting at something bigger. Why us, man? I don't want to take care of all those people. I want to have some fun.

My mentor turns me away from the fire and into the unknown.

We wander in the darkness for hours, I think, and during all that time, I can't figure out who my pioneer is. I know he must be one of the older boys but I can't guess which one. Too many are about the same height. Too many walk the same way. They copy each other just like we do. But I am so relieved when we stop walking—him pointing to mysterious markers, animals and trees along the way—that I don't care anymore who he is. We'll probably find out in the closing ceremony anyway. We stop me at the inductees' cabin and he gently pushes me toward its door. The walk is over. I try to look at my hunter but he turns away before I can see his eyes.

I am curious about a tent pitched beside the inductees' cabin. It wasn't there before. I wait until my guide leaves and then I walk to it. A flashlight is on inside and I can see the shadow of someone spreading a ground cloth. I look inside. It's Roy. He turns around just when I'm trying to sneak away. Roy looks at me the way I look at Lonnie on nights he spends over. He likes me. I freeze.

Roy quickly rolls out his sleeping bag, then sits down cross-legged at one end. Without breaking the vow of silence again, he taps the bedroll next to him and smiles, with one corner of his lip curling up. I get hard. I quickly look around outside and, seeing no one, decide to join Roy. The tent flaps close behind me.

Roy takes his knife out of his pack. He strikes a match to sterilize the blade. He lifts his shirt up above his navel. His stomach is flat. His waist is narrow and round, an exciting contrast to his thick arms and stocky, angular shoulders. Then, with quicker-than-the-eye-can-see precision, Roy unflinchingly cuts the tip of his finger, squeezes out some blood and draws an X just below his belly button. *Roy is weird.*

Roy reaches for my hand. *I don't like these rituals and I don't need another blood brother.* Instead of giving him my palm, I put it on his thigh. He smiles his smile and slowly looks down between his legs. He wants to play "Guess what part of my body I'm thinking of." I reach over there and rub a little. He gets hard. He leans back and I know that I can use him anyway I like. I guessed the right body part.

There is something that I have never tried. Something perfect to try during a vow of silence. Not only because we can't talk about it now, but also because nothing can ever be taken from this weekend into the outside world— even to other Scouts in our troop. We can never put anything we do on this retreat into words because none of it has words attached to it now. There is something that I read about in one of Daddy's college psychology books (my parents think I am too young to understand the books in the attic so they've never put them off-limits). It has always interested me. I really am curious and I want to try it.

I have tried many things besides playing with Lonnie. I felt my cousin's breasts. She let me. They were soft. I thought they would make noise like a milk bottle but they didn't. Last summer, Lonnie's big sister, Selma, and I sneaked into the woods to look at each other's private parts. We rubbed them against each other. It was exciting. I was hard as a rock. It felt good. I couldn't breathe fast enough. I kissed her, too, all over—on the neck, arms and new breasts—just like in the movies. I wanted to go inside her but it wasn't easy. The opening was very small. That skin thing I read about in my big sister's hygiene book (that only the girls get in sixth grade) was blocking the way. We were afraid that Selma might bleed and die or something, so we stopped. Maybe the opening will grow and we can try again some time. She promised to tell me if it did. I hope it does. I want to try. She's not my girlfriend. She's older than me. It's safe for us to try together because we would never tell anyone, not even Lonnie.

The book said that a man "penetrated another man." He was arrested. I don't know why. The man didn't die or anything. There was no skin in the way. He couldn't go to the bathroom if there were. I know that.

I never let any boy go inside me. None. We've played with each other. Talked about each other's booties. And one or two of us licked each other's thing. Some of us practice kissing together so we'll be good when we start dating. No one admits to it, though. Everyone talks about not bending over in the shower, or how using soap can make it easier, but I don't know anyone, anyone worth mentioning, who ever let one of us "do it" to him. Some of the older Scouts say that one old member their age, Lesley, let someone do it to him in the locker room. They said it went to his head. He acts more like a Leslie now. He thinks he's a girl. None of them will speak to Lesley anymore.

I'm just interested in how it feels, not in being a girl. If a boy puts his dick inside me, it's got to feel completely different from anything else. And since I won't be licking, I won't have to smell Roy's crotch rot. I imagine it will feel close. Exciting. Special. That's what I want Roy to do. I'll relax, like I had to get out a really big turd, only backwards. Roy is crazy enough to try anything. That's what I want to feel. His thing is definitely willing.

I reach for the flashlight, turn it out and loosen my belt. I pretend to go to sleep on my stomach. Roy does exactly what I want him to do. I guide him. Like I had to pull my pants down a little more than he thought. He moves back and forth, like a dog. He holds onto me real tight. I think the rumors that he's already gone all the way with girls is true. Not because he's got peach fuzz or knows how to talk to them or anything. He just knows the moves.

It's not exactly what I had expected. It hurts at first, but the newness makes it worth it. Then, it mostly feels good. Unique. Complete. At first, I bite my lip to keep from screaming, then I bite it so I don't moan out loud.

Roy shakes like he's been moved by the Spirit. Then his body stiffens like a board and he pushes into me, deeper than ever. Suddenly, he collapses on top of me, heavier than ever.

I push him off, sit up, straighten my clothes and leave. The chill smacks me in the face. I take a really deep breath. Stars twinkle. More brightly? I'm glad I tried it. Glad that I don't have to talk with Roy. Glad he's in a different Sunday school class and goes to a different junior high.

I don't want to do it or anything else with him again. It was an experiment. Good practice. He did all right but he weighed a ton at the end. I think it could be even better with someone I liked. But he was a good test. And since everyone thinks he's a real troublemaker, they'll never believe him if he blabs.

I glide over the frost-covered path to the cabin. The door squeaks open and I hope everyone is asleep. I step inside. Jimmy whispers, "Is that you?"

"Yeah, it's me."

He's great. I'm glad Jimmy risked breaking the vow of silence to check on me. He's always looking out for me. *If I ever had the courage to ask Jimmy to do it with me, I know it would feel better, really great, because I like him a lot and I trust him, too. I would get on top of Jimmy, too. He's fair: even Steven. He's not crazy like Roy. Jimmy is trustworthyloyalhelpfulfriendlycourteouskindobedientcheerfulthriftybraveclean andreverent. But I don't think I could ask him. I won't risk losing his friendship just to experiment. What if he hates me afterward? What if he makes fun of me? What if he plain ignores me? It's not worth the risk. It would have to just happen. By chance. Like we would both be thinking about it at the same time, we looked into each other's eyes and it happened. Like that. First him, then me or first me, then him.*

"Good night."

Jimmy grunts good night back to me.

I finish making the popcorn. Daddy lets me do it by myself now. It's Jiffypop. It's easier and I don't have to wash a bowl and a pot or wipe off the stove afterward, either.

Lonnie is in his pajamas. "Where did you get those, Lonnie?" His mother bought them, I can tell, but I want to tease him some. He would never buy any with small animals on them. Lonnie just scowls back, acting like he didn't hear me.

It's Friday night. Vincent Price and Boris Karloff are on TV. Lonnie jumps whenever something scary happens, then holds onto me. We get hard. We hold each other throughout the movie. Warm.

It's midnight and Mother taps on the door. That's her signal to turn off the TV. I do and its grey-green flicker is replaced by street lamp stripes squeezing through the upturned blinds and bouncing off the ceiling. I am thinking of a body part and I want

Lonnie to guess. He knows the rules. I always go first. He guesses right and holds my penis. I guess right and hold his.

"Let's go all the way, tonight. I'll do you if you do me. Let's see who can do it first. I already made stuff come from mine. Do you think you can?"

"I already made stuff, too. Don't you remember?"

"That's right, and you," I laugh, "you thought you had broken something. You thought you were bleeding to death. Whoever heard of white blood?"

"Mine almost reached the ceiling."

"If that's true, then you should be able to win this race and outshoot me, too." My thing is about to burst. I want to get started.

"Okay, let's do it." Lonnie gives in. Maybe he wishes he hadn't bragged so much about shooting his milk. "But tell me when your stuff is coming. I don't want to get it on me."

"Okay," I lie as I start to jack his thing. He moans, happily.

He does a good job of pumping me, too, I know I'm about to shoot, but I don't tell Lonnie. I win, and my stuff drips all over his fist.

"Ugh, man. I told you."

"It won't kill you, Lonnie. Just wipe it off on the sheet." I jerk him until he shoots and feel his warm milk all over my arm and hand. "See, I play fair."

"Yeah." Lonnie relaxes completely and turns on his side, facing the wall. "Thanks."

"Goodnight." I wrap my arms around him and quickly fall asleep.

Our right hands raised in the Scout sign, we recite the oath in unison: "On my honor, I will do my best to do my duty to God and my country and to obey the Scout Law; to help other people at all times; to keep myself physically strong, mentally awake and morally straight." The metal folding chairs barely clatter when we sit down like good, courteous Scouts.

Mr. Carpenter reads off the names of the new OA members. Jimmy, Lonnie and I make it. We each get a handshake reserved for members of the Order, first from Mr. Carpenter, then, after he's congratulated all of us, from our no-longer-secret mentors who led us on the thinking trek. "You're one of us, now," William, my big brother, congratulates me.

Everybody makes it except Roy. I guess laughing at the campfire was serious. I don't mind that Roy is not in the Order. He looks over at me and smiles, one corner turned up, then he walks toward me. I hope he doesn't expect to play that game with me again. Now that he's not in the Order, I won't have to camp with him anymore. If I never see him again, it will be fine, just fine.

"Congratulations." He winks at me.

"Thanks," I stammer.

William grabs Roy by the shoulder and lectures him. "If you were serious about studying and spent less time trying to get some tail from those hussies, you would be in the Order of the Arrow now, too."

"Women chase me. They ask me to mess around." He gives me a look.

I get very nervous. He might break the vow of silence. Instead, Roy just stares my big brother down for a few seconds then backs off and walks out of the meeting.

"Roy!" Mr. Carpenter yells after him, "Roy, the meeting is not over!" He catches Roy and grabs him by the shoulder. Mr. Carpenter lowers his voice but we can all read his lips. "There'll be another chance to try out for the Order in a few months, son. It's only a few months."

Roy looks Mr. Carpenter right in the eyes, doesn't say a word and then shrugs his hand off his shoulder and leaves.

He is hanging around outside when we leave the church basement meeting. Jimmy and Lonnie tell him they're sorry he didn't make it.

Roy boasts, "You guys want to meet some women? I can find one for you. Easy."

Lonnie drools at the thought, "Yeah. Are they nice?"

"Sure they are, Lon. What about you two?"

"No, thanks, Roy. I already know a girl I like." Jimmy tells the truth and breaks my heart.

"What about you?" Roy asks me.

"I already know a girl I like, too," I boast.

"Oh, excuse me." Roy turns to Lonnie. "Well, me and my man here will be leaving you love-struck Boy Scouts now." Roy wraps his arm around Lonnie like an older, wiser brother, and asks, "What time your mama want you home?"

"Before nine."

"Damn, how old you say you are?" Roy doesn't wait for Lonnie to answer, "Naw, man, I'm just playing with you. Let's get moving then. We got enough time."

I watch Jimmy watch them head toward Roy's neighborhood.

"I hope Lonnie takes care of himself," Jimmy mumbles.

Lonnie and I are walking to school like we always do. Just before we get to the store where we buy candy, pumpkin seeds and bubble gum with part of our lunch money, Lonnie stops. He wants to say something but I don't know what. So I wait a minute, then start talking. "There's a new horror flick on TV Friday. Well, it's the first time on TV, anyway. Want to come watch it with me?"

"Yeah, I guess."

"Well, you don't have to sound so excited."

"The movie sounds good, but I don't know about spending the night."

"Why not?"

"I'm too old for that."

"What do you mean? I'm older than you are and I still like it. You're my best buddy."

"I'm different from you."

"Yeah," I snap, "you're stupid."

"I mean, I don't want to play the guessing game anymore… or cut holes in our pockets or anything like that."

"Why not?"

"I want to do that good stuff with girls, man."

"Me, too. But that doesn't mean we have to give up our guessing game."

"It does for me."

I don't know what to say, so I snap, "Okay," and start walking again. I am not sure if Lonnie is walking with me. I wonder if he has a problem. Does he hate me now? Should I want to stop playing, too? Should I have given up the game first since I'm older than Lonnie? Maybe I'm some kind of retard? What does Lonnie think of me now?

"Don't be angry, man." Lonnie breaks his at-my-side silence.

"Leave me alone, dummy." There is nothing else I can say to him. "I think I'll walk a different way." That'll show him. Two can play at this changing-things-all-of-a-sudden game. I take longer steps; quicker, too. Leave him in my dust, I hope.

I'm angry that I feel so different. I must be from outer space. I bet some aliens put me in my family as an experiment. Substituted me at the hospital! Well, Aliens, the experiment is over. Rescue me! I can't play here anymore. Take me where I belong, where I can speak the language.

I turn right at the next corner and catch Lonnie tagging along after me. I stop and glare at him. I make my entire face frown at Lonnie so that he knows I *really* want him to leave me alone. I scowl like a man until he retreats and then disappears into the candy store.

I continue walking the new way to school. I like going down the curving sidewalk. I had forgotten about this block. It's quiet. The houses are cute and uniform, like the Scouts. The front yards are mowed and green. One is trimmed with chrysanthemums. They look good. I like watching the petals move in the breeze.

Out of nowhere, someone grabs my shoulder. It's Lesley. I didn't hear him coming. I didn't see him. He just showed up.

"Hi." Lesley looks much older than fourteen.

"What are you trying to prove? You scared me."

"Oh. Excuse me." His tosses his head back. "I didn't know I could scare a member of the Order of the Arrow." He puts his hands on his hips and looks at me with his lips puckered into a know-it-all smile. He must be imitating his sister.

"What do you want?"

"To talk. Maybe have some fun. I've been watching you. I think maybe you would be interested in some of the things I like." He bats his eyelashes at me.

I can't believe what he just did but I can't run away, either. So I rebut, "Like what?" I guess he doesn't know that I make jokes about him just like everyone else. Guess he hasn't figured out that I was the mastermind behind covering his tent with toilet paper the last, and final, time he came to camp.

"Like spending the night together. Like holding each other tight. Like kissing."

"Kissing! Are you nuts?!" If I had known Lesley lived on this block, I never, ever would have walked this way. "Boys don't do that."

"Not all boys. But it makes the guessing game a lot more fun if you kiss and hug."

"What? What are you talking about? What makes you think I'd want to do anything with you? You're, you're a sissy."

"'Sticks and stones may break my bones but words will never hurt me.' I know what I like and I'm not ashamed to tell you about it."

"That's disgusting. I don't want to hear about that stuff!"

Lesley shakes his head just like a girl. "Oh? That's not what I heard. Come on, you know what I mean. Stop faking. I know a place where we can go. No one will ever find us."

"No way."

"Meet you after school."

"You're not right."

"It takes one to know one."

"I'm not like you."

"Mm-hmmm. Well," Lesley breathes in very, very slowly, "if you say so, I guess it must be so." He-she tosses his head to one side.

"You don't know anything, punk!" I turn around, determined to trudge our usual route to school. "Get out of my way." I march away, head up, shoulders back and chest out, without checking to see if Lesley is following me.

Harry comes up to me after school. He is excited about his new project. "I think this one will win. I'm going to build a model refinery. Really, I'll build two: one like the usual ones and a second one with improvements. My improvements, based on things Dad tells me."

I'm glad Harry wants to talk. It gives me a good reason not to walk home with Lonnie. I have got to change as soon as possible because I don't want to feel the way I do about Lonnie or Jimmy or any boy. That's a bad part of me. I'm worrying too much to hear a word Harry has to say.

"And the judges will have to think it's great because everything will be based on current research." Harry has it all planned.

I "uh-huh" a lot so Harry thinks I'm listening.

I want a house, car, wife, children like everybody. I can't end up like Lesley. I'm no sissy. If I ignore it, it will go away. I can't be a punk. Never. That's awful. I'll act just like everyone else. Do what everybody else does. Then I'll be all right. It will be all right. "Uh-huh."

"I will have articles to support my choices and drawings, too." Harry could finish the project today.

Two big guys run up behind us. The light-skinned one grabs Harry by his shirt. "You're Roy's friend, aren't you?" He turns to his medium-brown buddy. "Look at him. Looks like one to me. He's got to be one."

I look as mean as possible and insist, "We don't know anybody named Roy!" But I know they mean frog-skinner, peach-fuzz Roy. "Let him go!"

"Who's talking to you, anyway?"

"Let me go!" Harry looks funny trying to talk tough. He swings at the light-skinned one.

"Let's get *him*, too." The darker one points at me.

"He's not even worth it. Roy said this one."

"Leave me alone!"

"Let him go!"

"You better go before I knock your block off!"

I kick the light-skinned one. He lets Harry go and swings at me. "I kill people for less!"

The other one grabs Harry before he can run. Harry struggles with him and tells me, "Get help!" Then he screams as loud as a police siren.

The brown one covers his mouth and warns me, "You better go home to your mommy while you still have the chance."

I want to help Harry. I look at him. His eyes tell me to go. Roy is crazy. *This is all my fault. If I just liked girls the way everyone else does this wouldn't happen. I lied when I said I was interested in a girl. I just copied Jimmy. I don't want to play with Jimmy. I want to be like him.* None of this is fair. Harry is getting it because of me. I don't want to get him in trouble. Lonnie is right. It's time to stop playing games and get a girlfriend. I'll make myself like her. These big boys won't make the same mistake twice: I could get hurt. I hope they don't hurt Harry. I need to help him.

"What are you waiting on? We told you to go!" The light-skinned one punches Harry while the brown one holds him still.

"Let go of him!"

Harry bites the darker one's hand. "Get my mother!"

The light one reaches for me. I dodge him and run toward Harry's house. I pass Lonnie walking our usual way home. *A wife two cars a dog maybe a cat too. Lonnie looks in the other direction. I don't need him anyway. A big house with a garden and a fence a good job and lots of vacations.* I run faster. I pass Harry's house. I don't stop. His mother's car is in the driveway. I can't go inside. I don't want to tell her the truth: what's happening to Harry because of me. I can't stop. I'll call from home. I keep going. I reach home. The screen door slams shut behind me.

Mother hears it. "How many times do I have to tell you not to let that door slam?"

"I won't do it again," I apologize as I catch my breath.

"Are you all right?"

"Yes, ma'am." I don't even think of telling her what is going on. "May I use the telephone?" I run to the one in the hall, barely hearing her answer "Yes." I dial the number quickly. It rings and rings. Harry's mother is not there. Just her car. Maybe she went to visit a neighbor. Shoot. I should have stopped and left a note under the windshield wiper.

I dial the police at the number on the emergency note pad beside the telephone. "I want to report a fight... two against one. Two big boys are beating up my friend. I called his parents. Nobody answered. Can you help him? On the corner of Jefferson and Nineteenth. Yes sir, near the vacant lot. Help him, please. Thank you."

I dial another number. I've known it by heart since before I was allowed to use the telephone. Sometimes I am lazy about it but I have to keep in touch with her. Let her know that I have plans for us. "Hi, it's me... Oh, you recognize my voice? That's good. When I'm old enough to date, I want to date you first. You do, too? Okay. I've got to go now. I can't wait until we're old enough." I hang up and rush to my room feeling better: since I'll date a girl, I won't end up a sissy. I'm worried about losing Harry as my friend. I hope he's okay.

It is a freezing Friday night. I don't know what makes the Scouts think that camping outside on the snow proves anything to anyone except that we can get very cold. I'm glad I got a new sleeping bag for Christmas and that we are going to use a cabin tomorrow night. It has a wood-burning stove. I'll help chop the wood. But tonight we sleep outside. At least we can talk this weekend.

Jimmy and I volunteered to take charge of making camp. We had all the guys arrange their sleeping bags in rays around the fire. This way the fire heats our heads—where most heat escapes from the body—and we heat each other by sleeping side by side, each boy in his own sleeping bag, of course. It's a good plan. I think it will work as long as Jimmy and I keep the fire going at a safe level all night.

Lonnie showed some new Scouts how to cook dinner. He did a pretty good job making beef stew from the freeze-dried rations. You can really mess it up if you add the water too quickly. Then you just get a bunch of tasteless clumps. Lonnie made the rice from scratch. He grins as he finishes his last spoon of stew, "Maybe next time, Mr. Carpenter will let us bring some girls."

We all laugh at the suggestion. I don't think it's funny, but I laugh with the rest of them. I know how dangerous it can be when I don't act like everyone else.

"I know which one I would bring," Jimmy adds.

All the guys look at Jimmy, except me, waiting for him to say who.

I end their anticipation. "But he's not telling," I explain my merit badge buddy's style, speaking, I think, as much like a ladies' man as any movie star.

"That's right because I don't want you guys all over her. Go find your own." Jimmy clears that up.

"I like Sharon Jones," a new Scout boasts.

"She's all right," Jimmy congratulates.

"You know who the best girl in the whole school is?"

We all turn to Lonnie and ask in unison, "WHO?"

"It's Charlane." And Lonnie leans back into a daydream about her.

"Yeah, man, she is fine." I agree with Lonnie, "I want me some of that!" I elbow Jimmy, who knows I'm just trying to make Lonnie mad.

Lonnie sits up and glares at me, "She's mine!"

"I know that, man. Calm down. I was just joking, but she *is* too old for you." I take in a deep breath, spread out my chest and smile mischievously like Bill Cosby on *I Spy*. I slowly look each of my fellow Scouts in the eye. "Anyway, Tanya is working on me," I brag. "And I'm working on her." I lied.

"My man!" Jimmy slaps my palm.

And the others echo his approval.

My Boy
by Laura A. Harris

As she stepped out the back door to descend the steps she felt an early morning heaviness in her body. Full and fat were the satisfying words that came to her mind as each step down emphasized for her a sensation of weighty pleasure. She lifted the thick metal lid of the trash canister with an ease that added the adjective strong to her list, and as she let the kitchen trash fall into the damp tank she brought her now free hand up under her left breast in a gesture of support and affection for its potent round presence. "Ripe," she silently mouthed to herself as she used both hands to trace her shape down to her proud potbelly and then to rest against her sturdy buttocks.

"I am plump and pregnant," she joked to herself as she turned back to the house. She stopped almost before the thought was finished, before a complete step had been taken, and like a small rabbit with its frantic heart beat as the only sign of life she froze in overwhelming fear. In front of her lay the canyon with its dense green and multicolored pattern, with the night's fog still and moist hanging low over the plenitude like a forbidding guardian of silence. Her anxious eyes searched the impenetrable shapes and turns for the figure of her fear, for the cause of its intuitive reasoning. But nothing moved. She took a deep sigh and admitted to herself that the danger was of her own making.

"Ripe, am I?" she chastised herself as she finally walked toward the house. "What for?" Her buoyant morning spirits dissipated and she felt with her whole being a frustration of such magnitude and confusion that she turned it inward on herself. She felt her body shrink back to its small frame with the too big hands and feet, with the long braid a heavy burden to her slender neck, and her pale high-yellow complexion of secret living. She wrapped her arms around her waist for protection and refused to allow her breasts to rest on them. "I trick myself with these feelings of expectancy, with these feelings of a grand promise to come." Tears began in her eyes as she harshly pushed the desire for fulfillment away, a cruel rock to be thrown into the canyon's dark growth. Punishingly, she reminded herself that she deserved nothing, that her solitude should make her grateful. It was her security.

Later in the morning, the gray skies never having faded into proper daylight, rain began to pour down in lashing steadiness. She was appropriately satisfied by the spectacle as she sat in the kitchen and looked out toward the canyon. From this distance its expansive contours and erotic texture were beautiful. From this distance she loved it and allowed its beauty to cajole and soothe her needy mind. She did cherish her solitude. Often when she went into town she would run into social acquaintances, friends even, who would rapid-fire ask her where she had been and when might she be expected to come out and fraternize. They recalled various occasions when she had done just that and how they had loved her energetic company and her affectionate toying. They had missed her lately, missed talking with her, and partaking of her friendship. Sometimes she would take the time to have a coffee with them, to listen to their woes and triumphs, to walk through their busy and jumbled lives with the sincere pleasure of a caring friend and the cautious distance of a voyeur. She rarely had much to reveal to them but this didn't prevent her from offering up engaging conversation and stories, a charming deception of a specific and emotional bond with her. And at these moments she did often feel a genuine bond with these people; she loved them and petted them and felt insulated by their obvious pleasure in her. They played an important role in the small world she had created for herself, and despite her careful distance they felt close to her and never quite grasped her separateness.

Yes, at moments like this, with the comforting thought of friends, she certainly cherished her ritual solitude. She was relieved, and no longer guilty about that relief, that they were gone. All of them. The father and sons to whose lives she had attended in every last detail for years. She had made her contribution, she had behaved like a dedicated race woman of which her father would have been proud. But the guilt grabbed her when she admitted that her own motives were not lofty. The only reason she had prostrated herself to these lives was in order to escape the terror of her own extreme passions and imaginings. A small world of lives to which she could be efficient and necessary, in which she could hide away from the danger of her life, of her need, and return it to others as a gift of nurturing. It had not lasted long though, and before she had made the final decision to part from them she had fretted as to why she was not able to sustain such an intimate little world. Maybe if they had been different. If he hadn't had maleness all over him like a dank mold. If they could have remained young and smooth-skinned and brave and sensitive. But as it was they grew older, taller, hairy and ruthlessly demanding. And as they did she began to dislike them, to think of them as nasty bodies with so many loathsome needs. She did better to consider them from a distance, to write them letters and think of them fondly, to think of those days when she had held them to her breasts in brief but complete rapture.

As she sat musing to herself she caught a blur of movement out of the corner of her eye. Out near the trash canister a slender figure was rummaging through its contents. From the raggedy outline she understood it was one of the homeless canyon dwellers who found refuge in the umbral foliage and food in the neighborhood trash. In her tendency to create imaginative fictions around the lives of other people she had a highly developed empathy that rendered her unafraid of strangers. She decided to tell this one to come onto her back porch where she would gladly give him some of the soup she had made only yesterday. Throwing on a sweater she ran out to inform this character of her benevolence and managed to get near enough without him hearing her due to the noise of the rain.

"Hi there," she began. But the startled stranger, whose face she could not quite see under the blanket wrapped around him, jumped back and moved to leave. "Hey you," she yelled out, "come to the house. I have extra food if you want." The figure stopped and, just as she had done earlier that morning, he seemed to freeze in order to assess the possibility of danger. She could barely make out large brown eyes under the blanket and a dusty stained hand grasping at the edges. "Really, it's okay," she reassured loudly. "I'm the only one here." Immediately she realized that may have been less than cautious but it did seem to encourage this character and, after all, she wasn't afraid. She had always proclaimed her fearlessness of possible attackers. "Why, just let someone mess with me," she would growl to friends and make them laugh as she boastfully strutted her publicly ferocious demeanor.

She ran back to the house, looking back once to make sure he was still coming. Enlivened by this person's dilemma she ran into the kitchen and put the soup pot on the stove to warm. She poured a cup of coffee and grabbed some chocolate-dipped cookies out of the cabinet. By the time she had done all this the small stranger was finally sitting in the furthest corner of the back porch by her plants. "Come closer, come under here where there is covering," she insisted. He didn't move immediately and so she put down her first offerings and ran back inside to get towels and a dark blue serape blanket. When she returned to the back door the stranger was now within arm's reach of her. She placed the articles down next to him and squatted to be in eye contact.

"Would you like some cream?" Shaking his head he pushed back the wet covering of the blanket and reached for where she had placed the cup and cookies. She was shocked by his youthful face. "Geezuz," she thought. "He's so young. He's just a boy!" She watched him intently as he drank and ate, and he silently, uninhibitedly returned her gaze. She took in all the details, the slight build of him, the copper-gold color of his skin, the dark curling hair hanging wet behind his ears, and the cliche long-lashed eyes that only real boys have. She saw the dirt on him, under his nails, shadowing his neck, the soaked clothing and she unknowingly stared at him, held in an awkward balance between his desperate beauty and filthy derangement. He was shaking from head to toe, shivering so violently that he could barely bring either cup or cookie to his mouth. She realized she had better take the situation into hand and find out more about this youth.

"Look," she said, placing her hand on his, "why don't you come in and you can take a warm bath and have dry clothes and eat. You can tell me about yourself and, well... I would like that." He didn't respond; he only continued shivering and looking at her with veiled eyes. She softly grasped his hand and rose to her feet, pulling him up with her. She wordlessly led him into the house; she had started down the corridor to the bathroom when he suddenly dropped down to the floor in a dead faint. She quickly knelt beside him and felt his forehead; he was burning up. She propped his head up against her and tried to awaken him. He opened his eyes a bit and moaned slightly. He seemed semi-conscious and she could feel his body was rigid with cold shaking tension and that his clothes were wet through and through. She supported him to his feet and half-carried and half-propelled him to the bathroom. Setting him down on the toilet she started a hot bath and then turned to begin removing his clothing. Just as she was getting the first layer off he came back to life and pushed her off while clinging to the tails of his shirt. Relieved that he was coming to life and thinking that he must be scared, she held her hands up to say "okay." She went to pull a dry flannel work shirt and plain worn jeans out of the bottom of her closet to give to him, and then left him to his own bathing. Back in the kitchen she sat in dazed anticipation waiting and listening in case he hurt himself by passing out again. She accidentally boiled the soup twice.

Finally she heard the door open and heard his steps but they didn't move in her direction. With more than a little anxiety now she went toward the bathroom but he wasn't there. She stepped into the doorway of her bedroom and saw him curled like a child in a corner of her bed as if he couldn't do more to find comfort. She carefully walked to the bed and as he looked up at her with ashamed vulnerability she couldn't help but respond. "It's okay, why don't you get under the covers? I'll bring you the soup." As she prepared the tray in the kitchen she found herself shaking, not from fear or nerves, but with a deeply felt emotional stirring for this strange boy. She brought him soup and juice and liquid children's Tylenol that she couldn't remember having bought. She filled him spoonful by spoonful with her delicate soup; she held his chin as familiarly as if he were her sick child as she gave him the juice and medicine. With one last soft look into her eyes, his lids closed and he slept. She arranged the covers closer to his frame and had involuntarily leaned to kiss his cheek when she caught herself. She sat near him, listening to his breath, looking at him, and wondering at her actions. At one point, reaching out to caress his worried brow, there arose in her the distinct feeling that she was in extraordinary contact with some feral creature the canyon had a claim to. She knew it was illogical but somehow she believed it possible the canyon had offered him up, as a gesture of approval or one of judgment, she could not decide. When she went to the kitchen to clean up she was surprised to see the dark night in her windows. She couldn't account for the time, and moving about her kitchen she realized her thoughts were dreamlike and disconnected.

And it was from a dream that she was later awakened by a low crying from her room. A dream she could never quite recall, since it was all imagery and tactile sensation, but a dream that bestowed upon her body that feeling of fullness and pregnant desire to which she often awoke in the morning. Sitting up on the couch, clearing her senses to determine the cause of the disturbing sounds, she had for a second the clarity of that dream and its lingering impact, but it slipped away as she quickly went to her bedroom. The young boy was restlessly tossing and tangled in the sheets; his long slender legs and arms seemed just as tangled underneath him. She climbed up over him to straighten the sheets and his body as much possible without startling him. Inadvertently he turned and clung to her, the weight of him pulling her down to his side. Not having the time to be taken aback, she allowed him to hold on to her and she held him back, stroking his short sweetly damp hair and neck gently, rhythmically. He lay in her arms crying quietly and so motionless that she believed him to be asleep. She lay there like this with him for how long she couldn't reason, and whether or not she slept was also hard to decide. Sometime during the night though, whether in sleep or in full cognition she had lifted his fragile weeping head to her breast. She had moved her nightgown down and pulling her nipple up between her thumb and forefinger, she had offered it up to his crying, swollen lips. Tenderly, ever so tenuously, he had wrapped his warm wet mouth around her nipple and began an exquisite and light sucking that went on interminably. Childishly he held onto her breasts with hands not groping but finding a need fulfilled and a dismay comforted throughout the rest of the night. Lying with the lambent light of dawn in the windows she wondered at her passionate response to this child. How did she offer it so completely? The timing of things seemed lost with his needs and hers in this past night. But she knew, she saw in her mind that she had had such extreme feelings, such compassionate desires with his head in her arms and his inconsolable soft crying against her breast. She ran the moment over and over in her head with its sheer delight and precious yearnings. She wanted to know it so well that it would be forever saved in her memory without one diminished detail.

Days went unaccounted for and the nights were an ethereal life. She never questioned the intimate exchange between them; it was there with a full delirious expression and always appropriate. It was an extension of her ministering to his physical sickness of a high fever and weakened body. It was as right as the foods and liquids she painstakingly prepared for him and brought to feed him in his waking hours. It was there in the books she read aloud to distract his pain, the combing of his hair, and manicuring of his hands and feet. It was an afterward to the massaging of his aching neck and cramped tightly muscled back. She poignantly, devotedly attended to his every need and once offering to bathe him she was intensely hurt by his rejection of this intimacy. He closed the door to the bathroom like the gates to a monastery. And she would wait patiently for him to emerge pleased by his cleanliness but regretting the temporary loss of the fixed wistful smell of his boyish body.

She didn't see him getting better, gaining in strength and health from her unwavering tending. She didn't want to see it for he was her own helpless lovely boy with whom the vague distracting dreams had been replaced. Each night now she did not have to wait to be affected by intangible images; instead, he made her body real and abundant with a weighty saturation of perfect fruition. If she noticed at all that he was healing she understood it in his now often taking of her breasts by his own volition. She might have considered his silent insistent pulling of her body close to him, the slow studied way in which he stroked her nipples through her gown before removing it, then the holding and lifting and touching of her breasts until she felt she could no longer endure her anticipation for his mouth to take her, as an indication of his recuperation. But she was far too enamored with his taking, that firm taking of her nipples in his mouth for long hours of tasting and sucking and licking during the cover of night.

Perhaps she didn't notice the changes because she herself was in a fevered state. So full of turmoil and frenzy that she no longer fell asleep after their intimacy. She waited for sleep to overcome him and then she quietly removed herself to the couch where she pulled down her panties and spread her legs. Astonished at first to find so much wetness there, to find it flowing over onto her thighs, and then becoming pleased with herself as she played and drew designs, and ultimately touching directly until she spasmed repeatedly. It was in this very state that he discovered her one night. So involved was she in her play that she didn't see him standing above her watching with those black unfathomable eyes. But when she finally opened hers she wasn't afraid for him to be there. She lay passive, captured under his look. She responded emphatically as he climbed on top of her and began a thorough and purposeful kissing of her mouth—as he took her body in his hands. She wasn't surprised at his masterful desire, somehow she had expected it and passionately she submitted to his every move. And when he slid his hand between her legs, to that overflowing wetness, she had a moment's shyness and started to move aside but he held her, kept her fear under him, and entered her with his fingers. She was at a loss at first with his persistent stroking fingers deep inside her and then she felt the deepness of herself as she had never before known. She left herself and came back only to realize that she was making sounds so incoherent and ecstatic they seemed like real words.

They continued in this way for how long, how many days, she was disinterested in calculating. At some point it was evident that she had to make a trip to town for basic supplies. She was thrilled to do so, relishing the free rein she would give to her desire to procure all sorts of dainty succulent foods for their pleasure. As she passed the canyon she stepped to the edge of its vast isolation and she exalted in the complexities and vagaries of its presence.

She recognized its movement and heard the power of its slightest wind against a leaf. She avoided every well-traversed spot in town and gathered her purchases to her like a private treasure while hurrying back to the house. When she returned she entered the kitchen and placing her parcels on the table she rushed to see where and how he was. The bathroom door was slightly ajar and the sound of running water explained his whereabouts. She turned to go back to the kitchen with the intent of preparing a luscious tray of delicacies. For some reason, for some whimsical curiosity she stopped and contemplated that bathroom door. It was an unclosed door, an odd detour from his strict boundaries. Without making a conscious decision she touched it with just enough pressure that the door deliberately, slowly swung open. Through the glass doors of the shower she saw her boy and she saw his body. His body that was formed different from her own but exact in its anatomy to hers. Their eyes met, he didn't react and neither did she. They searched long and intimately for their answers in each other's eyes.

As she fed him juicy apple slices, smelly cheeses, and sesame crackers in the kitchen she began speaking aloud thoughts and plans that until now she had not known how to formulate.

"It isn't possible for me to stay. You understand that, don't you? I can never be what I am, so I keep moving. Soon I have to leave, before that pile of mail and list of unreturned phone calls of yours grows much larger."

Never having heard his voice she couldn't make the connection for a moment's breath of time. The sound of it was like a melancholic melody that permeates one's senses. As she stood useless in the face of his words she had the sensation of waking, though she knew she had been awake for hours. She felt the weightedness of her body connected to the glossy tile of her floor. She placed a hand in the place between her breasts and reassured herself of their fulfilled vigor. Her heart didn't miss a beat but purred on steady and effective.

"We'll go together," she responded. "And you can be exactly what you are wherever it may be that we choose to go."

"Really?" he inquired. "And what do you think I am?"

She knew the answer in a flash. "My boy," she told him. And to his for once surprised expression she repeated it, allowing the image of it, the held hands of mother and son on a fast-speeding train, to tickle and tease her tongue. "My boy."

A House in the World
by Shawn Stewart Ruff

4F was still vacant six weeks after a race riot scared downtown. That was five weeks longer than its flustered landlord figured. Angus Short took losing money hard, and was stewing in Cancun with his brother-in-law-Bass when he phoned home for an applicant update.

"Few people've been calling," Cookie his wife said, screening prospects on his behalf. "That white couple you talked to, they saw it. They kept asking about the riot, though. They seemed antsy, said you should come down in the rent under the circumstances."

"What you tell 'em?"

"The community's talking about riot causes and healing."

"Tell 'em the police got these fools under control."

Cookie sucked her teeth, a sign she was bothered. "Police was cruising the block when they came, so I guess that took care of that."

"Good. Anybody else?"

"Hold on."

Pots clattered and the oven yawned. If he were home, the gurgle of frying chicken would lure him from paperwork and phone calls in the basement to the kitchen for a drumstick with Red Devil hot sauce, a Thursday dinner indulgence in a forced low-fat life. Angus had nothing personal against quesadillas and tacos, as long as he ate them near home.

"I'm back. I'm baking a healthy-cake for LaRoux's birthday—"

"I best go," Angus cut in, unwilling to chitchat at international rates. "Guess you can tell the couple I'll come down to eleven hundert."

"There was somebody else. Let me see. Yeah, this nice young man—he call and come by day before yesterday. His name is Mitchell Meeks, and he's a twenty-nine-year-old attorney with a fancy law firm downtown—the one that sued that air-condition company, Hendrex, remember?"

"You checked his references?"

"Spotless, he makes good money, too. His partner's coming here in a few months from D.C., I think that's where Mitch said. He just wants a year lease and they plan on buying if they stay in town."

"Fax his application and that couple's to me, here," Angus said, rooting around the hotel room for the fax number. "Tell 'em all I'll get back on the twelfth. Tell 'em to come by on the thirteenth. And don't schedule 'em all at once."

Cookie cleared her throat, then said, "That won't be necessary, I told him he can have the place."

"Huh?"

"Mitch Meeks is moving in at the end of the week."

"What? Cookie, I ast you to wait till I'm home."

"Forcryingoutloud, I know the perfect tenant when I see one. He's just what we're looking for."

"Ain't no such thing, ain't you figured that out yet?"

"You'll love 'em, such a sweet, proper young man. He lived in Cincinnati until he was ten. He knows the Chenaults, too."

"Knows the Chenaults? He black?"

"Yeah, and he went to Georgetown Law, so there!"

"That and a buck'll get him coffee and a jelly donut at Central." Angus snorted. "He ain't one of them... You know I don't allow that in my house."

"Angus, stop worrying me about this apartment!" Teeth sucking again. "And say hi to Bass."

Angus was percolating with anger, and so said "bah." If you wanted a thing done right, best to do it yourself. He paced his and Bass' beige suite, staring at stenciled sombrero-patterned wallpaper in guacamole green. The ugly room was on a low floor and festooned with a pool view. The pool's devotees were leathered flabby retirees, pale newlyweds from the Snow Belt and men with high foreheads from the National Association of Hair Transplantation. A sorrier sight there wasn't.

Bass was poolside too, jackknifed in a chaise under burning sun, his skin shining like coffee beans. One hand balanced a martini, the other fished his crotch, baiting the whores. He had an acorn-sized brain tumor of an inoperable kind. Cancun prostitutes seemed to know a man on a death furlough. They circled nearby, wriggling in Tidy Bowl-blue pool water or tottering on laced up Espadrilles, in bikinis no more than brisket string. Their pint-sized nakedness didn't matter much to Angus. He was in the last cycle of prostate treatments, with eight months since his last rise. The only thing worse than losing money was losing dick control. Bass was Cookie's brother, and for now the enemy—in sex overdrive.

Angus joined Bass just as a clay-colored prostitute in pink mules approached, but Angus' scowl was a scarecrow, and the prostitute kept going.

"Angus, man, you scaring everybody away. I'm gone send your ass home if you don't sit down and relax. Jolly up."

Angus did, but not without a fight. He tussled with a stiff white chaise umbrella to turn it against the sun. He felt burnt to a crisp after a day of walking the dusty Mayan ruins, outside Cancun proper. He lowered himself into the chaise, then sat bolt upright, the heat getting on his nerves. A fairway of sand led down to the beach, edged by foam like missed shaving cream along the Gulf of Mexico's face. A waiter came by for Angus' drink order of scotch straight up.

"Now you know me, I usually like a woman wid height and butt on her, but these little brown chiquitas get the juices going."

Angus grunted.

"What's eating you now?

"Your sister rented out the apartment. Every time I leave something for her to do, it goes wrong. She got bad judgment."

"That's what I said when she married you."

"Yeah, right."

Cancun had been Bass's idea to escape January cold. Winter brought on migraines so bad his tumor gave off heat vapor. Angus was not a man of sentiment, or one with many friends, but he was choked and torn over being somewhere he didn't want to be with a brother-in-law as good as dead. It should've made Angus happy that Bass was having a ball. And it should've made Angus happy the trip wasn't costing him a red cent, since Bass was picking up the tab to spend down his assets, decent after thirty-seven years with P&G. But even under normal circumstances Angus wasn't fond of travel, not since catching malaria in Laos, in the Vietnam War. Twice a year he packed up the Windstar and drove to Buffalo or Austin for his grandchildren's sake. That's about it.

Nine days was a long time to be "jolly up" for a man mad as hell. Angus pretended at having fun, but could only think about home. Friends shouldn't die on each other, and not while vacationing in Cancun—even friends of over fifty years. One trip goal was to convince Bass to move in so Cookie could send him off to eternity right. Cookie was a retired RN, a professional with the dying. Funny thing was, dying seemed to make Bass happier, so happy he didn't seem dying at all. A man with years of groaning about two ex-wives and six kids taking him to the cleaners was at peace, and at the ready with a wisecrack: "I'm going to see the world, but you can tell Cookie I ain't interested in a one-way ticket to no place, and I ain't moving in so she can kill me."

It took a week, but Angus relented to the pleasure of gambling. They ate like dogs, and drank like fish. A day trip into Mexico City to breathe brown air left Angus tight in the chest. Bass liked the resort best and wasn't so keen on touring no how. He had been here a coon's age ago, back in the Seventies with his first wife and her big titties "busting out her top. Even the chiquitas gave Brenda props. We didn't leave the room." Now Bass' headaches and hard-ons required of him a lot of time in bed, in a tense state. The chiquitas had sticky fingers, but what was a "fiddy" to a man being robbed of life.

Alone, Angus walked the beach. Calm crested his worries, but went out with the tide, as little brown people bobbed about like wine corks in the topaz gulf. He worried about money and tenant trouble. He worried about riots and fires. So hard to get good tenants in a siege climate, and he worried about shiftless, ignorant, unemployed black men prowling the streets bent on trouble—the real cause of the riots, Angus believed, having seen these fools reincarnated over the last forty years. He was jealous of Bass' erection and wished for his own—and that the chiquitas would leave him alone, with their mummy eyes and deep navels. Bob Dole's Viagra was dangerous for Angus' high blood pressure; all Angus could do was peek inside his shorts, yank and pull and palm his big balls for naught. Life's highlights were occasional pee hard-ons that refused to last long enough to take matters in hand. It was a terrible thing not to be able to fuck. Make a man feel dead—although, to watch Bass, death seemed to make a man want to fuck. It was all about control. Control is what gave life sense. Angus' control seemed to be slipping away, first in the newly riot-prone city of his birth, then in his shorts, now in his rentals. Had Cookie disrespected him like this because of his erectile dysfunction?

There wasn't shit to do about the violence-crazed city. Bass and life in his shorts were in God's hands. But the new 4F— Angus could do something about that. On the day they finally left Cancun he felt himself in sync with a drumbeat of action that would fix Mitchell Meeks, lawyer or not. But the violent flight back shook him up so bad he couldn't remember his own name. He wobbled into the waiting area, and as miffed as he was at Cookie he was never happier to hear her say "Here's my man, now."

"Hey Cookie," he said, lingering in her arms, his toasted nose and lips pressed against her neck gold chain. Not a man of public display, now he didn't give a damn. Didn't mind her cornrowed hair either; she looked like Cicely Tyson in *Roots*.

"What's wrong, baby?"

"He thought the plane was going down," Bass bubbled.

Cookie gave Bass a sisterly smooch, then turned toward a man standing a few feet behind her. "Angus, Bass, this here is Mitchell Meeks, he's the new tenant."

"Bienvenudos," Mitchell said.

"Hey," Angus grumped. He stared into a primped, clean-shaven brown face like Harry Belafonte's and whiffed the aftershave of money, the type that suggests a tenant who whines about everything from crooked soap dishes to frayed carpet. He was wiry like a sprinter and had Puerto Rican hair.

"How you doing, Mitchell." Bass pumped the man's hand. "You play ball or summin'?"

"For fun growing up, but not anymore. Bad knees."

"He just looks tall because y'all short," Cookie said.

"It's a natural question," Mitch grinned. "Tall black man, basketball."

"I used to be tall, but I've been shrinking since retirement," Bass said.

"Angus, Mitch was nice enough to drive me over. It got dark out like it was gonna storm, and you know I don't like driving in the rain, and so he volunteered. Ain't that nice?"

"Sure is," Bass said. "Cookie can't drive for shit."

"Oh, hush," Cookie said. "Angus, ain't that nice?"

"Hmm," Angus grunted.

"Mitch, don't pay my husband no mind at all. Angus just acts tough."

ℰℷ ℂℛ

4F was on the top floor of Angus' home. Two flights of stairs away from a showdown with the landlord. With over forty-two years in the commerce of units, Angus wasn't to be trifled with. A people person he wasn't, but he could pick a tenant. Mitchell Meeks replaced a Japanese whose parents went broke in a Nikkei downturn. Minus a yellow streak running her hair's length in skunk-like fashion, she was Angus' ideal—alone, mousey and short-term. Some years back, a clean-cut white man with TV-looks taught Angus a lesson. Turned out he was a cocaine dealer with a courier service catering to Mt. Adams, where known Bengals and Reds players lived. After a sting arranged by the FBI snared him and a running back, Angus realized bad was bad, no matter the packaging. An ideal tenant is one who feels the force of the landlord's presence like a threat. Little Asian women were just right.

Terrible to say, Angus never met a black tenant he didn't have to put the law on. Before 1977, when Over-the-Rhine was a middle-aging ghetto, twenty-seven of the thirty-five units he rented out were in court for eviction. Cookie feared they would get hurt living near so many people they were suing, but Angus was not a man for the suburbs, having lived all his life downtown, and he did not run away from threats. He figured he should be rich, instead of husbanding ends, and if he could dodge bullets in Vietnam, he could suffer the profanity of no-account nitwits up to no good. Still, he bused his kids to Summit Country Day School just in case, then shipped them off to college out of state. By then, whites started coming back, starting with the gays—men in crack-tight jeans and pink T-shirts. He got rid of the blacks, added a few gays but drew the line at renting to sodomites in his own house's rental units, and was no longer in the red. He turned sixty in 1995, and sold seven buildings for a profit that made him twice a millionaire. The two he kept kept him busy, with yard work or under sinks. He could do a little of everything, and always liked to be doing something, lest he fidget in time and grow useless. He was futzing with sidewalk weeds when news of the riot came in a shriek of sirens rushing to the projects blight less than ten blocks away. He was not surprised. "Sorry niggers," he complained to Bass, and perched in the window with his shotgun, ready for the wave of violence should it surge to his block.

With Mitchell Meeks Angus got the sense it could go either way. Early Sunday morning a jetlagged Angus read over 4F's application, with emphasis on handwriting and the check, then climbed to the fourth floor to take Mitchell Baines Meeks' measure. The door was wide open, the entrance stacked with marked boxes, with an opera choir singing on the stereo.

"Hey, Mr. Short," Mitchell said, again primped. He carried a coffee mug. Angus followed a T-shirt that said Harvard, but he did not sit down. He told of why he was there, that all tenants sign a document attesting to the condition of the apartment. Tenant and owner walked from room to room, and when the tenant signed the paper, Angus noticed blunt fingers, a wedding band and a college ring. Cookie only mentioned a partner, not a wife.

"Normally I do the interviewing, but I'm sure my wife told you we don't go in for a lot of commotion around here. Partying, drinking and such. Do that at the club, not here."

"Don't drink or smoke, and I'm very respectful of the people around me. I'm the quiet type."

"Good." Angus nodded. 'What aspect of the law you in?"

"Real estate. This is my first job out of law school. I'll stay a year, learn the lay of the land, and, if I like it, I'll start my own business developing commercial property."

"Oh." The furrows in Angus's face bunched. The tenant talked about the World Trade Center and anthrax business and how it changed his mind about Washington and New York in favor of Cincinnati.

"Mrs. Short says you used to own a lot of property."

"Did a few years back. Too much for me to handle now."

"It's good that you realize that. My dad owned property, too, in D.C. His holdings were near Capitol Hill. After Mayor Crackhead left office, values took off. But dad never slowed down. He died last year; he had a heart attack. It was a bad year. But that's life."

Angus frowned on the swapping of personal stuff. "Can't lose with real estate, I don't care what nobody say."

"That's just what my Dad used to say. He was street smart and self-made, like you. I admire that."

Tell his dumb-ass sons that. Angus had a beef with his Austin, Texas son always asking him for money, with his MBA in bad investments. Angus may not have finished high school, but he had a head for business—and knowing when he was being conned by a tenant.

"So what you want to live around here for?"

"I'm a downtown kind of guy. I like walking to work. Lots of good food around."

"Don't go wandering over to Ezzard Charles. Dangerous over there. Lot of lowlifes, same ones I been seeing for all my life, only with different faces."

"Your wife warned me already."

Figures, Angus thought.

"Mr. Short, you ever need any legal advice, let me know."

"Got a lawyer, but thanks."

Angus was halfway down the steps when 4F said, "Mr. Short, you into football?"

"Take it or leave it."

"How about the game tomorrow night, you want to go? The

company gave me welcome-to-Cincinnati tickets. I've got an extra."

Angus hesitated but said "naw."

Back in his office, he felt good about two things he recognized: the tenant was no dope head and he talked like Lester Holt on CNN.

Later, Cookie said about the football game, "Would it hurt you to live a little?"

"I don't mix with no tenants. They goose you every time."

"He's all alone here."

"He ain't alone there, a lot of people be alone. BJ in 3B's alone, so's that nutty woman in 2A. You go, you so concerned!"

It was the wrong thing to say. He certainly never meant for her to hang out with somebody who owed them money the first of the month. Angus had rules, but Cookie had a mind of her own. Angus stood firmly against entertaining tenants in their home, and Cookie abided, but that's about it. So of course she went to the game with 4F, and they started doing the gym together and by spring were taking in concerts and plays, when the tenant wasn't rushing to the airport for overnight work trips to Columbus and Cleveland or who knows where. Cookie fretted over his travel. She was maternal to the tenants who let her be, but seemed to lactate for some more than for others. Angus didn't mind her giving chicken soup to the flu-stricken law student last year in 2B in the building next door, or sharing a slice of their thirty-fifth anniversary cake with the newlyweds in 4F, also in the building next door. She was qualified for one aspect of his job that scared him to death: Nothing worse than discovering a moldering corpse. Cookie used to look in on indigent tenants until they died off, back in the days when it was a struggle to squeeze profit from downtown real estate. Merciful heaven, times had changed, and these new tenants had aspiration and education and never stuck around for longer than two years anyway. Bankers, architects, graduate students, teachers. Some left to set up house nearby. One tenant, a giggly gay Angus once saw struggling to the car in a sequin gown at midnight, outbid Angus on a house he wanted to buy as an investment for his grandkids in Buffalo. Angus couldn't stand Muncie, but Cookie and he went to block association meetings together. But that's how it was. Christmas cards showed up from tenants of ten years back, always addressed to Cookie. Nobody liked Angus, except for a manless pretty girl with two kids and a pussy for bartering rent. Angus negotiated, once or twice.

Even Cookie didn't seem to like Angus much these days either. His erectile dysfunction maybe stressed her out, too. The last year she was nuttier than usual, in a constant state of change. One minute her hair was ironed and pretty, the next in crisscrossing cornrows or in a fade, looking like the sharp-tongued lesbian truck driver four doors down. The couches moved or changed colors two or three times since Christmas. Ham-and-black-eyed-pea soup, Angus' favorite, got replaced with bouillabaisse. For ten years she played hymns at the piano for her church, tying the loose chords of a raggedy Baldwin upright together. Then out the blue, six months ago, she quit, saying she needed change. Nothing was sacred.

"It ain't God," she said. "It's the church. I'm tired of the hypocrites, the folks in glass houses who throw stones, and that jackass preacher and his new Lexus bought with our money. And I'm tired of being me."

Her abrupt change followed D'Artagnon's death last Christmas day. D'Artagnon was her organist, choir co-director and best friend of ten years, a man given to processed hair and diamond rings. Some sunny afternoons, his jewels set off a light show above the keyboard, his fingers afire like sparklers. He died bone thin with splotches all over him, his caramel complexion gone old-steak gray. He had AIDS—although the jackass reverend called it vengeful cancer. He had lived in Mt. Auburn in a house with turrets, a lacquered grand piano and a pipe organ rescued from the Regal Theater downtown. The organ pipes poked clear up to the attic of the Victorian three-story house. The choir rehearsed there when not at the church. God's praise was their business, but sometimes it seemed like Dracula worship. D'Artagnon often dropped by Angus' for gossip and to encourage Cookie's redecorating schemes, and dressed in capes with crushed velvet insides. Angus always felt D'Artagnon was staring at his privates, so he cut the organist a wide berth. He couldn't imagine how the two got on so, and even wrestled with jealous notions. He himself knew there was no accounting for taste. The decorating and her friends were Cookie's business, but the AIDS thing bothered him to no end, especially when Cookie nursed him straight to death. At news of D'Artagnon's last breath, Angus breathed a sigh of relief.

No sooner was the organist in the ground than Cookie joined a gym. Young men called to set appointments, and a dreadlocked man in athletic pantyhose dropped her off with carrot and beet juice. At the crack of dawn Angus would find her doing updog and downdogs with the TV because the then-alive one-hundred-plus-years-old Delaney Sisters said stretching and breathing were the secrets to long life. Oprah and Dr. Phil helped Cookie find herself, and helped Angus to understand she was lost. She refused all pork, turned her back on baking pound cakes, and dropped thirty pounds. After all these years of marriage, Angus worried he would be shed next, for a gym man stiff to pleasure her. If she could drop God—and it seemed to Angus she had—what chance did he have? But he was still welcome in the bed they shared all these years, and every night she snuggled against him with a goodnight peck, these days sometimes with incense burning. He was grateful, as he'd always been, just butter in her arms—the secret to a good marriage was knowing when to melt. Angus believed he married a woman of good sense. Last Halloween she attended another church, to pray for Bass, she said, somewhere in Clifton.

℘ ℭ

4F's rent was paid on time, he was pleasant enough and did not nag. Angus occasionally saw the tenant running to the car with wine and flowers on Saturday evenings. Proper-talking folks his age, mostly white, stopped by from time to time. One morning before sunrise, Angus heard a commotion in the entryway and saw the front door close. He peeped through the blinds of his office in time to see a tanned man with magazine muscles and a buzz cut disappear in a weather-beaten jeep. Angus had a lot weighing on his mind, and so did not think much of it at the time. A pee hard-on had tricked him, not for the first time, to start what he couldn't finish with Cookie. She said what she usually said: "you lucky to be alive" and "it'll come back." But Angus skipped bed and skulked to his office, fed up. There, naked, he stared at his body, not understanding its betrayal. A little disk had been planted above his balls to feed on the cancer. Suppose this condition never ended? Slack black skin, stomach sag, grizzled hair on his privates, dusty legs and crusted feet foretold of stroke, Alzheimer's, or worse, something more murderous growing inside him, more cancer, only untreatable, like Bass'. Behind a locked door he took a bourbon shot, put on a porn video and pulled out a new pump gadget called The Shaft, and with it tormented his dick to the size of a bologna loaf. Still nothing, and he hurt like hell for days afterward. So bad that he went to the doctor. No harm done.

The idea of illness picked at him. Angus was a cross patient, not the type to sit idly by when he could be doing something, only he did not know what to do. He put his computer online and learned the ins and outs of prostate problems, the success stories and failures. June 12th marked a year since his treatments begun, but it passed with his plumbing still broke. Again the doctor said be patient. Angus posted a desperate message to a man calling himself Stiff, and Stiff said get in shape. A guy named Jerk suggested lipocine and other alien stuff. Angus was determined, and even started eating Cookie's tofu. He quit going to Minnie's Soul Food for pork chop sandwiches on the sly, and upped his exercise. He usually bowled Wednesdays with Bass in a league, and weather permitting they played golf Sundays. Bass, who was supposed to have died from seizure back in April, tried to talk Angus into buying a Stairmaster. They stopped at an athletic store on the way to Kenmore bowling lanes.

"That's all I do is climb steps. What I need more steps for?"

"Let's look at the cycles."

"Had one and threw it out?"

Angus climbed on a ski machine and liked it. That's what ended up in his basement, for $1,400.

Just before they got to the bowling alley, Bass asked if he got The Shaft yet; it was his idea.

"I did, and I just want to tell you that damn machine liked to kilt me. It turned my pecker purple. And it looked like it was about to explode."

Bass laughed for a good minute. "Now, it ain't the kind of blow job I like no how. Like I told you, I got that recommendation from a pressure sufferer. Viagra'll kill ya you got the pressure."

"So will that contraption."

"And what color is your dick that it could turn purple anyway?"

℘ ℘

3B next door went empty in August. BJ the tenant, the only other rent payer to like Angus, died while hiking with a friend somewhere in Grand Canyons. Word came in a teary phone call from a Mrs. Margaret Hampson, the tenant's mother, of Portland, Maine. Angus was not the type to pry, but his imagination, set to morbidity, demanded answers. "He was taking pictures and fell down a canyon," she said. "My husband and I will be in town this weekend to collect his things."

Tenants had died before, but Angus was troubled now. Usually the rent was unpaid in these tenant death situations, and Angus had to haggle with the deceased's family over security deposits. But BJ had paid up before leaving town. He was an earnest, sleepy-looking young man with bright acne. He worked at the museum at Union Terminal. Sometimes he would take pictures of Angus gardening, hoeing or hammering in a nail. He gave Angus and Cookie a pumpkin last Halloween, and a Christmas ornament made of matchsticks. His L.L. Bean-looking parents arrived with grief's puffy eyes. They smiled a lot, showing gold fillings, said, "Our boy spoke of you kindly, and we thank you for looking after him," boxed his things up, and that was that. Angus went to a riot prevention meeting that night. Picketers against James Brown's upcoming concert blocked the entrance. "Bunch a idiots," he snarled, and went home.

Angus placed an ad, then fell into sleeplessness. Here it was August, fourteen months later, and he still couldn't get it up. It seemed like his world was coming to an end, even as the pounds dripped away on the ski machine. To make matters worse, he was sitting in his office fussing over his accounts, thinking of selling the other building, when he heard a car door slam. He peeped through the window and saw that jeep and the tanned man with a Marine buzz cut. He could tell where the Marine was going: 4F. Angus was in the kind of mood to have the worst about humanity confirmed, and sneaked up the back stairs to the third floor, right under Mitchell's living room. But that is not where the faint noise was coming from. Its source was the bedroom, just above one of Angus' guest bedrooms.

The next morning, Angus encountered both men in the hallway.

"Morning," Mitchell said.

Angus grunted.

"By the way, Mr. Short, this is Skeet. Skeet's my ... my friend."

Grinning, Skeet stuck his hand out. Angus grudgingly took it.

"Got any buildings for sale?" Skeet said. "We're thinking about buying a house around here."

4F frowned. "Well, I…"

"Naw." Angus left.

For two days he could hardly speak to Cookie, he was so mad.

He told Bass about it, and Bass was surprised. "Shit, didn't he say he was a baller? Didn't he invite you to the Bengals game? It takes all kinds, Angus. Guess that's what happens when you see that kind of stuff on TV, everybody starts doing it. Live and let live, that's what I say."

"Yeah, right."

"His old man's dead?"

"That's what he say."

"Maybe he'll ask you to give him away at his wedding."

"What's the world coming to? I could even hear them carryin' on."

Bass laughed. "How long you listen?"

"What kind of bullshit is that?"

"Well, maybe that's why your pump ain't working…"

Angus hung up. He stayed down in the cellar on his new ski

machine, and later painted and polished the floors of 3B without the help of laborers, and bowled one of the worst games of his life.

Things came to a head with Cookie over breakfast.

"What now?" Cookie complained.

"Nuttin'."

"You ain't gonna worry me none, Angus Short." She stood up, in black exercise tights. "Bass is the one dying and even he ain't half the misery you are these days."

"He ain't going nowhere. We'll be dead before him."

"Speak for yourself. And you're on your own tonight. Mitch's mom's flying in, and they're taking me out to dinner."

"Fine," Angus grumped.

"There's some crab salad and slaw from last night."

"Where's this girlfriend or wife of his anyway, this Pat?"

"What you talking about?"

"The wedding ring."

"Patrick isn't coming. They broke up."

"You knew he was one of them people, didn't you? That's why you rented the place out to him so fast."

"He's good people, that's what I know. And you better be careful what you say, he's a lawyer, remember?"

"I know a little about the law, too. Sodomy's illegal in this town."

"Not anymore. Get your facts straight. And half the people living around here are gay, in case you haven't noticed."

"You know I don't allow that in my house."

"This is my house, too, Angus Short. You do anything to hurt that sweet man and I'll... I'll never speak to you again."

Angus chewed leftovers but couldn't swallow pride. Cookie dined with the tenant, Mrs. Abigail Meeks, a fifty-something woman in lace gloves and strong gardenia perfume, and Skeet in a suit that strained against his muscles. Angus stayed clear, and it took two weeks, Cookie buying a plane ticket, Bass booking a Hawaiian cruise, and a new tenant to replace BJ, a plumb Taiwanese woman with cat's teeth, before Angus backed down. Even then he wasn't that nice. He saw the two men leave the house, then Mitchell shortly return. Angus was in his office, but came out, stopping the tenant on the landing. If he were Angus' son, he'd be smacked into tomorrow. Why, Mitchell Meeks was only a better rent than the niggers tearing downtown apart, a sinful disgrace. His mind had hurtled to the moon and back for words, but what came out was, "Did your daddy know about you?"

"What?" Mitchell said. He looked mad, but then his lips twitched and his eyes pooled. "Yeah, he did."

Seeing hurt, Angus walked away, and that was that. Soon enough 4F would be an empty unit, with Mitchell Baines Meeks sending Christmas cards addressed to his Cookie.

Tenth of November, Bass flew to Miami for a few days of fun before boarding a cruise that cut through the Panama Canal on its way to Hawaii. Angus drove him to the airport, and choked up at Bass' saying: "I'm ready to go, just sail away, shit, and never come back." On November 13th Cookie planned to head to Austin for the grandkids, but without Angus. Angus usually gave her 24k gold or silk to smooth over a rough patch, leaving the gift at the breakfast table, in shiny Saks wrapping. Not this time, though. More than a lifetime of marriage had written out the rest of their lives, but Angus still wondered how it would end. What if she flew away and the plane went down or some crazy Mexicans busting through U.S. borders kidnapped her for ransom? The death of sex was already killing him. How much could a man stand? In a panic, he phoned the airlines and put himself on the same flight. But he mentioned nothing about it to Cookie. Two nights before she was to leave, they were watching the news, and he was ruminating on what to say, when he felt a long-forgotten tingle.

"Mind if I come to Austin with you?"

"Not if you plan on being fussy and mean. Life's too short, Angus Short."

"Stand up," he said.

"What?"

And not long afterward he was sweating on Cookie twice in the same night with the bed squeaking something terrible, loud enough that 4F could hear, he hoped. "You ornery old goat," she purred. "That's what's been eating you." At breakfast he felt giddy and his lust panted. "From now on, I'm charging," she winked.

"I've been paying since you was fifteen years old."

"It's gonna cost you your bad attitude."

Later, with his hand in his boxers and thoughts on nookie, Angus cell-phoned Bass with the news. No answer, and Angus got scared. But ten minutes later, Bass called back, ready to abort Hawaii for Cuba with a certain Altagracia with golden titties. Of Angus' news, Bass said, "You just in P-zone, that's all."

It was more than that. The little about life Angus figured he did understand he was all right with.

Sons
(excerpt)
by Alphonso Morgan

ONE

When the sun slipped into his room and cast a perfect white rectangle mask onto his eyes and forehead, Aaron didn't suspect a thing. The anticipation which had begun needling him from the moment he flickered his eyes open into the blindness of the light he attributed simply to the call of summer, which began, officially, on that day. Not officially, in the haphazard manner with which the months and years are delineated by the stars or by the angle of the earth tilting toward the sun, but o-ficially, because the New York public schools commissioner had said that it was so. It was June 17th.

Aaron sat up and rubbed his eyes, angled out of bed and into a pair of rubber sandals parked beside it. The room was dark except for the finger of light that pointed down at him from the paned square of glass at the top corner of the room. He wiggled his feet in the sandals and stood, took three familiar steps to the little mirror leaning against the wall of his small square of a room in the basement. Normally, after a few seconds in the dark, he would reach for the switch to the right of the mirror and pour a hundred watts of hard light into the situation to get a clearer picture. But today he felt somehow unprepared for what he might find in the harsh reality of light, so he stared into the shadowy reflection of the mirror, faintly recalling the way his waistline curved down into his too-loose boxers, unable to make out the ridges of his stomach or the outline of his still broadening shoulders.

At sixteen Aaron was small—compact, it could be said—but unmistakably reminiscent of a man. His brown body had yet to take on the full flavor of manhood, but the promise of it wafted from every pore, mixed subtly with the colognes and aftershaves which, he thought, masked his adolescence. His muscles, though not fully developed, were sinewy and lean and pulsed under his skin. His thin arms and legs curved out at the biceps and calves just enough to say that the little boy who had inhabited that body months before was gone, and that a full-blown man might just come pounding out at any minute.

To Aaron's eyes, though, peeking through the darkness, he was the same skinny kid he had been years before, except for the shadow which gathered now above his lip and trailed imperceptibly down his jaw. He no longer wanted to be that skinny kid, no longer wanted to weigh a hundred twenty pounds or wear two pairs of sweat pants beneath his jeans to disguise his little waist. He wanted to be six feet tall and look down into the eyes of other sixteen-year-olds instead of up. He turned away from the mirror and lifted an abandoned T-shirt from the foot of his bed, pulled it on and went out of his room, down the hall, toward the creaking staircase, leaving the fading white rectangle on the bed near his pillow.

In the kitchen his mother stomped frantically around sipping and choking into a broken coffee cup, inserting items into a black leather bag. Aaron recognized this: her effort not to be late for the third time in one week to the bright tiny cubicle under the clocktower of the Republic National Bank where she worked.

"What you doin' up so early?" she said and looked at him. "Forget you ain't have school today?"

"Sun woke me up," he said quietly, sitting down at the table.

"The sun?" she said, and stood for a moment in front of him. "I guess you think you too old for me to slap you 'cross the mouth?" They stared at each other.

"I ain't got time to play with you," she said after a moment. "I am late for work." She went out of the kitchen, and from the front hallway said: "Your Uncle Jack is dropping Anise off at 5:30. You better be here to let her in, or you going to be in trouble. You hear me?" The front door opened. "And stay out of the streets!" It slammed shut and Aaron could hear her scuffed black pumps clomp away down Newkirk toward the D train.

Anise was his sister. She was nine years old. She had the exact round head her brother had, and his exact color, with exact black hair twisted into geometric configuration by her mother on

Sundays. The style, whatever it was, was intended to last all week, until the following Sunday when she would again get her creative juices flowing and invent a totally new series of flips and twists for her little daughter's hair. But Anise had her own ideas, and had usually, by Tuesday or Wednesday, reduced her mother's weekly ritual into a lone unicorn twist down her back. Anise liked the *idea* of getting her hair done, and would sit in front of the mirror those Sunday nights admiring and examining that week's creation. But a head full of ribbons and whatnot was unconducive to a week's romping and Tom-boying.

Aaron liked his sister. The amount of control she seemed to have over her little life infuriated him. But he forgave her because he realized there was something of it in him too—a basic ability to handle almost anything life dished up, maneuver in whatever predicament. But there were times when he doubted himself, when adolescent uncertainty crept in to blur his vision and put a choke hold on his confidence. A neat combination of aloofness and brand name clothes was Aaron's cool camouflage, his very effective way of projecting a more perfect version of himself onto the world.

But today Aaron felt only anticipation, a prickly urgency to step out into the world and feel against his skin whatever was in the air. Quickly he showered and dressed and stepped coolly out onto the stoop. He could hear the jingle and chimes of the ice cream truck dissolving odd into the morning. He breathed the Brooklyn air, considered his mother's admonition, and dropped off the steps, kicking his black and brown gore-tex boots down Newkirk toward Flatbush Avenue.

TWO

At 9:45 in the morning, Sha sat on gray cement steps squeezing a spark into the tip of a Newport. By that time he had already pulled three cherry embers down the white shafts of three previous Newport cigarettes, pushing his jaw forward and pressing the smoke out of his lungs in short, forceful breaths. Everything Sha did, he did exactly in this manner: Forcefully.

Quickly. Decisively. All of the daily processes of life being done with force and decision to mask the limpness of life in its greater scheme.

The steps he sat on were attached to a row of brick apartments. The owner of the steps, Mrs. Barbara Beckford, left for work by eight o'clock each morning and he would plant himself on her stoop, which was closest to the Avenue, and sit for hours smoking weed and cigarettes, watching the brown bodies move through the sun up and down Flatbush Avenue.

Sha took a last pull of his cigarette and flicked it to the ground. His eyes scanned the Avenue, past the old Jamaican ladies in their printed hats and dresses, and the young men in their blue and gray uniforms delivering produce and Coca-Cola and cigarettes. Down the block, past the blue and white ice cream truck with its sunny jingle and chimes sounding before any cones or sundaes or bombpops would be wanted in the day, a familiar stride was making its way down the Avenue in his direction. He had seen Aaron before, carrying himself through the neighborhood on his manicured teenage gait, going to the store or back and forth to school.

They had collided one afternoon that winter. Aaron was coming out of the bodega with a carton of milk for his mother. His headphones pounded against his ears and he hadn't noticed Sha stepping into the store as he was stepping out. Their bodies came together, and startled Aaron dropped the bag containing his mother's milk and started to fall back into the store himself. Sha had instinctively put his arm around Aaron just at his waist to steady him until he felt the hard little body regain its balance and stoop to pick up the dropped package.

"You alright, son?" Sha had said, looking at him.

"I'm cool," Aaron blurted too loudly over the headphones. He slipped past Sha and flew around the corner toward his house.

Sha had stepped backward out of the store and watched through the clouds of breath for a second before Aaron disappeared around the corner. It was his first glimpse of the boy. He had liked his small, purposeful hump-walk, a slight variation of that one employed by every Brooklyn boy alive in the decade. Later he thought about the boy, visualized his face and triangle nose, big eyes and round head and low haircut, the small tight body hiding and the layers of clothes. *Perfect*, he had thought.

Fuckin perfect, he thought again as Aaron came closer, the jingle and chimes whisking up from the ice cream truck, the combination making his mouth water. But Sha was surprised to detect something else creeping in along with the attraction he felt for the boy. There was a thin innocence with which the boy lifted and lowered his eyelids to take in the world, something about him Sha wanted in his life.

He was fifteen or sixteen, Sha guessed. There was nothing overt in the boy's demeanor that should have made Sha think he messed around. There was nothing there that showed. But there was something: he way Aaron's eyes lingered a second too long on certain young men on the Avenue and not at all on others. The familiar resigned solitude in those eyes when they looked. Something caught Sha's eye, something not altogether quantifiable that danced slightly and incongruously in his ever-discriminating peripheral.

It had not occurred to him immediately. But Sha, who, at twenty, had not yet accustomed himself to the traditional types of employment, had had plenty of occasions in the months he had been staying in Flatbush with his sister to observe Aaron from the Beckford stoop. Most of the time, Aaron would avoid his pregnant glances—too hard, Sha thought. One more clue, according to his impeccable logic, not only that the boy had it in him, but that whatever it was, was bubbling closer and closer now to the surface. Maybe he didn't know it yet, or understand it; but he felt it, Sha bet.

To Sha it seemed that the ones seeming *not* to pay attention were generally the ones paying the utmost attention. A nigga with nothing to hide would just nod and say *what's up* and go on about his business. No big deal. But the ones who doubted themselves, who read too much into the casual exchanges which occurred between men a million times a day on avenues all over Brooklyn, those were the ones who were suspect. Those were the ones you could shake down and assault and unmask, which was usually the way he thought about the whole process—as a tactical maneuver, an exercise in strategy. Sometimes he didn't even want the boys.

But he wanted to say to them *I see you, you're not gettin over on me, I could get you if I wanted to.*

But he didn't regard Aaron in this way for some reason; an unfamiliar impulse was stirring in him. Right there, with the taste of nicotine swirling in his mouth, Sha swore that if he ever got hold of the little boy, he would never let him go. Shocked as he was by this, he had said it and he guessed he meant it.

THREE

Anise got down out of her Uncle Jack's black El Dorado, twirling her jacket string around her finger and thinking of stupid Keisha Armstrong who lived across the street from her Aunt Jesse's apartment on Kosciusko. She had gone to fourth grade at P.S. 126 with Keisha and had hated every minute of it. Not school. Just Keisha. But Keisha had figured so prominently in the scholastic experience of the preceding nine months that it was hard for Anise to think of one without the other.

Standing on the corner of Kosciusko with one foot planted in the mother-approved sidewalk and the other thrust rebelliously into the forbidden cement of the street, Keisha had put her hand on her hip and yelled, "If you let a boy put his thing on you, you'll have a baby!"

CeCe Miller, age 8, immediately dropped the red plastic handle of her jump rope with a click onto the cracked cement. "Keisha, my mother said for me to come home if you start talkin bout that kinda stuff."

"Don't listen to her, CeCe," Anise had said. "She don't even know what she's talkin about anyway."

"For your information I do know what I'm talkin bout, Anise. You always think you know everything." Keisha threw her hand out in front of her. "Anyways, my cousin Trina let this boy rub up on top of her and she bout to have a baby in two more months. And *she* only fifteen." The last point she added vehemently as if it strengthened her argument.

"He has to do more than that, Keisha," said Anise. "The boy has to put it *inside* of her for the girl to have a baby."

CeCe whined. "Ya'll nasty."

"Least I know what I'm talkin about, CeCe. Keisha's confused.

"I *do* know what I'm talkin about I *told* you!" Keisha moved her head on her neck. "The boy, Anthony, did it on her leg and they just went in, and now she's gonna have the baby in two more months." She formed a V with her fingers.

"Keisha, that's the dumbest…that's not even…" But secretly she wondered; and she admitted to herself, substituting certain of Keisha's laymen's terms for technical ones, her inability to disprove any of it. Now all the secret books she had read and all the piecemeal information she had amassed seemed useless.

"Anise," Keisha said then, tilting her head thoughtfully, "you need to try to find out something for yourself sometimes. Some people is smart in school but don't have no *common* sense cause all they do is read books all day. That's what my mother says."

That's why your mother works the cash register at Caldor's, Anise thought. *And if she had any common sense…* But tactful Anise kept this to herself, knowing it would be wasted on Keisha, and not forgetting that Keisha was eleven and had repeated the fourth grade twice already and would pound her if she did not. Anise said nothing, just raised her eyebrows in glib acceptance of her status as one of the smart, no-common-sense people.

"Dummy," she now said lightly to herself, making long circles in the air with the string of her jacket, raveling and unraveling it into the air. She climbed the stairs and pulled at the heavy outside door of the house. Locked. She slammed her little thumb into the doorbell. *Ding.* Waited a moment and let go. *Dong.* She heard nothing from inside, rose to her tiptoes, tried to peep through the glass. *Ding…Dong. DingDongDingDongDingDong.* Anise sighed, exhausted from her long series of debates with Keisha Armstrong, and the ominous negotiations she engaged in always with her Aunt Jesse for what privileges were allowed her. She sat down on the steps. The jingling chimes of the ice cream truck trickled up from somewhere and the new summer sun slanted into the street through the trees. Her uncle Jack had already accelerated the big El Dorado down the street. She was not worried, not *afraid*. But she was irritated now, and wondering where her brother could be. He didn't have *friends*. There was the set of girls that called giggling on the phone but were never seen. There was the vague occasional teenage boy for whatever period of time, each identical to the next and identical to her brother, seen at some point, but vanished thereafter. But now—there wasn't one now, and she knew in her heart he was walking aimlessly to spit her and remind her he was free.

The the bolt clicked behind her and she turned and squinted into his eyes. "What took you so long?"

"Sorry," he said.

"You're not sorry. You did it on purpose," she said. "Just to be mean."

"I did not," he said weakly. "I didn't even hear the bell."

"What do you mean you didn't hear it," she said, lifting herself off the step.

"I said sorry, Anise."

"I rang a million times. And, if you didn't hear it why did you answer the door?"

"Because it's five-thirty."

"Shut up." She shoved through the door past him and punched him in the stomach. "What's *wrong* with you?"

Anise slammed her bright book bag into one of the chairs at the table and began tearing her arms out of her jacket. She dragged the jacket half-on through the apartment and slung it into her room in the back. She came back into the kitchen, pulled out one of the chairs. Aaron stood at the sink, his back to her.

"What happened?" She sat down at the table.

"What do you mean 'what happened,'" he said and glared over his shoulder at her.

"I mean," she said very slowly, mocking, "what did you *do* today?"

"Well then why did you say 'what happened'?"

"A lot of people say that."

"Well, it sounds stupid."

"Not to me."

Aaron stared menacingly at her for another moment and

turned away. The dishes clanged in the sink. Anise smiled to herself.

"So, what did you—"

"Don't worry about what I do, Anise," he said, without turning. "I do what I want to do. I'm grown."

"You think you are," she said under her breath.

He turned on her then. "Get out!" He came toward her, pulled her out of the chair by her arm. "Get out of here!"

"Let go!"

He shoved her out of the kitchen then and she turned and screamed at him. "I'm telling!" she said.

"Tell, I don't care."

"I didn't even *do* anything. I was just asking a question."

"So what."

"That's why I'm gonna tell, and you're gonna get in trouble. It's not my fault. You probably got beat up."

He lunged at her then and hit her hard in the arm. She screamed and ran wailing to her room, slamming the thin door behind her.

A wave of guilt knocked into Aaron at that moment, swirled and frothed with the other emotions that bubbled inside him. He wanted to redeem himself but the swirl in his head distracted him and he knew it would be insincere. He felt sorry for Anise, but the most significant event in sixteen years had transpired that afternoon, ending not ten minutes before with the back door closing behind Sha's lean silhouette even as Anise punched her little finger into the bell at the front. All he wanted was to be alone and reflect, mull excitedly over the images of the day's events crystallized in his mind. He was giddy with excitement, but racked with fear and uncertainty at the same time. He couldn't fit the square peg of what had happened into the sphere of context he understood. He didn't have time to be sensitive.

Aaron had learned to guard his feelings viciously and always. Every indication from the world suggested that whatever he felt really at whatever significant moment was the exact wrong thing at the wrong time. His affinity for this sister was all wrong, he knew, knew without ever being told or warned or chastised. So he did what he could to disguise the truth. He taunted and tracked and insulted her, hit her with snowballs in the winter and stripped leaves off mulberry branches in the summer, switching her little legs until she screamed. But whatever he did and however she screamed or hit back or told her mother, there was always, below the noise and confusion, some little gleam in her eye, faint but unmistakable, that said that she knew. She knew that her brother was crazy about her and was laughing at him all the time. She understood—this was the fear. And the threat. Because he had never allowed anyone to understand. His grandmother and aunts who doted over him. His friends who praised his cool and whom he allowed to be drawn into his world briefly. The girls who laughed and smiled. He never once doted back—on any of them. He rarely even acknowledged their praise of him, because to do so would require him to affirm some feeling within himself. He could no more easily admit to believing he was cool or smart or cute than he could admit believing he was not. Either way, he thought, would open him up to ridicule. If he thought he was okay he could be picked apart by those who might suspect that he was not; if he did not, he would be eaten alive by the vultures who lived on self-doubters, or pitied to death by those who felt sorry for them. Better to remain aloof, never to reveal his exact feelings on *any* matter to anyone. Always hold on to just a little piece for himself.

Aaron finished in the kitchen and the stairs creaked as he dropped quickly down them to the basement. He wanted to be out of sight before his mother appeared to compose himself and wipe away whatever trace was left of it all on his face. His mother did not come down the steep stairs and he knew he would be safe until dinnertime.

In his room he closed the door and snapped on the light, changed his mind—snapped it off. The television was on, and he lay back on his bed under its glow. As the participants of the program taunted and screamed, Aaron floated back to Flatbush Avenue.

The sun had felt good on his back. Even at nine forty-five in the morning it was warm enough to send tiny beads of moisture onto his forehead and into the small of his back. The anticipation he had felt since the sun first seeped into his eyes and woke him that morning was still alive and poking around furiously in his stomach. He felt the sun and the light breeze in the air and wondered why it felt like Christmas morning or his birthday. There was something in this day for him, in this summer that was just beginning, but he did not know what. Life was calling and he meant to answer. That's all he knew.

He had come around the corner onto Flatbush and walked for some time breathing the Avenue's early air before he saw Sha squatting ahead on the stoop. He knew who he was. He remembered the bodega and his mother's milk and Sha's arm around his waist. And something about the way the boy had looked at him with those dark eyes that shook him.

Later, he had seen Sha around the neighborhood; there on the stoop, on Church Avenue, near his school. He would be on Church with the slim vocationless boys who were always there, talking with their hands and shifting their weight on their feet. He had never spoken to Sha. He had nodded at him once when it was unavoidable but always said nothing and evaded the dark eyes. He didn't want Sha to think he was looking. Didn't' want him to think he noticed. But he *had* noticed of course, and when Sha wasn't watching, let his eyes follow Sha's body down the block or rest on him there on the stoop. He was taller only a bit than Aaron, but sturdier, he could see, even under his clothes. He was dark, with those almost black eyes and quarter inch of perfectly unkempt hair.

Sha was good-looking, yes, but he had never said this to himself. He had never thought this thought. And even if he had *thought*, Brooklyn swarmed with them—with brown boy wonders like Sha. He had only ever to look around. But there was something else about the way he moved, the way he placed one foot swiftly and solidly in front of the other when he walked, cocked his head and showed his white teeth when he talked, that drew Aaron in. Sha seemed so comfortable in his world, so in command of it. Everything drawn to taut perfection.

Aaron moved down the block closer to Sha. He did not look at him. He wanted to know Sha, but his awareness of the fact made it impossible. He couldn't speak to the boy because he wanted to speak to him too much, and for Aaron, and for the mind trained never to take any thing out of its box, here was the problem. The most he could do was admire the boy's clothes. And in his mind he left it at that.

As he passed the bakery shop and the corner store and the blue and white ice cream truck with its happy jingle and chimes his eyes were cast downward or out, but he sensed Sha there on the stoop.

"Son." He heard the voice.

Aaron did not stop walking. He heard the voice (the gravelly tenor) and knew it must be Sha, but he couldn't be talking to *him*. The tingle in his stomach grew out of control. He thought he missed a step.

"Yo son," the voice came again. Aaron hesitated, instinctively wiped all trace of expression from his face and turned with vacant eyes toward Sha. From the stoop Sha peered into him, motioned Aaron toward him with a single quick flick of the wrist. Aaron took the careful steps back toward the stoop, concentrating to keep his balance. He raised his eyebrows with easy disinterest. He could feel his heart beat the blood into his ears. The sun got hotter and the shine on his forehead got brighter. He could hear the ice cream truck. What could the boy have to say to him? What had he done?

Aaron looked at him. He kept his eyes steady.

"Eh. Let me ask you something," Sha said.

Aaron panicked. *Why would he want to ask—*

"You know who got trees on this block?"

Trees? Oh. Aaron thought for a minute. He knew where the weed spot was; he didn't understand how Sha didn't.

"Yeah," he said. "You know that little store down on the next block across the street? With the yellow sign? That's a spot right there."

"Yeah?" He looked vaguely out at the avenue. "They got nicks?"

"Just dimes, I think."

"That won't do me no good today," he said and stopped. He sat there calmly. Aaron squirmed in the silence. Sha tilted his head then and looked at him again, showed the white tips of his teeth. "You live around here, right?"

"I live on Newkirk," Aaron said.

"Yeah. I thought you looked familiar," Sha said. "What's your name again?"

"My name's Aaron."

Sha nodded and moved his hand through the air. He said his name.

Aaron stretched his arm, cupped his hand into Sha's. He relaxed. Sha had spoken to *him*. He had not noticed anything, then.

"You got a light?" Sha shook a cigarette up out of the pack and took it between his teeth. Aaron shook his head.

"Don't smoke, huh? Don't start. It's a pain in the ass." He grinned up at Aaron, the cigarette between his teeth. His hand shot down into the pocket of his jeans then, came back with a silver lighter, squeezed a spark into the tip of the cigarette.

Aaron looked strangely at him.

"It don't work sometimes," Sha said, and laughed.

Aaron showed his teeth. He liked Sha's voice, the way his cords clipped together when he spoke. "You live here?" Aaron motioned toward the building.

"My sister lives right there," he said, tilted his head. "I stay with her."

"What school you go to? I never seen you at Erasmus."

Sha laughed. "I'm grown. I'm out of school."

"Oh."

Sha pulled on the cigarette. "I'm twenty-one." He blew the smoke out hard. You bout, what? Nineteen?"

"Be seventeen next month. I'm graduating next year."

"Yeah? You look older," Sha lied. "I thought you were nineteen or twenty at least. But you just a young buck, huh?"

Aaron stifled his smile.

Sha looked him up and down. "Why ain't you in school right now?"

"Yesterday was our last day."

"Oh, so you just chillin now."

"Basically."

Aaron felt fine now. There was always that surge at the spring of a new friendship. And it was happening already. He could feel it.

Aaron had had a long series of what could be called best friends, all of whom had eventually been cast by the wayside of his somewhat twisted emotional path through the teen ages. It began in the eighth grade. Tony Bias was light brown with squinted cat eyes and a curly taper haircut stuck under a blue Knicks cap. He was the first boy in the eighth grade with that year's ulitmate Air Jordans. Navy blue and black. Shipped direct from the factory. The Jordans, and the fact that he was easily the cutest boy in the eighth grade had made him infinitely popular at J.H.S 137. Aaron could not keep his eyes off Tony. He had spent the first semester of the school year staring at him secretly, watching the way he moved and acted. He wanted to be *like* Tony. But he knew it was more than that; somewhere, below the fear and confusion, he knew. By the time he was in eighth grade, he had been aware of his problem for some time.

When he was five, he had heard one of the older kids at school say faggot on the playground, and when he asked one of the other kindergartners what it was, his little classmate answered confidently that it was a bug. When he asked his mother she told him that it was a very bad word for a boy who likes other boys and that he never should say it. He thought he understood, but a boy who liked other boys seemed unworthy of its own cussword.

By the time he was ten he knew just what a faggot was and knew *he* wasn't going to be one. They were those men with women's ways, punks, sissies. Disfiguring and distorting the mannerisms and speech that made women so fluid into something else. Something that everyone hated. And he hated them too.

Eventually he learned that men who were fags slept with other men. He was sure he was opposed to this. All the faggots having sex together—this was a crime, certainly. Or did they do it with other, *regular* men? And if they did, he wondered, what were those other men? Fags too, or something else? And what did any of them *do*, exactly? Suck each other's dicks? It seemed nasty, but he did find the bodies of men...interesting.

By the time he was thirteen and found himself sitting next to Tony Bias in Civics class he had realized the severity of his addiction. He thought about boys all the time. And men. He had masturbated looking at the men's underwear section of a Montgomery Wards catalog that had been delivered to the house for his mother. The symmetry of the lines stamped into those stomachs and the lean power of those tan legs jutting out of the white briefs and boxers had kept his attention for hours. He had kept the catalog under his bed for weeks, until the recurring nightmare that it would be found there became too much. He threw the thing away rather than take the chance that his mother would notice it creased open to that page. He knew he could never unmask himself, never tell how he felt, but his attraction to boys was becoming so integral to his existing, to his feeling *anything*, he thought. It was so much of what he felt in total. At first he didn't want the feeling to go away. It felt good: the passion, the infatuation he felt for boys, the desire to see and to touch their bodies. But he just did not see how he could ever work these feelings into his reality. He had never had sex with a girl. Women hypnotized him with their grace and femininity, and he liked the sensibilities of girls, but he didn't want to *sleep* with them. But then, he wasn't sure he wanted to have sex, *per se,* with other boys either. He had heard, by this time, that gay boys fucked each other in the ass: and the idea made his stomach turn. And he decided at this point that the men who did this were all like the fags he had learned to hate. Pussies. And something changed in him. A part of him disappeared. Or he pushed it down so hard and so far, so deep into the dark recesses of himself that it was unrecognizable. He raised a dark wall in himself, blocked his thoughts and blanked his mind and he was numb. He resigned himself to a life of celibacy and clandestine masturbation. But he was sitting there three feet away from the best-looking boy in the eighth grade.

When Mr. Thomas had told the class that they needed to copy the information he had written on the board, Tony had leaned over and asked Aaron if he could borrow a piece of paper. Naturally, Aaron had obliged, and they started cracking jokes on Mr. Thomas' too-tight clothes and long bald spot. Over the course of the weeks that followed the two became inseparable, Tony evidently not realizing that his new best friend, though good-looking and well-dressed, was nowhere near his own social stratosphere. Aaron wasn't a geek, exactly. He was a loner, and for the most part didn't participate in the mandatory grouping patterns of J.H.S 137. But Tony loved Aaron for his wit and quiet ways, the few words he said always cutting right to the chase of things, and always said over an ambiguous half-grin. Aaron was cool and reserved, and somehow seemed above the fray of teenage angst. In reality, he was far from above it, and went home from school every day dizzy with thoughts of Tony's dash and charisma. He ruled over the rest of the kids and was by all accounts, and perhaps by some fluke of fate, his. *His.* Everyone knew that Tony was his, and the special clenched-fist pound they gave each other every time they met or parted company sealed their status as *boys* to the rest of the world. They would talk on the phone and go to dances and play basketball after school, and when Tony spent the night at his house, he would sneak looks at his smooth, hairless body. In private, he would fantasize about Tony—not sexual fantasies exactly, but he would visualize the bronzed tan skin and slanted eyes and imagine what it would be like to touch him. Not the way they touched each other usually— hands on each other's backs and shoulders, patting each other's stomachs, speaking into each other's ears. He wanted to really touch Tony, to feel his skin next to his own, but he had resigned himself that this could never, ever happen—not under any circumstances he could imagine. So he satisfied himself with being Tony's friend and confidante and spent every possible waking moment with him, patting and playing in the only way boys were allowed to.

But Aaron was not dissatisfied with his relationship with Tony. He loved Tony, and the oaths Tony repeated to Aaron that they should always remain together, as boys, reached deep in and touched a new part of him. He was experiencing the profoundest joy he could conceive of at the time.

But eventually, much to Aaron's surprise, he began to lose interest in Tony, and by that summer, the infatuation he had felt at first had wilted into a pile of discarded feelings, and a mountain of regret for having shared even the tip of his own iceberg of emotions with Tony. He was as confused at his sudden change of heart as was poor Tony, whose own feelings had evidently continued on the same course as before. He had sensed a chill in Aaron's demeanor toward him as the jokes and hand smacks in Civics class came less and less frequently, but he had kept trying until summer came, and when Aaron hadn't returned any of his phone calls for two weeks he gave up, finally, heartbroken.

By the time he stood there on Flatbush Avenue, shooting the shit with Sha, Aaron had repeated this sequence half a dozen times with unsuspecting boys he met at school or around the neighborhood. He would fall madly under the spell of some precious, good-looking brown Brooklyn boy, and they under his; and then, with sometimes as little as a few hours notice, the magic would disintegrate and the boy would be left to make whatever sense of the situation he could. Aaron would be characteristically non-communicative. But what could he say, really? That he'd fallen out of love with them? He didn't even think of it in these terms himself. And it was usually something relatively insignificant that sent his emotions spiraling imminently downward: something they had worn or said, a new friend or girlfriend he didn't approve of, a quirk or imperfection that suddenly became a glaring annoyance. He couldn't point these things out to them the way teenage couples cruelly pointed them out to each other when they broke up, so he just disappeared as quietly as possible and told his mother to tell whoever called on the phone that he wasn't home.

But he had learned to value these relationships for all they were worth. They gave him joy while they lasted, and each time he would swear he had found his new best friend for life.

"You smoke trees?" Sha asked, shooting ash off the tip of his cigarette onto the ground. "You don't really look like the type."

"Sometimes," he said gloomily. *What did he mean he didn't look like the type?*

"So, what? You want to get a bag? If you got five bucks on it I got five."

Aaron did not want to spend his precious five dollars on weed. He knew how his mother was, how unrealistic about the money she gave him, but he wanted to stay with Sha and five dollars seemed a small price at the moment. "It's whatever man," Aaron said casually. "Shit, I ain't got nothin else to do—I'm free!" He raised his arms above his head like a victorious prizefighter and laughed.

They walked down the block side by side, talking and laughing, weaving in and out of the people on the Avenue. They stepped into the tiny store where weed was peddled at all hours of day and night. The dirty yellow sign above the door said GROCERY, but a few faded boxes of Brillo pads and Kraft macaroni and cheese were all that were on the shelves, and they had been there as long as the spot had, attracting dust, and not attracting, conspicuously, the attention of the protectors and servers of New York law enforcement. No one ever came out of the place with anything even vaguely resembling groceries, only tiny plastic bags of weed with pictures of marijuana leaves or chocolate kisses on them. No one seemed to notice, or they didn't care, or had decided long ago that there was nothing they could do about it, so the steady flow of tiny plastic bags, and nothing else, continued from behind the filthy, bullet-proof glass inside.

On a rusty aluminum stool inside the store, a tall man with matted hair and worn clothes sat fingering his hair with one hand. When he saw Sha he pounded his fist against Sha's familiarly. "Peace," he said, monotone.

"What y'll working with?" Sha said.

"We got the chocolate back there now," the man said slowly, without intonation, and motioned toward the glass.

Sha stepped to the glass and tapped on it with his knuckles, slid his five-dollar bill and the one Aaron had slapped into his palm on the way up the street through the little window. He bent down to speak into the opening and Aaron could not hear what he said. Old lotto tickets and candy wrappers were pasted up around the opening in the bullet-proof glass, and the person behind it could not be seen. A weathered brown hand came down on the bills and slid back inside, came back pushing one of the decorated plastic bags.

Aaron watched the exchange from the door. Sha seemed to

know them. Or maybe his apparent familiarity was only directness, an exact understanding of his role in the scenario. He didn't think Sha had hustled him for the five dollars; he didn't seem that petty.

"Now what, little man?" Sha had said to him as they stepped back out onto the Avenue. "You don't have nothin to do, right?"

Aaron shrugged and shook his head.

"Well, you with me today, then," he said. "Let's go down by the courts and blaze." He pulled a Dutch Master from somewhere, tapped it on Aaron's chest.

Again they weaved through the sunny streets, moving slowly toward the courts on Ocean. When they arrived, Sha threw himself up onto the back of one of the benches facing the court; his feet rested on the seat. Five young men ran back and forth on the half court in a breathless game of twenty-one. They wore the names of five different superstars on their feet. Three others stood near a second bench, talking loudly to each other and glancing occasionally toward the court. Sha expertly broke open the Dutch Master and spilled the tobacco out onto the ground. He emptied the brownish crumbled contents of the bag into the cigar.

"You ever wonder why they let them sell these little bags," Aaron asked, taking the clear empty bag from Sha. "You can buy em at the Chinese store in packs of a hundred. The only thing they good for is to sell weed."

"Jewelry," Sha said, not lifting his eyes from his task. "Earrings and shit—that's what they supposed to be for."

"With weed plants on the side?"

Sha laughed. "Yeah, well, they ain't tryin too hard to keep *this* shit off the streets, let alone the bags. Jakes go by that spot ten times a day, man, you think they don't know what's goin on? They pay them niggas off,. Why you think they never busted that spot? It ain't like they don't see it. Shit, half of them be gettin smoked out *inside* the squad cars, eatin donuts all fuckin day. They don't wanna get rid of it. Too many people makin money off it." Sha licked the blunt. "Giuliani probably got a cut of this bag."

Aaron nodded and made a face. Sha finished the blunt, licked it a final time and set it on his lap, took his lighter and ran the blunt through the flame to dry. He lifted it to his lips and lit the end, pulling the weed and tobacco smoke deep into his lungs. He puffed several more times and passed it to Aaron.

They sat and smoked silently, watching the men on the court dip and pivot in strong graceful movements. Aaron blinked. The drugs swam in his bloodstream. Things seemed surreal. He wondered how was he even sitting there talking to Sha, whom he had seen and thought about so often, and whether their meeting was as simple as it seemed? Sha had to know about the weedspot, he thought. It must have been the five dollars. Whatever it was, he didn't care. He was glad to be with him.

"You want to play?" Sha motioned toward the court.

"In these?" Aaron lifted one of his brown and black boots off the bench.

"Man, what? You afraid to get em scuffed? Those goretex old as hell already. Look what I got on."

Sha dropped off the bench, called to the next bench. "Can we hold your ball?"

They played alone at the other end of the court, both of them stomping in their boots, touching each other too often. Sha had taken off his shirt and sweat gathered at the nape of his neck and trickled down his dark body in a thin stream, over the ridged stomach and into his white boxer shorts. Aaron tried not to look at Sha's body, but there it was, twisting and glistening in the sun right before him, jumping and bumping into his own. He looked like a boxer, Aaron thought, a bouncing brown featherweight floating past his opponents, sticking and moving with fearless precision. Aaron had already been attracted to him. But now, with Sha's half-naked body slamming into him every few seconds, and his senses heightened by the weed and the heat, he was excited beyond comfort. The blunt had made him paranoid. He was afraid something might show.

"Let's go, man," Aaron said gasping. "The weed is makin me tired."

"So what you wanna do, little man? Anybody at your house right now?"

"Nah. My mom's at work."

"So we can chill at your house? You got cable?" Sha grinned.

"Yeah, we got cable." He laughed. "Come on."

For the third time that day, they wound through the crowded Brooklyn streets in their boots and jeans and T-shirts. The afternoon sun was hotter now and they walked more slowly than before. When they reached the house, Aaron unlocked the door and led Sha into the dark hallway.

"This whole house yours?" Sha asked. They descended the creaking dark staircase to Aaron's room in the basement.

"Nah. We just have the first floor and the basement. Somebody else lives upstairs." Aaron led Sha into his small room, turned on the light and closed the door, punched the little button on the remote.

Sha sat down on the bed, one booted foot hanging off the corner of it. His eyes changed; they were different now, looking up at Aaron as he emptied his pockets of change and lint and dollar bills. Sha grabbed the crotch of his pants and pulled it toward him—a gesture familiar to Aaron, but one which now took a foreign flavor over Sha's obscure accomplice eyes.

Aaron had just averted his own eyes nervously. Sha broke the silence. "So what's up with you, Aaron?"

Aaron lifted his brows as if to say *huh?* Sha licked his lips. "I'm sayin. What's up?"

That was it. Those few words, carefully phrased and intoned so that Aaron could disregard them if he needed to and whatever happened could not claim later in some moment of desperation or denial that Sha had made a move on him, were his sole proposition. They rang in Aaron's ears. It was a simple phrase, one which Aaron had heard a thousand times, and which typically required a stock response, if any. But a real question, with all the urgency and precision of wanting to know floated in those words the way Sha looked at him and said them. And Aaron, who would never have dreamed of divulging even the most trivial piece of who he was or how he felt to anyone, was terrified by this; and there was a pertinence in Sha's voice that went right to the very heart of it, that asked Aaron to tell exactly who and what he was, and that said *I already know; I see you.* But at the same time, he seemed to be offering up something of himself, to be saying *here I am, if you want to look.*

Aaron smiled nervously. "I don't know," he said, keeping his voice steady but averting his eyes. "You tell me."

"I was about to in a minute. I just wanted to know how you felt." Sha spoke slowly and kept his eyes fixed hard on Aaron's. He could see the hopeful panic come into his face. When Aaron did not answer, Sha lay back on the bed and cradled his head in the crook of his arm.

"Why don't you turn the light off," Sha almost whispered, still keeping his eyes on him. Aaron still hesitated, standing there looking down at Sha lying there looking back up at him, one hand behind his head and the other under his loose T-shirt stroking his stomach. Aaron's own stomach twinged; he sensed something strange and familiar, something he knew instinctively, but had never experienced. A familiar melody played in his head; he knew the rhythm and feel of it, the runs and riffs and mighty crescendo of it, but not the words, and not the moves that went with it. It was something that he understood, but could not express, and certainly had no way respond to.

Aaron had never had a boy come on to him before. He had never flirted with a boy, never winked and smiled at one in math class. He had never, when he was younger, gotten a card from, or passed a note to a boy that said *I like you, do you like me? Circle yes or no.* He had never hung up the phone with a boy and said *alright baby, talk to you tomorrow.* And he had never, ever, and would never in a million years have thought that he ever could like someone and possibly have them like him back in the same way. It simply could not happen, and he had given up on the idea a long time ago.

And still he could not believe it. Sha could not be lying there on his bed stroking his perfect stomach, looking up at him with those black eyes, meaning what he could not be meaning, telling him to turn off the light. So he stood there hesitating by the door until Sha spoke again in that rough, reassuring whisper: "Turn the light off. It's mad bright."

Well, it *was* bright, he thought, as he flipped the switch, and moved through the darkness and uncertainty toward Sha. Aaron's feet moved on their own, his mind still frantically evaluating, weighing every possibility, so that he did not notice them becoming entangled in the wires of his video game, stereo, television, he only felt himself falling and his knees coming down on the floor. Sha sat up to catch him, and as Aaron came down between his legs, their mouths came together and, against the light of the television, they kissed, as it were, by accident.

∞

Aaron lay there listening to Sha's steady breaths, wondering what he would say to him when he awakened. He watched his chest move up and down under the gentle radiance of the television, which neither of them had bothered to turn off. Aaron had lost track of the rest of the world, and at first could not place what should have been the very familiar sound of the doorbell ringing.

"Oh my god," he gasped when the sharp *Ding-Dong, Ding-Dong, Ding-Dong* of the bell finally forced itself upon him. "It's 5:30! Sha, get up! It's my sister! Come on, my sister's home, shit! Shit!"

Sha rose with an initial start, then very calmly, very quickly, stood and began to reassemble himself. For the split second Sha stood there with his nakedness illuminated by the television, Aaron did not believe that his sister was at the door, or that he even had a sister, or that anything he had ever known existed. Sha continued to dress, quickly and calmly, like someone participating in a routine fire drill. Aaron struggled and twisted hopelessly. When they were finally dressed, Aaron led Sha quickly into the dark hallway toward the door in the back. Neither of them spoke. Aaron unlocked the door and pulled it open. He focused his eyes on the handle of the door. He was dumb. He could not speak. Sha slipped past him and patted his ribs. "Alright, son. Talk to you later," he said, and disappeared.

ℬ ℭ

Even now, Aaron could hardly believe it. He lay on his bed, smelling Sha all around him, wondering what to do, what to say when he saw him. He didn't know if Sha would speak to him now. But however confused or terrified he was, however much his brain sloshed in his skull, Aaron knew that he *wanted* Sha. He wasn't sure how he wanted him, precisely, or what it would mean, even, to have him. But he knew what he had felt lying there with Sha and, for now, that was enough.

On the television two huge drag queens tugged each other's hair in front of a studio audience. Aaron sighed and lay back on his bed; he hit the button on the remote and the room became dark. He could see the brown brick of the house next door, and wondered how the sun had shined so brightly that morning.

Ridge 479
by J.E. Robinson

The number was almost too impossible to read. Mrs. Archer found it doing the wash, tried burning it, and scorched the edges. She soaked it in bleach, but the ink ran a little. When Roger discovered it, part of the number had faded. It had been written in Mr. Kirkendall's best hand. Roger remembered enough of his idiosyncrasies to reconstruct it. He told his older brother Rudy he knew about the number, and what it meant, and Rudy told Roger to say going was the principal's idea, should anyone ask.

Mr. Kirkendall lived on Ridge 479, over fifty kilometers away. Everyone at the school knew where he was. No one dared visit him.

Getting to Ridge 479 would prove a task. The terrain was a harsh mix of red clay desert and sharp brush. The ridge itself was part of the foothills of a mountain range notorious for being a killer. And, once there, no one would be around for ten kilometers.

Rudy bartered for transportation and pulled rank on an underclassman, a forger, for visitor's passes. In print shop, as an independent project, the underclassman manufactured the passes, hand-copied the principal's signature, along with that of the settlement's administrator, and used an antique nutcracker as a notary's seal. It took two days.

Rudy and Roger planned to go on a school day, after attendance. That morning, however, Rudy met Roger in the boys' room before assembly. He told him he knew the principal knew. When the official summons came a few minutes later, Rudy told Roger how to handle himself. Roger listened and did as he was told. Before the principal, he remained cool, played dumb. None of the principal's questions came close to prying even the slightest confirmation of what was to transpire. Toward the end, the principal, a big man, sat on his hands and rocked.

"I know how you feel about Mr. Kirkendall," he said in a soft voice. "You liked him, didn't you?

"Yeah."

"A lot of people did. He was real nice to you, too?"

"Yeah, he was." Roger hung his head and pretended to snivel. "He was real nice to a lot of us, you know? Real easy to talk to. A really good guy."

"Yes, he was. But he hurt you, didn't he? He did a real bad thing to you and a lot of other kids. And that's why he had to go away. You know that. I know that and you know that and everybody else knew that. But, what I don't understand is why you'd want to go where he is. Do you think you can tell me why?"

"I don't know." Roger wiped his eyes and nose on his jacket sleeve.

The principal smiled a bit to himself. "I don't know, either. How do you feel?"

"I don't know."

"Mad," the principal said. Roger nodded. "Mad at him." Roger nodded, then shrugged. "I understand. I think anyone would understand. You liked Mr. Kirkendall, he was nice to you, but you're mad at him. You're mad at him for what he did to you. Right?" Again, Roger nodded and shrugged. "You feel confused. That's OK. Feeling confused is understandable. And, you know what, good man?" The principal leaned forward and touched Roger's knee. Roger shied away. "Feeling scared's OK, too."

The principal was finished. He made Roger exchange the forged passes for authentic ones, and he excused both Rudy and Roger for the day.

Rudy and Roger made one stop, at the greenhouse, to pick up a spade, water, plant food, and a redbud sapling to plant once they got on the ridge, if the ridge would take it. At the settlement gate, the sentry examined the passes, gave them a pistol and some shells, and warned them to be back before night.

Ridge 479 was west. Rudy got them there within the hour.

Though he understood it to be the exile's ridge, Roger had not imagined its bleakness. Unlike everything around it, Ridge 479 was limestone. Its face was almost completely flat. At the ridge's summit, jutting over the edge, was Mr. Kirkendall's house.

Getting out and standing alone, Roger looked up at the

house. "You bastard," he muttered. He wiped his nose and eyes on his jacket sleeve. "You bastard."

Rudy waited until Roger looked ready. Since he was old enough, Rudy loaded the pistol and stuffed it in his pants. Roger carried the spade, slung over his shoulder, and the water, slung over the spade. Rudy carried the sapling and plant food.

Then, they began the ascent. The footpath began at the road, wound its way to the ridge's back, then went up. The ridge's back was more hospitable than its face (it, at least, had grass) and climbing it felt like climbing yet another hill. Near the top, the footpath flattened and ducked between a pair of evergreens so thick they embraced. Roger stopped and looked back at Rudy.

"It's OK," Rudy said.

Roger nodded. He peered between the trees. Setting the water down, he pointed the spade into the branches.

"All right now," he shouted. "I'm not alone here, and we got a gun. So, ready or not, here I come!"

Flailing the spade, Roger ran through the evergreens. Rudy simply ducked under the branches.

Mr. Kirkendall's house was not far from the evergreens. It had been built as part of the observatory, more functional than punitive, but a succession of residents had added little things (a garden, a bird bath in the garden, colored pebbles around the bird bath, and so forth) that, as a whole, turned the place fancy. Like the houses in the settlement, this house had a slate roof, though its roof's slate was marked with the skull and cross bones. Anyone flying in would see it for kilometers. Earlier, it had a keeper's shed, but, once the settlers had perfected the electronic eye and monitoring system, the keeper was pulled. Now, the keeper's shed kept tools.

Mr. Kirkendall had been sent there less than five months before, in time for the frost. He had no time to add anything to the place.

"You go on ahead," Rudy said, sitting on a bench in the garden. "I got this rock in my shoe and I just got to get it out, so I'll wait here and you go on in."

"By myself?"

"Yeah, by yourself. I'll be right here, if you need me. Don't worry."

Roger watched Rudy set the pistol on the bench and remove his shoe. Leaving the water, Roger took the spade, just in case. He knocked on the door. He knew it had no lock. Then, he pushed the door in.

"Are you from heaven or from Earth?" chimed the electronic greeter.

"Neither," Roger said. "I'm from the settlement."

"Name, please."

"Roger Archer."

"Roger Archer, victim?"

"Yeah. And I got a right to be here, too."

"Uncontested," the greeter said. It turned on the lights.

The place had Mr. Kirkendall's feel. During the time he was there, the walls were painted a strange, bland gray and he had hung pictures of each of his classes, taken at the end of each year. As it had been in his classroom, papers littered every flat surface, including the floor. Among the papers were clippings his family sent from far-off Nebraska. Empty supply boxes were stacked in a corner near the door.

"I guess nobody wants his stuff," Roger said as he set the spade against the wall. He craned his neck into a side hall. "Hello?"

"Hello," said the greeter.

"Not you. Hello?"

No one answered. Roger was alone. For the hell of it, he opened the old rolltop desk the settlement administrator let Mr. Kirkendall keep. Inside was his collection of pins, pens, and pencils. A jar of Louisiana cockroaches sat on a salad plate between a knife and fork. Beneath the plate were cobwebs.

They let him keep his art supplies. Used watercolor trays were stacked to one side of the desk, and on them were fine point brushes with that hardened feel of dried paint. Watercolor, Mr. Kirkendall always said, was meant to be used. He used his often.

Mr. Kirkendall's most recent work, though, was gone. No fresh sketchpad was anywhere near the desk, and a space on the writing surface was marked off with masking tape and sat empty. His old sketchpads were bundled together by a single thick rubber band. They were stuffed into a pigeonhole. Roger examined them. They were bird and insect studies, landscapes, a few seascapes, but none he did in class. Perhaps, as talk had it, they made his disgorge them.

The bedroom was next to the desk. It was unlit. Roger peeked.

"Do you wish to enter this room?" the greeter asked.

"Yeah."

"Why do you wish to enter this room? Please state in a single, complete sentence of twenty words or less beginning, 'I, Roger Archer, wish to enter this room because...'"

Roger rolled his eyes and mumbled something about electronic greeters. "I, Roger Archer, wish to enter this room because I see something there."

The greeter mumbled something about humans. It turned on the light.

Roger stood in the doorway. In his entire life, he had never seen one room so completely and so thoroughly trashed. Everything was on the floor. The nightstand, end tables, and dressers were turned over. The trunk dumped. The futon mattress separated from its frame and ripped open. Duck down dusted the room, and it looked bloodied. A photograph of a billboard declaring "!ATOYOT" hung crooked on the wall, its glass smashed. Watercolors seemed among the stuff, but they had been torn into so many bits they were part of a single, all-summer jigsaw puzzle.

"Guess nobody wanted any of his stuff."

"Is this a serious question," the greeter asked, "or is this a pubescent human's idea of sarcastic irony?"

"Huh?"

"Never mind."

Walking in, Roger tried being careful about what he touched, since talk had it no usable prints were found. Mr. Kirkendall was killed there. Anywhere from two to fifty men did it.

The details got out fast. Two hours after the monitor beeped him dead and the authorities recovered the body, the entire settlement knew what bones were crushed, where he crawled, how long he stayed alive. Everyone knew the why. According to the version Roger heard, the men found the watercolor he said Mr. Kirkendall painted, but Roger knew that was a lie. No watercolor was ever made of him.

Roger couldn't take being there. He puked in the bathroom. The greeter asked if he needed help, but he said no. He sat on the toilet until he felt ready. That took a while. Then, taking the spade, he left.

Rudy was still on the bench. He had removed his shoes and socks and his toes were in the dirt. At first, Rudy didn't say a thing (Roger still looked a little red), so he watched his toes making semi-circles. Roger came right up to them, looking away and moving when they came close.

"Sorry," Rudy said a couple times. Each time, Roger moved his feet.

"What a mess in there," Roger finally said. "Everything turned over, and all. Just a mess."

"Find anything?"

"Yeah. I burned 'em."

Rudy nodded. He put on his shoes and socks, then picked up the sapling and water. "The soil looks pretty rich, so I don't know if we need plant food a lot." He looked around. "I think they scattered his ashes around here, since nobody claimed them. So, anywhere around here'd be fine, I guess. You got anyplace in particular in mind?"

Roger shook his head. "Anyplace. You pick the spot."

"I don't want to sound dungy, but—" he tapped the sapling roots against he ground. "I mean, it is your idea, after all. And, he was your teacher. You pick the spot. It's OK, I'm here. Anyplace's fine. All you got to worry about is it's got to have enough room for it to grow."

Rudy took the spade and pushed Roger toward the center of the garden. Roger wandered. He stopped at a space where some indigenous white flowers grew low to the ground.

"Here?" Rudy asked.

"He always liked these," Roger said, pointing to the flowers.

"He'd say they remind him of the ones back home."

Measuring depth by the roots packed together by dirt, Rudy dug. Soon, the hole was substantial enough to oblige the sapling. Roger set the sapling in the hole and Rudy centered it. Rudy's sense of balance was better. Between the two, they watered and sprinkled plant food over the roots. Then, Rudy headed for the bench.

"Where're you going?" Roger asked.

"I'm tired. I'm going to sit down."

"But the tree?"

"C'mon, I dug the hole. You can cover it up, can't you?"

Roger took the spade and, struggling to keep the sapling in place, he filled the hole. He tapped the dirt down, as he had seen the settlement's groundskeeper do, and he lumped the dirt around the trunk after pouring water again. Then, he stepped back.

"Sorry," Roger said. "Really, I'm really so sorry."

Rudy watched. He stepped onto the bench to get a clear view. He saw Roger pause after planting, sigh, lower his head, rub his eyes, then stoop down for the water jug and plant food container. Before Roger rose, Rudy eased down. He was sitting when Roger returned. Rudy looked at the sapling.

"You got it in OK," Rudy said. "Good job. Looks good. Real good. Good man."

Roger was unimpressed. He hated "good man." It was the principal's phrase. Roger shrugged. "Maybe it'll grow."

"For sure, it'll grow," Rudy said. "Believe you me. It'll grow real good. Just you wait."

They went back down the path and returned to the settlement. The sentry clocked them in. Per regulation, he and a dog searched for contraband and noted on the system things were clean. The sentry unloaded the pistol, sniffed the barrel. He counted the shells and gave Rudy a statement to sign that the trip went without incident, though Rudy was hardly legal. Then, the sentry set the visitor's passes in acid.

The spade, water jug, and plant food container were returned to the greenhouse. Rudy and Roger left their transportation in a pre-arranged spot for its owner to reclaim. Before leaving Roger sifted his soles to tissue paper. The paper went in his pocket.

They walked home. Most were pleasant. In his room, Roger pressed the tissue paper in his school yearbook, at the page autographed "Best, Todd Kirkendall." Rudy excused himself, bolted the bathroom, and turned on the hot tap. As he had done several times a day each day since Mr. Kirkendall's death, Rudy scrubbed.

Bees

by Curú Necos-Bloice

In my girlhood there were butterflies and bees, as well as other things. I cannot remember many things, but the feeling of butterflies in between my fingers, shedding their resplendent dust of colors, made me weep. I never kept these creatures which I found so utterly irresistible. Each time I saw one my impulses were the same: I would run after it, wait for it to alight on the petaled laps of flowers, and while it inhaled the breath of nectar I would capture it. Thus I hoped to own its beauty forever. Instead, each time the same thing happened: I would see its beauty shedding and I would cry before releasing it.

Water... falling from faucets that, despite being tied up with ropes, would not stop dripping. Under it I found my other love. Small and chubby as the babies we loved. They were there, I suppose, drinking. Bees, whose honeycombs I had never seen or touched, but still already appreciated. It was their wings of amber and the fluffy body striped like a polo shirt from America that made me love them.

I had attempted to imprison these as well, several times, disregarding Abuela's warning that though bees were peaceful they deserved freedom and would guard their liberty like all living things. I listened only when a feisty bee stung my eye as I chased it. I thought someone had come in the bee's defense and set my eye on fire. I wept then too, forgetting the bee, full of regret but not anger.

The boy.

I had watched him pass by the first time, selling coconut drops. He was like nothing else I had seen: brown as molasses, with eyes like ginger and teeth white as fresh coconut meat. I did not know why, but my mouth watered for him. Not for the candy. I was going to talk to him but I remembered who I was—la java, the yellow, ugliest little girl whose hair didn't grow and whose eyes were so huge and bulging that people believed her mother had seen the devil during pregnancy. Her mother's fear had become the child's permanent expression. I stayed behind the partition peeking out shyly from the flower-print curtains while Mami counted coconut drops onto a plate, as she took them from the beautiful boy's tray. Next time he came, barefooted, with midday sidewalks burning my soles, I followed the solemn boy, wondering what someone who walked all afternoon alone thought about. I followed him down the road and three streets away from my home, till he looked back at me, standing still. I ran away frightened, unwilling to hear him call me ugly.

There were also birds that I couldn't resist. I caught one, one time, and kept it inside till Abuela made me release it, saying birds had to be free. It was blue of body and gray of wings and it made my heart full as if it were the day of the three wise men, and I had just received myriad toys.

I am there. Different to all my kin. Different to my mother. Looking nothing like my sisters or brothers. I'm a middle child who grins and grins because at least I have white teeth, and because I know that people always ask "where did she come from?" when they see us all together.

Miss Hayworth looks like Papi, but has Mami's eyes. Ramoncito looks like Mami, but has grandfather's smile. Pilar, now sixteen, they say is grandmother at twenty-three. Junior is Papi except for the tan color he gets from Tio Pepe. But no one can say anything about me. So I watch Mami. I copy everything she does. Soon they'll have to say I have her walk.

My name is Cleopatra, thanks to Mami's craziness. She named an ugly, poor little girl after a beautiful, rich queen, in a town where people laugh at everything. I don't dare say my name to anyone. I got tired of the laughing. Now I say my name is Patria, which is what Mami calls me herself. I think she knows she was wrong to name me after anyone beautiful. So people think I'm named in honor of our country and no one laughs anymore. After all our country is poor, and I don't know what the rest of it looks like, but Papi's always saying, "This country's a mess. This country is just a mess." Even though he's never been in any other.

One day I'm watching the neighbor's monkey. They say he brought it from St. Kitts where he was born. He's a Cocolo like

Mami. Mr. Mc. I laugh with the monkey and throw it some hot peanuts I got from the vendor. Men walk by and say, "Look at that little girl laughing at the monkey, like she doesn't know she's uglier than it." They laugh. I run. I run to Abuela who is washing in the yard she shares with us. She's washing because it's Thursday and it's sunny. I stick my hands in the soapy water. She says, "You want to wash? Here." She passes me Abuelo's handkerchief which is stained with blood. Work is Abuela's solution to everything. If she sees you crying she hands you a broom and yells, "Go, go sweep the corners of the house."

The sun follows me. Wherever I go it insists on going, like a stray dog waiting for you to throw it some food. One day I ran as far as to the Beach of the Dead trying to get away from it, but no matter how I tried I couldn't get away. From then on I accepted it following me around, but I don't like it. I don't like it one bit. Mami always tries to get me to use an umbrella, but when I do I have to listen to the tigres yelling, "Hey, java, get some color! Shut that umbrella!"

Miss Hayworth has a lovely figure for her age, everyone says. She doesn't wear panties and shows us her privates when the grown-ups aren't watching. She especially likes to show it to Junior who always looks like he's going to cry when she does, and one day he did. She had been lifting up her dress and taunting him all day till he finally squatted in the corner of the yard and burst into tears. She looked at him puzzled and then started laughing.

Pilar is screaming again and I like to see her scream. She who's so beautiful that no one notices her darkness, because the truth is you can't get away with being too light or too dark here. She who's so beautiful she makes me look even worse. Mami is beating her again, even though Pilar is a señorita. Pilar's rough hair is out and all around her head like mountains. She sits on the ground looking like she's seeing something other than Mami's hand with a stick from a tree beating her. But I love Pilar. I'm glad she's my sister. It comforts me to know that someone so beautiful is related to me, is my sister.

Ramoncito and I are playing with dolls under the floor of the house. We don't want anyone to see him doing this. Papi has already beaten him twice for combing dolls' hair, but he can't help it. When he doesn't play with them his big eyes—beautiful big eyes, not bulging like mine—look so sad. After a while I can't take it. I tell my little brother, "Go meet me under the house and I'll bring Deedee and Maylen," my North American dolls. We stay there for hours making believe these dolls have lives like the women in telenovelas.

I like clouds, especially when they look like arroz con leche, because I love rice pudding, though Mami hardly makes it. Instead she keeps giving us oatmeal which only Cocolos eat. I used to think I could reach the clouds by climbing our sea grape tree. I knew that if only Mami wasn't watching, and yelling, "Get your butt down from there! Little girls shouldn't be climbing," I could make it to the highest branch, stretch my arms and get some clouds. One day I did, I did climb all the way to the top of the tree, just like Junior had done over and over, but I couldn't touch anything. Junior had told me I couldn't but I never listen to boys, because they never want a girl to know anything.

I've been out of school for years. Maybe three, or maybe just one and a half. I'm not sure. At first I was glad, but now I'm sick of cleaning out chicken coops and the duck pond and always going here or there to get salt or sugar, verdura or salsa, vinegar or olive oil. I think I want to go back to school, but not to the one I was in before. Not to that one in Sister Bea's yard, where no one wears a uniform. I want to look like Ivelise the Cocola who's an india, who looks like a dominicana, who wears white ironed tops and blue pleated skirts and even has a bag made from some poor dead goat. I want that big yellow bus to drop me off for siesta. I'd like to sit looking pretty on a porch, looking through books that are full of pictures, instead of having dirty feet and dusty legs, bringing this for so and so, or doing this for that. Pilar and Miss Hayworth also go to school. Well, Pilar doesn't just now, but Miss Hayworth still goes. I don't like her uniform though, it's khaki and dull, like my father's work uniform.

The rain is my biggest love. I like to bathe in it in our backyard. I do so without any clothes on since I'm still young, though there're few girls my age who do this. It makes me feel like

Sunday is the following day no matter if it's happening on Tuesday. The day we moved to this neighborhood and all the kids chanted, "fea, java, ugly, ugly, yellow girl," following me around, I hoped it would rain. It didn't, though, so I sat at the corner by a ditch that still had some water from the last rainfall and cried. Parents came out from somewhere and made the children stop their taunting since it seemed that Miss Hayworth, and Junior, could not.

Some mornings there were so many butterflies in our yard that I didn't know what to do. I would spin and spin from joy 'til I could only see their colors around me in motion, not the world, not our house that needed painting, or the outhouse that smelled no matter how much it was cleaned. Once, I spun until I fell in a heap exhausted, and for some reason, maybe because I was bathed in sweat, the butterflies landed all over my arms and legs. Oh, how beautiful I felt then. Just for that moment I was so beautiful, as beautiful as Maria La O, which is what we called the sea, as beautiful as the sky, as beautiful as Pilar.

The night is hot. As usual the light has gone. In the dim light of the storm lamp, we quarrel with each other for no apparent reason. There are also a lot of mosquitoes biting our legs and faces. We have mosquito nets, but they're old and full of holes. Mami and Papi start arguing about I don't know what, and this is really strange because Papi hardly talks. Then suddenly Mami gets out of her bed and runs past the partition into the living room. We are all real nosy so we follow her to the living room. Though she's just in an old slip, and though she's not churchgoing, she opens the front door wide and yells, "Satan, I know you're in here! Now get the hell out of my home!" Just like that, just like when she throws out her friend Tana, because she's gotten on her nerves. That's what I like about Mami: She doesn't take crap from no one. I don't see the Devil leave, but I'm sure he was here. Papi wouldn't have been yelling if he weren't possessed. Now we can all get some sleep.

Junior still sleeps naked. He has always done so as far as I can remember, but now his body is different. He's bulky as Jack Veneno, my favorite wrestler, and almost as hairy. I like to see him in the morning when he runs out of bed, all sleepy-eyed with his binbin standing up, pointing at the sky as he makes his way to the back of the yard to pee. He used to call me fea all the time, but as he gets bigger and more handsome he gets more kind. Now he comes home late all the time and I've heard Mami chiding him while he strips for bed. She's really worried because they're arresting boys from the neighborhood. He never says a word. He finds his spot in the bed next to Ramoncito and the minute his head hits the mattress, he sleeps. I wonder if maybe he has a job, one that makes him work as hard as Papi's.

Papi wakes up earlier than Junior, so early that I never see him go. He works real hard at the electricity plant every day, except Sundays. Ramoncito and I usually take him his lunch. It's always the same: white rice, beans, beef, and a beverage which Mami makes from some fruit or other—sometimes it's guanabana, sometimes it's chinolla, a lot of times it's jagua. Each food is placed into a separate canteen that stacks one on top of another.

When we go to take the food around eleven thirty Ramoncito and I do not stray or dillydally because the food has got to be warm or Papi won't eat it. Once, we got distracted and stopped to watch some boys playing with marbles; when we got to the electricity plant Papi's lunch was cold and he refused to eat it. He showered us with boches that made us stare at our dirty feet, and sent us home with the cold lunch. We didn't know how to face Mami with the food. We knew she would beat us with the stick she now uses on Pilar if Papi hadn't eaten his lunch, so we sat on a hot sidewalk and ate Papi's food with his drink.

It was then that I realized how different Papi ate from us. His share of the same food we ate every day and that we would've eaten later that day, was not just more, but so much more delicious, as if Mami placed special ingredients in his canteens— ingredients that she considered too good to be wasted on us kids. As for the drink, we of course loved it since we usually only got water. I felt cheated, though I loved Papi and understood we were less important than him. I did not share my feelings with Ramoncito who was still worried that we would be found out when Papi came home and probably beaten worse for trying to deceive Mami.

Pilar is screaming and sobbing. Her hair is again loose, her eyes somewhere other than in this yard we share with our neighbors. Mami is beating her again, at intervals because it's Thursday. At the same time, Mami is washing Papi's clothing— the clothing that, according to Papi, only she can wash properly. Pilar and Rita wash everyone else's. Even though she's crying, Pilar doesn't stop scrubbing the clothing against the washboard.

Miss Hayworth is watching her sister. She's looking deep into Pilar's runny eyes like she knows what Pilar's seeing. When Mami's not exhausting her skinny body hitting her oldest daughter, she's fretting. "Una hija cuero," she says. She says she can't believe her own child, who she has taken to church, who she has presented to God, could turn out a whore. She's been talking this craziness since Pilar returned—well, since Papi brought her back. The neighbors tell her to forget it. They say forgive her, forgive her. She's young. Children make mistakes. But my mother just keeps fretting until it seems she's about to explode like a balloon stuck by a pin. Then she rushes at Pilar with that stick she used on Ramoncito and me the day we ate Papi's food. Pilar stops washing because she's suddenly convulsing under Mami's violence. Andrea and Maria, our neighbors, finally intervene. They get Pilar away from Mami. While Andrea tries to calm Mami down, Maria takes Pilar into her section of the house.

I'm suffering for Pilar. At first I was happy to see her scream. I don't think I wanted to see her beaten, but I enjoyed seeing her beautiful, black face become ugly from pain. My mother was furious when Papi brought her back, saying that no daughter of his was going to be in no brothel while he still lived. I wondered what a brothel was.

"So you bring her home to shame us all!?" Mami screamed, with a fist on each hip. It was the first time I heard her speak to him like that, but Papi wasn't surprised.

"She's still our child," he said calmly.

"No child I raised would do that! She's no daughter of mine!" Mami screamed, walking away from Papi, shaking her head, and waving her hands like someone was trying to give her something she didn't want.

"Hija, don't say such a thing. God will punish you," Abuela almost whispered, trying to avoid the neighbors' sharp ears.

"And this isn't punishment, mamá?"

"Child, you must forgive." Abuela spoke to no avail. Mami wasn't listening, just shaking her head, rejecting the whole episode.

"Listen to your mother, Dinorah, because either way Pilar stays." Papi was holding the hand of a now crying Pilar.

"Manuel, do you want Miss Hayworth and Patria to turn into cueros too?" My mother persisted, with her fists back on her hips, looking at Papi like she was about to box with him.

"She stays." Papi wouldn't give in. Mami sat on the vinyl sofa crying. Pilar was afraid to budge, but finally she approached Mami and said, "Perdón, Mami. Perdoname." Mami looked at her daughter and they embraced even though she sucked her teeth. It seemed then that we would have peace.

I was happy to have Pilar back. I had missed her. During her absence I was very confused about where she was and why she had left. Since Mami would not allow us to mention Pilar's name, I couldn't ask any questions about her. I decided my beautiful sister was in a hospital, 'til the rumors started saying otherwise. When she returned I couldn't be upset about her being a cuero because I was too glad that she wasn't dying. Besides I wasn't sure what a cuero was.

Abuela is walking Abuelo in the yard. He likes the sun. While I wish for rain, he wants the sun on his face. He says it makes him feel alive. He's moving at snails' pace, diffusing his smell of sickness all over the yard, holding on to Abuela and to a cane. She is all tenderness with him. She is always all tenderness with him. Even if he wakes her at three o'clock in the morning because he can't sleep, Mami says you can hear grandmother's voice through the crack of the walls, patiently comforting him, asking him if he wants her to read him a Bible passage. Mami says that this is truly love. She hopes to someday love Papi that much.

Many people say that the most beautiful women in our

neighborhood are found on the Calle Sanchez and past. This is where the tutunpotes live and this is where you see ladies with hair as smooth as a horse's tail and skin like the Virgin Mary. But I think the most beautiful women are three streets behind ours, in the area called the Arena. I've never been to the Arena. No decent girl would be caught dead there, though they say that's where Pilar was for the month she was missing. That's where you find cueros. Every woman I found beautiful, sooner or later someone would say, "Oh, honey, she's a cuero." Now I know who they are before anyone tells me. When I see a girl with a skirt shorter than a boogaloo dancing girl, with lips as red as a hot pepper and hair as bright as fire or gold, I say to myself, "Look how beautiful; she must be a cuero." These women are seen rarely and somehow they always remind me of lost birds, walking around in high shiny heels in our dusty streets. My grandmother calls them fallen women and they do look like they fell from Heaven and are just waiting to be taken back home.

I wonder if my sister also looked like this when she was a cuero? Pilar sure is beautiful enough to be one of these women. Maybe that's why she went to them? Maybe she was called to go to her kind? I don't know. I can't picture Miss Hayworth and I belonging to that group. I know they would never call me to them, me with my bulging eyes, skinny body and almost hairless head. I really don't think Mami has to worry about that, but I can't tell her this. She won't listen to a kid. Pilar returned to us wearing one of her old dresses, without lipstick and the same black hair. This left me confused. Was she really ever one of those fabulous cueros, this girl who used to bathe, comb and change me?

On the day the lunch got too cold for him to eat, Papi came home around six, which was his normal time, and as soon as he arrived he started complaining about the cold lunch he couldn't eat. Ramoncito and I tried to run out through the backyard, but Junior blocked our way. He must have sensed our guilt. Mami didn't ask for any explanation. She did not trust kids, especially not her own. She went to the corner of the kitchen and found her deadly stick. Before we could protest it was on us. Papi did not interfere. Junior still blocked the back door. In the past he used to protect us, but it seemed that the more he resembled an adult the more he sided with them when it came to our punishment. Later on, though, when Mami had ended her fury, because she had finished cooking another meal for Papi, Junior tried to console us with pan de fruta. While chewing these we at least could not cry. I don't know what Ramoncito was thinking, but I kept picturing Mami being bitten by mosquitoes, and that night she was. I could tell by how many times she cried out "coño!"

I like the moon, maybe because I feel sorry for her, because every morning the sun comes and chases her away so that only he can enjoy seeing people awake, fighting, playing, working or whatever. Poor moon, she only gets to see us sleeping, and that's just boring, but sometimes I see things walking on the moon, scary things.

I saw my molasses boy again. He came out of Johaira's house. I couldn't stop grinning and he didn't say anything. He didn't say ugly or anything. So I was glad.

When Rita found out who her namesake was she became a pain. We, like the other kids on our street, go to El Gremio, the wharf workers' lodge, to watch TV each Monday night. One night they gave *Gilda*, a movie that Rita, Ramoncito and I loved, but that Junior and all the Gremieros hated, because they said the guy was a pendejo. Gilda was of course a beautiful Rita Hayworth. My sister had known she had been named after an actress, but Mami had not explained that this actress was a Hollywood goddess. Well, Rita went home with her head in the clouds. After seeing that movie, for days, if you asked her to do anything, she would respond by saying, "Would you ask Rita Hayworth to do that?" and refuse to oblige. She even told Abuelo this when he asked her to get him his slippers. She didn't even care that he was sick. Abuelo couldn't believe it. He sat on the bed looking dumb and barefooted.

I don't know why, but Mami allowed Rita to keep up this nonsense for several days. On the following Thursday, Rita refused to do the laundry. When Mami asked her if she felt sick or if she had her moon, Rita said that she was not sick or anything. Mami said, "Then you know you have to help Pilar do the laundry." I don't know where Rita got the courage, maybe she was already crazy at that moment, because she responded to Mami the same way she had been responding to everyone who had asked her to do anything dreary since seeing *Gilda*. "Would you ask that of Rita Hayworth?" she said, tilting her head back, and walked away from Mami. Well, needless to say Mami was enraged. In Mami's eyes children had no rights or opinions but the ones she said they had. She had been holding a broom while speaking to Rita, so of course she beat her with the broomstick. After that, in mock we referred to Rita as Miss Hayworth. She did not appreciate it, but had to get used to it.

> *They won't let us open the door*
> *Because we'll see Balaguer on all four*

Young men with dusty faces, faces that look like the faces of ghosts—gray—march down the street chanting this as well as:

> *Balaguer is an assassin!*
> *Balaguer is an assassin!*

Mami stops Ramoncito and me from going to deliver Papi's lunch. She tells us to come into the house. I take one last look at the gray men chanting. Their footsteps make my heart excited. Mami has gone inside already and has closed the front door. Ramoncito has also gone inside, though he used the alley that leads to the back door. I'm mesmerized by the beautiful men, 'til I see that one of those gray faces is none other than my brother Junior. I freeze from fear. I'm only nine, but I already know that it's dangerous to say these things about the president. I already know it can get you killed. I run into the yard afraid for my brother. A moment later I hear gunshots and running. I run into the house where we throw ourselves on the floor or under a bed. We had done this before. I thought it fun during the revolution, but I was about four then and Junior was not a protestor.

Johaira makes ten, and even though she's a girl her father is giving her a birthday party. The only one in my family that had a birthday celebration was Junior, when he was one, and I was cheated of it since I wasn't even born.

There's no record player so the radio is turned all the way up, and we have to wait for the music to come in between commercials. We have to hope the DJ feels like playing a merengue so we can dance. Johaira and I wait together, singing the commercial jingles, then I see him come in through the front doors. It's the coconut drop boy! It's the molasses boy! It's the ginger-eyed boy, coming straight to me. I'm glad he gets to see me in my party dress, in my arroz con coco dress, which is ice cream yellow lace. "This is my cousin Chago, Patria," Johaira says. "He just moved here the other day from the country."

My molasses boy smiles, just before Joseito Mateo's merengue "Cana Brava" comes on. "Vamo a baila," he says, pulling my arm. He's older and taller than me. I'm too glad to dance to be embarrassed. I like my hand in his hand. I'm close to him. I think he smells like coconut and pomade. I like it. I can't stop looking down at my skirt hem. The drums get louder, my hips move faster. His do not. I'm a good dancer. He's not. He moves like a Cibaeño, slow and without rhythm. I try to lead him. He says, "Hey what'd you think this is? The girl has to follow." I try this for a while, 'til the drums make me crazy and I get away from him. I won't miss my chance to have fun, to show off, not even for my coconut boy. I know I can dance, and what if the radio doesn't play another merengue. I dance by myself, while he looks at me surprised. Someone yells, "Man, that ugly girl can dance!" And I move even more. I feel really proud.

Like the females of the house, while Junior and Ramoncito bathe outside, Papi takes his bath at nights, in the kitchen. This isn't announced, but somehow we know to give him privacy. Today, however, I'm about to go get water from one of the water containers. I see Papi squatting, naked and scrubbing himself. I have seen him naked before, but today I do not say a word, I do not want him to know I am there watching. I see that he is beautiful. His skin is smooth as Ramoncito's or even

Pilar's except right above his backside. There, there's a bunch of hair, wild as grass. When Papi finally sees me he's not surprised or ashamed like I am. I blurt out, "I want water," like I'm dying of thirst. He simply says, "So get it, chiquita. Get it." He still thinks I'm a baby, so I act like I am, but deep down I feel bad because I know that I'm not. "Call your Mami, Chiquita; it's time to scrub my back." I go get Mami, trying to forget my shame and feeling happy Papi still calls me chiquita, though he's never called me cutey the way Johaira's Papi calls her.

I've never seen a man naked except for Papi and Junior. Lately I've realized that I would like to. I wonder if they all look the same. I know Junior looks quite different to Papi, but I do not see them as men, not really. Even though he can't dance, I wonder what Chago looks like without his pants.

Before Pilar disappears for the second time and forever, she starts receiving letters. They are scented and the scribbling on it hard to read. She keeps these letters in her bosom, the same place Mami keeps the money Papi gives her. These letters seem to come every day through her friend Casilda, the only visitor Mami allows Pilar, because Casilda's family owns the store where Mami takes food on credit. The two señoritas—I still call Pilar that though Mami says she's now a mujer—chat for hours in whispers while Pilar does her many chores. Casilda is very kind to me, though she's very beautiful and as white as people on TV, but she wouldn't tell me what her and my sister talk about. "Tu eres muy jovencita." She says I'm too young, and this burns me up and makes me more curious. I see her give the letters to Pilar, which Pilar takes to the outhouse to read. I know better than to ask Pilar about the letters that I'm not supposed to even know about, so I watch and wait to see where she might hide them, but it seems they never leave her side.

To get a hold of these letters, I begin to offer Pilar assistance throughout the day and especially when it's time for her evening bath, when she has to completely undress. I bring her warm water from the anafe and I scrub her silky, black back, from her shoulders to the curve of her waist, all the while eyeing the papers in the brassiere. I manage to take one of the letters and leave the kitchen.

My life,
I know your mother does not want you there.
I'm sorry that I hit you. It pained me much more than you. I don't care about the brothel.
How I miss you. I realize I can't live without you. Please come to me soon.
I'm being placed in Constanza. I want no other woman with me but you.
Morena, please be compassionate and come.
I love you more than my own life.

Your prisoner, Rhadames

"Compassionate." I do not know this word, but the rest of the letter I understand. I am jealous, and at the same time glad that my sister has such a man. Only someone as beautiful as she could get a man to love her like that. I see Rhadames in my dreams, on a horse coming to save Pilar, just like the prince in Snow White. His woody smell is everywhere. He says "I love you" to my sister and he sounds just like Ramo Ramo, Pilar and Casilda's favorite radio DJ.

A week went by after I read the letter. I managed to place it back in the bra before Pilar could notice it. I wished I knew what the others before that letter and the ones after contained, but I was too afraid to find out. Pilar had always been kind to me; I did not want to betray her trust. Casilda had continued her daily visits, and between the flipping of her long black hair, dancing to Johnny Ventura's "El Floron" each time it came on the radio, and her chatting away about Sandro and Rafael the most popular foreign singers, she would invariably slip a letter into Pilar's quick hands.

Ramoncito's taking advantage of Mami's good mood. He's dressed up in Miss Hayworth's pink ruffled dress, and does the boogaloo, yelling "yeh, yeh, yeh" like an American go-go girl. The whole yard is in an uproar with laughter and applause. I can't believe how pretty my little brother looks, and I realize God had meant for him to be a girl. I think Mami knows this too and that's why she doesn't punish him for playing with dolls, or swishing his hips or dressing in my or Miss Hayworth's clothes. Papi blames her for Ramoncito's "weakness." He says she made him that way, but I know it's not true. Ramoncito is just that way.

When the errands are done Johaira and I go to the back of the yard, behind the outhouse and ignore the stink, because there we find the ant nests. Ramoncito comes with us sometimes when he gets bored with my dolls. I capture red ants and Johaira catches black ones, and then we put them to fight. Ramoncito just watches. Even though the black ones don't bite they always seem to win. When we get bored with the fighting we destroy the nests with a bucket of water and stand back laughing while we see the ants drowning. After the water is swallowed up by the earth we give the remaining ants stones and sand so they can make themselves a new home, so that we can have some more fun in a few days. Next time maybe we'll use fire. Ramoncito doesn't like it one bit. Not at all. Strange boy; everyone knows boys like to destroy and kill, but not him. Johaira and I love it, even though we're girls. I guess life isn't always how it should be.

Mami's anger toward Pilar had not ebbed over the month of Pilar's return. She controlled it each night when Papi returned or while Abuela was visiting, but almost every day she felt compelled to call Pilar a whore and to slap her if not out and out beat her. That last week had been no different. For that reason as well as because I loved Pilar and believed that Rhadames would save her, I did not say a word when I awoke to find my sister with a bundle, making her way out of our bedroom. Our eyes met. I was about to tell her something, I'm not certain what, when her pleading, incredibly clear, black eyes silenced me. That was the last time I saw my oldest sister.

Constanza is a very faraway place. I know nothing about it when I figure Pilar has gone to live there. I hear that it's high up in the mountains, that it's close to Pico Duarte, the highest mountain in the Caribbean. They say that it snows there. I see

Pilar's black skin freckled by snowflakes that adorn her like pearls, instead of melting.

Weeks later I ask Casilda about Rhadames. She looks at me surprised, and says, "How do you know about him?" "Pilar told me," I lie. Then she tells me all I want to know without my asking. I think she was tired of keeping this secret.

Rhadames Teofilo Ramirez Cepeda is a captain in the army. He saw Pilar at Casilda's store and it was love at first sight. Casilda says that Rhadames is quite a man—tall, indio and handsome, with eyes no girl can resist. I'm not sure what that means. Are his eyes like Chago's? I wonder. He was stationed in La Romana temporarily, and had come to town to visit an aunt. On that weekend, he convinced Pilar to leave with him. Casilda then told me that my sister was not happy at home. She said that Pilar felt like my mother hated her. I think she added the last part to be dramatic. I know Pilar probably felt like a prisoner because Mami hardly let her out of the house, except to go to school, and then she had to hurry back or risk being whipped, but Papi was the one who made the rules. He said he did not like the way men looked at Pilar. He said she had to be protected.

In La Romana things went as wonderful as Pilar and Casilda expected, 'til a month later Rhadames brought home a little boy, his only son, for Pilar to raise. Pilar felt betrayed and slapped him, calling Rhadames a son of a bitch, as well as the kid. Supposedly, the gentle Rhadames was enraged and struck her repeatedly. With nowhere to go, but refusing to remain with the man that beat her, Pilar found herself in a local brothel.

Casilda is certain that Pilar and Rhadames belong together. I want to believe this, too. I try to forget about the beating, the way Pilar has. I recall the captain's letter. That beautiful letter convinces me.

We ate the same meal everyday, unless it was a special day, or unless Papi threw a tantrum out of the blue and decided the menu had to be changed. He didn't do this often, though. I think he knew Mami didn't really have a choice. So white rice, stewed red beans, stewed beef, and fried ripe plantains were the midday meal. No one enjoyed this food. We just ate it not to be hungry.

Ramoncito and I usually pretended to be eating something so exotic that in real life no one would eat it. One day we pretended we were in a fancy restaurant in Caracas. We must have seen something similar in a telenovela at Ofelia's home, which was where we went nightly, along with half the neighborhood's kids, to watch the telenovela, no matter that Ofelia was not happy to have so many kids in her house, and that sometimes without warning she threw us out. Ramoncito and I went on and on about how delicious the snake stew and fried lizards were that day. No one paid us any mind. Mami let us go on and on while she busied herself serving the rest of the family, and taking out food for Abuela, who only cooked soups for Abuelo and nothing for herself. We admired the tables in the restaurant and the beautiful china. Our imagination got the best of us and we found ourselves yelling at Mami, "Waitress, what do you have to drink!" Well, Mami didn't like this one bit; before we could snap back to reality we were showered with flying forks and spoons.

It is nearly dawn when the guardias come. They knock on our door like the mad, but even before that we were awakened by the sound of the jeep. Lately jeeps have been roaming the dark; their engines make the songs of crickets and frogs disappear. Junior, especially, is awakened by them, and this dawn he sits up in bed with eyes wild from fear or excitement. It's Papi that greets the army men, but Mami is the one who cries out when they read out the name of whom they want. Manuel Luis Munoz. It's my father's name. It's also Junior's name. We all know who they want, but it's my father they handcuff, half dressed as he is, and push him into a jeep full of guardias. Junior remains on the bed paralyzed, naked but for the sheet that's wrapped around his lap.

Sunny days mean nothing to me. I like the rain. I wait for it while Papi's away.

Junior gets dressed and is ready to go to where he thinks they took Papi. He knows it's him they want. He's scared, but he wants Papi free before they beat him. Mami throws herself at his feet, like Mary Magdalene at the feet of Christ, begging him not to go, but he doesn't listen. He kisses her and I see tears leave his eyes as he opens the front door.

Hours later Papi comes home and we all surround him, all of us except Abuelo who is bedridden. Even our neighbors, Maria, Johaira's mother, and Andrea. We are all crying except for Papi 'til they ask him about Junior, then he loses all control and I see my Papi cry for the first time. I don't like this sight. I envy the crying of women, maybe because I see it so much, but I don't like this.

It's windy. The leaves of mango, plum and sea grapes are forced to the ground, making our yard look like a sea of leaves. Lizards come out from their hiding place and scurry over the ground while our ducks and chickens chase them, excited for a meal. It will rain, and plenty. I'm hopeful. I walk back and forth in the yard waiting. I regret the fact that I can no longer bathe naked in the waters that will come. Miss Hayworth told Mami about the blood in the sheets, about my moon. So though I have no chest and no hair on my body, I am a señorita, a prisoner. I can't climb trees because I'm in "development." I should not play with boys, I am not to be seen naked by Papi or even Ramoncito. I cannot play with Ramoncito under the house anymore, and the list goes on and on. I do not like this: I do not like being a señorita. I understand why there's blood when you become this because I feel like I have to kill the old me. It seems that everything fun has to cease and I notice that Papi is not the same. He doesn't tickle me anymore because Mami warned him the last time he did. "Don't you know she's not a kid anymore? Don't you know she's in 'the development'!?" she said with a scowl. Papi laughed nervously and hasn't touched me since. I don't want to be this señorita thing. I want to be me. Just me. And the way everyone says I'm "in the development," like everyone knows what that means, makes me mad as hell because no one has told me crap.

The wind stops and it doesn't rain after all. It doesn't rain. Frig it! And the blood comes down again while I'm talking to Ramoncito. He's under the house playing with my dolls that I'm too old to play with and he the wrong sex to play with. I'm talking to him without seeing him because I can't be caught under there anymore when the damn thing comes. I have this thick cotton pad between my legs but I feel like it's not thick enough, so I run in the house to put more cloth down there, just in case. I'm nervous as a kitten without a mother because I'm also afraid that the cloth between my legs can fall out as I run.

When Pilar and Miss Hayworth became señoritas they no longer went to the stores on errands, and if they went out they had parasols to protect them from the sun. I expected that as a cursed señorita, at least I could enjoy this privilege, but somehow Mami did not add making errands, no matter how hot the sun was, to her long list of prohibitions. I continued getting salsa, olive oil, cilantro, whatever at Casilda's family's store without any parasol. I guess Mami didn't think there was much point in protecting my yellow face.

Junior has still not returned. To me it's been years since he left, but Papi says it's thirteen months. Mami used to take him food every day, but then he was taken far away. She can't go to him anymore. Since they took him Mami's face looks like skin and bones. Her eyes are nearly as big as mine, and her mouth looks like it has too many teeth. Thank goodness they're white.

The Sunday after our older brother was taken away Miss Hayworth became a born-again Christian. She took off all her bangles and earrings and lengthened her skirts. Mami tried to stop her, saying, "What happens when next week you change your mind? Then you have to raise the hems of all your skirts." Miss Hayworth wouldn't listen. Mami was furious, but she couldn't beat her child for giving herself to Christ. She sucked her teeth and let it go, mumbling something about the waste of thread. I myself agreed with Mami. I couldn't accept the idea of the exhibitionist Miss Hayworth being pious.

The following September I went back to school along with Ramoncito, who much to Papi's distress, and despite his nine years of age, was looking more and more like a girl no matter how closely his hair was cropped. His voice was also unusually high, and his walk, well, there was no correcting that incredibly delicate and graceful way of his. Next to the cueros he was the prettiest thing in town. We were placed in the same grade, third, even though I turned twelve, and thank goodness because I spent most of the days protecting him. We never left each other's side, and usually held hands. Soon the kids got used to him and he became quite liked. The teachers adored him, except for the nuns. I relaxed my vigilance and he began to make friends, even with some of the boys. Still we always went to school and back together, holding hands.

We advanced quite quickly in our lessons and pretty soon it became obvious that we were too smart for the third grade. A month later we were both placed in the fourth grade class. At first we were a little scared, but with Miss Hayworth's help we caught up and again were at the top of the class. Since I was in school and doing well, Mami no longer insisted that I do errands. She was so proud of me that she did the errands herself, for the most part. Since Pilar left, however, I still had to help Miss Hayworth with the laundry, but with Junior gone and Mami washing her and Papi's clothing, it basically amounted to my washing my clothing and a few of Ramoncito's—who wanted to wash his own clothes, but Mami wouldn't have it. My little brother was extremely neat so none of his clothing was ever very soiled. So being a señorita was looking better, even my hair for some reason began growing, maybe because Mami began using the hot comb on it. I also took to wearing Miss Hayworth's jewelry.

We're under the house again, Ramoncito and I, sitting on the damp earth because the sun never shines under here. Maybe that's why I like it here so much. I hear the drumbeats again. I had heard them all morning. Close, far, far, close, but now I was certain they were finally coming down the Presidente Jimenez, coming down my street. I'm excited, but afraid as well. I can feel the drums in my chest, right in the middle where they say the heart is. I can't control myself. The drums are closer, and then I hear flutes, tambourines, whistles and the sound of whips. It's becoming real hard to just sit still. I glance into Ramoncito's eyes and then I know neither can he. We drop Maylen and Deedee and run out on all fours from under the house, feeling like dogs, yelling, "Lo guloya! Lo guloya!"

Out on the street it's crowded with people who've been following los guloyas all morning, and with our neighbors now trying to get a glimpse at the beautiful dancers. Ramoncito and I hold hands and push our way through the throng 'til we get to the edge of the dancing circle.

We see mirrored skirts in motion and colors of the rainbow on the skin of men as black as Haitians, men as dark as Abuelo. We see scarves, crowns, gloved hands cracking whips and dancing. So much dancing! We begin to loosen up. I smile at Jural, my favorite dancer, as he stops in front of me moving like the sea. I let go of Moncito's hand. I know damn well a señorita shouldn't be doing this, but for the last time, my feet are stomping, I'm laughing real loud, looking at Primo the king of the guloyas, and then my hips, my hips…

The old tree is a giant. It has whispered at night of danger, it has sung in the morning of joy, but today it fell without warning. It fell on the roof of our house and then rolled off 'til its branches lay on the ground. I thought, looking at the sea grape tree, of a woman with her dress upturned and her underpants exposed. At last I can reach the ripe grapes, eat as many as I choose without flinging one stone, but my stomach feels like I've just swallowed a basket of pebbles. Burdened, I sit down next to the tree watching the caterpillars roam over its branches. Ramoncito sits next to me and hugs me while Maria and Andrea's children strip the tree of her fruit. Johaira, in her usual effort to outdo the boys, gets a machete and starts breaking off the branches with the most ripe fruits. Seeing her do this makes me wonder when the hell is she going to be "in the development"?

I notice that men watch my brother. They say "cuidate lindo" and give him candy. I hold onto his hand even tighter. Some approach us to talk about his lashes, others talk about his lips, some have the nerves to talk about his toosh and try to touch it. They confuse Ramoncito. They frighten me, but I don't know why. I hate them all and I don't know why.

It's Sunday. The sky is full of tiny clouds that seem to run into each other, but it's very sunny and hot. Mami wants us out of her hair. She makes us go to Sunday school—Ramoncito, Miss Hayworth and me. We get to the church door. I see that the teacher for today is the one that likes to hit when you can't remember what she says you should. I never make it in. I tell miss

Hayworth I have to pee and head west 'til I reach the sea. Here I curse at the sea and dare her to wet me, until she gets angry and does. My Sunday dress gets drenched. Now I know I'm going to get it. Mami will know that I missed church and that I took my fresh self to the sea. I should've just gone to church since Mami is sure going to beat me worse than the Sunday school teacher would have.

I walk back home counting clouds. I see that some are almost blue while others are white and round. There are many of these; they make the sky look like a giant upside down bowl of rice pudding.

When I get home Mami and Papi are both in a good mood. They are giggling and laughing, but when I enter the living room Mami still says, "I sent you to church, young lady? So where did you go?" While asking these questions Mami doesn't take her eyes off Papi, who's playing with her wild derizado hair like men do in telenovelas. This makes Mami look like a loca because her hair is everywhere. "So do you have an answer, señorita?" Though Mami is actually speaking softly her hair makes me think she's screaming. I start to stammer out an excuse, but Mami cuts me off. "Ya viene con su cuento. With you it's always something," she says, still not looking at me, and sucks her teeth. "Go get your father a beer at viejo's." I almost run to the store relieved at Mami's good mood and leaving that strange telenovela behind.

The sun is strong. My dress has already begun drying. Though I still smell like the sea, I feel good. I start naming clouds: Pilar is the pretty one, Junior the thick one, Ramoncito the delicate one, Miss Hayworth the fast one, Papi and Mami the twins and, lastly, I name the twisted one Cleopatra after me.

It's time to go home from school and I can't find him. I cannot find Ramoncito. I look all over the school grounds, but I do not see him. I ask everyone including Esteban, the janitor, if he has seen my brother, the beautiful one, the quiet one, the one that reads too much. They say, "No, not since the bell rang." Even Esteban says, "No, I have not seen the beautiful boy, not since the bell rang." Finally, I ask did you see him then? Did you see him right before it rang? "Yes, I saw him right after. He was running with some boys toward the gate. You should look for him at home," Esteban says, not at all worried. But, though he's an adult, I am still worried because my little brother would never leave without me.

I run out of the schoolyard, through the parted, wrought-iron gates—ignoring the nuns who yell with their weird Spaniard accent, "Niña! Sin correr se llega!"—into the street and down the block. Two streets later there's still no sign of Ramoncito. I'm out of breath. I hope he's home, but I feel he isn't. He would not leave without me. We are to go home together. Mami insists on this, and we've never thought to do otherwise since this suits us fine.

I slow down. Turn a corner Ramoncito should've turned to get home. I seem to be strolling, but I'm not. The street is bordered by Mexican creepers. There are bees buzzing all over the purple flowers. I remember how my left eye had swollen after the bee I was trying to trap stung me. Junior laughed at me, saying, "Well, at least now that your left eye is halfway closed, it looks almost normal. "Up ahead, in front of the abandoned house, there's a crowd of boys. They're looking in through the broken windows. I was going to pass them by, but I notice they're wearing school uniforms. I see that I know them. I see Andres, Isidro, Ramiro, Enrique, Abraham, Gregorio and Luis. These are the boys from fifth grade and up, and when they see me they stop their laughing. They stop pulling at their crotches. They stop looking through the broken windows. They act like I'm dead and walking still. My heart is in my mouth. I do not ask them if they've seen my little brother. I walk onto the shaky porch. They scatter, and when I look through the window I want to die. My heart turns to blood in my throat. It tries to choke me, at least I think it must be choking me because I want to scream, but can't. I barely breathe, but I jump through a window into the house. I pick up a broken bottle of Cerveza Presidente. More boys scatter, but these have trouble doing so since they are half dressed, since their pants are down to their ankles, since their penises are hard and exposed.

I am stabbing one of them. I do not know who it is, I just

know he's the one hurting Ramoncito most. His screams cover Ramoncito's sobs. I see blood. I see blood, but I can't stop the stabbing 'til finally the boy is on the grimy floor, and off of Ramoncito. I still cannot scream. I still cannot, though this is what I want. This is all I want…

I do not care for the sun. I do not care for sunshine. Give me rain anytime. Leave me jumping over the ditches of muddy water that are circles and squares all over town, where mosquitoes wait to suck blood.

I clean off my brother with the slip the foreign nuns say girls have to wear, even though it is hot as hell here. I dress him again and make him look as neat as he likes to be and I do not stop kissing his forehead 'til he's silent, 'til the sobs have stopped and his black eyes once more are incredibly clear. I wonder what they focus on now, though? It scares me to imagine.

We leave the abandoned house. We leave the bleeding Amado whimpering there, surrounded by his kind. They do not touch us. They make room for us to reach home. Ramoncito and I will arrive home holding hands the way we should, but he's sort of limping and I am wild-eyed, still swallowing blood, uglier than ever. But today I'm glad to be ugly. Today I want to be a monster. Today I want my eyes to bulge, I want them to look like they always have because if my mother did not see the Devil while I was in her belly, then today I certainly have. Today I could yell at the world "my name is Cleopatra!!" Today this name suits me because I know that to save my brother and anyone I love I have the strength of a ruler, I have the strength of a queen.

The nuns say that I'm a bad girl—monstrous even—for trying to kill a boy. They're afraid of what having me in the school will do to other girls. They do not know if I should be allowed to remain there. They have sympathy for Ramoncito, though they feel he needs to change his ways, and even have sympathy for Amado who took a few stitches, but none for me. Is it because I'm an ugly girl, I wonder? Would they not feel rage if they saw their brother suffer? They call Mami in. They shouldn't have. Mami does not like to leave her home. That's another reason why I always made the errands. They tell Mami that because of what

I did I'm not a normal little girl. Mami says, "Well, I thank God for that."

Mami said, "Don't tell your father what happened to Moncito. I mean what really happened. Just tell him he was beaten by the boys. Understand, querida?"

I didn't understand, but when Papi asked why his chiquita attacked Amado like a tigre, I let Mami tell her story. Papi looked at Ramoncito, shaking his head, and said to me, "I wish you were the boy." My little brother's eyes could've killed me with his sadness then. I wanted to offer him Deedee or Maylen, but I knew I couldn't then. I knew I couldn't. When Papi went into the kitchen, Mami stared at the floor. I didn't know whether she was ashamed of us or of Papi.

Ramoncito and I are no longer in school. I'm cleaning chicken coops and the duck pond again, but I'm glad to be away from San Antonio, a school for thugs. I want to forget those khaki uniforms and I know Ramoncito does, too. At first I was afraid that the guardias would come for me like they did for Junior, but Papi said Amadito's father was a good man and that I shouldn't worry. Everyone wants to hear the details of what happened. "Was it really twenty boys?" "Is it true Ramoncito wanted it?" "Who could've known there's a killer in you!" "Tell us how it happened, Patria!" "Ramoncito, come on, talk!!" "Hey. Ramoncito, can I get some, too?"

I spit at the kids, and kicked a few asses, but I don't know what to do about the gossipy, nosy adults. I wish Junior was home; I would have him deal with the adults. Miss Hayworth was useless since she joined the church. If she wasn't preaching, she was singing a hymn. If she wasn't singing a hymn, she was praying.

Ramoncito and I say nothing to anyone, not even to each other. We want to forget, but I know I won't. How I wish Ramoncito, the beautiful one, could. Oh, but in this town...

Of course it rains. Of course it has rained. We do not live in a desert, but it's been a long time since it's rained when I needed it. Today it looks like it might. I don't want to get too excited. I don't want to be disappointed, though the lizards are scurrying around, the ducks are flying from the roof of the outhouse to the roof of the house, and the coconut fronds are whistling. I tell Ramoncito to come out from under the house. "Don't you see God has punished you for playing with dolls!" Miss Hayworth yells at him. I want to slap her, but I don't want to be a bad girl. I don't want to. I just look at her and snap, "Shut up! Your mouth looks like a snout!" She looks stunned and hurt, like she really believes that it does.

It rains! And I can't believe it. I run out of the house in my dress because now I have breasts, though they are tight and hard looking. Now I have hair under my panties, just like Miss Hayworth. At least my feet are still bare. I love the wetness of the soil under my feet. I love letting my feet sink into mud. I laugh and I laugh until Ramoncito joins me. We hold hands and spin in circles under the rainfall, hearing only the roar of the water crashing against the zinc roofs of Miramar.

During this rainfall Junior returned. Wet as a stray dog and just as thin. His eyes were wide, like someone still in shock, and, more than anything, Junior returned silent. Ramoncito and he resembled more than ever. I did not want to think about whom I resembled then.

That fragment of a house—our house— that we rented from a greedy old man was now full of a heavy silence that was only broken by screams in the dark. When ugly is kept silent it will talk in nightmares, even if unintelligibly. There was hardly a night that ended without one of us screaming in our sleep. Papi screamed the worst and the most often. I wondered what frightened him so in his sleep, but Mami said he could never recall his nightmares. Miss Hayworth was the only one who seemed at peace in the dark. I was beginning to think the church was her protection.

But a week after Junior's return Miss Hayworth woke us screaming. She was in the backyard pulling out her hair and shedding her nightdress as if finally her old habit of exposing her private parts had come back stronger than ever to reclaim her. Before anyone could respond to what was happening Miss Hayworth ran through the alley at the side of the house and out into the street, screaming all along. Terrible screams. She would not stop screaming and spinning herself into a blur of brown flesh, not when the neighborhood awoke and surrounded her, not when Mami threw cold water on her as if she were a bitch in heat, not when Papi bared his chest to try and cover her with his pajama top, not when Junior yelled out her name in a strange cracking voice, not even when we tied her to a coconut tree in the yard, not even when they came and took her. She did not cease screaming. She would not be covered. Miss Hayworth, we lost her. We lost our star.

Abuelo did not see the next morning, though his eyes were open wide, and he was holding onto Abuela's waist 'til Mami and Papi pulled the scared old lady away. "He wants to take me with him. He wants to take me with him!" Abuela kept mumbling even after she was in our section of the house, sitting on Papi's and Mami's bed.

Abuelo was buried the next day, pretty quietly, which was surprising because in our town when anybody dies there has to be screams. But maybe we were all too tired from screaming at nights to cry out over an old, old man who had been bleeding to death for some time. Instead of crying we worried about Abuela who never stopped murmuring, "He wants to take me with him." She never stopped shaking, convinced that Abuelo was coming to get her. She said that even though she had given him the best years of her life while he was alive that wasn't enough. Now he wanted her to follow him and serve him in the grave. Because he brought her from St. Kitts to this country he felt she owed him her life. Well, he was seventeen years older than her and she wasn't ready to go. She wasn't ready to go! He never thought of anybody but himself. Never!

Mami tried to tell Abuela that no such thing would happen, that Abuelo was dead and that was that, and that Abuela was still here and nothing was going to change that, but the old lady wouldn't listen. She wouldn't. She worried herself for weeks, not eating, refusing to sleep, because she said she knew he would wait for her to fall asleep and then come and drag her with him. She said she knew he was a sneaky son of a bitch. That was the same way he had gotten her pregnant over and over again, by waiting for her to fall asleep and then riding her like a horse. Mami tried to shut her up, but Abuela was in another place, lost in her fear. The last time I had seen something so scared was when I cornered a poisoned mouse in our kitchen. It was too weak to go anywhere, but it still knew I was its enemy and that it shouldn't just sit there trembling while I glared at it. I felt sorry for the mouse, but then its cowardice annoyed me and I ended up throwing it down the latrine. I wish I could do the same for Abuela, but I knew that wasn't possible.

Mami talked to Abuela 'til she was blue in the face, and so did my aunts and uncles that came from all over the country to try and get their mother to eat or to at least get out of her rocking chair, but the old lady was tough and hard-headed like she had always said we kids were. She stayed rocking herself day and night, watching for her sneaky husband, prepared to fight for her life I supposed, though she was shaking so much I couldn't imagine her fighting anything, let alone a ghost. I guess she couldn't after all because Abuelo came and got her. He came and got her. And though I had thrown that scared mouse in the shit hole, and though I forgot to shed a tear for my sickly grandfather, I cried for my grandmother. For my grandmother I cried.

"He came and got her, Johaira! He came and got her. No matter how hard she tried. I wonder if she fell asleep? I wonder if she fell asleep? But her eyes were open this morning. They were wide open."

Abuela's funeral was as dramatic as it should've been. Mami and myself got more than the expected ataque. We screamed ourselves into unconsciousness, and each time we were revived we woke up yelling, "Why?! Why?! Why?!" I knew that's what I wanted to say, but I wasn't sure what the hell I was talking about.

My period of mourning ended when Mami said she had no money to make me more black clothes. I liked being dramatic, and the respect running around in black got me, but after two weeks I was totally bored with my three mourning outfits. So Mami said it was okay to go back to wearing colors since I was, after all, barely out of Pampers. I didn't remind her about her señorita sermons. I gladly gave up mourning.

We had no seasons. We never spoke of spring or summer. Definitely not of autumn or winter. Maybe Christmas was winter, spring was Easter, summer when school stopped, autumn when it began again, because even if you didn't go to school yourself you missed the uniforms by July and were happy to see them again in September. Johaira was going to school next September—finally, she was declared "in the development." I began to miss learning. I wanted to read about Anita and Pepe, about the fox who couldn't reach the grapes, about Blue Beard, I wanted to know what happened to the Haitian girl who had been converted by the Puerto Rican missionaries. I even missed division and fractions.

I approached Mami gingerly. I begged her to send me back to school and Ramoncito, too. She said, "But to which one? We can't send you to San Antonio, and the nuns are everywhere."

I was glad with her answer. I knew Mami well enough to know she had been thinking about the same thing. I trusted her and knew that next September this woman who threw the Devil out of her house would make sure that Ramoncito and I were back in school somewhere, somehow. It was because of her insistence that all her daughters had gone to school in the first place. Papi had only slightly cared that his sons learn how to count. "Ay, mi Cleopatra!" I knew that by calling me by my proper name Mami meant to remind me that I was meant to be something special. In private the name didn't embarrass me. I actually liked hearing it. Since the day I stabbed Amadito I had been hearing that name in my dreams. "You and Moncito were such good students. Too bad that happened… But we have to get you back in school. Maybe you could even be a doctor. Do you know your abuela wanted me to be something? That old lady had wanted all her girls to be something, but with what and how?"

It's September. Ramoncito and I are sitting in La Mixta's fifth grade class together. We are not the oldest kids there. The teacher is young and pretty. She looks a little like Pilar, with her dark skin and clear black eyes. She's about to begin history class when suddenly it starts thundering. The kids start to laugh from nervousness. Johaira is one of the loudest. Ramoncito laughs too.

I am glad to see him once more in a uniform and laughing. I don't laugh. I'm anxious. I wonder if the thundering is a false alarm, but the sky goes gray and then black. The almond trees by the windows make a ruckus. The scent of the ripe fruit enters the classroom, as does the smell of flame trees before the aroma of wet earth overwhelms me. It's raining. Without a doubt it's raining, just as it should be.

abuelo/a: grandfather, grandmother
anafe: charcoal Hibachi-style grill
Balaguer: Joaquín Balaguer, president of the Dominican Republic 1960-1962, 1966-1978, 1986-1996.
boches: curses
Cibaeño: person from mountain region of Cibao
Cocolo/a: pejorative term for English-speaking Caribbean migrants who arrived in early Twentieth Century in the Dominican Republic; dark-skinned person of West Indian descent; poor blacks, usu. pejorative
cuero: whore
cuidate lindo: take care, pretty boy
derizado: relaxed, straightened (hair)
fea: ugly girl
guardias: soldiers
los guloyas: Cocolo carnival dancers
la java: high yellow girl
querida: dear
sin correr se llega: without running you'll arrive
telenovelas: soap operas
tutunpotes: people with money; used in the 1960s and '70s

nothin' ugly fly
by Marvin K. White

i am a black bird
two and three winged cessna
beat sound like night falling
call and caw
sound like no bird heard
sound like tickle and pain
crushed between lid and lash
sound like tear held in breath
sound like rock thrown at god
sound like rock thrown at god

i am black bird
i fly
all night
never tired this way
didn't know north
still don't
felt like counter clockwise circles
was no stopping
no perch
might end up somebody's chicken
some greasy ass sandwich
some two piece with a biscuit

i am not that
i am bird
i fly all night
soon as sun crash
soon as people become they shadows
soon as skies have eyes
i fly
i fly
i fly

to your house
like uninvited omen
you not there
house empty
you not there
door click
you not there
what bird you think i was
some come here
tch tch tic tic tic
some come here
eat seed from mouth
not a kiss
not a kiss
not a kiss
rest on finger
sit on swing
inside your cage
inside your window

i bird
i fly
nothin' that fly is ugly
just wing and air
nothin' that fly ugly
just small
swallowed up by sky and god

i bird
leave feet
leave hurt
leave leave
leave life
leave you
imma fly
nothin' ugly fly
imma go

find up
find way up
can't find it
not from here
not with you
can't find lightness
can't find me
cuz you always trying to catch me
and i always get caught
in your fist
in this lie
so i go up
imma bird
i fly

Dreams
by Ayodele Christopher Dana Rose

He spoke to me
of dreams.
Spoke of them
with sadness.

Then he spoke
to me
about my
dreams.
Wanted to know
if they were
broken.

I thought for only
a moment,
then answered him,
"I prefer to say
I have
'unrealized' dreams."
To lend potential.
Hope.

"Broken"
sounds
defeated.

I have yet to learn
not
to run up against
jagged rocks
stones.
I have yet to learn
that.

Later, he spoke
to me
again
of dreams.
He asked,
"Can you dream
for me?

I have no strength
To do it
For myself."

I answered,
"I cannot.
Will not.
But I'll
gladly
encourage you
to dream
again.
Live as if I
have hope
even when I don't,
so that you
will
know hope
through me.

Eventually,
Dream your own
Dreams."

He spoke to me then
sadly
of dreams,
as he walked
slowly
away.
Not knowing
how difficult
it was
to see that part
of my dreams
go
with him.

first anniversary
of my brother's death
by Letta Neely

the day before my father left
he took them all to dinner
and then shadow boxed on the patio
his bare hands built
he threw his cigarettes in the trash
and willed us the rest of the world
he woke up really only once
in the hospital room
sat up straight in bed at midnight
his skin sagging arms in the air
shouting "I won, I won"
and we who had not been sleeping
laughed and celebrated the good fight
and then he was gone again
soon for good

Cycles
by Barbara Stephen

I remember Mama
I was six
When she left
For America
She was beautiful
Red shoes
Black bag
Over left arm
Waving from the
Airplane's door
And so I cried.

I remember Daddy
I was eight
He returned
From America
Hair blacker than
Midnight
Slicked straight back
Gray polyester striped
Suit
Shoes and socks
To match
Thought he was
F-i-n-e
And so I laughed.

I remember Auntie
I was ten
Hunched over the
Tub and washboard
Scrubbing the clothes
Her head tied with

Floral scarf
To protect from sun
Hands worn and aged
From hard work
And so I helped
Anointing them
With oil
She smiled
And whispered
Thanks.

I remember the years up
To eleven
Always being sick
The many absences
From school
The long walks to the
Clinic with my cousin
Pain from my chronic ear
Infections were so intense
The nurse with a lollipop
In one hand and the needle
In the other
I wanted the candy but cried
Anyway.

I remember my first
Kiss
I was twelve
It was behind the
Old chicken shack
I was there with
Nicholas
We bucked teeth
Hard
Thought mine got
Cracked

Tried several times
Until we got it right
Wow!

I remember feeling
Isolated and hollowed
Inside
The constant crying for no reason
Being teased by my
Classmates
Expressions I have
Never heard:
St.Vitus Dance, Stella Morris
As I got older
The expressions became clear
They were making fun of my
Muscular twitches
I just wanted to
Wither away and die
Years later I would
Discover the medical reason.

I remember leaving
Belize City
For America
I was sixteen
Standing at the
Airplane's door not
Wanting to enter
Hard
Saying good-bye to all
I knew...
Finally waving
But not like Mama
I shook and
Cried
Then exited.

I remember my first
Day at high school
In the tenth grade
Still sixteen
Accent weighed heavy
On my tongue
Trying hard to fit in
Smoking my first
Cigarette
In the girls bathroom
Coughing so hard thought
I wouldn't stop
Ended up in the
Nurse's office
Letter accompanied me
Home to
Mama and Daddy.

I remember too many
Rules at home
So I left
To stay with a friend
School in the daytime
Baby-sat for her at
Night
While she worked
Mama came and got me
I cried all the way
Home
And so new rules
Were set.

I remember my first
Suicide attempt
I was seventeen
Waking up the day after
The fact

Tied to the hospital bed
With tubes coming out
From every corner of
My body
Mama was there she
Wept
Daddy came after
He aged
Ten years.

I remember being in the
Mental institution
It was hell
"Don't belong here, made
A mistake."
I told the doctor
Month followed weeks
Then days and minutes
Followed by seconds
Of therapy with the
Bearded pale face doctor
Freedom finally came
I returned to
Mama and Daddy
Promising never to do
It again
But I lied.

I remember the
Years from eighteen through
Thirty-five
Suicide
Institution
Addiction to prescription
Medication
Rehabilitation
Illness

My own
College
Graduation
Starting over
Aged
At thirty-six
Feeling old.

I remember all the
Medical testing
To find out why
My muscles felt
So weak and tired
Why they twitched
The doctors
Said "Polymyositis"
One of Muscular Dystrophy's
Many diseases.
Lots of medication
Lots of discomfort
But happy to know
I was not crazy
When the children were
Teasing me.

And so I write
This at forty-two
Feeling very
Nostalgic
Longing for the tangible
On a quest for
Spiritual
Emotional
Physical fulfillment
And life
Goes on...

west coast east
by Carlton Elliott Smith

i wanted him to say
words of comfort
words that would assure me
that there would always be
room for me
in the body

surely in his wisdom
from our motherland
there would be some black pearl
he would release
from a tightly closed shell
that i could hold on to forever

and each time
the powers and principalities
of this world
scrutinized and denied
my experience of god
i could take out my black pearl
a gift from our ancestors spoken
in some ancient tongue

their voices would speak
and my heart would know
that i would always belong
among the people
my people

but my brother
the scholar
the theologian
from the west coast

east of the atlantic
said
those whose behavior
is unacceptable
will be put outside of the community
this is our custom

afterward
walked out into the mist
under the limbs of barren trees
under the skies of endless grey
and i searched for shelter
yet in that moment
i knew
that no locked shell
held the pearl
the promise
of a place
where all that i love about me
and all that god made me to be
would be seen as a blessing
and not a curse

walking along the shore
where my streams of thought
flow into the sea
i found a shell
somewhere between my heart
and my soul
it looked like the face of my mother
glowing whenever i go back home
it felt like the hands of my father
spinning his child around in circles

it tasted like a lover's kiss
breaking through my solitude
its scent was that of a dying friend
held close in my arms
when i held the shell to my ear
it sounded like
laughter
and tears
and daybreak
a voice inside me
saying
you are a part of me
you will always belong

Nothing Looks
the Same in the Light
by Reginald Shepherd

Sucked him off at the End of the World
in Bennington, Vermont, where it was
cold, a tumbledown stone barrier
held off the shallow drop, held on
to moss and townie kids' graffiti,
damp grass and trampled dandelions
soaked through my denim knees, late
March, 1982, he said *I take a long time
to come,* then came, left, and the bitterness
surprised me when I expected salt,
so I forgot to spit it out, everyone
was sleeping or drinking or getting off
inside where lighted windows in dorms
said this is warm, this is locked doors,
walls and no moon, but better the dark
you know I thought, I swallowed and didn't
get off, got up, swallowed my doubts,
and in the morning we pretended
not to know each other, it wasn't big enough
for that, but room can be made,
there's always room to pretend by day.

All of This and Nothing
by Reginald Shepherd

As if there were nothing,
or nothing but this: you looking away
again, embarrassed by noon
or the sound of my voice:
as if we had been lovers,
or could have spoken to each other
openly. On days like this light seems a poor excuse,
marking your face as you drive
me home, marking and measuring the struts
of the bridge. White buildings
of a city I intend to leave
make promises they mean not to keep,
but we move toward them
anyway. Too many things
I should have known, or realized I knew, things
to know better than: the shadows
lining your hands, shadows bisecting
your face. Look: that line beneath the water
is pure quartz. Why should you
care? The light shifts
with a sudden swerve of the wheel:
we're almost there.
I let the day do what it must.
As if it were all
equal to this, a car backing into
a one-way street.

Unfinished Work
by Colin Robinson

(for Zola & for Shawn—and now for C-FLAG/ Curaçao, for Rohan,
for Godfrey, for Mario, for Ian, for André & for Kelvin)

I shall go without companions
And with nothing in my hand
I shall go through many places
That I cannot understand
Until I come to my own country
Which is a pleasant. . .*

¡Maricón!

Cuando gritan *maricón*
Yo oigo *cimarrón*
I remember Michael
We were buddies, sisters
That summer of my first return
I remember Michael
Long before I could conceive him as a friend
I remember Michael
Dropping curtsy to
Buller
Crossing St. Mary's schoolyard
(St. Fairy's was the other name)
I remember Michael's
Thank you!!
Neutering insult
I remember Michael
We've both survived
We're still alive...apart

---

*The Countryman

So I remember Michael
Through this story
Though truth may vary—somewhat
It's this version that becomes
The myth for me
Llamaron maricones
Oímos cimarrones y viniendo
At this quilombo we arrived
From different places
Other countries
Cities, villages, plantations
Bantustans and ghettoes
Other colonies and nations
Old and new
From strange lands
But not strangers
We carried tongues like oil and
Flames of pentecost
That linked and licked
The darkness of past wounds
And heels and opened holes
Of memory
In passion whispered
Buller batty baby
Faggot maricón adodi
Magic words
And some were
Kings and Queens of colour
Come from other galaxies
Whose suns had failed
Some wearing black hearts
On their cheeks
And foreheads
History
Twisted in their hair
Emblazoned on their eyes
Painted on their lips

Like scars
Of heritage
Brave outriders' trumpets beckoning
Like Joshua's
Jimmy   *Godfrey*
Adrian   *Andre*
Essex   *Ian*
Joseph   *Mario*
Yves   *Kelvin*
From Babylon
From Babel
Coming
In procession
Under canopies of breath
A chain of tongues unchained
Refashion rotten
Syllables and poisoned
Metaphor and broken
Roots and metonyms of
Pain and
Flickering light the journey further
Home

I remember
Home
Remembering Michael
Ah see Miss Ting
De Zola Hole
De odder day
De tiefin' ho
In a fete in Brooklyn
Michael, I did not remember him
The queen who ruled our schooldays
Then remembering I refused
I am afraid of forgetting
Michael
Forgetting our language

Afraid of these new words
Not ours

Gritaron maricones
Nos oímos cimarrones
And we came
Arrivants
Awkward migrants
Changing territory
Heard ourselves
Eager muffled voices
Learn to sing
In their full range
Falsettos deepen
Basses soar
Some uttering first words
Like "Gounda"
Grunts and groans
Gasps and moans
Laughs and sighs
Shouts and cries
Voices echoing echoing
Questioning the silence which they slay
Griots
Shaping language into power
Food
And substitute for sex
Into tools like weapons of survival
Rage and passion
With the clarity of spit
Language of retention and of hope
Daniel hungry
Always hungry
Your hunger like a brilliant knife
Touched and left untouched
Donald
Blackheart brother

Mentor and best friend
Tossing dreaded head and laughing
At my foolishness
With Grimke sisters' tales
Shawn, my batty, my beautiful
First double double brother
Cary tender bangy
Breaking hearts
But we have learnt
The limits of our love
Yours is quite another poem
Unwritten
La Yves
Arriving like a loa
Charles in brooding silence
Len no longer flirts
We fashion verses out of clay
And sail on champagne seas
Mark first friend
Still friend
Madame DouDud D'Histoires d'Afrique's
Imperial tales of boys
And Allan
Who knows the treachery
Of my love
Michael, I have grown away from you
From roots
From childhood's sturdy trunk
From branching adolescent boughs
From anchors in the soil of Trinidad
Like seeds arrived in boats, Michael
I have flown away from you
Back turned to the Gulf of Paria
Seatbelted in the coffle of the jumbojet
Across a modern middle passage
Overflying backyard islands never walked
To glittering North Atlantic ones

Michael, I have been away too long
Left ripe with promise
For a land of promise
With promises to soon come back
With more
Intention is not meaning
Cuando gritan maricón
A past and future abandoned
Prematurely in the jetstream over Piarco
I feel in ripeness
Rotting

Cuando gritan
When they call me
Maricón
Like *antiman*
Like *faggot*
Battyman
Massissi
Buller
Remembering Michael
My ears resound instead with
Cimarrón
Echo *marron*
Reverberate
Maroon
Like steelpan
Drumbeats
Maroon
Like curdled blood
Maroon
Like black and lavender when they fuse
Maroon
Like memory

Cuando griten maricón
Pervert the language

Oigamos cimarrón
The simplest acts are the bravest
Like rearranging syllables is
Revolution
Rewrite history
Redecline the past
And conjugate a future
Reinvent etymology
Grow new roots

Until when I have found a home
In this quilombo
I must return
I must remake my history
Re-member Michael
Que griten
They will call me
Maricón
Shout *buller*
I will curtsy
I remember Michael
With the passion that remembering brings
Come like *cimarrón*
Cracking my tongue
Lashing it free
Like a whip

the dancer
by Gina Rhodes

she is standing on the corner of 125th street
in front of bobby's records tapes and accessories
wearing old white keds
a hole cut out for her corns to breathe
they are perfectly round and hard
the size of small gum balls
her costume is graying and wrinkled
a skirt and a shiny mint-colored blouse
her hair is a wig
tossed on
dark brown
matted into the ashes and scars of her face

and when the music starts
a slow '60's ballad
her eyes flutter
she plies
taking the edges of her skirt
pirouetting several times
her eyes are just barely parted
her feet kissing the stage
just swaying and twirling
swaying and twirling
into the last gray note

and when the drooling men come
offering to be her partner
offering her drinks from their bottles
her face grows indignant
she turns completely from them
and stands
straight and tense
waiting for the next song to begin

Fourteen
by Mistinguette

Wrapped in the glistening lips of night
her shoulders shrug one invisible lover
closer. Willie Colón pours out like streetlight
each time someone swings in the door.
Tamarindo sweats cloudy in its glass.
Her naked belly shines and winks. I
cannot find her footsteps in the dark
loose way her ankles step and turn.
Shut the door bellows Papi, *you're letting in
the whole night.* Too young to go
out in it, she dances the whole night in.

No, I Haven't Heard.
by Antonia Randolph

No, I haven't heard them.

But I do remember hearing Claude
read to me in grade school
in a voice I have always imagined to be my mother's.
The words are spoken in my mind
with the tone she uses when brought to anger,
her Costa Rican accent puncturing the shrink wrap
of a British education.
If we must die,
her voice reasons flatly, as flat as unleavened bread,
let it not be like hogs.
And the words would collect the moisture in my mouth.
The words would rise with a rapid and oblique heat,
the heat that radiates from the bottom of a pot
to where your hand is resting,
leaving you burned beyond the doctor's care
before you even realize there was danger.

And I remember hearing Nikki's voice
filling my parents' room on Saturday mornings;
occupying the mirrors on their bureau
now taking residence in their dresser drawers.
Her voice would carry the spirit everywhere.
And James Cleveland would be percolating beneath Nikki
Peace, be still
affirming the holiness of both death and niggas.
The truth was indeed on its way.

And I remember me unlocking my doors to Nina
because her voice was so alarming.
So nasty sweet and mean tender
that I had to see who was there.

Her voice that is implacable.
And she entered and walked by me
while I stared at her voice, unable to move.
And she searched through my refrigerator,
while I was peeled and cored by her words.
And she walked out
without me ever being able to say who had been there.

And I remember finally giving in to Audre,
after trying not to find her
in gay white Gore,
and later in gay black James.
I remember being afraid to find her
because to do so meant confirming my longing for myself.
I can still feel the grain of the poems of my surrender;
the sanded thought of her sentences,
the words burnished to insure durability:
I am,
are you
ready ?

So, no I haven't heard them.
But I managed to find my voice in other places.

Après Midi a Isabel's: Deux
by Alexis De Veaux

Was never determined
by clock or calendar
this country between friends
she became one
of those women
old world
planted in laugh lines
and forgotten language
women of her tribe;

You can see her, evenings
passing shuttered windows
opening like portulaca
when no one is watching
she re-bakes the world
dainty as whispering;

Threaded fingers
carry back
a tapestry of
memory from
market to ocean to
safe-keeping;

In her country
in my country
perhaps, she was one
of those women
on horse back or
was it camel
and men were unsure
and could not conquer
what they could not
define;

Going Down Bluff Road
by John Frazier

To the home where your father raised you, that burned
one summer with the sweet corn, you always discovered

some animal, upturned, usually a deer, still
breathing as steam rose from the belly.

Left there with blood more black than red and dogwoods
calling from the forest, the white blossoms scattered in the air,

lifting so with wind. You are reminded
of them—father, animals, trees

—now walking to your own modest house,
the streets littered with invitations to dance, invitations to,

come, undress before me. You are the age of grown men,
older than when he made you. And when

you drop your clothing in the moonlight,
the body shimmers so.

Living to Live Again
by Tony Ray Brown

I

The coffee cup refuses to hold steady at my lips. My hands tremble as if I'm naked and wet in the cold. Not wanting to believe the shaking has anything to do with my being upset, I stare at the cup as if it and its brown stains are to blame, absently wondering if they come from coffee or something else. I hold the cup by the hook waiting for my hands to stop shaking. When they don't I try cupping it firmly in my palms like people do when they're trying to keep warm. I'm trying to keep calm. As the shaking slows, I rush the cup to my lips only to have coffee spill down my chin and onto my shirt and the table. The coffee's hot, but I don't jump or move. I sit alone, seemingly calm, wondering what Sean will think if he returns, wondering if he'll think that these are tears rolling down my face onto the table.

I'm crying coffee because one day when I was younger and could cry real tears, I cried myself out of them. And Sean said, "Someone who can't cry, can't share. And if you can't share, you can't love. That, James, is what the game is all about—loving. If you ain't loving, you ain't alive. And you don't seem to be loving no one, least of all yourself." That's exactly what he said as he was putting on his jacket. "What happened to you to make you so cold?" he asked before he walked out the restaurant, leaving me shaking with a cup of coffee in my hand and staring down at the check on the table. Hearing the truth screamed at me in hushed tones while sitting at a cafe should have made me angry. It just made me sad. He didn't just walk right out after saying his piece. He gave me a moment to respond. I could only hang my head and look at the check as if there was something pressing there.

I was taught that boys should not cry. Yet I've learned that men must. But what could I say? I already know that I have only opened myself to someone once. That one time ended in such a disaster that I didn't think I could ever do it again. The memory of how my love ruined my first love's life causes me deep pain. I can never forget what I did to him or rather did not do for Benny, my first love.

Thinking of him freezes me. I sit confused over the someone I lost long ago and the one I lost a few moments before. I know what I have to do. To get him back, reclaim the self that was lost one teary afternoon, I have to go back. Back to that afternoon when I locked myself up and never came out again. I know how to do it, too. I realize that I've known for a long time but was too afraid to try. Now I'm afraid not to. I sit the coffee mug down exactly as I picked it up, stand and put on my jacket. Everything I do, I do slowly and precisely the opposite as I did when I arrived. After my jacket is buttoned from the bottom up, I walk backward—out of the cafe, backward—down the steps, and backward—along the street. I stop after I cross the street as if I am waiting for the light to change. I walk until twilight turns to day and spring falls to winter. I walk back so far and so long that I pass places I had once been and people I once knew. I pass the source of my guilt, the loss of my self and stop in a time and place where tears flowed as freely as love.

II

"Is something wrong?"

"No." My voice shook only slightly.

"Why are you crying then?"

"I don't know. I think... well... I think it's because I'm happy."

Lying there in Benny's arms, I felt warm, safe and loved. The feeling of comfort was so total and overwhelming that I could not imagine being anywhere else or doing anything else. Benny cradled me within his larger body. My feeling of satisfaction was not sexual. It was like the way a comforter felt on cold mornings when my mother woke me to go to school. Snuggling deeper in the soft folds, not wanting to get up just yet, I would hold on to the last few moments of comfort.

Other boys and men in the neighborhood weren't like Benny. When they were hanging out in groups or with their girlfriends, they called me a fag. When they were alone, they took me to their basements, garages, cars, parks, or even parking lots and tried to make me feel like what they named me. Benny never talked bad about me just because other people were around. After church, he would always come over to me to say, "Praise the Lord, Brother James. How's your walk with God going?"

"I'm saved, Brother Peters," was my standard reply. Then we'd shake hands and Benny would be on his way to greet other members. I always allowed my hand to linger in his. I guess I should feel guilty for this, but I don't. I have no shame about how it started—only remorse over how it ended.

The beginning to the end happened that night as I lay in his arms. Neither of us heard the front door open. Both of us had just enough time to jump and turn toward the bedroom door with startled expressions when we heard it creak apart. And I'm sure even God in heaven heard Benny's wife screech, "My God! My God! My Lord, Jesus Christ! What? Benny? Is that? Benny, what is going on?"

I wanted to answer. But nothing could come out.

She looked at me as if I were evil. For the first time with Benny, I felt dirty. I jumped out of bed, quickly unwrapping Benny's arm from my shoulder while cupping a sheet to my body, and ran toward the chair where my pants and shirt were thrown, stopping to pick up socks, sneakers and underwear. I guess the sight of me with only a sheet draped across my body was too much for Sister Peters. She fainted before I made it to the chair. I looked at Benny, wondering what he was going to do. I didn't want him to be mad at me. But I didn't see how he could not be.

He was hiding his eyes from me, covering his entire face as if to shield himself from what was happening. I whispered his name as if Sister Peters were asleep and I didn't want to wake her. "Benny?"

He moved his arm and looked at me. His eyes were sad and wet. "James, you better go home now." He said it softly as if he didn't know what to say. Yet, those words hurt as if he'd screamed them in my face. It wasn't what he said. I knew I had to go home. It was how he said it. I thought I heard abandonment, as if he were banishing me from his life.

I didn't want that. So I said his name again, this time more imploringly: "Benny?"

I forgot to whisper. Sister Peters whimpered on the floor where she had fallen and Benny flicked his right hand—the same one that had just been holding me so tightly—and said rather harshly, "Hurry up, get out." I snatched my clothes from the chair and ran to the other room to dress. I ran all the way home, wanting to get there before Sister Peters called my mother. I stopped at the door, caught my breath and walked inside. I walked into my room, fell on my bed and started crying.

"James, is that you in there? What's all that noise you're making? Boy, I know you ain't crying."

I quickly recovered myself. I thought I was alone. "Yes, mama, it's me. And no, I'm not crying."

She appeared at my bedroom door. "You sure sound like you were crying."

Trying to change the subject, I asked. "What're you doing home? You're supposed to be at church."

"Lord have mercy, if the tail ain't trying to wag the dog. When I got to start answering to you? When I left, you were in here studying. I come home, you ain't nowhere around. You decide to show up and you start asking me questions. Don't think just because you're turning fifteen next month you gone run things around here. I ain't had a man that stupid since your daddy left."

"Mama, please. I was only asking. I just passed by Brother Peters' house and saw Sister Peters walking in and was wondering if she had finally gotten thrown out of a church meeting." I begged God to forgive me for the lie.

"Oh, no, nothing that drastic," she laughed. And I was happy I got her to smile, knowing she wouldn't be smiling much soon. She started telling me what happened. "Evangelist Hill is suppose to be chairing this women's committee for Pastor Turner's birthday celebration and she claimed she was sick…"

As my mother talked about the meeting, I thought about how I would tell her about Benny. She wouldn't understand. She would blame him. She would say "that lecherous man," and "My baby this, my baby that, my baby's only fourteen... how could that man..." and go on and on. For her to understand, I would have to tell her about the other men that go back as far as I can remember—my uncle, cousins, the Jackson boys next door, that Foster boy who is married now and lives down the street. I would have to tell her that there was a time when I didn't want them to touch me, a time when I didn't know if I wanted their touches and later when I couldn't wait for them. I would tell her that when I prayed at church, sometimes I prayed for God to deliver me— take this conviction away from me. And sometimes I prayed that he would deliver me straight into someone's arms, someone nice who wouldn't hurt me. When Benny started to talk to me, I thought that finally my prayers were being answered. That's why I started going over Benny's house when I knew his wife wasn't there—on the pretense of asking his advice about things. For her to understand, I would describe one of those days to her.

"Mama, I knocked on the door and he answered wearing a pair of old jeans and a white v-neck T-shirt. You know how tall he is, Mama, taller than me, about 6 feet 2. I had to look up to him. I always got lost staring in his dark eyes with those eyelashes so long they seemed to touch his high cheekbones when he blinks. My eyes wandered from his eyes to his warm smile and dark brown skin. You ever notice how hard his body is? It's from baling hay, picking cotton, and doing stuff like that when he was growing up in the country—working when and were he could.

"That day, Mama, he answered the door, as always, very politely, 'Hello,' then he noticed it was I and he warmed up even more. 'Hey, James, it's you. What's up, man? How's it going?'

'Hi, Brother Peters, I just...'

'James, I told you. Call me Benny. We're not in church now.'

'Benny,' I savored pronouncing his name, 'I just wanted you to help me with something.'

'Well sure, come in.'

Up until that moment, I had been standing on his porch. He was leaning in the doorway, holding the screen open with one hand. The sun was beaming on my head. The heat from the wooden porch was penetrating my shoes, entering the soles of my feet and traveling up my legs. All this heat joined with the heat emanating from Benny's body and left me with a knot in the pit of my stomach, not to mention a hard-on. As he held the screen door open for me, I walked in and past him. I always tried to brush up against him, innocently, of course, when I was near him. This time, I only allowed my shoulder to touch his forearm.

'Thank you, Brother... I mean Benny. It's not a big problem. It's just that tomorrow I have to go to a speech contest and I need to wear a tie. And I notice in church your ties look different from everybody else's. They look neater somehow. And I don't really know how to tie one properly as I'm sure you've noticed.'

He laughed. 'I'll show you what I do. It's not too difficult. My ties just look better because I do a double knot.'

Benny retrieved two ties from his tie rack in his bedroom closet. Mama, we stood side by side in his bathroom mirror practicing the art of putting together a tie. It made me feel good—doing something with him. After I mastered the art, I thanked him. I was about to leave when he stopped me. 'You can't leave yet.' I took a deep breath, thinking, 'finally...'

I looked up at him and breathed a husky 'yes?'

'Tomorrow,' he said, 'you might be so nervous that you'll probably forget everything I taught you. Let me tie one on you. When you take it off, just loosen it and pull it over your head. That should be no problem with your skinny self. That way in the morning you can just slip it back on.'

He hardly touched me, just once when he grabbed my chin and raised my head. 'Look straight ahead,' he said, capturing me with those eyes, forbidding me from moving. I watched him, his face, as he put the tie around my neck, looped it twice and pulled it through. Then he touched me again. As he was tightening and adjusting the knot, the back of his fingers brushed the top of my chest. I was drowning in the sensation and I think I must have moaned or something because he asked me what was wrong.

'Is it too tight?' He was looking deep into my eyes.

'It's perfect. I just wasn't expecting that.' And at that moment, Mama, I knew that he knew that I loved him. And I also knew that one day he would love me.'

I would have to tell her about that event and so many other similar events with Benny for her to understand that it wasn't his fault at all. It was mine.

My mother was still discussing Evangelist Hill, "...so she just ended the meeting like that. Like she's the only one can make any decisions. Can you believe it?"

"No, ma'am. How dare she," I responded on cue. Before she could continue, I said, "Mama, I have something to tell you."

"What is it, baby?"

I took a deep breath. "I…" The phone rang before I could go on. My mother ran to grab it. I held my breath, thinking it's too late. When she came back, I asked her who it was.

"Just Sister Peters." I was ready to cry and beg her understanding. "She wants to know if I'm going to attend church tomorrow. I told her, 'of course! Don't I always.' Lord have mercy! I swear that woman tries my very soul acting like I just joined church and she got to call me up and remind me to go."

Well, she might be attending, I thought, but I sure ain't.

III

When she came to wake me up the next morning, I mumbled that I didn't feel well. "You was fine last night," she said as she placed her hands on my forehead, "and you don't have a fever."

"My stomach hurts," I pleaded.

"Go take your bath and put on your church clothes. You'll feel a lot better. Church will pick you up. You know how you love Sunday mornings."

I knew I couldn't argue with her. As much as I didn't want to go to church and face Sister Peters, I also realized that I wanted to be there when Sister Peters told my mother. Plus, she was right. Church was exciting to me and obviously to a lot of other people. I guess that's why many of us stayed in church five days out of the week, and about five hours out of the day. It seemed as if we went to service to get happy.

When we walked in, as usual, my mother went to the women's side and I went to the men's. I had been promoted from the children's section last year when I turned fourteen. I was happy because I didn't have to deal with the noise. Plus it gave me a better chance to be near Benny. When I saw that neither Benny nor Sister Peters were there, I gave a sigh of relief, praying that they had decided not to come. I was hoping that Benny had convinced her not tell my mother what she saw.

Praise and Worship service was just starting as we walked in. Praise service is always my favorite part. And today, Sister Ross began, as she did every Sunday, in her strong voice with "Praise the Lord, Pastor Phillips. Praise the Lord, saints. You know God is a good god. I just want to thank God today for waking me up in my right mind and starting me on my way. Many of you think the alarm clock woke you up this morning. But I'm here to testify that God woke me up. Ha-ha. You may not know it, but I know that God didn't have to do it. Hallelujah! Praise God! I thank God today that I'm saved, sanctified and filled with the Holy Ghost. I thank God today that I'm living to live again. Then she broke out singing, "I don't know what you've come to do."

In the middle of her song, when half the church was standing and singing, and I was praying quietly to God to please make Sister Peters stay home, I noticed them walk in the door. Sister Peters filed right up to the front on the left, Benny stayed in the back to the right.

After the church quieted down some, Pastor Phillips decided to ask if there was anyone who wanted to testify. Now they don't have testimonial service all the time. But today when Pastor asked if there was anyone who wanted to tell about what was going on in their life, Sister Peters stood up. No, she ain't. I thought. No, she ain't. God, please make me invisible. No, make her invisible. Make this whole thing disappear. I prayed to God for everything, anything. I even prayed for him to make us Catholic so Sister Peters' testimony could be quiet and anonymous.

She began in her loud alto voice, "Praise the Lord, Church, Saints. I thank God that I'm a Holy Ghost-filled woman. The devil's been working long and hard in my life. You know he can't stand when you love and I mean really love the Lord."

"Oh, yes," shouted Brother Randall, loudest and most boisterous of the amen corner members.

"Come on Sister Peters," intoned Sister Ross.

"Y'all know, I've been a good church member..." continued Sister Peters.

"Well," sang a few members.

"...attending to the sick and shut-in, ministering to those behind bars, always being here for church meetings, shut-ins, tarrying for someone to get His Holy Spirit, prayer service on Wednesdays and praise and worship on Sunday and Thursday nights. As the Lord is my witness, I try to be a good servant to Him and a good wife to my husband." Here she stopped, took a deep breath and paused as if she just couldn't go on.

During the silence of Sister Peters' strength gathering, I looked back at Benny. He was seated with a look of absolute shock on his face. It was obvious he had no idea his wife was going to take these measures. Obviously, she had led him to believe that they would settle the matter some other way. Probably pray it out. I'm sure he didn't know she meant to pray out loud.

When this happened the first time when I was fourteen, I started crying as soon as Sister Peters stood up, not knowing what else to do. But this time around, I was ready. I've walked back ten years to change the past and unlock the person that I know I could become. The current me joined spirits with the boy I used to be and waited for my world to blow up in my face. This go around, I would make sure the shrapnel didn't all land on the ones I cared about. I didn't cry this time. I saved my tears. I would need them later in life.

"Help her, Lord," from Sister Ross, and "It's all right. Take your time," from Brother Randall, prodded Sister Peters to continue.

"...but the devil can't stand a saved woman."

"Amen, amen. Oh, no, he can't. Ha Ha!" chorused the amen corner.

"And he normally strikes at what's closest to your heart," she continued. "Last night, the women's committee meeting ended early and I went straight home. Lord, as I walked up my steps and into my bedroom, I just felt something wasn't right. I felt the devil's presence all around me. The Holy Ghost was telling me something wasn't right. I walked into my bedroom and there in my bed was my husband with someone else." Now she broke down in dramatic sobs.

For a second, there was silence except for Sister Peters' sobs. Then the women in the amen corner whispered fervent "My God, my god, my god. Lord have mercy. And Jesus, Jesus, Jesus." The men, even Brother Randall, were all quiet.

The pastor, not nearly expecting this, piped in, "Help her, Lord."

"And church, I think I could have taken it," she cried, "I really would have tried if the devil hadn't made it sick and loathsome to my stomach. The devil invaded my household and this church and spread his foul, sick behavior around here like weeds in a field of pure white lilies. Alongside my husband, in bed with him, naked as the day he," she screamed, "was born, was a young man."

Now the church was completely silent. The children even seemed to sense the seriousness of the testimony because not a sound came from their section. In fact, I believed that everyone had stopped breathing and was waiting fearfully, anxiously for the next tidbit of information.

"To make matters worse, he's here today, Saints. Lying in bed with my husband was Sister Philips' son. James." She said my name as she pointed at me. The whole church followed her finger to me, then to Benny.

When this happened the first time—when I was fourteen—my tears turned to sobs. Benny was standing by this time and the church stared at him. A silent man looked back at them without guilt or seeming remorse, taking their condemnation, too honest to deny the accusation, ready to take all the blame, and leaving me, the child, innocent in their eyes. When they looked at me I was broken before their silent censure. The events that followed led to Benny's complete rupture with his family, his church and eventually society. The church condemned him, completely and unequivocally. He was a broken man with no community, an outsider to society. He ended up on drugs and homeless and died in the street two years later from a drug overdose.

This was the shame I came back to rectify. Benny's silence and the way he took the blame upon himself was proof of his love to me. Now I had to prove mine to him. That is why I walked back ten years—to exonerate Benny and proclaim my own guilt, thereby freeing the little boy that locked himself away, not daring to love again.

With my matured spirit speaking out of my younger body, I was ready to say what I wanted to say that day but was too afraid. I stood up wiping tears from my face, holding them back. With this bold display, eyes that before were sympathetic turned accusing. I looked across the congregation, stopping to lock eyes with Brother and Sister Peters, my mother and the pastor, all of which were standing, and I began very loud and strong, "Praise the Lord, Saints. I want to thank God that I'm here today. I thank God for having the opportunity to share with you today, I thank God that I too am living to live again." The congregation gasped. They were left stupefied. They never expected that I would stand up and give a praise testimony. They expected me to deny the accusations or to cry and beg their forgiveness at least. They got neither. They bridled at what they thought were sacrilegious words coming from my unholy mouth.

"How could you be living right while sleeping with another man?" their unspoken thoughts screamed.

I continued. "And I want to share with you today the trials that I've been through. Yes, Sister Peters did find me in bed with her husband yesterday. Church, for me, Benny was the salvation from your censure, the shield from your vicious tongues. He was the antithesis to your hypocrisy. I'm sure it's no surprise to any of you that I prefer men. You have been discussing it for years among yourselves. Telling me in what you thought were coded messages, 'Be careful, Brother, something's trying to get you. The devil has many faces and means. You need to exorcise those demons within you.'

"You told my mother outright, 'If you don't watch it, Sister Phillips, your son is going to be living a life in the city of Sodom and Gomorrah.'

"I've heard it for as long as I can remember in your voices and seen it in your actions—longer than you've been cautious of them. At school, your children echoed your thoughts. Before they knew what sissy was, they had named me one. You tolerated me when I was singing for you or playing the piano for you, clapping for you or stomping for you. But you never welcomed me. In a home full of Holy Ghost fire, you left me cold and without shelter. I had hoped the Saints were different, that they weren't like people at school. Teachers even that sometimes laughed at me. Kids on the school bus who ridiculed me. I had hoped the Saints would embrace me like Jesus embraced the untouchables. The only embraces I got came from your brothers, sons, nephews, cousins and husbands. They were unsolicited. They were harsh, brutal and accompanied with whispered threats. These same guys that abused me were the ones that talked about me. They spread rumors about what I had done and they were right, because they were right there along with me. I'm the town fag, the church sissy, known by all, liked by few and loved by none. Least of all by you. So when Benny reached out to me with his kindness like he does with everyone, I latched on to it. I turned that kindness into love and turned his love into an armor, an armor protecting me from you."

I then turned, looked at Benny and said, "I'm just sorry you got hurt."

After that, there was nothing more for me to say. As abruptly as I had started, I ended. I turned to walk out. My mother met me in the aisle. She was crying, she grabbed me and hugged me, whispering over and over again, "I didn't know, I didn't know."

Sister Ross came over, touched my hand and said, "Maybe we've all been living so holy and sanctified that we've forgotten what life's all about." I glanced at Sister Peters and she seemed more upset than ever. Mad that her moment of victimization had been stolen. Her head was back. Her palms were up and open. Her eyes were closed as if she were beseeching God to strike me down right then and there. I felt sorry for her. Then I looked at Benny. He was looking at me from across the room. Our eyes locked for a second. His seemed to say, "Thank you."

Mine replied, "Yes, and thank you." Most of the church didn't know what to do, how to feel. It is easier to feel anger and hurt than it is to feel guilt. They didn't want to blame themselves for what happened but they didn't know who to blame. But now all of them would wonder if there was something they could have done, some care they could have shown, some godliness they could have performed. I had done what I came to do. It was time to move forward with my life.

IV

"James, James... hey, James. Are you there? Come on man. James, what's wrong with you?" Sean says as he shakes my shoulders and snaps his fingers in my face.

"Sean, is that you?" I whisper.

"Yeah, James, it's me. Man, what's wrong? You look like you've been through hell. And you're crying, too," he says, surprised. "Damn. I mean gushing. I didn't know you cared one way or the other if I left. I'm sorry for doing that to you. Walking out like that." He's seated across from me. He takes my trembling hands in his and says, "James, calm down, O.K. I'm here. You can tell me all about it."

We reach to hold each other's wrists across the table, like people do when they're trying to rescue someone or pull them up. "And I will," I answer, "finally I can. I thought you were gone for good. Why did you come back?"

He looks down at the table, then back into my eyes before mumbling, "I forgot to pay the bill."

Come Mourning
by Christopher Adams

This day is a blight, thought John Rose's mother. She sat poised behind drawn curtains, her face hidden in shadows. Her eyes focused on the gauze slither separating the red velveteen fabric, which let in a blade of sun that split her body into halves—one light, one dark. She twisted her head back and forth as if the light were an insect buzzing about her, as if it could illuminate the dark thoughts she kept returning to. This new day and her empty house.

Dawn had come with her sitting, as did the men from County who took the enshrouded body away. Now she turned her face from the day, remaining behind the drawn curtains, waiting, wondering what came next.

And with that thought the front bell rang. She rose from the comfort of the couch, with some effort, left the bookmark that said "Jesus saves" to hold her place in her Bible, and went to answer the door. There in the foyer she stopped before the hall mirror and straightened the doily pinned on her head.

The door, some fifty pounds of heavy oak and neglected copper hinges, resisted her pull, then creaked open, and suddenly there was the daunting light of day, dancing in her face as unrelenting as a prize fighter, and nestled, nearly translucent in the glare, was a slender figure. A pale hand pushed out of the shock of sunlight and extended itself toward her. The figure stepped in revealing teeth and nails impossibly white, whiter than new china. John Rose's mother struggled and failed to put a name to the familiar face.

It was a fanciful image before her. Tall, black riding boots. Tan jodhpurs. A black lamb's wool waistcoat with embossed, brass buttons shaped like tiny wings. All high quality. The shoulder-length hair was fine and black, oiled close to the scalp, and pulled back in a neat, French twist. Handsome was the word John Rose's mother thought of the stranger.

She began breathlessly, "Are you...?" But the question died on her lips. In her confusion she almost asked the ridiculous question if the stranger was from the apostle board of Friendship Baptist. But she could never have forgotten someone so extravagant. "Oh...oh," she stuttered, "I'm not buying anything today."

The stranger added, "I'm not selling," and presented a toothy grin. John Rose's mother stood blinking, beguiled at the brilliance of those white, white teeth, new like baby's teeth.

"Then you're..."

"...here to offer my friendship," the stranger finished for her.

She nodded, and, squinting, made a stronger effort to identify who the stranger could be. "You're one of John's friends, right?" she guessed. "He brought you by the house before?"

"Guilty. On both counts." There again was the beaming smile that matched the glare of the day. It calmed her and she felt a familiar ease with the stranger. She accepted the smile with an upturned wrinkle of her lips and with a timid hand beckoned the way in.

The stranger walked ahead of her into the living room and she followed behind, breathing in the perfumed trail that reminded her of honeysuckle and newly mown grass.

"Thank you for coming by," she said. Then in a whisper, "John passed last night."

"Oh yes. I know." The stranger sat in her place on the couch, immediately curling legs and feet onto the cushions.

"Do you mind?" she asked. But the stranger didn't react. "Your feet? Could you take your feet down please?" She felt peculiar reprimanding this unknown person. "My son bought that couch for me."

The stranger laughed—a light, rippling chuckle.

"I expect this place'll be full of my church members soon. The sisters of Friendship Baptist really let you know how they feel after a loss. They'll try to bury you in covered dishes." She opened her mouth as if to laugh—but didn't. She began to consider more carefully the absence of her church family. She'd often told John the wonderful thing about having a family in

Christ, a church family, was that whatever answers you sought in the Holy Spirit, they would add their voices to your own and somehow the burden you bore seemed lighter. So, why, she questioned, were they absent and this new face here.

"Well," the stranger began, "there must be something you need in the meantime." John Rose's mother looked up expectantly.

"I'm so embarrassed at the state of this place. Them men from the County dragged all kinds of filth through here." She pointed down. Dark burgundy stains in the white carpeting at the bottom of the stairs led toward the front door.

"Yes, I see."

"You know I don't keep this kind of house. Cleanliness is next to godliness: That's my motto."

The stranger didn't reply. Just bore down on her with a pointed gaze she could not decipher. Fear flickered, just behind her eyes, that she had trusted too fast, too soon, this person. She began to chide her foolishness, when the stranger said, "Yes, you need to get your house in order. You'd like that, wouldn't you?"

John Rose's mother bobbed her head in agreement.

"Then, why don't I see if I can straighten up before your company arrives?"

"That would be lovely." She sighed again and sank back into the cushions. And that quickly she sank into a deep sleep.

"You're gonna have to lift up, honey," the stranger shouted to John Rose's mother. She woke to the stranger wedging the nose of the vacuum under the sofa, where it rumbled and snuffled.

"Heavenly father," she murmured, eyes shut, her voice buried in the noise of the machine. He went out praying, she reminded herself, and bundled herself in that reassurance. Still, she hoped that her church family would arrive soon. Add their voices to hers. Ask the Lord to take mercy on her son, that he be redeemed and ascend to a heavenly reward. "He went out praying," she said aloud.

"I found him," she said, raising her voice above the machine's noise. "Day barely breaking and there he was, looking as sweet and calm as he did in his crib." The vacuum stopped abruptly. "'Cept he was dead—God have mercy on his soul."

"You can put 'em down now," the stranger said and she did, then watched as her armchairs were sent spiraling into the next room, revealing tiny clumps of hidden dust wheeling like tumbleweeds. John Rose's mother bit her lip and blushed, blood lighting her face like neon. The stranger placidly said, "When I finish here, love, then I'll straighten the kitchen a bit. How 'bout I put on a pot and you meet me there for some coffee in a few, all right?"

She smiled up, then wondered if this was an invitation or a command. She realized that had her life depended upon it, she could have reported little about the stranger, sex included. Sometimes, the voice was an airy flute and the mannerisms graceful, and she was convinced that the stranger was a woman. Then, light would frame the chin and she'd be reminded of Deacon Edwards. At the thought of the deacon she wrinkled her brow with worry, then, inspired, she called the operator.

"Excuse me, but I'm expecting a call and I was wondering if my line could be faulty."

"Well, I am hearing you quite clearly, ma'am," the operator replied.

"Yes, but the ringer could be broken or something, right? Could you ring me back to make sure?" she said, nonplussed. "Y'all still do that, don't ya?"

"Yes, of course," the operator said and hung up. Seconds later, the phone rang.

"Thank you, operator," she said, suddenly remorseful that she'd confirmed her suspicions. No one had even tried to call. She'd heard the bell when the stranger came, so there was no question about it. This ain't Christian, she thought. It ain't Baptist. The Reverend Hall had practically rushed her off the phone that morning like he was tired of praying for John. Or that it was a futile pursuit.

She blamed herself for a moment, wondering: What exactly did I tell the Reverend? Their talk had been brief and simple this time. If nothing else, she remembered saying, "John Rose is dead.

My son is gone." Like it was the end of a story.

Now, she thought, strange hands were up in her kitchen cupboards doing Lord knew what.

Still pulling the skein of sleep from her eyes, she stumbled into the kitchen moments later and found the stranger kneeling, leaning headfirst into her refrigerator. Rubber-gloved hands were reaching in and emptying her vegetable crisper into a trash bag placed nearby. Pulling out things that she hadn't remembered buying, amassing a volume of putridness that staggered her. How had she avoided looking in there? How had she not noticed this herself?

The stranger stood quickly and whipped off the gloves, which snapped in retort. "Ready for a cup?"

"I'm so sorry, dear, but tell me your name again?" she said. Instead of a direct answer, she received another chilly stare from the stranger, who then wiped his hands, pulled a kitchen chair from the table and elaborately gestured for her to take a seat.

"Tell me," he said, "about your son's death," then reached in the cabinet to the right of the sink and pulled down the blue ceramic mug, her favorite, the one John Rose had given her back in junior high that said "World's Best Mom." The stranger filled it halfway, then spooned in cream and sugar until it reached the top—just as she liked it.

She didn't pause in her reply: "He went out praying. I take that as a comfort. Yes, yes, Jesus Lord, your lost lamb found its way back to the flock."

She didn't mention how long she'd prayed for such a happening, for John to one day cleanse himself in the Lord's blessings. She'd run her voice raw preaching to him that he'd misstepped his path.

Come home to Jesus, son, she'd begged. He is the Way and the Light. Sonny, you think this virus is a coincidence? It's the Lord trying to tell you something. "You shall not lie with a man as with a woman." Johnny? I'm talking to you, boy. Here's supper ready for ya. John. John.

When she saw him next, he was in the hospice ward of Grady Memorial. She'd remembered how, once, people had joked that they looked more like brother and sister than mother and son. And she'd always laughed loud at it, but had in a small way thought it true, when they'd stand side by side, with their ripe eggplant cheeks and soft, round tomato bodies.

She hadn't laughed in the hall at Grady, couldn't. All similarity was gone. He was so desiccated then that he reminded her of an apple left to shrink and rot. He even smelled of decay.

She'd followed him on a tour through the ward with his IV trailing behind, though they were forced to stop before they made the first corner of the floor, so he could rest. She'd helped him get to a chair nearby and he'd grabbed her arm, digging with thin fingers as he eased down. His eyes were covered with a film like dirty water as he'd looked up and asked her if he could come home. Come home to die. And it was wrong of him, she thought. A son asking his mother to nurse him into the grave.

She didn't answer at first, just took her small, leather-bound Bible out of her handbag and held it aloft between them. "You wanted to do what you wanted and I let you." Her voice had quivered. "Now I'm asking you to do what God wants."

He'd surprised her, her baby did. He put his lips to her cheek, hugged her. "I love you, Mama," he'd said.

"He must've been in a lot of pain? Right? Toward the end he must've really suffered." The stranger's voice suddenly broke her reverie.

He seemed to demand details of the sorrow that she wanted so much to shelve. He had no right, she thought. Some deviant from her son's past. She was saved. A Baptist. The reverend had once said that "the church could not exist without the fellowship of sisters like her." "Sisters like her," he'd said, and he was a minister of the Word.

"I'm real proud." She ignored the stranger's last questions. "Yes, sir. Not even two Sundays past my son asked to be given absolution and my pastor, Reverend Hall, went into that bedroom at the top of the stairs and prayed with him for that very thing. He may've misstepped, but John found his way back to the Word." She resisted the temptation to add that the stranger could too.

"But the end? His last night. What do you remember?"

She fought, but the stranger kept taking her back to last night. She didn't want to keep thinking about it. Or what she'd lost when her son came back home. Gone was her routine of watching the late news, reading the Bible, then falling asleep with it, curling it to her body like a lover.

He kept her awake with his unflinching testimonies, loud like revival meetings. John would punctuate each with, "It was wrong, Jesus. I pray for your forgiveness," then with a clap, wail, "Jesus, Jesus, ah-HA, ooh-ah-HA."

"John's last night?" the stranger repeated, seating himself across from her.

"Yes," John Rose's mother replied, then focused her gaze through the kitchen window as if something moving outside had her attention. Her eyes roamed from left to right and back again, faster and faster, until they were like those of people heavy in sleep. The dream state.

That night John's voice was loud, as vast as a choir soloist. His voice, almost hysterical, filled the house: "Heavenly Father, sweet Jesus, hear my prayers. I have sinned. You have given me life and I have profaned it by committing acts of sodomy." The way he lingered on the word sodomy made it sound like something good.

John Rose's mother knelt at the foot of her bed, hands clenched, the nails biting into the skin of each. "Save me," she asked and pushed her Bible across the bed. "Save my son. Forgive him. Have mercy. Have mercy." John Rose's mother knew of folks who'd been healed of afflictions, released from temptations, who'd risen reborn from their sick bed after giving themselves to God. Her son should live, she told Jesus, a new life because he believes. Come judgment, she and the reverend would vouchsafe his soul before St. Peter himself.

John's voice shattered her meditations. Forgetting her amen, she pulled herself to her feet, and as though his words were a call to worship, she obeyed the summons. She took up her robe and cautiously made her approach.

John prayed: "Precious Lord, sweet Jesus, all knowing, all seeing." She listened with a full heart to her son's words. She'd waited so long for him to come back to God, but something in his voice sounded like an accusation. "Deliver me into your sweet embrace."

All the lights in his room were on. John Rose was lying on a mass of sweat-soaked bedding nearly naked, his pajamas practically torn from his body. "Oh, I know you, Jesus," he said. "Your wisdom, Lord, is like something inside me breaking, but I don't feel no pain; I feel like laughing." It looked like he was trying to laugh, but instead his body just convulsed and heaved.

"And when I was on my knees taking his cock into my mouth, you saw me. I sucked it and liked it even from the first. Lord, I know it's wrong, but why do you make it feel so good...so good to do? You wept for me, Jesus! When those veins pulsed against my tongue and I felt him coming, I almost choked. I knew that he was unclean and that I was unclean, but...have mercy, I wanted him to never ever stop.

"I understand, Jesus. I know you. You welcoming me into your immaculate bosom. Wash my body clean in the body of Christ."

She stood, now inside his bedroom, listening until his voice was still and the house began to fill with the strained rasping of his breathing. His teeth chattered and his body pulsed with violent shivers. Turning to her, he seemed to be searching for words that would not come. His pupils dilated and contracted, seeming to beg. And she was suddenly reminded of times when he was a boy, when she'd open her closet and find ruin piled up around him, while his eyes brimmed full of spirit and joy. She had let him play and just replaced the nylon stockings, the lace blouses, the alligator purses. Anything. Just so he might be happy. Now she had a feeling that something precious was crumbling that she could never replace.

Seeing him she knew the many things that she could do for him. Change his bedding and clothes. Give him oxygen. Bathe him. Read to him. Perhaps even call for an ambulance. She had done them all before. She did none of these.

She turned off the light. Avoided his eyes. For a moment she stood in the doorway listening to the sound of his clogged breathing.

"Goodnight, Johnny," she said, "sleep well." And closed the door.

"Are you all right, ma'am?" The stranger's voice brought her back.

"Yes, fine."

"You were saying…"

"Nothing happened. One moment my son was here and then he was gone. One never knows when death will come calling. And tomorrow is never promised. We both just slept right through it." She didn't notice the stranger move, but when she looked up, he was at the window with his back to her. She continued, "What else is there to say?"

"Not a thing," the stranger offered in a low voice. "And at least it's over for you—right?"

John Rose's mother looked away from the question with its strange gravity, as if she was to be judged by her response. She stumbled, "Well, there is his burial to plan and…I was hoping that the reverend would be here by now, say something, help make this…" She didn't know what she'd hoped the reverend would do.

"Words? We can say some words together, can't we?" the stranger said.

"You're saved?"

"I think so," he said.

"Well…yes, that would be lovely. Let me get my Bible. I believe I left it in the other room."

She left the stranger at the table, his face twisted in a vague smile, and returned to her resting spot, making a slow, deliberate circle around the stain in the hall. She was surprised not to find her Bible in the living room, but decided to check her bedroom. Approaching the stairs, she saw a long, jagged strip of black fabric lying on the carpet. Stooping, she picked it up, and recognized it as leather. She turned it over and pondered the inscription raised on the surface in gold. Just a series of short, parallel lines suggesting the letter E. Climbing the stairs, she saw more: one small oval read B-I-B. She wanted to call to the stranger and ask him what these strips meant, then realized she still didn't know who the man in her kitchen was.

"Excuse me," she called over the side of the banister. "Sir, excuse me, can you hear me? Hello. Mister. Hello." The only response was the hollow echo of her own voice. Supposing that he couldn't hear her from the kitchen, she climbed on.

Waiting for her at the top was her son's room. John Rose. She'd turned her head when his body, strapped on a board, wrapped in winding sheets, left her house just hours before. Now she held her breath and looked in. The room was immaculate. Not a sign remained of his medical supplies. The bed was freshly made. Stepping in, the air smelt fresh like a mountain of pine, though the windows were closed. She was reminded of hotel rooms—how they try to trick you into thinking that no one has ever lived in the room before you. How the maids give the illusion of cleanliness with scented aerosol spray. But there is always some detail that breaks the spell: stray pubic hairs and piss stains on the bathroom tiles. She continued on to her bedroom.

Funny, she thought, I don't remember closing this door.

She stopped just outside, sneezed. The air was heavy with dust and rank, like the smell of an animal left to die and rot. Her hand trembled and slid on the wet knob.

She had to lean with all her weight before the door gave. It flew open and a cloud of thick, scratchy soot flew into her eyes and face. Something that was not the wind blew past her and shut the door behind her. She gasped, as the air became immediately thin. She tried to blink her eyes clear. Though they strained to focus past the whirling mass of dirt, she was sure she saw John's entire sickroom scattered there: soiled bedding, clothing, his IV and medical array. The bedpan was overturned right upon her bed. Paper was strewn in balls around the room.

She moved to open a window, and almost lost her footing. Perhaps it was the emptied contents of the bottles of John's medication left underfoot like stray marbles. She picked up a large, bloody wad of paper at her feet. She unraveled it and peeled off a page that read "The Book of Ezekiel" across the top; another page included the 23rd Psalm; the first page of

"Genesis" was another; and seeing the page heading "Revelations," she dropped it horrified.

"My Bible. Sweet Jesus. Oh my Lord."

She reached for the doorknob and it turned and turned in her hand, but the door would not open. Her lungs plunged up and down, snatching for air, but it only confounded her by whirling and beating the grit into her face. And each time that she felt for the walls they seemed to fall away from her grasp. She realized that she had nowhere to lean—she could only go down. Then came the terrifying realization that even if she could reach the phone—could call someone for help—they would arrive too late. She would die alone.

Was this what her boy had felt in his last moments, she wondered, as he lay in a sweaty clump, fighting for a few moments more before the final embrace?

It wasn't a real thought, more a reflex, but she called out his name: "John, my sweet baby John." And the storm about her responded by doubling its fury. She knew that it was too late for sweet murmuring. "Forgive me," she added.

And the biting dust came abruptly to rest. There was mud on her face made of her tears and the dirt. A clicking sound told her that the lock had been released, and she knew that the door would open again for her.

She wasn't surprised that no one was in the kitchen when she returned and didn't notice the single sheet of paper waiting for her on the table until an errant breeze lifted it up. It hung there one long moment, suspended a few inches mid-air, then returned to its original position. She didn't pick it up, just leaned close enough to read it. The writing on the page was covered with thick black markings like a child's angry scrawl, but one line was perfectly clear: "The stranger who sojourns with you shall be to you as the native among you, and you shall love him as yourself."

Words from Leviticus were coming back to haunt her.

"John, I'm sorry." She wheeled around, searching. She was alone.

She braced herself against the chair that had held the

stranger, suddenly feeling as empty as her house, remembering the handsome stranger, remembering her son, pounding the table now with the aching awareness that as if she'd turned the last leaf in a book, she'd told the reverend true: Yes, John Rose was dead.

No Beauty Is Native to Us
by John R. Keene

"But it's not a problem..." Elliot repeats, the words barely registering above the din of his twin eight-year-old sons Carver and Carlos, who romp air-conditioned behind an almost-shut door a room away, their shrieks melding with the squeals of the videogame-plied TV. The whispered words, like the thought they carry, sink beneath the heat-muffled jam and hum of car stereos and human cries swelling the nearby thoroughfare of Washington Street, flowing in through Elliot's study's growling window fan from outdoors. In here, in the dim lamplight, he can feel the syllables in his throat crumbling to the distant rumble of the train now shuttling from its underground harbor at Shawmut in a red line bound for the outer reaches of Cambridge.

Tonight his wife Carole is away, attending the first fall term class of the certificate in human development degree program she enrolled in, and as they agreed when classes began at the beginning of this past summer, instead of the babysitter they had from June to August, he's now watching the twins. Though they spent an hour after school at their Dorchester Youth League soccer practice and ought to be laid out, completely exhausted, they're jumping around and screaming loudly, the zaps and blasts of their videogame resounding through the closed door. As soon as he brought them home, he took them along as he walked Mavis, the family's German shepherd puppy, around the neighborhood, and then helped them with their math and reading homework, but not only are the boys still hyped up, Mavis is now cavorting and barking as if ready for another stroll.

"But it's *not* a problem," he says once more, firmly yet softly, almost whispering, into his cell phone. Grabbing one of his workout tees from a nearby chair, he mops his brow and chin clean of sweat. Despite a late-afternoon breeze, this September evening has alighted in a mid-summer swelter, scorching the edges of everything it touches. It's settled beneath Elliot's elbows and thighs, soldering them to the worn leather of his desk chair, smothering everything not on ice or under air conditioning in its heavy, stifling embrace. He grabs a newspaper and begins fanning himself as he waits for a response on the line's other end.

"Daddy, Mommy's at school tonight, right?" Carver yells, bounding into the room and roping his small, supple arms around Elliot's. The door to the living room ajar, he can feel the chilly air seeping out, and more clearly hear Carlos' laughter, the videogame's blips and bleeps, the air conditioning unit's steady murmur, Mavis' intermittent yawps.

"When are we going to get dinner, Daddy?" Elliot sets the open phone on the bookshelf and hoists Carver onto his lap. He frowns at his son, but before he can say anything, Carver continues, "Carlos was cheating again, Daddy. I caught him!" and spots the phone. "Daddy, are you still talking to somebody?"

"Yes, Daddy's on the phone." Elliot shifts in his seat, smiles with acknowledgment. "So I need you and Carlos to keep the noise down, okay? I can't hear anything when you're so loud. So you'll be good and quiet for Daddy, right?"

"Mmm hmm," Carver says, his scrunched-up face striking Elliot at that moment as a near-exact replica of his own at the same age. So desultory, fluid, usually more eager to compromise than to battle, until Elliot learned, as his father had said all black men who wanted to get anywhere in life must, to press all that deep beneath the surface, to bury it carefully and fully, so that nothing was visible at all, unless he wanted it to be. "Yes, Daddy," Carver repeats, returning Elliot's smile.

Elliot uses the T-shirt to wipe away the sweat beading on Carver's round forehead. You're always such a good boy, Elliot thinks, the same as I was when I was your age, but doesn't say this, not wanting to butter him up too much. As he pulls his son to him, generously caressing the wiry cap of curls atop his small head, Carver looks up, and again Elliot sees a version of the face that stared back at him in countless mirrors, like the full-length one his father had hung on the inside of his bedroom door when he was almost the same age as his sons now are and his family had first moved into this house twenty-five years before. How often he and his sister, Pamela, who was only a year younger than him, would stand before the mirror when they were little, she posing and primping and making funny faces, as Elliot glanced anxiously away from his own reflection that was always threatening to reveal too much. A few years later, for an entire month, she took to reciting a rhyme to torment him whenever she saw him even passing in front of the mirror, before dropping it without comment for no reason he could discern.

He's the one you can't really see
Elliot Invisible Kennedy
He got your nose and he got your eyes
But the face you see is a big disguise...

"Daddy?" Elliot feels the pressure of the palm in his stomach, then notices his son, his forehead again glazed with sweat, corkscrewing between his legs, staring at him. "Mommy promised us McDonald's tonight. When are we going to go?"

"I'll tell you as soon as I get off the phone." Elliot gently lifts Carver up and guides him toward the cooler family room. He grabs the phone, which nearly frees itself from his moist grip. "Go finish playing with Carlos and then we'll go get something to eat, okay?"

Carver takes two steps, then wheels around. "Is that Mommy?" He pauses in front of his father, then slips back into his lap.

"I said go play with Carlos now, Carver, and tell him to let you play some, okay?"

"Is that *Mommy*?" Carver leans back in, re-looping his arms around his father's forearm, locking on as if never to let go. Elliot pries him off, and pushes him toward the cracked door, which he pulls open a little bit more. "Who is it, Daddy? Nanda?" Annoyance tickles Elliot's throat. "Papaw?"

"It's a *business* friend of Daddy's, Baby." Elliot can hear a buzzing on the line's other end, but through the moist muffler of his palm he can't tell if it's just regular talking or shouting. "It's a very important call, so I have to have my conversation and can't talk with you right now." He and Carole agreed when the boys were infants never to yell at them if they can help it, but he can hear his voice tightening and creeping upwards. "Go play with your brother." Elliot brings the phone's mouthpiece to his lips. The boy doesn't move. "Carver, I said—"

"Is it your friend who you called when Mommy went to Auntie Pam's house last week?" Elliot cringes, his face scrambling momentarily before settling on a grimace. Carver shrinks behind the door crack, pulling the door backward with him. "When you went to the bathroom I said hello to him, Daddy. He asked me how old I was. Is it that friend?"

"N-no," Elliot stammers. "Not that...no. You shouldn't ever pick up Daddy's—" He realizes he's almost screaming, so he stops to regain his composure, his serious mien. "It's a call from work, for Daddy's *job*, Carver. You know how hard I work. Now get back in there and tell Carlos to let you play and not to cheat, okay, and stop being so loud, OK?"

"I'm sorry," Carver says, nearly invisible behind the door at this point, before closing it. Then Elliot hears from the living room, "CAR-los, Daddy said let me play. He said so!"

"Jerome. Are you there?" Sweat rills down Elliot's lips as he speaks into the receiver's silence. "Are you still there?"

"...Elliot, why do we keep—"

"Jerome? God, it's so loud down here and my son came in, and—"

"—having this conversation, wasn't I clear enough for you? Wasn't I? Someone else is calling anyway, so I've got to go."

Through the fan's roar, Elliot can now hear outside a trio of loud voices in conversation; a bottle shattering; a whistle. He pushes the computer keyboard out of the way and steadies himself on the edge of his desk. "I'm going to go upstairs where it's quiet and I'll have some privacy, and I'll call you back, so we can talk this through, Jerome." Laughter; a car alarm; the whistle trilling again. He wipes his chin and throat. No answer. "Jerome?"

"No!" Carver blares over Carlos. "You keep holding the button down too long, it's not fair! Plus it's my turn anyway! Daddy said to tell you stop being so loud too!"

"Wasn't I clear enough for you? I seriously have to take this call."

"Stop, Daddy said so!"

"Jerome, wait, this is how I see it—"

"Got to go—"

"Wait. In half an hour—I'll call you, okay? Thirty minutes—"

"Daddy!" Bounding into the room, Carver and Mavis brake at Elliot's knee. "Daddy, Carlos keeps on firing when he's not supposed to, he won't stop. I told him what you said, Daddy. He won't!"

"I promise," Elliot breaks off into the receiver, and quickly snaps the phone shut, placing it in his pocket. He stands and, grasping his son's hand, heads into the family room, the puppy tagging behind them.

"Carver, it's too hot to be acting up so, why aren't you getting along? Isn't it nice in there?" In the cool darkness, which Elliot brightens by lighting the torchiere, Carlos, his other son, is sprawled out on the couch, the videogame remote tucked under his elbow, his entire form burnished by the shifting, multicolored glow. "Carlos." His other son doesn't budge or even acknowledge his father, Carver, or Mavis, but continues furiously jerking the joystick as the screen jingles and cackles on.

"Carlos." The boy, the same height as his brother but stockier, more robust, bolts up. He too resembles Elliot, but less so: different forehead, mouth, his eyes lighter, less deeply set, like his mother's, after whom he was named. Even when still smeared in blood and mucus and amniotic fluid, as the doctor was bearing him aloft to whack the phlegm from his lungs and the world into him, Elliot had noticed these marks of physiognomy tying him inexorably to Carole, her father, all the Shaws. The tinier one we can name after my side of the family, Carver, he thought as he looked at her lying in her postpartum grogginess, and the bigger baby, who looks just like you and your father we can name—"Carlos? Why aren't you letting your brother play? What's going on?"

Carlos twists his lips in a scowl and leans back into the couch. "Daddy, he's just being a baby, like always! Every time I beat him, he claims I'm cheating. But I'm not, he can't play, that's the problem." Carlos sits forward, as if he's about to spring at his brother, who's leaning against their father's leg. "He can't play anything, it's obvious he's a little sissybaby!"

"I am not a sissybaby, *punk!*" His arms and legs whirling like a daisy wheel, Carver lunges at his brother, who yanks him to the ground and starts pummeling away. Mavis surges forward as well, leaping around their writhing pile.

"Carlos, Carver, stop it!" In one sweep Elliot has grasped both boys by their collars to spread them apart and set them at opposite ends of the sofa. He plants himself between them, his arms falling upon their shoulders like the ends of a broken cross bar. "What is all this fighting about? You know you're not supposed to talk like that about each other." He looks at both boys, who are sulking, their faces screwed into little bolts. "You don't hear your Mommy or me using those kinds of names, do you? Do you?" They shake their heads. "And I don't want to hear either of you use them either, you hear me? What did you learn in Sunday school about Cain and Abel? If I hear you calling each other names or fighting again I'll give both of you a real whooping, and I mean it, do you hear me?"

Both boys turn toward him, Carver's face a scene of tiny spasms, as if something hidden beneath the surface of the skin were trying to escape, Carlos' steeled in sullenness. "Yes," they say in unison. Carver slumps back into the fabric, covering himself with a pillow.

"But Daddy," Carlos blurts out, taking his father's hand in his own, "I wasn't cheating, I swear to God, he—"

"OK, I know, but I don't want any fighting." Carlos too slumps back into the sofa, his eyes glinting, rolling. "He's your twin brother, you gotta *love* each other! Now give me and each other a hug." Immediately, Carver slides closer to Elliot, but Carlos does not budge. "Carlos," Elliot says, then repeats it, with a bit more force: "Carlos." Slowly, the boy inches forward, extends his arms, holds Elliot lightly. Pulling them both in a close embrace, Elliot continues, "This is what I want to see. You know Daddy loves you, right?"

As Elliot speaks, Carver winches his father around the waist. "I love you too, Daddy." Carlos leans against his father, silent and still as a blade, his eyes trained anxiously on Elliot's.

"Don't you love Daddy too, Carlos?" The video game, having run its course, emits a long, loud razz. "Don't you?"

"Love you too," Carlos replies in a barely audible voice. Elliot kisses him on the top of his picked-out afro, then applies the same kiss to Carver. My beautiful boys, Elliot tells himself, remembering the first day he held them both in his arms. "You just don't know," he starts, wanting to add something more that suddenly is just beyond his ability to vocalize it. For a second, in his throat he can feel his heart's vibrato, a deep stirring now welling, bringing him to the verge of tears, but he inhales deeply, recovers, stands up.

"Can we play on the computer?" Carlos says, sounding once again like himself.

"Not now," Elliot answers, since he or Carole always supervises them closely when they go online. "Why don't you two watch TV so Daddy can go take care of some business upstairs? Let's get one of your favorite movies or shows."

"When are we going to McDonald's?" Carlos pounds his hand into Elliot's thigh; Carver is still draped against his leg. "Mommy promised us. We're hungry."

"Very soon, and if you both act real good and don't bother Daddy for a little while, I'll get you each an extra box of cookies." The boys respond with broad grins. "But you've got to be good like you always are when Daddy's busy. Okay?" Carver and Carlos jump up from the sofa to plant themselves in front of the TV set. "Let's see what we got here." Elliot extracts an unmarked DVD sitting beside the TV set from its case, pops it into the machine. "Is this one of them?" A scene of a young white man and woman, pressed against a kitchen counter, passionately kissing, fills the screen. He winces and pauses the DVD.

"It's Mommy's show, *Loving!*" Carver giggles, collapsing on top of Carlos. Elliot nods, realizing he's never watched this TV show with his wife and doesn't know half of what Carole tapes when he's out. Carlos abruptly clicks from the DVD screen back to the cable display, landing on a commercial in which a tall, striking young black man with a low cut is striding across what looks like a playground set. The image freezes Elliot, who catches himself as he's about to note the resemblance: Jerome.

"It's Dwyane Wade, Daddy!" the boys say in tandem. "Miami Heat 2006!" Elliot feels his heart re-jogging after a brief skip; he watches Celtics games from time to time and knows who this player is, though for a second... Finally, at the bottom of the stack of DVDs and videocassettes, he finds the ones on whose jewel cases Carole has clearly marked "Kids' Shows."

"Now you two are going to be good and not bother Daddy, right? And no rap music shows and nothing else like that, OK?"

"Yes!"

As the boys sit engrossed in the DVD, the dog now curled placidly at their hips, Elliot slips into the hallway. He climbs the plush stairs, the heat trailing him, along with the abrupt, relative quiet. On the second floor landing, he checks his watch and emits a sigh of relief. It is 7:30, and Carole will not get home for at least another hour.

After shutting the door and settling on his side of his bed, Elliot pries off his shoes, then shucks off his polo shirt and tank tee, which the heat has plastered to his torso. He sheds his socks and pants and tosses them onto the pile, leaving him in only his briefs. He runs his hands over the black star of fur covering his pecs and upper abdomen, his aureolas' tight purplish pins, the open trap of his ribs. It's cold, his fingertips are cold: The air conditioner in this room is ratcheting out an arctic breeze, indifferent to the tropical temperature outdoors. He tries to recall the last time he lay in this bedroom, on this bed, by himself. At first he can't pinpoint it, then he remembers the last time: It was one evening about a month after he and Carole and the twins had first moved in here, four years ago, shortly after his parents had decided to retire to Wilmington, North Carolina, where many of his father's people were. He and Carole and the boys had been living in a two-room apartment in Mission Hill that was too small anyway, and since his two older sisters both lived out state, and Pam had just bought a new condo near her South Shore job, his parents asked him take over the house. He'd also just been promoted to District Deputy Supervisor, so he could cover the taxes and still have some money left over every month.

That evening, Carole had taken the twins to visit with the children of one of her coworkers who lived in Cambridge, and Elliot had stayed at the house to finish off the last of the unpacking, stack up things to be stored in the basement, and prepare a little meal for when she and the boys returned. As soon as he heard the car's ignition turn over, he'd headed upstairs, locked the bedroom door, stripped down to his underwear, and spread himself across this bed to surrender to the moment of aloneness, just as he'd done periodically all through junior high and high school while growing up, though back then he'd done so in the bedroom down the hall that was now his sons'. Unlike all through his teenage years, that evening he hadn't needed to imagine that he was somewhere else, to dream of getting away, out in the world, away from everyone and anyone who really knew him, and he sometimes felt as if, though flat on his mattress, he were actually airborne, taking flight. The respite from Carole, from the boys, from his parents and work, from the unending noise of a life that he sometimes felt was devouring him whole, alone satisfied and invigorated him. He did not move for a half-hour, lying silently in the same spot, savoring that rare opportunity to be by himself, be himself. Then, he'd gotten up, emptied several boxes of books and albums, created neat piles of furniture, clothes and other household goods that would be consigned to the basement, vacuumed the stairs and hallway, and set an immaculate table by the time Carole and the boys got back.

He momentarily thinks about Pam, who for several years, as she was entering adolescence, had often pestered him as he lay in his room just like this. For a time she'd tried to jimmy his door open to find out what he was doing. *What are you doing in there, Elliot, something so freaky you gotta be sneaky?* If he didn't feel like telling her to go away, which would provoke her even more, he'd respond by feigning sleep, or if he was listening to music to turn it up as loud as he could without making the walls vibrate, and she would usually leave him alone. One evening, with both his parents out, however, Elliot had remained silent and assumed she'd found some other interest to amuse herself, like chatting on the phone or watching TV. Pam, however, had deftly worked her makeshift hairpin key up and down to the exact demands of his lock's drum. She'd turned the knob so slowly that he would not notice, and then burst in, to find him quivering atop his blanket, his briefs twisted about one of his ankles, his left hand strumming his spit-slick sex, his head turned toward the wall from which stared out a row of album covers, of male hip hop and R&B stars, his eyes peering upwards at them, his open mouth emitting a deep grunt. How long had she stood there, without uttering a sound, before backing out of the room and shutting the door, whose sucking sound announced her departure? That evening and for several weeks after, Elliot tried to persuade her that what she had witnessed hadn't happened before, wouldn't happen again, and in any case didn't mean anything. At first she refused to say anything about it at all, then she eventually denied witnessing anything at all. Once he ceased mentioning the incident, she never again brought it up, even abstractly, nor did she bother him if his door was closed. He'd nevertheless kept it locked, and gone cold for a while, but after graduation from high school, and before his stint in the Army and then at UMass-Boston, he'd discovered the Fens, and Combat Zone...

Carole, he thinks, hears himself say, automatically. He met her at a party given by Pam's sorority about five years after he'd finished school and had gòtten his job at the state agency. He'd just broken up with his then-girlfriend, who'd been so clingy that he couldn't bat an eye without her asking 100 questions. A few weeks after the party and several phone calls later, he and Carole began dating and quickly found their rhythm. Unlike the other women Elliot had gone out with, Carole was independent, easygoing and took everything in stride, her personality and emotions always in balance as if by an invisible, interior level. He admired this, as he believed it almost a perfect reflection of his own personality. They rarely argued, and if they did and he didn't resolve the problem with a little butter-talk, she'd become the diplomat. Elliot especially appreciated that she didn't appear to mind his occasional silences and moodiness, or his need to just get away from time to time. He'd noted right away that Carole neither tried to order him around and remake him into someone else nor did she need his guidance to make it through the day. Pam, who'd gotten to know Carole through their sorority functions and then through her brother, told Elliot she thought his new girlfriend was aloof and ingenuous, joking that he liked her because she'd let him get away with anything, and probably was doing the same thing herself. Elliot's parents, however, called Carole a godsend, as did his older sisters, and around six months into their relationship Elliot proposed. Despite her visible elation, Carole asked him to consider three things before she would say yes: Would he be willing to be as much a partner as a husband, was he eager to be a good father to the children she wanted them to have, could he give her the time and space she imagined she might need at various points down the road? Yes, he'd answered without hesitation—for wasn't she asking him what he had always imagined, hoped, his future wife would ask?—to all three questions. Three months later they were Mr. and Mrs. Carver Elliot Kennedy, Jr.

So far in their married life, Elliot muses, he's held up his end of the bargain: Doesn't he treat Carole as an equal? Doesn't he set a good example as a father? And doesn't she control her own space, the orbit of her life? Everything she's asked for, he's given her: time for her family and friends, their boys a year earlier than he'd planned, a house with a front and back yard, the opportunity to go back to school. She never complains about anything, except that he seems too preoccupied by work, spends too much time there, and even then, after he's talked her through what the extra effort is for, she completely grasps it... The hairs prick up on his fingers, arms, thighs, which he claps together as he does sometimes when he and Carole are lying in bed together, playfully munching her between them. Carole: Elliot traces her name onto his stomach, wipes it away. He's not surprised that now that he's lying here, all by himself, he's thinking of her. He wonders what she thinks of when he's not around, if she's thinking of him and what exactly comes to mind. He realizes for the first time that if they were on one of those reality marriage shows where he had to answer this or a similar question, he'd draw a blank.

Elliot slides his hands down between his thighs, trying to picture his wife beside him, on her side, wearing as she does to excite him only her burgundy panties, her face buried in the pillow, and him sliding in behind her—but instead, what he sees is Jerome lying there, his arched back turned to Elliot, his legs splayed open and welcoming, and Elliot recalls with a start that he's supposed to call Jerome. He's supposed to call Jerome and convince him for the second time in the last few weeks that he's getting worked up over nothing. There is no problem, Elliot's told him, he shouldn't keep saying that Elliot is making demands of him when it's obvious to Elliot that it's Jerome making all the demands, but it's all so foolish anyway, Elliot's been clear, he hasn't mixed messages as Jerome keeps claiming, all the complication is unnecessary, Jerome's just misreading him again, he's been as clear as harbor daylight.

As he sits up, a clearer image of Jerome's body, which is what caught his eye in the first place, which is what always draws him to them, fills his head: tall, he appeared almost superhuman the first time Elliot stood beside him in the elevator at the District office six months ago, Jerome's shoulders pitching straight out like the crossbeams of an immense building, the impossibly long arms falling from the white short-sleeved shirt of his uniform down to his lean hips, later swinging darkly alongside the black, etched tank of his torso like extension cords seeking to electrify anything they landed upon; the lacquered-smooth cheeks and throat, bald head, chest, stomach, back, back of the thighs, buttocks, all materializing in Elliot's consciousness as if memory alone could transport the body here. He sees the thick shank between Jerome's legs, how it meltingly curled against his own sex the first time they got together. Before that first evening, after work, at the Chandler Inn, a few weeks after Elliot had exchanged e-mail addresses and cell numbers with him as they were waiting on the platform at the T station for the trains to take them home, Elliot had envisioned Jerome being a throwaway, but instead he'd proved more intense and at the same time tender, than any man Elliot had previously gotten with. It was not supposed to continue past that first night, it never was, but then Elliot would see Jerome when he stopped by the District office to log his hours or meet with his supervisors, and Elliot would end up waylaying him in the bathroom or dropping him an e-mail or call, just to say wassup, and somehow weeks, a month, four had passed.

Yet, Elliot reminds himself as he fishes his phone out of his pants pocket, he was clear about things from the beginning, he, he'd laid it all out for Jerome, because he could tell the first time they chatted that Jerome was probably the emotional type, all that vibrato in the voice and his emphatic mannerisms, which threatened to give him away if he didn't watch them. Elliot also knew it was a risk to hook up with someone at work again, as he'd done with that brother who ended up securing a new job and moving to Atlanta. Elliot no longer remembers his name, only that he'd cut him loose like a laser after he'd started calling himself *bi* and telling Elliot he'd thought about leaving his wife so that— the ones he's met on the Net aren't like this, they don't bother or mess or ask questions or try to dig, as if they've got to find something that should see the light of day in the first place, but with Jerome it was a relief to get beyond the made-up names and IDs, the avatar and pornographic images circulating endlessly throughout cyberspace, and unlike the ones in the theaters or the department store bathrooms, who want nothing more than to open their mouths or have him open his, with Jerome something else had clicked, at least at first, though it had taken a different and uglier tack of late.

He slips his socks back on, then his T-shirt, which is cold and dry, and glances at the clock. It's 7:57pm. Not a full half-hour has passed, though he can't remember exactly what time he'd come upstairs. Even if he's a few minutes late, he's sure all it'll take is a little butter-talk, and Jerome will calm down and they'll figure out when they can get together again. Except with Pam he's always known how to resolve any situation, mend any disagreement, right upset feelings. It was as true with his mother and father and older sisters as with his friends in high school, in college, with his commanding officer, his fellow GIs. Carole, he's certain, has never stayed angry at him for longer than a few hours. He'd even been able to end their last argument, a month ago, over his resumption of long nights at work, within a few minutes, by persuading her that the extra time was to their benefit and would pay off in the long run for the boys. He'd underlined, as he had so many times before, that he was one of the few black district deputy supervisors in his company's history and on his way up, knowing she couldn't quibble with that line of reasoning. He'd promised once more to spend less time at work, more time with the boys, with her, and had iced the situation by taking them all out to dinner and agreeing to do even more than he was already doing around the house.

As he's about to dial Jerome's number, the phone rings. Jerome is calling him, Elliot knows, he's calmed down.

"Hey," Elliot says loudly, almost giddily.

"Elliot?" It's Carole's voice on the phone.

"What?" Elliot hesitates, then says, "Oh, hey Baby."

"Hey. Is everything okay? You sound strange. What's up?"

"What? Nothing." Elliot's diaphragm contracts, he feels the muscles of his face darting in different directions like a shoal of tiny fish fleeing a predator. "Nothing much, Carole, everything is fine." He is trying to settle himself, though he perceives too much tremolo in his voice. "What's going on with you? Your class isn't over yet, is it?"

"No, it's break time. I was just calling to...you don't sound...like yourself." Elliot hears Carole sigh.

"I was just, Carole, the boys had gotten into an argument, and it kind of, I was thinking about it, they were fighting, that's all. Everything's cool, Carole, really."

"What were they fighting about this time? They didn't hit each other, did they?"

"Carole, everything's fine. Really."

"Was it over that video game again? I told Carlos to let Carver win once in a while, but he doesn't listen. He didn't beat up Carver, did he?"

"No, no. Carlos won a game against Carver and then they started calling each other names and yelling, but I broke it up.

They just got me a bit worked up is all. I hate to see them fight like that."

"That's good. They've been calling each other names and arguing a lot lately, especially when you're not..." After a pause, Elliot hears, "Let me talk to them. Put Carlos on the phone first, he promised me he was going to behave."

"Hunh? They're, oh, the boys are downstairs. They're watching TV right now—"

"Where are you? I called you on your cell because I thought you'd be out getting them something to eat and the few groceries you said you'd pick up."

Elliot momentarily clears his throat, which he can feel his heart creeping into. "Upstairs, in the bedroom. I was coming out of the bathroom up here when you called—"

"Mmm. You know, remember, we need to do something about that air conditioner. It's too cold, it's been keeping me up a lot."

"Right. I'll look at it, but it might make sense for us just to get a new one. I thought about getting one for the study but it's already September and it'll be much cooler soon enough, so...but maybe I can pick up a new one after work tomorrow."

"You're sure they're watching TV and not on that computer? Because Carlos pulled up one of those sites and I mean...they're too young to see that stuff, and I don't know how they found it. It was just... And none of those music videos either."

"Yeah, yeah, I got one of the DVDs you'd labeled, the computer's off. I was planning to take them to get something to eat in a few minutes."

Elliot hears Carole sigh again, this time more demonstratively.

"So how's your class?" He can feel his voice evening out, hear it.

"Oh, class? Fine. It's always hard getting started up, but it's fun. My teacher's great, he's so...smart. And thank you for the pens. I opened my bag to pull out a pen and what did I find in there but a whole package of them, with your note!"

"I'm glad you like them."

"You can be such a sweetheart sometimes. Oh, will you make sure Carlos doesn't just pick at his food? You know how finicky he can be. I've got to get back to class. Tell the boys Mommy said hello, okay?"

"I will."

"I'll see you in about forty minutes. I *love* you."

"See you soon and love you too." Trembling in the room's chill, Elliot reaches for his pants, belt, shirt. He slowly slides them all on, lies back down, sits up again. What is he supposed to be doing? Taking the boys to get something to eat, picking up a few groceries, which he'd completely forgotten about. Damned Jerome. The bedside lamp, beside him, haloes on the ceiling in the half-darkness. The boys' dinner. He stands up, slides on his shoes, Carole's sighs ringing dryly inside his head.

As Elliot gets ready to leave the bedroom, his cell phone rings again. He opens it, expecting a follow up from Carole, even he could tell he sounded odd. Instead he hears a man's voice, raised, tapping out words like drumsticks.

"Elliot? You promised to call me back in a half hour? It's *8:15.*"

Jerome! Elliot wants to cry out with relief, but instead he says, "I'm sorry, I swear. I was...I came upstairs to get some privacy, some quiet to talk to you, and you had the phone call, and I stretched out—"

"Look, Elliot, I don't want to hear it. I have been sitting here, doing guess what? Waiting for you to call. Waiting. I'm always waiting for you, to call, show up, do what you say you're going to do! The same tired games. That's why one month ago—"

"Jerome, okay, please, listen. I swear, I was just going to call you, I was waiting and I laid down for a few minutes, you know the boys can wear me out—"

"No truer words have been spoken by you tonight, and you'll find a new one soon enough. Look, I told you a month ago I was ready to get on with my life, you're the one who keeps calling me, e-mailing me, bothering me, so if you can't—"

"Jer-ome."

"—understand after repeated, polite attempts, maybe I need

to—"

"Baby—"

"OK, that's it. I've heard enough. Just hang up first and—"

"*Jerome*—"

I can smooth it all out, Elliot reassures himself. He's trying to think of what to say now, he's been here before, Jerome's adopted this tone quite a bit recently, but he knows he can make it all better, if he can only find the right words.

"Jerome," he starts in, "let me say something now, come on. There's no need to go so far. Don't we—"

"Don't we what?" Jerome's voice is rising, each word popping more sharply, breaking off, reverberating in Elliot's ear. "One minute you're talking about how it's not a big deal at all, the next minute you're promising me the Nile and the Congo. One minute you're dialing my number every time a thought comes into your head, the next you can't even dial and at least hang up to let me know that you called, or send me damned hello by e-mail. Don't we what?"

"Jerome. You know it's not, it's not that easy for me, I, there's a lot going on in my life, you know that, you know I don't do things intentionally to make you so upset"—he thinks of the dark velvety flesh, those shoulders and arms spreading across the bed sheets like gigantic wings—"I don't want us to have these fights, things have been so good, Jerome, I was lying here, thinking about you lying here right beside me, I was running my tongue across your chest, and I could smell your sweat on my fingers, and—"

"It's not going to work this time, Elliot, so please hang up first or—"

"I'm not BSing you, I swear. I'm not sweet-talking you."

"Is this how you treat your wife? Do you put her on an emotional seesaw? What's her name again? Carole? Do you subject Carole to this same level of crap, Elliot?"

Elliot begins to say something but it stalls on his lips, he can't get it out. He tries, but it won't crystallize as words—I, I...

"Goodbye, Elliot. It's been great but..." Jerome pauses, then in a voice tipped with frost, continues: "No, wait, put Carver on the phone, he's smart enough to explain it all to you so you understand. He can stand you in front of the mirror and break it down so you can see it all very clearly."

"Jerome!" Elliot's voice shatters. "You leave my son out of it, you hear?" His voice swings between falsetto and bass. "Say what you want to me, but you start bringing my boys into this—"

The line goes dead. Elliot punches the seven-digit number he knows by heart. It rings, it rings. He lets it ring five times, ten times, fifteen times, twenty times. It rings thirty times. He knows Jerome is there; he is just not answering. He stands up, turns around, dials again. This time the line is busy. Jerome has taken the phone off the hook. He dials the operator: Is there a problem on the line, is there someone on this number...? He waits, hears that the line is working fine. He dials again: Busy. He dials again: Busy. He's crossed the lines. Busy. He's crossed... Busy.

He dials again, and slowly his chest starts to heave, his entire torso heaves as though wrenched by unseen hands. As the phone slips from his grip, caroms off the bed table's edges, and as Elliot reaches to grab it, jarring the lamp to rocking so that it paints deranging swirls upon the black ceiling overhead, something else starts to pull away, from inside him, that captive thing tries, vies to break free, take flight, but can't. Jerome, Elliot hears himself mumbling, to no one, to the empty room. He rubs his temples, which are on fire, then picks up the phone, sets it down on the bed table. He will make everything better, he will smooth this whole situation out later, Jerome will listen, things will be back to the way they were, it will all be fine soon, soon. Dinner: The boys. He pats his pockets. Butter talk. Jerome, he stammers, Carole, it will all work out, as he stands, stuck as if frozen to his spot. Then, a moan, so soft and hoarse that it can hardly be heard, so that it nearly drowns amidst everything around it, the air conditioner's roar, the ticking clock, the other sounds of the body, the room, the house, the night, the din—

—of his twin sons, Carver and Carlos, followed by Mavis, their German shepherd puppy, bounding up the stairs, screaming out what they want for dinner, how in the movie they just watched that was based on the video the Black Ranger defeated three monsters with the same kick, that they have been waiting and calling out for him for a while now, their opening the door, treading into the room, freezing momentarily before the bowed and moaning form, as they call out in their children's voices, "Daddy? Daddy? Daddy?"

Flint:
The Story of Sean and Floyd
by Cary Alan Johnson

"Shall we stop to make a list of the dead?"
from "taking stock," by G. Winston James

Maybe this will quiet them down. It's been almost fifteen years since our paths crossed, but recollections of Sean and Floyd still knock about inside my head like cowry shells in a shekere. They keep me awake at night, noisy in a way they never were in life. Rattling around like buff ghosts, they nudge my memory in a hundred crazy ways. Pick-up trucks racing down the Beltway, houses in mid-construction along a highway, wrong numbers on my telephone. Louder than the others lost along the way, their voices hammer, demanding that their story be told. And I'm the vehicle they've chosen to do it.

Melodramatic? Egotistical of me to think such a thing? Maybe. I only know that I can't sleep lately. Four a.m. finds me sitting on the living room sofa. TV turned down low not to disturb the neighbors. Just staring blindly into a screen that might as well be blank. Seeing... nothing, just the black and white emptiness of the "Late Late Show" through the foggy vision of the insomniac who knows that tomorrow he will pay.

Now it's lunchtime and I'm yawning, standing in front of my office window watching the expressionless hordes goose-step down K Street. If I stand here all day, I will see them trundle off to lunch then back to work, then home to friends and families and hobbies and secrets that maybe, just maybe, make their lives bearable. I know because I'm one of them. In a few minutes I'll ride down in the elevator and take my place among them. Fifteen floors above, I can feel heartburn rising from the baking concrete. I see MacMillan come out of the lobby downstairs, talking to a client, a fat white guy who owns a string of hardware stores in Ohio. MacMillan is gesticulating in his measured tones. He has absolutely no idea that he is being watched, but he is always on stage. Hair, tie, suit—everything just so.

Think I'll skip lunch today. Maybe it's time to talk about the coincidences that brought us together. Time to get real about the deception—theirs and mine. Sean and Floyd want honesty, finality. They want the world to know how close they came to perfection; how they were the most imperfect of all.

1. Floyd

It was 1987 and I was a rising star at my law firm in New York. With fifty associates and ten partners, it was a small operation by Wall Street standards. It was an open secret that if I kept setting up transactions the way I had been doing, I'd be a partner by the time I was thirty-two. I had graduated from NYU Law in '82, one of only two blacks the firm hired that year.

Everyone knew that MacMillan, one of the senior partners, was grooming me. I remember the first time I met him, when he interviewed me at the NYU Law Library, its narrow, rectangular windows looking out onto Washington Square Park and the West Village. It was the fall of my second year and we were all posturing, preparing for that all-important summer placement that would make all the difference in our careers. MacMillan met with me for less than twenty minutes, asking a few easy questions about corporate reorganization, and property transactions, things that didn't take much thought. Then he paused, took off his wire-rimmed glasses and asked me, "Mr. Christopher, why have you chosen to be a lawyer?"

I looked homeboy square in those crystal blue eyes of his and said, "Cash and prestige, Mr. MacMillan. I am interested in using the law and the smarts God gave me to generate cash and prestige."

MacMillan smiled, and I knew that I was *in like Flynn*. I started at the firm later that summer.

Though he never formally agreed to mentor me, MacMillan made it clear that he was interested in my progress. He was always looking over my shoulder and commented on everything from my wardrobe to how I handled my closings. He offered suggestions (rewrite that transaction report, Mr. Christopher, it needs punching up) and criticisms (never, never cheap shoes with a good suit, Mr. Christopher!). Sometimes I wondered if he had bet the other seniors that he could turn a black boy from the projects into a top-notch mergers and acquisitions lawyer. I was determined to help him win that bet.

MacMillan put me to work on important deals that he was personally managing. At the end of long days and even longer evenings, Macmillan would lean back in his oversized oak and leather swivel, the lights from Jersey City twinkling like diamonds behind him, and say, "Mr. Christopher, you're a smart young man, and one day you'll be a fine attorney." A few times he even said it in front of the other partners. That shit made me feel good.

I didn't mind being his protégé, as long as my salary kept increasing—and it did.

One day in the spring of '87, MacMillan called me into his office. "The firm is opening a D.C. branch, Mr. Christopher. I'm heading down to get it started and I want you on the team. This is a great career opportunity for you," he said. "Who knows what it might lead to?"

I knew and so did he. I wanted to be a partner so bad I could taste it. And I wanted it soon. I was already picturing the house in Long Island I was going to build for my grandmother once I was clocking six figures.

"You're single. No family yet. Why not make the move with us? Are you ready to make it happen, Mr. Christopher?" MacMillan said, leaning back.

A porter appeared at the office door. He was a Jamaican man, gray-haired and stoop-shouldered, who'd been working for the firm since he was a teenager. He carried a bottle of Perrier and two Waterford crystal glasses on a silver tray. He poured MacMillan and I a fizzy glass and silently left the room. His eyes never rose above chest level.

MacMillan took a sip and folded his hands over the vest of his Armani suit. I figured MacMillan to be nearly 50, but he had a trim waist and a handsome face. His full head of salt-and-pepper hair was short and layered and he had a measured but affable smile. I began to wonder if underneath the façade of the coiffed wife, the kids at Dalton, and the toney Westchester country club, MacMillan was a queen. He had never hit on me and I suspected he never would. But I had a sneaking suspicion that MacMillan knew *my tea*, that he'd *been there and done that*, that he was trying to make the road a little easier for me.

Mergers and acquisitions is a conservative field and I knew that being openly gay would have been a real career-sinker. Maybe the white boys could get away with it. But I already had one strike against me. I couldn't afford another badge of courage. I kept the gay thing on the hush-hush—the down low—and that worked just fine for me.

I didn't have to think long about MacMillan's offer. There are three places in the United States in which young blacks yearn to live—New York, Atlanta, and *Chocolate City*. That's what everyone was calling D.C. back then. Washington had a history of black achievement. Negro lawyers, doctors, and teachers had lived there in style since the 1920s. Black mayors had run the city for years.

A few weeks before my move, I flew the Pan Am Shuttle down to D.C. Get the *lay of the land*, McMillan had said. It was a fine and balmy April. The cherry blossoms were holding out longer than usual, lining the Tidal Basin with gentle color and draping the city in a cloud of pink perfume. The unbearable heat that I would come to know as a staple of a D.C. summer hadn't yet arrived. Everything around me was vibrant and I felt young and invincible. I spent two days with lawyers who'd been brought in to staff the new office. We strategized on a few new prospects. I meet my new secretary and set up my office. By Friday evening I felt I'd made a good first impression and now the weekend belonged to me.

I bought one those *Spartacus Gay Guides* that listed all the bars and cruise spots in the city. I looked for the one that had the little symbol for rough trade, knowing that would be how the black bars would be described. There must have been a good half-dozen clubs and discos (yes, we still called them discos back in 1987) that catered to blacks. The clubs were still pretty segregated, but mostly by choice. Most of us didn't mind. In the workplace, we fought for total equality and that usually meant integration. We spent the whole day explaining ourselves to our white colleagues.

Christopher, what do you put in your hair to make it so shiny?

Christopher, can black people get a tan?

Christopher, what do you think of that Jesse Jackson?

Come five o'clock, the time for mixing was done. We wanted to be with our own, to cut up with our friends, to let our hair down.

I chose a bar in Southeast called the Bachelor's Mill. The guidebook said that the bars in D.C. closed at 1 a.m. so I decided I'd fall up in the piece about 11. Despite being the nation's capital, D.C. was a cow town. In New York at ten o'clock on a Saturday night, I would've just been waking up from my party-nap, choosing my outfit, and deciding what drugs to take.

I took a cab to the address printed in the guide and paid my three dollars to a bruiser at the door. I walked up some rickety stairs and entered a crowded barroom. Now I'm not saying that *the men all paused* when I walked in, but a few heads turned. I'm not a bad looking guy—tall, slim and dark— my look is in these days. Black folks have finally bought into that *blacker the berry* adage, and I ain't complaining. Maybe forty men were propped and posed around a huge rectangular bar behind which bottles of all shapes and colors glistened, promising miracles or maybe just the promise of a miraculous night. There were four card tables off to the side, where men were playing bid whist and drinking. A half-dozen guys were having a billiards tournament near windows that looked down onto a street that led to Pennsylvania Avenue. It was a good-sized space, larger than the cracker box firetraps they usually cramp us into. The Fire Department doesn't care if there are enough exits in places that cater to black faggots. We can learn not to burn or not.

I could hear music pumping through the floorboards, so I went downstairs to investigate. A second but smaller bar stretched across one wall, and there was a raised dance floor with ample room for the sissies and drag queens to twirl and to vogue—with space left over for the B-Boys with their Philly fades to do their rock steady.

Lord God, it was hot down there! I started sweating just watching the twenty or thirty guys on the dance floor tearing up Whitney Houston's "Love Will Save the Day." The music was throbbing like something alive and the hot hands of desire seemed to pushing folks closer and tighter in the heat.

The lights were low and the whole scene reminded me of the blacklight basement parties at my cousins' house in Queens. When I was a teenager there was a whole lot to prove to the girls and to the other guys in my crew. I hated those parties, because they let me know just how different I was. That no matter how well I fronted, I would never be a part of that scene. When I wrapped my arms around the slim waist of one of the girls at the party, or felt her pointy breasts pressing into my chest, I felt nothing but the weight of an empty pain in my soul. Nothing but pain sprouted from a place where I knew I was supposed to be feeling something, reacting to this physical closeness, but wasn't. So I went undercover. And I've been doing okay ever since.

"Hot enough fer ya?"

I turned my head wondering who could possibly be using this tired line to get my attention. In front of me stood this pecan-colored pit bull with the warmest smile I'd seen in a long time. I gave the guy the once-over, throwing on the New York attitude thick. I was the new kid in town and wanted everyone to know it. "For me and you both, partner."

"You sweatin' already and you ain't even been on the dance floor," he said with a twang as thick as his neck. He was a pug little thing—cute as a button, and as country as scrapple on a Sunday morning.

"Where you from, brother?" I said.

"Why? *Ya thank* I have an accent?"

I laughed. So did he. Turns out, he wasn't even from the south, though his family had originally come from Tennessee. During the Great Migration they rode the rails to the factories of the automobile industry and settled in Flint, Michigan. I conjured a series of images of black men with broad backs working time-and-a-half and driving Fords. Green suburbs with modest but comfortable homes. Smokestacks. Cookouts. Pensions. He told me that *yup*, that pretty well summed it up.

I asked him to dance and we made our way to the floor. We were all doing the Patty Duke back then. He had his own version that was a little clumsy, but butch. His two-step made me smile.

His name was Floyd, he told me as we danced. Later, he drove me out to his place in Alexandria in a red pickup truck. As we crossed the bridge over the Potomac, he put his hand in my lap and gently squeezed me. I was hard from just being with him, and this seemed to get him going. His breathing got heavy.

"You all right?" I asked.

"Right as rain," he said with a straight face. This guy was too funny for words.

He had a ranch-style house in a middle-class development outside of Old Town. He was a contractor, I learned, and had built the house himself. That's what he did. I scoured the room for a hard hat. I wanted to see him in it before we went to bed. Just the hardhat—nothing else. But I didn't see one and I thought it might be too outrageous to ask, at least the first time out.

He had rough, calloused hands. As he turned me in one direction and then another, I imagined him handling pine and oak, mounting rafters, chugging two-by-fours into place. I looked up into his face, the round eyes, the pecan complexion, and the slight smile that had changed into something much more serious as his passion had risen. His skin was lustrous. His shoulders were like a crossbeam. His caresses were the tender crush of a man who knew a thing or two about making love.

The next morning he drove me back to my hotel. D.C. was gonna be cool. Yeah, I was off to a great start in my new home.

Months passed. Probably closer to a year. MacMillan was busting my chops at the office, but I was still turning the job situation out. I knew that I was a work-in-progress in MacMillan's eyes. He was still molding, creating, and transforming me into something I wasn't sure I wanted to be. I drew the line when he even offered to sponsor me for membership in his country club in Virginia.

"They prefer married couples," he said, "but I think we can

make it happen."

I respectfully declined. I wanted to get paid. Not to sell out.

Floyd and I would run into each other occasionally, mostly at the Mill. Sometimes we'd meet at the Brass Rail, a little bar downtown. It was the watering hole preferred by two out of three drag queens, but Jeez, they poured a mean rum-and-Coke. When we'd meet, I'd buy him a beer, or vice versa. A couple of times we ended up back in Alexandria at the end of the night, but most often we'd go our own ways. I still thought he was hot, but I was young and good-looking. My career was zooming. There were too many fine young men in D.C. to focus on just one guy. And to be honest, though I liked Floyd, I thought he was kinda country. He didn't fit in with the Capitol Hill image I was cultivating.

Besides, I was a committed *playa*. I'd seen too many of my friends get cheated on, lied to, and ripped off by guys they thought they loved. Men made great friends, but lousy partners. I wasn't fooling myself about my sexuality. I knew who and what I was. But I was not about to get caught up in the drama of trying to make a home with another knucklehead. I had a great family back in New York, lots of friends, and a challenging career—that was enough.

I bought a condo on Sixteenth Street. Not the Gold Coast, mind you, but in Adams Morgan down near Columbia Road. It was the hipper part of town and as close to a New York feel as D.C. could muster. I called Floyd and asked if he and his pickup would help me move. Being the good brother that he was, he agreed and showed up bright and early Saturday morning. But he didn't come alone.

When I got down to the curb with the first load of my stuff, I saw this gorgeous black woman sitting in passenger seat. She was *all that*, really she was. *Essence-, Jet-, Ebony*-fine, what they like to call a *redbone* in D.C. She had skin the color of honey blossom and shoulder-length hair that looked naturally straight to this untrained eye. Now, don't get me wrong, I'm not one of these people who's hung up on skin color and "good hair." But the sister was slammin'.

He offered her his hand as she stepped her fine self out of

the cab of the pickup. The gesture was very boyfriend/girlfriend. Not the kind of thing you do for your hangout partner, or your dyke-friend. "Tamika, I'd like you to meet J.C." Floyd made the introductions.

She shook my hand. "Hey, J.C. So pleased to meet you. Floyd says you're from New York." Her voice was sweet and educated.

I was a little nervous. Floyd had told me he had a lady and I had seen evidence of her at his house. A pair of pumps on the floor of the closet. A flowery robe on the back of the bathroom door. Most of the guys I was meeting in D.C. seemed to see no contradiction in shacking up with a sister all week and then stepping out with the fellas on Saturday night. But Jeez, I wish he had warned me.

Floyd looked a little nervous himself. He was counting on me not to let her peep his hole card.

"Nice to meet you, Tamika. Thanks so much for helping me with the move."

"That's southern hospitality, J.C."

"I wasn't aware D.C. was considered the South. When did we cross the Mason-Dixon line?"

She laughed with this upper-16th Street giggle, all proper, but warm. I could see Floyd relaxing. I could carry it. He knew I could. That's why he'd felt safe enough to bring Tamika with him.

Floyd and I got busy moving boxes out of my apartment and loading them onto the pickup. Tamika stayed on the street and watched the stuff while Floyd and I hauled and hoisted. On the last trip down in the elevator, Floyd and I were alone.

"Damn, man, you could have told me you were bringing your Old Lady. What's the deal?"

"I wanted you to meet her. She's fine, ain't she?"

"Hell yeah, she's fine. But that's not the point. What if I got jealous or something?"

"Jealous? Boy, you got more brothers coming in and out of your apartment than Hecht's has bottles of cologne." He grinned at me. He had a tiny gap between his front two teeth. I'd never noticed it before. It was what some folks refer to as *fetching*.

"But what if *you're* the brother I really want?" I said,

wondering for the first time if maybe he was.

Floyd looked at me and his small round eyes clouded over for a second. Then he sucked his teeth, grinned and grabbed me playfully in a headlock. Horseplay seemed to be the only answer he could give to my feeble attempt at elevator intimacy. We'd been moving heavy boxes for a couple of hours. His shirt was wet and I could smell the rugged exertion in the hairs of his chest and under his arms, the southern hospitality. The elevator door opened and we hoisted the last carton onto the truck.

2. Sean

Memory is a funny thing. It consists of the pieces of fiction you choose to believe. Sometimes I can recall just how I felt on a particular day or at a certain moment, even if it were years ago. Or I'll hear a song and I'll feel this rush of emotion deep inside my chest. Not because the song was any good. But because suddenly I'm transported, I'm there again, reliving the moment of first contact, when the song first dug its hook into me. I'm feeling that sensation right now as I tell you about Sean and the unlikely way he stepped into my life.

It was early one Saturday morning and I was asleep, way into some really nasty dream. I usually dream when I can sleep late enough to sense morning creeping into the room. That's when I feel pampered and spoiled and I let my imagination start spinning.

So the phone rings and I'm off in la-la-land somewhere. I didn't need to look at the clock to know that it was too damn early for someone to be calling me on a Saturday morning. Then the thought crossed my mind that maybe it was MacMillan. He had a habit of calling me at all times of the morning or night. That damn firm thought they owned me. So I put on my I've-been-awake-for-hours voice, 'cause I was bucking for partner.

"Good morning," I chirped.

"Yo, yo. Kunda, my man. What's up?"

What the fuck? "No. No Kunda here," I said. "You've got the wrong number."

"Are you sure? Is this...?" the hefty baritone on the other end read off my digits.

"Yes, it is," I said, wondering if I could still slip back into my dream. It was something about frat brothers and an X-rated hazing. "But there's no Kunda here."

"Are you positive?" The voice was laid-back. The attitude was thorough.

"Listen bro, I'd know if there was a Kunda up in here with me."

"Yo, man, I'm sorry for waking you."

"No problem."

Neither one of us hung up.

"So, uh, I hope you reach Kunda," I said. "Is he usually this hard to find?"

"I don't know. I just met him."

Silence again. Crisp, like an invitation.

This time *he* spoke up. "You've got a nice voice."

"You sound kinda good yourself. From D.C.?"

"No, Detroit."

"Ahh... City of raging steel."

He laughed. "What are you, a poet or something?"

"No, just a wise ass."

He told me that his name was Sean and we exchanged vital statistics. Age, height, weight. I listened attentively but without much confidence as he described himself. Men lie. I don't care what anybody says, that's just a fact. I've done the phone lines, the personal ads, and the Internet for too long to believe anything a man says. If a guy says he's got a football player's build, it means he's fat. If he says he's slim, it means he's skinny. Sean's physical description sounded proportioned, but I reserved judgment. A sexy voice is one thing. A proper body is another.

"Can I call you again?" he asked.

I thought about it. To be honest, this *wasn't* the weirdest way I'd ever met a guy. Besides, it wasn't like he didn't already have my phone number.

"Sure, bro. You got it. Later." I forgot about my Kappa Delta Sigma dream and went off to my day with a cocky grin.

I think Sean and I had about four or five phone conversations.

He would call early in the morning before I went to work or else late at night. It never pissed me off, because it was exciting. The whole thing felt scandalous—like some kind of Ma Bell-orchestrated blind date. I told my buddy Dwayne about him and we began referring to him as the *"Right Numba."*

After a couple of weeks, Sean and I decided to kick the thing up a notch. We had discovered through our conversations that he lived on Maryland Avenue, not far from the District Supreme Court. He was in real estate, so his schedule was flexible. He invited me over for lunch. I was purposely casual about the whole thing because, like I told you, I half-expected to walk in and find some homely three hundred-pounder munching on Doritos.

That is not how it went down. Not at all. As I walked up the block I could see that the front door of the Capitol Hill row house was open. Through a locked screen, I gave the place a thorough once-over before I rang the bell. I was ready. If the guy was not my type, I'd have a sandwich, shake his hand, and be back in court in under an hour.

When he came to the door, I thought I'd died and gone to heaven. Everything about the guy was correct. Medium build with a tapered waist. Medium brown skin with soft, large eyes. Medium length hair—curly and thick. The only thing that wasn't medium was his smile—it was high-voltage. I was glad that I had come hungry.

He invited me into a comfortable living room, with thick oriental rugs and lots of heavy wooden furniture. Lunch was all ready on the table and homeboy fed me lovely. He served some leftover oregano chicken and a green salad. Back then, radicchio and arugula were pre-trendy. He had done his homework and was offering up major style without being pretentious or haughty.

We talked about everything under the sun, but mostly sat smiling at each other in awe of our good fortune. Turns out, Sean had been as suspect of me as I had been of him. We laughed about it as the compliments flew back and forth over the homemade lemon-coconut cake.

"This is delicious," I said. "Did you make it?"

"No, a friend," he said.

"Oh," I said.

I didn't hit it that day. There was really no need to. I had gotten all the sexual rush I needed just watching him walk around his house serving me lunch in a pair of white tennis shorts and a tight-fitting Polo shirt. Built and packed, he was a man's man and I loved every minute of being with him.

When we finally did the deed, it was over at my place. With my futon on the floor (the mortgage on that place was eating up my salary) and a sandalwood-scented candle, Sean taught me ways of pleasuring another man that I never knew. The amazing thing about him was his intensity. He'd dive into loving me and what felt like hours later he'd still be loving. He was as single-minded as a general. He didn't seem to need to breathe. He breathed through me, sucking air from my lungs as he kissed me. Sean started coming by two or three times a week, usually unannounced. I'd put some blues on the stereo—Nina Simone or Irma Thomas— and we'd kick back. I'm gonna be honest. I was hooked. I was what the kids call *open* behind that brother. I began to want more from Sean—more than just sex. Despite being thoroughly convinced that a relationship with another man would never work, I began wanting to feel attached, maybe even to build something permanent.

But I wasn't a fool. I saw the signs. I knew there was someone waiting for him at home. Sean and I would spend wonderful evenings together, but by 2 or 3 a.m. he always had to go. *Why*, I'd ask, *can't you spend the night?* He never answered.

One day an appeal judge I'd been pleading in front of issued an injunction against a merger I'd worked on for months. I was fit to be tied. MacMillan was pissed and insinuated that the brief had been less than persuasive. I needed to be held, to hold back, to have me and another brother scream at the world in unison, *go fuck yourself.*

I took a chance and stopped by Sean's house during a recess. I rang the bell readying my apology for dropping by unannounced. That was Sean's style, not mine. A chocolate princess opened the door.

Not another one, I thought. "Hi, is Sean home?"

"No, he's at work. Are you J.C.?"

Once again, I was nervous. I've read all of E. Lynn Harris' books. I know the scene where the scorned woman takes matters into her own hands and confronts *the other man*. I didn't want to return to court with claw marks on my cheek.

"Uh… Yes." I said tentatively.

"I'm Jasmine. Sean's fiancée."

"Oh," I said, trying to keep my expression bland.

"Sean told me you raved about my cake."

Her cake? Oh, yeah, her cake. "Girl, that cake was out of this world." Whatever. All I knew is that I wanted to get off this stoop.

"Would you like to come in? I was just having some lunch. I teach music at Sidwell Friends and I decided to come home for a bite." I looked through the door. The dining room table was set for one. A casual bouquet of purple irises and snapdragons were tastefully arranged in a long black vase. Jasmine's shoes were kicked off in the living room. She wore a sleeveless dress, black and form-fitting.

"Thanks, Jasmine. But I was just passing by. I've got to get back to work. Tell your old man I came by."

"Sure, J.C. By the way, I hope it's not too personal. But if you're single, I've got a couple of girlfriends who'd love to meet you."

Many times I'd considered finding myself a little Spelman honey to take to the company picnic, to have some gorgeous chocolate babies with. But when I imagined the prison of a loveless marriage, for me and for her, some part of me just couldn't do it.

"Maybe we can all go out to hear some music one night," she went on. "Sean tells me you love the blues."

"Okay, Jasmine. That sounds like a winner."

That night, around three in the morning, my doorbell rang. It was Sean and he was drunk. Very drunk. I let him in. I always did. I was glad to see him whenever I could. I wasn't angry. I was resigned.

"What's up, my man?" I asked once I'd woken up a little and had gotten him settled on the couch.

"It's all a big mess," he said.

"What's a mess? Tell me what's wrong."

"Everything. My life."

"What's wrong with your life, Sean? You're a good-looking man with a great job. A beautiful fiancée. You're living the American Dream. Get over yourself." I didn't know if I meant all that or not, but I didn't want to kick the guy when he was down.

"But I'm lying. I'm lying to Jasmine, to my parents. I lied to you."

"You didn't lie to me, Sean. You just left out an important detail."

"And that doesn't make you mad?"

"I can't get all bent out of shape every time a brother lets me down." I was serious. I couldn't. Life was too short. Men were too shady.

"Brothers are trifling," he said.

"Yeah, trifling that's the word."

"You're right, J.C. I don't know what's wrong with me."

"Atta boy. You want something to eat? Are you staying the night?"

"I gotta go home. J.C., can you do me a favor?"

"Sure, man."

"Can you put on some Nina?"

"Of course. That all?"

"No... Then can you hold me?"

"Sure, Sean. Whatever you need, man."

I thought about putting on "Trouble in Mind," but chose "I Put a Spell on You" instead. I took that medium-brown, medium-build, curly-headed heartbreaker into my arms and held him for what felt like hours. First, he cried. Then he slept. Then he went home. I never saw him again.

3. What I Know Now

Toward the end of that winter, MacMillan called me into his office. He was all smiles and congratulations on the work I'd been doing. Business was great. Yes, he'd been hard on me, but only because he saw my potential, he said. The firm had plans to expand. There would be more new lawyers hired and hence more space at the top.

"We like your work, Mr. Christopher. This may well be your moment."

"Thank you, Mr. MacMillan. I think you know the level of my commitment to this firm."

"Of course I'm not promising. It's not my decision alone. But if you play your cards right, there may be one more name on our letterhead by the end of the fiscal."

I was giddy and light-headed. I could barely contain the joy I was feeling.

"Just one thing, Christopher." He came from behind his desk and sat in the chair next to me. "How old are you now?"

"Thirty-three," I responded, wondering where he was going with this line of questioning.

"Don't you think it's time you put down roots, started a family? That's the kind of thing that builds confidence in your stability."

My stability? I looked at him like he was crazy, then remembered that he was my boss—the man who was offering me something I'd been preparing for since college. Something that was at the core of achieving my dreams.

"I haven't really thought about it," I searched for words. I said something about the right moment, the right girl, and the right relationship. None of this was any of his goddamn business.

"Of course a man's affairs are a man's affairs," he said. "But I'm sure you'll be getting married at some point. Why not make it sooner rather than later?" He winked at me and returned to his big chair in front of that big window. He sat down and started reading. I was dismissed.

I went back to my office and sat at my desk. My head was spinning. I didn't know whether to be ecstatic or morose. I was scared. Success sat outside my tenth-story window grinning, inviting me to grab it, to take the plunge.

I hadn't heard from Sean in months, and I decided to call him. The number was disconnected. That evening after work I went to Mr. Charlie's on Columbia Road and did a few too many tequila shooters. I didn't want to think about work. I felt lonely. I needed a shoulder. I wondered where in the world Sean had gone.

I called my buddy Dwayne. He knew just about every good-looking guy in town.

"Do you know a brother named Sean?" I asked him. "Brown-skin boy. Lives on the Hill. Drives a red pickup. Works in real estate?"

"You mean Floyd's boyfriend?" he answered.

"Floyd's boyfriend?" *Floyd's boyfriend?* Slowly I started putting the whole thing together. Referring to home as "Detroit" was Sean's way of citifying his image. They were both Flint boys. They had moved together to D.C. to see the world and find their fortune. Floyd would build the houses and Sean would sell them. Their relationship was the ultimate in openness—each was available to other men *and* to women. They had set up separate homes—Sean in D.C, Floyd in the suburbs. They had collected matching trophy girlfriends. In the city of duplicity, they had set about the task of living double lives. It was all so perfect.

"Floyd is sick, you know." Dwayne said the word in a way that left no doubt as to what illness he was talking about. AIDS had a code back then. Unwritten, but easily decipherable by its victims. It was a tone in the voice. An unmistakable drop of the head. A hesitation between words. "Sean took him home to Michigan."

I panicked a little at first, thinking about the sexual gymnastics I'd engaged in with both them. But then I reminded myself that I'd been using condoms since '85. Even so, the next week I went to the Whitman Walker Clinic and got tested. Twice. I turned up negative, but somehow that news didn't provide me with the relief I thought it would.

I got Floyd's address and sent a card. It wasn't a get-well card because back then we pretended not to know too much about someone's status. It was a thinking-about-you kind of card, with a picture of kids having fun on a beach. Six months later I got a note from Sean. It was written on a piece of loose-leaf paper that looked as if it had been torn from a kid's notebook. The handwriting was scraggly and tortured.

Sean thanked me for the card. He said that Floyd had died

earlier that winter after doing a mighty battle with this bitch of a disease. He said that Floyd had been happy to be back in Flint, home, among the things and people that were most familiar to him. He wrote that somehow Floyd's last year had been beautiful. They had been together—that had been the most important thing. He promised to send me a picture of Floyd taken in happier days. I never received it. Sean himself passed away that spring. I guess he never got around to sending the photo. Dying can keep you pretty busy.

Folks are saying that the epidemic is almost over. The most optimistic say that in a few years AIDS will be a manageable chronic disease. I've seen friends of mine change from walking skeletons back to the healthy foxes they had once been. God is good, no doubt.

I don't know much about religion. In fact, I don't give it much thought. I do know that Jesus loves me. I learned that from my old grandma. And though I'm a big city lawyer now with degrees from Ivy League colleges, that old lady's truth has never steered me wrong. And if Jesus loves us, why would he do something merciless like give us a disease that tears us up from the inside out. No. AIDS is man's doing, not God's.

I sometimes wonder what became of those two fine sisters. Those sepia goddesses, Lena Horne wannabe/oughtabe/couldabeens. Did they wither like the men they loved? Did they die spindly and ashen on a bed of needles and morphine? What was worse? The horror of their senseless deaths or the realization of their deception? Could Flint, small town that it is, contain the magnitude of their rage?

I've decided to quit the firm. I am so tired of MacMillan and everybody telling me how to run my life. A group of young black attorneys who do entertainment law picked me up. Sure I'll have to take a salary cut, but they've got big plans and I'm along for the ride. The work will be real different, but I'm a fast learner, and the clients are bound to be a lot more interesting than these corporate moguls. They've got an office in L.A., but they need me in New York. So I guess I'm going home. I'm even considering having that conversation with my grandmother. You know what conversation I'm talking about. The one we all dread and covet at the same time. The Big Talk. She's known for years anyway, ever since the mornings after those blacklit basement parties when she'd make me my favorite breakfast of cheese grits and pull me to her and tell me how much she loved me *just the way I was.*

I've been re-thinking my commitment to the *dawg pound.* Maybe my brothers deserve another chance. Maybe I owe myself another opportunity to go deeper, to find the guy that's right for me. Full time. Long term. I was living a lie, thinking that my narrow life would be enough. I thought I was on the "down low" to protect my career. Truth was, I didn't want to risk my heart. But if Sean and Floyd taught me anything, it's that there's only one risk worth taking, and that's the chance for love. Right, fellas?

Right, fellas?

Curtis
by Ernest Hardy

On the morning that I woke up with the clarity to know I could never be in a love thang with an ofay… On the morning after the night that a friend pointedly told me that Dorothy Dandridge once said, "Some people commit suicide by booze, guns or drugs. I did it by marrying a white man." (I don't know if she ever really said this, but I know in my bones that she felt it…)

On that morning, I ran into Curtis after two years of not seeing him. He was wearing sunglasses and dark blue, baggy nylon sweatpants. An azure, short-sleeved cotton T-shirt (folded lengthwise) was tucked into his waistband, dangling like a sash. His upper body was exposed and gleaming, like truth at the root of cliché, in the sun. Passersby snatched glances.

His naturally wavy, almost-straight brown hair was sun-streaked with blonde highlights and sculpted into baby-twists. He'd been tanned to a nice golden brown, and smelled of beer and *eau de crack*. It was a new fragrance for him: pungent/acrid/bitter. His previous scent was never any stronger than a dab of weed & forty, wafting gently from his pores as he read his poetry.

His gestures were more flamboyant, more queeny than before. Gone were the sturdy lines of hetero-mulatto, surfer-boy machismo that had been girding him when we first met. Gone, too, was the baby-fat that had once padded his face. The crack, in a perverse but familiar twist, was razoring his beauty into high relief before destroying it altogether. Showing what could have been before cruelly wasting it away.

There was a hardness to him, now. The melancholy that had hung from him when I first met him—melancholy made all the more potent by the childlike optimism that struggled to sustain itself within him (he wanted to be an important writer)—had coarsened into a bitter, palpable sadness.

After hugs and small talk, he slipped on his shirt and we walked back to my place, talking of agents and writing, New York vs. L.A., porno and poetry, and what he grimly grinned and called his "long, dark descent into self-annihilation" before he said, harshly, "Can we talk about something else? Thinking about writing only makes me depressed and angry."

He paused.

"It's so funny," he began again. "Last night, I told myself that today would be the day that I seriously thought about this shit, about my writing and my life. Then I woke up this morning and didn't want to." He looked at me. "Funny running into you, again. It's like an omen or something."

He told me that he and his girl D_____ had spent the morning drinking forties and getting high. He'd been on his way to Benito's Taco Shop when I ran into him standing at the bus stop on the corner of Santa Monica and Western. Now, he was going back to my place with me.

When we got to my apartment, I put Lewis Taylor in the CD player (*"Whoever is the love in your life, he got a hard time ahead of him..."*) and opened a window. A breeze blew over his chest as he sat on my sofa, absent-mindedly fingering his twists. "I gotta put some beeswax on my shit when I get home," he said softly. "I haven't been home for days."

"Where are you staying now?" I asked.

"With my sister. Or, I guess I should say, brother. No... sister." He smiled. "My brother's a pre-op transexual, now. Stays up on DeLongpre and Vine. I love my sister. She's so cool... so fucking cool. She's always making me laugh. She just knows shit, you know?"

I sat next to him and he slid down on the sofa until his head rested on my shoulder. I put my arm around him. He took off his sunglasses and looked up at me with glassy blue-gray eyes. We talked about the low-end modeling gigs he'd been working...

"That's not my thing at all," he said with disgust. "People always trip off how I look. I hate that shit. This photographer I know is always telling me how I could have a big career. Based on my fucking looks. Nothing to do with talent. Nothing to do with substance. My fucking looks."

...about the porno he was tempted to do, and the minorceleb porn stars (men, women, and all points in-between) that he'd been fucking since I last saw him.

"I'm not a writer, I'm not a poet. I'm nothing, okay?" he said suddenly, looking me square in the eyes. "I'm just another fuckin' Hollywood waste. A pathetic excuse for a human being. Don't think of me as anything other than that, okay? I'm serious. That's all I am."

He inched closer to me and I kissed him. His lips were sticky. He kissed me back,

then leaned down to untie his shoes. "I forget," he said, looking up and chuckling, "the last time—did I ravage you or did you ravage me?"

"It was a mutual thing," I replied, wondering if he meant *ravish*, then remembering there was no difference.

I knelt before him to help him with his shoes, then slid his pants and underwear off. His tan line was so pronounced, it looked like two different bodies—a bronzed torso and a white man's pale lower half—had been sewn together. I'd forgotten how fair he was.

"I like being touched," he said softly, as my hands stroked his body. "Keep doing that. I don't even care if you're only doing it because of how I look," he said, smiling crookedly, "or if you really like me. Nobody ever just touches me." He closed his eyes and Mona Lisa'd to himself.

For a flash, I wondered if his brother-sister had the same coloring he did or if the white mom/black dad combo had fallen on the sibling differently.

I stood up and took my clothes off, then lodged myself between his generously opened thighs, licking his nipples, his navel, his chest. He stroked my chest and stomach.

My dick accidentally slid between his ass-cheeks and his whole body stiffened. "Oh, no... uh-uh... That ain't happening."

"I know," I smiled. "I remember."

I was about to pull away when he said, "No, it can stay where it is. That feels good. Just no deeper."

I started sliding in and out, getting harder. He laughed softly, kinda sadly.

"I'm a bottom but I like pussy," he chuckled. "How fucked up is that?"

He had a light faggot-lisp when he said it. Something else new. I was surprised by both the confession and the accent.

The last time we'd gotten together, he'd sucked me, I'd sucked him. I'd played with his ass. But he'd made it clear that he wasn't getting fucked. "Never been penetrated... never will," he'd stated firmly at the time.

Suddenly, now, he raised his legs up and guided my dick to his hole.

"Put it in," he said softly. "Just a little bit. I wanna feel it."

It wouldn't go in, so he spat in his hand and rubbed it against his asshole, then took my dick and slid it in. His dick got rock hard as I entered him.

Thoughts flashing through my head: Oh, shit/AIDS/death /illness/my friends' consternation/bliss, bliss, bliss...

This is why bare-backing is back in vogue, I thought, being too much the observer, critic, detached social commentator, even in my own life.

"Here, let's try it this way," he said, getting on his hands and knees on the sofa, with his round, light-yellow ass jutting in the air.

I was tempted to run get some lube but was afraid he'd snap out of the moment. So I stayed and slid it in, semi-dry.

He moaned and gyrated, the muscles in his back rippling as he arched and ground back into me. After a while, I came all over his back and he quickly jumped up. For a moment I was stunned into stillness by the beauty of his body, a body only now starting to go the slightest bit slack but with muscles still defined, still breathtaking. I got him a towel and he wiped himself off, all while looking at me blankly / shyly / smiling / a little coldly.

As he got dressed, he asked for my number. "I lost it when I moved," he said. I wrote it down and handed it to him.

"Hey," he asked, "you think you could give me, like, a little something? Since I let you play with my asshole... and all."

"Um, yeah," I said quickly, caught off guard. Reaching down to grab my pants from the floor, I rifled through the pockets for the crisp new twenty-dollar bill that was supposed to last me another five days.

I gave it to him and he smiled. "Thanks."

He slid on his sunglasses and shirt, then kissed me and started to leave. "Hey, I'll call you later this week and maybe we can get together, read each other's stuff... just hang out like we used to. I'd like that."

"Yeah," I said, "so would I."

I walked him out into the building hallway wearing only my shirt.

"Dude," he laughed, "you're naked."

"Yeah, I know," I grinned.

He nodded appreciatively and gave me a thumbs-up.

"Freedom," he said evenly. "Freedom."

Then he was gone.

I went inside and closed the door, then sat naked on the sofa for a long time. The music had stopped and the place was entirely quiet. I wondered if Curtis could have ever found the freedom to get fucked if he hadn't been defeated and degraded elsewhere in his life. I wondered if he really liked getting fucked or if he simply saw it as deserved debasement. Or if there was even a difference. Shame, self-anger and self-hatred manifested in a hard dick and shoved inside you. Sometimes that's the greatest aphrodisiac of all. I pondered if the cost of his new carnal freedom had been worth it, if sometimes freedom can cost too much, and if he was truly prepared to be free... with all the repercussions, responsibilities and fallout that entailed.

I stretched out on the sofa and closed my eyes. I hoped he'd call. I knew he wouldn't.

Infidelity
by Bruce Morrow

We met on the subway—which in my many years of experience is never a good beginning. We met again the next day by my apartment—which like all coincidences should have drawn a bright red flag. We had brunch together the day after that, fucked, fucked again a few times more, and then I never saw him again. I've been sitting around waiting on his call ever since, waiting for a voicemail or e-mail, a text message or simple smiley face. Waiting and wanting. Even as I wait to be seen for my appointment, I feel consumed, possessed, like a spell's been cast on me and only he can set me free.

Let me start from the beginning again. We met on the subway. He stood only a few feet away from me on the crowded rush hour platform. We waited side by side for the train door to open, then entered the air-conditioned car at the same time. Was that fate, a coincidence or totally random? I'm not sure. We held the same pole, our hands only inches apart as the train rumbled into our future. Was he reading a gay novel? *Before Night Falls.* I remembered only the movie and not the book. He closed his eyes for more than a moment and I finally had the freedom to stare at the slope of his nose and folds of his ears and the red fire in his brown skin. Attached earlobes are sexy as hell. Did he turn away first or did I try to ignore him, not let him see me looking at him or me see him looking at me? I put away my newspaper and pretended to read a book I'd been carrying around for months, *Rabbit at Rest*, which was part of my investigation into flawed American characters. What do Nick Carraway, Holden Caulfield and a used car salesman have in common with our president?

We got off at the same stop and then transferred to the same train. I studied the back of his head, looking for a flaw. A bald spot. A mole. A bishop fold at the base of his sculpted skull. But even the back of his head was attractive. Slim but muscular, leggy but not tall, his feet looked too big for the rest of his body. He didn't really seem trendy even though he had all the trappings. Grey-flecked goatee. Close fade. Flat-front khakis. Silver earrings, hanging like commas from both ears.

When this guy, who didn't seem to be cruising me, but didn't seem to be ignoring me, and had now followed me all the way from Harlem to Union Square, got off at the same stop as me, I sort of let him see me smile. He smiled back, bashfully, then put his book away and quickly exited the train.

We reached the top of the stairs at the same time.

Was I trying to catch up to him or was he really following me? Was it synchronicity or coincidence or plain old random luck? They all make me nervous. They make me feel like somebody's pulling my strings, forcing things to happen before they have to.

Spooked into action, I cleared my throat and said, "Hey, wassup? I see we have the same commute."

He looked startled but not alarmed. "Oh," he said then paused. "I just moved uptown. It's not bad. The commute, I mean. I mean the neighborhood." He started all over again. "I love it uptown." He seemed to have a hard time putting his thoughts together, which is always a bad sign. Which is probably why I felt like being a little more provocative.

I laughed. "Well, for a minute there I thought you were following me."

"What?"

"Just joking," I said and shook his hand. "The thought just crossed my mind." We both imagined that for a while and then I said, "See you later," and quickly walked away. I lost my courage. I thought I heard him say something, but I didn't want to get something started that I couldn't finish, especially with a neighbor who I'd run into all of the time.

I had to keep reminding myself: I'm married. I'm in a long-term relationship. I've got a good man. Mitch, I love you.

So there he was the next morning, Saturday morning, in *my* neighborhood, walking out of *my* deli as I'm running in to get coffee and milk for me and my man. A vision in blue sweatpants. What a coincidence! If only I could've turned around or snuck by. But he stood in my way, waiting for the secret password.

"Hey. What's up?" he said, smiling, not letting me by. "We met on the train yesterday. On the way to work. Downtown. You called me a stalker." He chuckled but looked me right in the eye. When it was clear that I wouldn't stop staring, he gave up. "I'm Okolo, by the way."

Okolo? What kind of name was that? It reminded me of okapi and I couldn't help but imagine him eating mangos in a lush Congo forest. It was eight thirty on a Saturday morning and I felt so guilty for having an active imagination. No one should be put on the spot during a quick trip to the deli. One should only nod at neighbors and quietly continue one's errands. One doesn't start a conversation. One just shouldn't do that.

It took me a while to get my name out. "Jimmy. Nice to meet you. Again." You hunk, I wanted to add. Me? I'm a mess. Me need to comb me nappy head. I couldn't decide if I felt more like Tarzan or Jane. Possessed. Not myself. I tried to recover. "I'm just running in and getting a few things. This place gets all of my money. I'll probably be back later to pick up more things. I really should just go to a real supermarket." With no caffeine in my blood, I babbled.

"I like it. It's so neighborhood-ie," he said, shifting his weight to his other foot and shifting my world upside down. I'm married—or as married as gay folks can get. Fifteen years in a relationship is a lifetime in gay relationships.

He smiled. "I love the name of this store, Mee Happy Deli. And," his disarming smile miraculously widened, "I ran into you. So what's up?"

I told him I lived right in this building and I needed to buy some milk and coffee. I've said this enough but I repeat: I really, really don't like coincidences. Or someone sweeping my feet. Or a hat on a bed. Or anonymous sex. I didn't add: and my boyfriend's waiting upstairs for me to fix breakfast. Okolo's smile made it easier for me to forget. He had this way of smiling; not only his mouth but his whole face seemed to be smiling at me. Even his ears. When we shook hands I noticed how nicely his hand fit inside of mine. Like the binding of a book glued to its pages. I didn't want to let go.

What spilled out of my mouth next, I couldn't believe:

"You know there's a concert at Grant's Tomb tomorrow. Jazz, I think. Roy Hargrove. Wanna check it out?" It was as if someone had made me say that, as if a spell had been cast, a mojo worked.

"Oh, yeah. My roommate told me about that. We were thinking about going. You want to join us? Maybe take a bottle of wine?"

I definitely didn't want to make a commitment. Not this early in the morning. Not before a cup of coffee. I pulled my hand away from his. Finally. The pages took to the wind. Leaf by leaf. I noticed his was trembling, his fingers shaking. Was he as nervous as me?

"Sounds great, Okolo. We'll see. You know, I've just got to get some caffeine inside of me," I said. But what I really wanted to say was, I'll worry about fitting you in later. I gave him my business card and rushed to the back of the store to pick up a can of Café Bustelo and some 100% Lactaid milk. It's so much easier on my stomach.

When I got home I closed the door and leaned against it to ensure that Okolo hadn't followed me and wasn't going to knock the door down even though I wished he would and was—*knock, knock, knocking on my back door.* I wanted to know everything about him. What he did for a living. Where he got his name. Did it mean anything. Did he like to kiss. Just the basics.

"Did you get some bananas?" my boyfriend Mitch yelled and I jumped almost to the ceiling. He was sitting on the toilet with the bathroom door open. He must have been watching me the whole time. "Did you get some bananas?" he asked again. "I need some fruit for breakfast. Some fiber. I'm trying to keep up with this five servings of fruits and vegetables a day. It really works."

For a graduate of Georgetown Law, Mitch can be a little wacky at times. He's what you'd call a little hyper. But it comes with the territory. He represents teenage multimillionaire hip-hop entrepreneurs and haggles over half million-dollar kill bonuses— to start their own labels so they won't guest star on a music video with an artist from another label. He's done well for himself—for the both of us. We own this cute condo and we're thinking about buying the building on the corner to develop some rental income. Real cute.

But it's getting to the point when I want to smack anyone that ohhhs and ahhhs when I tell them Mitch and I have been together for fifteen years. "Bless your hearts," they say. "Let me rub some of that on me," and they take my hand in theirs and squeeze so tight that I have to look to see if there's any juice coming out. Even though I think it *is* a big deal—a true long-term gay relationship's a rarity—it's now weighing me down. Our history together isn't holding me up anymore, keeping my head above water, lifting me up over that traffic jam of sexy men walking the runways of Christopher Street and Eighth Avenue. I'm stuck in a gridlock and I don't care if I get a ticket. I've become a compulsive looker. It's hard for me to concentrate in public places. Like the subway. Mitch, of course, always points out how rude I'm being.

"What are you doing?" he asks. "You look so dramatic standing there, like you're holding the door against some big hurricane or tornado or something."

"What?" How'd he know? Hurricane Okolo is expected to reach land at any moment now. "Oh. Nothing. Aren't there bananas here? I could have sworn there were some," I said, trying to change the subject of the conversation that was going on in my mind. So loud and clear. "I just need a cup of coffee."

"You seem so flustered," he said, washing his hands. "You all right?"

"Sure, I'm fine. Don't test me until I've gotten some caffeine in me. A'right? I need an IV. You want a cup?"

"Naw, that's all right. Can you make banana pancakes? And bring me the phone. Please, sweetie, can you make us a little breakfast? Pretty please?" He kissed my cheek and turned away.

"We'll see," I said, knowing full well that I was going to make a big breakfast because I felt so guilty. Big pancakes, the size of Frisbees, with lots of cinnamon and creamy chunks of bananas.

All while I was cooking, I thought about running into Okolo

and my good fortune at seeing him yesterday, today, and perhaps again the next day. What wonderful coincidences! Would he call me tonight? Tomorrow? Not giving him my home number might have tipped him off. When I closed my eyes I saw his face, smiling—even his ears—as he floated closer and closer to me. I burnt two pancakes that way.

With two cups of extra strong coffee in me, I finally started getting on with my Saturday routine. After breakfast I made a few calls, cleaned the kitchen and bathroom, and then went over to my friend Paul's house to do some more of the same. I've been making weekend visits to Paul's for about two years now. He has full-blown AIDS. Until a couple of months ago Paul was nothing but bones held together by Scotch Tape skin, hallucinating and sinking deeper into dementia. Another new protease inhibitor combination drug helped him bounce back. His T-cell counts had gone up and his viral load had zeroed but he was going completely bonkers, hallucinating at night, having bouts of nausea and aching neuropathy in his feet and hands. It's like he's on both sides of the net, playing tennis against himself. He has to worry about eating so he can get better, so he can seize this moment of being relatively healthy and just live for a little while. He got his libido back too—or maybe he's gotten a prescription for Viagra—because now he's not satisfied with telling nasty stories and watching porn all day. He's actively seeking. He can now walk up to that nasty part of the park twice a day and get a great workout. And does he tell that guy he's kneeling in front of, "I'm almost undetectable now?" Paul's crazy. I can tell him things I would never ever tell Mitch and he doesn't flinch.

My Saturday routine ends with Paul giving me a quick haircut before I sweep and mop the kitchen. He's an amazing hair stylist, even though there's not much to trimming and fading my hair. He's always talking about when he used to do hair at this fabulous Upper East Side salon, and how those high society party girls would send a car to pick him up and take him home so they could have their hair done right before stepping into the limo.

"Paul, I think I'm ready to have an affair," I tossed in the air like a tennis ball. Serve! He was putting the finishing touches on my cut, snipping away at those little hairs that never act right. All of a sudden his scissors stopped in mid-snip. Ace!

"Miss Thang," he said dryly, "I'm so glad you've finally come to your senses. You've been in a daze for years."

"But I've only known you for two."

"Well, I could tell the first time you walked in that door that you hadn't had a passionate moment in years. I could smell it. Just joking." He thumped me on the back of the neck. "Seriously, he must be something if he got your attention." I told him all about the coincidences and the stalking joke and the thick feet and the funny name. "Okolo," he repeated, exaggerating the vowel sounds, "like Ricola, 'Nature's way of soothing a sore throat.' I'm having a hard time fitting that one into my mouth." Like schoolgirls, we couldn't stop giggling.

When I asked his opinion on what I should do, how I should proceed, he said just let it happen. "You make the choices. Don't let fate do it," he said. "That's what my psychic keeps saying. You should get a consultation. The first one's free because you're a friend of mine."

I could tell he was excited about the prospects of my having an extramarital affair because he helped me finish cleaning up the kitchen after my haircut. As if he were born in a manor and accustomed to being served, Paul usually doesn't lift a finger to help me. But that day he said, in a very dry soprano voice, "Let me give you a hand now that I can. I might not need you for much longer. But why get rid of cheap help?"

Before I left he gave me a big hug and I could feel that he'd put on a few pounds and was working on a little potbelly. The excesses of life when heaven is resting on your shoulders.

The next morning, right after I checked the refrigerator and found nothing in it, I checked my voicemail. There was a message from Okolo inviting me to brunch. I didn't hesitate. Didn't have second thoughts. Mitch had left early in the morning to go to a hip-hop networking breakfast, to which I, being his homo DL lover, was never invited. I called Okolo back and set a time and place. His place.

Okolo made a wonderful breakfast of omelets, toast, home fries, coffee, and fresh-squeezed orange juice. With no ulterior motives at all, I brought over a cheap bottle of champagne that had been sitting in my refrigerator for months. We made mimosas. There's something about drinking with breakfast; it makes your head go snap, crackle, pop just like Rice Krispies. With each drink it became easier to talk to him. I asked if he'd finished *Before Night Falls* and he said yes, he liked to read fast. He was reading *The God of Small Things* now and loved all the flights of fancy. I asked about his name and he said his parents met in the Peace Corp in Africa and—get this!—his name means "one who is loved by all in the village."

After we finished eating and freshening our drinks, we moved to the living room. I plopped down on the couch. Before he put in a CD, he asked if I liked Mary J. Blige and I said sure. For some reason she'd always rubbed me the wrong way, too much sampling with too much ghetto girl posturing.

"I don't think I could stomach reading *all* of Updike's books," I shouted over the music, "but I'm almost finished with his Rabbit series."

"You're a better man than me." He touched my shoulder as he continued. "Just because he wrote that *Witches of Eastwick*, in my opinion, he should never be allowed to publish another novel or win an award. The Nobel Prize is out of the question. I'd rather re-read *Beloved*. Or *Autumn of the Patriarch*. Or *Herzog*, for that matter."

"Really. Are you sure you're not a literature professor?"

"Nope. I'm a dancer. Mostly modern. And you? What do you do?"

"I'm an architect, but I work for a firm that doesn't build buildings. We design interiors more than anything else. Theme restaurants and casinos. Cruise ships and museum collections. I specialize in all things African American. I'm the black face of The Spencer Group. Besides heading the team that designs the narrative flow of museum collections, I do a lot of writing of proposals and, in the end, writing the information on the panels in the exhibits."

"Cool. So you're a real architect. When I was little I always wanted to be an architect. Then my teacher told me architects had to be good in math."

"That's not really true," I started but got distracted by the music swelling, filling my head with more snap, crackle, and pop. Or was it the champagne or the taint in the room? "Who *is* this?" I asked even though I'd seen him put in the CD. Her voice was seeping into my blood, grinding into my hips.

"Mary J."

"Really. She's changed or something. This is like real music. She can really sing." He told me he thought that Mary J. Blige was our modern-day urban juke joint singer with a touch of church and I had to agree. It's a wonder what perseverance and life experience can do to a voice.

By this time, I was leaning on him or he was leaning on me as we sat on his couch, pressing against each other, balancing against each other's weight. We kissed. I kept thinking that it should feel strange to be kissing someone other than Mitch, we'd been doing it for so long. Fifteen years. But that thought lasted as long as the moment before I pulled Okolo into my arms. I surrounded him and he enveloped me. We stitched and glued ourselves together like pages in a book. Bound. Sex hadn't been like that for a while. I read him. He read me. We didn't skip a word. He pressed my head against his chest, covered with soft downy hair. I'd never been attracted to a man with a hairy chest before. *When would it start getting in my way?* I asked myself, already leaping ahead to the future. A future? There wasn't going to be one. Really!

After he'd gotten up and gone to the bathroom, I thought, *Now what am I supposed to do?*

Lost in thoughts of what if and if only, Okolo appeared with a bowl of plums. Large. Purple black. The size of tennis balls.

"How'd you know?" I asked, taking a wet plum and rolling it in my hands. "I'm hungry again."

"What's that?" he asked, getting back into bed. He tugged on my anklet and fingered the little silver charms. I noticed that his hands always trembled. As if he were nervous or standing on a fault line. "What are these? Initials?"

Caught. Testing the ripeness of my plum, I gathered my thoughts. I told him he didn't want to know, but he kept asking while playing with the little silver letters dangling from my anklet. It was a silly gift Mitch gave me when we were in the Bahamas. He went to one of those tourist trap junk shops and bought two silver charm bracelets with our initials on them. MTM and JSJ. It was very sweet. We laughed at the symmetry of our initials and where the "charm" in charm bracelet came from. Miss Manners' protocols or voodoo rituals? But I had no intention of ever wearing a bracelet until one day, on a whim, I put it on my ankle. It felt nice, looked nice. Like I practiced some cultish religion. I liked the way the anklet felt in my socks and how it looked when I wore sandals or took a shower. Like a charmed snake. At first I thought about lying to Okolo, brushing it off, telling him it was to remind me of my mantra or something, but I couldn't.

"You don't really want to know," I said.

"Come on." The ball kept bouncing back to me.

"You don't want to know."

He tried to laugh it off but he had a serious look on his face.

"Well, I have to tell you this. And I hope you're going to understand. I never thought this was going to happen even though I wished it to." I took a deep breath. "I've been in a relationship for fifteen years. I have a boyfriend." He raised his eyebrows. "But I don't know where we are right now. He's all into his business. Right now he's at some meeting negotiating some million-dollar deal for some ignorant rapper that's not even old enough to vote and is too stupid to do so even though he's always talking about rights and the wrongs done to his people. I want to tell you this because I want to be as honest as possible. I don't think it would be fair to not tell you. I could've just said something stupid but I want you to know, Mitch gave me this. I don't even know why I'm wearing it. I hate jewelry." I turned so I could look directly at him. He held his small trembling hands in front of his mouth. "So what do you think?"

Even though he looked away, I felt him still eyeing me. "I wasn't expecting that. I mean, I like the way you're talking about this. You sound honest. And to be honest with you, I don't want to be a mistress. I don't think I'm made of mistress material." He must've been thinking about a future too.

"That's not fair. You're right." I didn't know what else to say even though I wanted to tell him that one sex act doesn't necessarily make this an affair or him a mistress. We were both leaping ahead to the future, some future we were going to share together. Without Mitch. Without the home I've built for fifteen years. How could I have done so wrong? With all lost, all gone, would I suddenly have a heart attack and die? I tried to think of a better literary reference as quickly as possible. "Have you ever read *Madame Bovary*?" No, she poisoned herself. "*Anna Karenina*?" No, she threw herself on the train tracks. "Someone like Colette? I guess she's the writer I think of when I think of affairs. Always the mistress. Never content, really. She never seemed to get the love she wanted the way she wanted it." This wasn't turning out to be a good choice either.

He said flatly, "I've never read Colette."

"Oh, she's great. I guess she completely covers the position of the mistress and their stake in love affairs." I bit into the dark purple skin of my plum. Bitter tart quickly changed to honey sweet. Okolo ate a plum too. We put our pits back in the bowl and I hugged him, I put my head on his furry chest and tried to match my heartbeat with his. We stayed like that for a while. I fell asleep. We dozed. Darkness stretched across the room and somehow we ended up reading chapter one again, unsticking the pages, leaf by leaf, only to get them stuck together again.

It was a short walk from Okolo's apartment to mine. How convenient, I thought. With each step I became more determined to tell my boyfriend everything. Finding Okolo wasn't just a coincidence. He'd understand. Mitch would get that and give me time to figure things out.

Instead of stopping at the store and picking up something for dinner, I found myself on the train, headed uptown to Paul's. I should have called Mitch, but I didn't feel like facing reality or making any excuses yet. Perhaps I could spend the night at Paul's, maybe even move in, become the live-in maid and cook and clean in exchange for my rent. I should've called Paul, too, because he wasn't home. I rang several times, but he didn't answer. So I let myself in with my own key. His apartment smelled of lavender and sage and burnt toast. What a great old apartment. Beautiful moldings and painted wood paneling in the living room. Too bad it was all painted over, cracked and chipped. If this were my place, I'd lay it out, strip all the woodwork and, because the apartment's in the back, paint the walls a light yellow to give the appearance of sunshine. With grand visions of a complete renovation, I fixed myself a cup of peppermint ginger tea and sat at the kitchen table. I rummaged through Paul's old mail. Bills. Donation letter from the Lesbian and Gay Community Center, GMAD, and Teaching Tolerance. Calendar of events from the Asia Society. Catalogues from Abercrombie & Fitch and TLA, which by the looks of it, were both gay soft porn distributors. Paul's a collector. He has newspapers stacked almost to the ceiling, books stacked in chairs, magazines stacked on top of the toilet tank, and CDs and videos stacked four feet high in the middle of the floor. Didn't I just straighten up in here yesterday?

"It's me," I yelled when I heard the keys jiggling in the door. I didn't want to startle Paul or scare away one of his little Latino johns from the park. Paul's weakness is Dominican *platanos*.

He stood in the kitchen doorway, taking off his jacket and cap. "Let me guess, it happened."

"How'd you know?"

"I can tell by that ecstatic look on your face. You're blushing just at the thought of him. I hope you're not feeling guilty. I told you: Monogamy is not only boring, it's a fallacy. You think Mitch has been faithful the whole time?"

"Yes. But that's not the point. It's more about truthfulness."

"Yeah. Yeah. Yeah. Chil', I just had Truth and he was so quick to whip his dick out, it almost poked me in the eye. All that meat and no potatoes. I've been having a streak. Can't stop. Can't stop. Just let me hang this stuff up. Fix me a cup of tea, would you please. We need to talk." He disappeared down the hall but he kept talking, raising his voice while hanging up his jacket in the closet. "I've got something to tell you. I didn't say anything yesterday. But I'm dying to tell somebody." He giggled at his inappropriate exaggeration. He sat down at the table and as he wrapped his hands around his cup of tea, his face went blank. Then he blurted it out. "I stopped taking my medicine. Two days. I didn't tell you yesterday because it was too soon."

I didn't understand. He looked really good now. All those drugs had really worked. He looked great. Thin, but in that I-work-hard-to-be-thin sort of way. His hair wasn't so baby fine anymore and it had a cute reddish tinge to it. I'm sure he'd tinted it to accentuate his eyes, which have a thin sky blue ring around his golden brown irises. They sort of looked otherworldly. Mysterious. And Paul knows how to work it. "I don't get it, Paul."

"See, nobody's going to understand." He didn't act angry or upset. "I've just had it. I can't take it anymore. Everybody thinks I look great but I feel like shit. All the time. I'm tired of being saturated with drugs. It's like taking poison everyday. At first it was only at night. I'd sweat all night and become coated with this thick mucous-like stuff. And I'd vomit. And I have what can't even be described as diarrhea anymore. It's like every pore in my body is vomiting, shitting. I'm so tired."

But not too tired to walk up to that park, I wanted to say but didn't. "Can't you switch drugs? Can't you decrease your dose?"

"Oh, I've tried it all. They all make you sick, one way or another. It's like voluntarily giving yourself poison every day, every single day of your life. Might as well go to a witch doctor. And I'd rather just get it over with and die."

That wasn't a threat. Was it? It was just a statement about his present condition. I wanted to cry but I also wanted to help Paul hold everything together, keep everything in place, be logical. I can't even take Claritin for more than four days without getting sick of the medicine. And now that he had stopped the drugs it was probably better that he not start again or decrease the dose himself or take only part of it. Everything causes cross-resistance.

"So enjoy your affair," Paul whispered, and across the top of his table covered with bills and junk mail, our hands, warmed by our teacups, touched. "It sounds nasty." A sly smile spread across his face. Like a jack-o-lantern, his smile was missing a front tooth, which made him look even more mischievous. "Enough about me. I'm sick and tired of me and my HIV. Let's not say another word about it for a while. You should keep your little tryst a secret too. Keep it safe. And keep it a secret."

"But I've got to tell Mitch."

"Well, it's not an affair if you tell your husband."

I couldn't believe that I was already contemplating having sex with Okolo again. Already. It had taken over my life, this clandestine operation. This affair. I was struck by the idea that this affair was really happening to me. Correction: I was having him. An affair. They really happen. Like in books and magazines, they take over your body and your mind, possess you, and make you do things you'd never imagine.

I bought a six-pack after I left Paul's and started drinking in the subway station. I took a piss at the end of the platform, in the shadow of the tunnel, but I had to cut it short because the train pulled into the station. The wind almost blew me over and I panicked. What would it feel like after I'd gone under the train? The front of my pants was stained and had to hold the bag of beer in front of my crotch. Having finished the first six-pack on the train, I bought another one when I got off. Just a little something to wash down the bad news I was going to tell Mitch.

Nothing was simple now. When I got to the front of my building, I saw a parked ambulance and my heart started racing. I don't know why, but it must have been the beer. I'm such a lightweight. I can drink whiskey or wine or champagne and I'm fine but beer goes right to my head. The ambulance looked like a shining omen; it was parked, not running; there were no flashing lights or EMTs, no stretcher with ailing patient attached to IVs and respiratory devices. As innocuous as an ice cream truck, the ambulance just sat there. And yet, I panicked. I couldn't get in the building fast enough, couldn't wait for the elevator, so I ran up the stairs. I dropped the beer while trying to wrestle the door open.

I found Mitch sitting in the living room, listening to the radio with the lights off. He never listens to the radio; the commercials drive him crazy with their constant jabbering which competes against his constant jabbering. But when I finally realized the ambulance out front had nothing to do with Mitch's life, I started worrying about why Mitch was sitting in the dark, listening to the radio. Sunday night slow jams. Old Dinah Washington. New Jill Scott.

He asked how my brunch was and why I hadn't called. He'd been worried. "If anything," he said, "you should have just called and let me know you were all right and when you were coming home.

"You were too busy with your case. I didn't want to interrupt you."

"Bullshit. That's bullshit, Jimmy." I wasn't expecting anger even though I should have.

"Well, I have something to tell you. You want a beer?" I asked and, without waiting for an answer, I handed him a bottle. He looked at it as if a genie might fly out of the cold green glass and grant him three wishes. I didn't want to take a guess as to what he would wish for first.

When I opened my beer, it sprayed my face. A cold wet slap. "Just let me clean this up," I said, wiping my face with my sleeve.

"No, Jimmy. It can wait. I've been waiting all day for a call, the floor can wait to be wiped up."

For a person sitting in the dark, Mitch looked illuminated, as if light, a bright white blanket, had gathered around him, ready to protect him from the cold truth I was about to tell him.

"I had sex with someone."

"I knew it. I knew it the minute you walked in the door."

"Well you had your brunch and you can't bring your wifey to those kinds of functions, can you Mitch. Let me finish," I said, even though he wasn't trying to interrupt me. "I feel trapped in our relationship. I can't move. If I want to talk with you, I should call your cell phone. Or send an e-mail. Or send a FedEx package. But it's not really that. I just want to make sure we're together because we love each other, not because we're on some marathon to see how long this will last, not because we're setting an example for the rest of the gay community. For GMAD or something. For our friends to gush over. I'm losing myself. I don't want to be an architect that doesn't build buildings forever."

He rushed to me. Just in time for my head to rest on his shoulders. So my tears could be absorbed by his blanket of light. He took the beer out of my hand and whispered that it was all right, everything was going to be all right. "It's going to be all right now. I knew this was coming. Like a storm out at sea. It's all right, Jimmy. Just let it go. Let it out. It's time. We can"—he quickly corrected himself—"I can help you get help, if that's what *you* want. Therapy. It's time."

I didn't know where it came from. All this emotion. It must have been the beer. Was Okolo already not everything I thought he was? Was the sex really good or was it just new and different? Or did I just need someone who didn't see me as a "we"?

Okolo and I have gotten together three times since then and now—now that Mitch has moved out and rented a loft space big enough for him to live and work in—now he says he only wants to be friends and we'll both have time to think about it because he's going on tour with a dance company. California. Three weeks. I send him e-mail almost every day, but he hasn't replied. He hasn't returned my calls either. I'll call him again after this appointment and fill him in.

I never thought I would be here in this psychic's office asking for help. The lamps are covered with black lace. A yin-yang sign hangs over the door. The whole waiting room smells of frankincense and burnt orange. Paul talked me into trying his psychic before getting a shrink. He said all those signs, the coincidences, the charmed anklet, the blanket of light surrounding Mitch really added up to something that therapy wouldn't be able to handle. Maybe Jungian therapy but not psychoanalytical. Therapy wasn't right. Yet. I keep remembering that Mitch might not come back. I keep going over how I'm going to tell this story to some woman dressed in a satin turban sitting in front of a crystal ball. I don't want to come out looking like the selfish one. The asshole. Like that asshole Rabbit who deserved to die all alone, without his sister, without his son or grandchildren or his "nut brown" wife who drowned his baby daughter in the first book and stayed with him through three more volumes of tragedies. Infidelities. What an awful man! I finally finished that book on the way to this appointment and Rabbit is dead.

PATH
by G. Winston James

Who knew that it would take such a long time to fill so few empty minutes? I did. Or would have normally, but I guess it's understandable that I might forget when so immediately in the moment. That is, in the heat, crush and press of the moment. The amnesia of sweaty, logicless seconds compounding so mysteriously, forcing the rational and the remembered to disappear so soon. Perhaps it was the crush, after all, that caused me to forget how long it can take to silence my lust and to get moving back on my way.

It wasn't a very crowded train that morning—the PATH from Journal Square. Not any more densely packed with commuters than on most days. Still, I knew immediately when I got on that that day's ride would be more eventful than usual. More intimate than the norm. As if there was something almost tangible moving among the passengers. Lifting women's skirts, brushing the denim of men's crotches, stroking everyone's nipples. Resting finally on him. Pulsing there.

Or perhaps it was more that there was something in his half-closed eyes, or in the shine and slow-sliding silent question on his lips, than there was anything physical about the train itself. There was an energy, a revealing. A pulling. But all of that is relatively unimportant. What was most important, though, was that because of it all, I knew. With no rainbow flag pins or protesting pink triangles, or even the quickest adjustment of his trade, I knew that this man in business attire could be had if I played my fifteen minutes on the rails between New Jersey and New York just right. A short commute too often mitigates the effectiveness of nonverbal communication, but still I had hopes. And there was that energy. Palpable. Vibrating. There.

He was tall. Much like myself, but olive-complected, where I am a deeper brown. As slender as he needed to be to attract me, dressed in a suit of material as fine as it was well-tailored, he was simply handsome. Beyond that, sexy. It was summertime; he glowed. Warm. I wanted to touch him. To feel the color beneath my fingers that a passionless, silent sun had left behind. To stroke him in a way that said, "This skin of yours, it matters. I care deeply about hue." I moved further in his direction.

I'm not sure where he was from—Latino, Arab, Israeli or some multi-culti mix—but at 8:35 in the morning I could see that he would only be more lovely at noon, and someone else's erection by three. I'd have to work fast and be direct, yet somehow subtle. Like a twenty-dollar bill on a dance floor, I hoped I could entice him to stoop low enough to pick me up in a way that none of the others on the train would see.

He was standing to the left of the door opposite the one I'd stepped through. Leaning against the wall and the faux-wood decorated divider at the end of the row of seats. I walked directly toward him. Eyes to his eyes. To others it would look like we were going to speak. If the move worked as I hoped, then he would straighten as if he knew me. Focus on me to remember a face he would believe he had forgotten. By the time he realized that he hadn't met me before, it would be too late. I would be inside that sphere of personal space outside of which the rest of the world dissolves into dim shapes, shadow and murmur. I would be in that blind spot that most men possess, but of which few take advantage in public. If I was right about the energy I felt around him, he would stand stock still in order to time just right our eventual collision.

When he did as I expected, I ran my stare like fingers down his face and chest to his zipper, then back to his eyes as I stood closer to him than was necessary on a leisurely ride like that morning's.

The fact that he didn't adjust himself in response to my nearness was a very good sign. His eyes yawned and fluttered as memories of sleep still held him. He crossed his hands over his crotch. No doubt to test and to draw my attention. I let my right hand fall to within two inches of his knuckles. Waited.

I wondered then whether wishing could make a man rub his dick against the back of my hand on a train. Whether my wanting could cause our trip along the turbulent tracks to rock my fingertips momentarily beneath his testicles. Whether desiring it could make me bold enough to keep my hand there. Kneading his genitals slowly. Surreptitiously. I wondered simply whether many things and hoped.

If ever I'd doubted the power of creative visualization before, I became a changed man that morning as he unclasped his hands, put one behind his back (bringing himself closer to me) and moved his feet even more forward. My heart moaned. Blood surged like evening tide just beneath my skin. The man seated at the end of the row next to where we stood heard my blush. He glanced over at my hand lightly grazing the material of my conquest's trousers. I glared at him where he sat and saw jealousy clenching little fists behind his eyes. He was as gay as I am and as desirous. I noticed then that every homosexual on the train had looked up at us at almost the same moment. They knew that sex had uncrossed his muscled legs and was slowly standing in that train. That energy filling the car, obvious and sweaty to anyone who could feel and smell it.

With our faces fixed in the humdrum expression of morning, I rubbed his dick with the back of my hand, and slowly moved my right hip between his thighs. When he could, he stroked my ass. By then we were uncaring, believing that only other homosexuals—creatures so attuned, like wolves—would see. We were impossibly bold. Cavalier in our not-so-secret touching of balls, dicks, ass and eyes. It was strangely beautiful to be so unthinking, to feel so free.

When we arrived at the World Trade Center, though, I found myself suddenly in a quandary: to continue to pursue or not to pursue. To get to work on time or to fuck the establishment and blow him as I wanted.

He headed toward the restroom on the first landing, just at the top of the escalators from the train. I hesitated only a second before—as it would appear to any onlooker—I too suddenly realized I had to pee. I couldn't believe my eyes as, entering the restroom, I rounded the corner, hoping to stand at a urinal next to him, and found that at 9:00 a.m., every single, solitary toilet was occupied. Men with eyes darting down and into the urinals next to them. Arms moving when to my knowledge urine needs no external help to be freed. Perhaps they didn't start work until 9:30, but I was not so lucky. I wanted to ask them to leave, but realized as the words touched my lips that I had little right to be so demanding.

Instead of fighting, I motioned with my head that my new friend should follow me upstairs to the smaller restroom behind the escalators, to the left of Duane Reade in the mall. There were three stalls, two urinals and one resident homeless man bathing in the sink. I stepped into the stall for the physically challenged— and wondered for an instant if, all things considered, I might not be handicapped myself in some way. With a quick flick of the hand, I silently asked him to join me in the slightly larger than usual stall.

There was true fear in his eyes then. "We can't do that," he said. "What about the cops?" he asked. Yet each word had somehow brought him farther into the stall. I simply stopped listening. Knowing this variation of "Don't stop. Don't stop" all too well. I closed and latched the swinging door behind him. Fortunately, he left his chatter outside.

He shut up, unzipped his zipper, fished in his boxers and spilled his fucking dick all over my arm. "No, ma'am!" I thought. I wanted to call the homeless man in to see. His trade was longer and more girthy even than my own. One of the rarer of treats. With a dick so big and chicken eggs for balls, I couldn't have chanted "Nam Myoho Renge Kyo" enough times in my lifetime to ask for that.

I literally dropped to my knees with a thump. Looking at his dick. Almost waiting for it to speak, then realized it was mute. He began speaking in sign. One of his hands touched my head and the index finger of the other motioned me to climb on. I opened my mouth and wet it as far down as I could go, then withdrew. I held it in my hands, gave a requisite, whispering "umm, uumm, uummm" and licked the parts my restrictive throat and tonsils hadn't allowed me to pursue. Then I sucked his dick like I was late for work.

One hand just as wet as my tongue, following behind my

mouth as I let those inches slide out. Stroking circles around the head for good measure. I stopped only once to wipe away tears and to make sure that his eyes were glued on the space at the hinge of the stall. It wouldn't have done to be caught by the police on my knees munching bird in an Armani.

He smiled and said, "Just suck my dick. You gonna make me cum."

That was the point after all. When he roughly moved my hand and started fucking my face, I knew he was close and I loved him as one does trade in such moments.

"You want it in your mouth?" he panted.

"Ahhhh, no," I thought. It's Tuesday morning. I have no toothpaste. No mouthwash. And I'm not crazy enough to think that cum doesn't smell like cum when it's laying heavy on the breath. I shook my head urgently so he'd know. Thankfully, he understood.

As his streams of cum fell into the toilet, I wiped the corners of my mouth and looked at my watch for the first time since I'd first genuflected in the stall. 9:30! Oh my God, I thought, imagining the department heads gathered for the meeting that I had called the day before and should have run. The one that should have begun right then. I didn't know what I was going to do.

My new friend was gone by the time I looked up. Taking his sexiness and my sense of satisfaction with him. I imagined that later he would dry the thin layer of moisture from his dick and wonder if his boxers smelled of my breath, stomach acids and his cum. He would think of me and I would think of him, even though I hadn't seen him leave. Hadn't really cared to watch him go.

Minutes and men, I thought then. Minutes and men. So little to hold onto when encounters with them are done.

I gathered myself and headed home to be sick. From work, of course, though there was the option of feeling better by the afternoon. I really had forgotten that it could take so long to get so little accomplished. As the train doors closed behind me, I realized ruefully that I still hadn't cum. I looked at the fellow seated next to me and wondered.

A View from Flatbush
by G. Winston James

God's hand has covered the sun
Made solid the clouds like clay

Darkness deepening this morningtime
The atmosphere thickening

> Flavored
> like standards
> burning

At the broad corner of Parkside and Ocean
West Indian women push their laundry in carriages

> Seemingly unaware
> some end
> has come

The tree-head screams, "Oh, shit, man! Oh, shit!"

The sky is falling
    there are shoes in it

Cumulonimbus hailing
    blood
            money
                    power
            securities

How many
    (secrets?)

Parts of bodies

9-1-1

Miss Agnes' Middle Son Was Mine
by Duncan E. Teague

March 24, 2002,
Just before the Oscars came on.

Beat-up old leather house-shoes still stink
His lazy Saturday afternoon smell
Tried to box them up
Tried so hard, so hard
"I'm not doing nothing today" smell.

His brother phoned: the big, nice, younger one
We pleasantly talk 'til we can't
Still got things they should have
The potted flowers from the service still smell pretty.

They look too much alike
Brothers
It's scary looking at him, so hard
Wears that same cheap cologne I hid away
Smells too much the same.

So proud of his mom, Miss Agnes
We kissed, hugged at the service
Not too long
He would have smiled, laughed and hit me.

Nervous about calling Agnes, "Miss Agnes"
She just plain wilted after the attacks
Aged instantly.

Arrived early to get her hair permed, washed, set, teased and sprayed
9:00 every Tuesday, Nine-Eleven no exception
Watched it on the hairdresser's little set
Shocked, all rolled up

Permanent wave cream stinking up the shop
Almost went bald.

She knew, she knew, she just knew somehow
Pentagon, brand new job
Early morning on time
Like to the hairdressers every Tuesday
Early morning
I knew.

Her middle son
My one and only

Brand new tie, new citrus musk cologne
New job.

Scared to call Miss Agnes
Scared to put these nasty, sacred slippers away
Scared to check with the Department of Defense
Gays all up in the military
Scared to erase that greeting off the voice-mail
Scared to send Miss Agnes this box
She's too scared to ask for it.

Glad the firemen found most of him
In his new office chair wearing the new tie
Happy for Miss Agnes.

Be fine!
Going to visit my folks Friday
Mom loved him too, afraid for me
Dad's angry at all of it, scared to be this scared.

The terrors creep back again
Going to put these slippers on and
Be fine.

I'm Slipping
by Warren Adams II

I'm slipping

Through your fingers
Your hair.

There is no real sound but wind
Being disrupted,

Being stopped by things standing in its space

Causing it to go around picking up dirt,
Shifting it, spitting it into your eye.
This I know for you can barely see me.

I'm slipping,

through your fingers,
your hair,
down your mirror.

There is no real security but love being habitual,

Prolonged by things,
Never being able to let go—never sure how because
your mother breastfed you too long one night.

Light became lighter lifting into morning.

Your lips still attached to her hardened leaking skin.

I'm slipping

through your fingers
your hair
reminding you of breast milk dribbling down your chin,

down your mirror
out of your vision

into another.

In the Silent Bathroom #2
by Warren Adams II

We dreamed a lot those days about sex
In stairwells
Abandoned buildings where we all met
Black
Our penises erect
Excited by the darkness
The sounds of bodies
Crosshatched
Walking the planks
The stares attached

There were so many men
Lovers kept quiet by the awful sounds of silence
I brought people to this place
We waited in line
    waited in love
    waited in abandoned buildings

To be picked
Fucked clean of our shame
Forgetting the feel
The hands
Just remembering the heart pounding against our backs

It was the way they ravaged our bodies
Climbed our skin left marks
Left dreams of themselves with us
Inside the body

Native American Hustler on Greyhound

by Jerry Thompson

Henry leans in to remind me that the big picture of unseen miracles is at my fingertips. The moon is gone and the week is coming to an end so the unavoidable hunt for shoulders without heads, tongues without mouths is on.

I count the breaths the night takes away. I sleep with my eyes open to watch the moon nod out. I am careful not to disturb the stars. They have watched me grow into an insane man with no sense of home or recovery.

The greasy plate of deviant swashbuckling is alive with man-eating precision. I begin unloading those broad, drunk moments in the sun of my ambitious appetite for bookstore sluts onto every loser town that will have me.

I pile on the freaks like the mashed potatoes of some funky night that invites us, pours in like a brown gravy from all the turkeys that licked my contagious drive for the impossible distance in between strangers.

Henry rolls up his sleeves to begin swallowing the days and nights that betray him.

Suicidal Ideation
by Michelle Sewell

Eight years later
still not convinced
he is meant to live
he surrenders to ideation

       prepares his tomb

begins the shedding
friends
house
guilt
Armani suits
The job
that took him from
Richmond to Capitol Hill

       Transitional replacements
       blanket
       television
       stash
       solitude

It won't be messy
No mop
or gallons of white paint
to make the room livable
after they find him
No pills

       He will simply surrender
       Make this intentional and final
       Needle to vein
       Heroin, brain
       Finally
       end.

Dead Man Song
by malik m.l. williams

Heard a dead man sing
on the radio
tonight:
first anniversary
of the day you succumbed.
Dead man sang
about my life
without you now.
Suicide dead,
he must have known
this pain.
Must have clutched
impotent pill bottles
and unanswering
yellowed old photos
like these.
He must have agonized
at the knife twist
in his heart
from just this kind of loss.

Shut off the radio
with my tears.
Went out.
Out of range
of the dead man's voice
his pain
pricking my anguish.
Across town
found a spot full of life
voices, rhythms, movement
and song.
Stayed late to avoid

my suicide flat.
Stayed long enough
to hear a pretty brown girl
sing the dead man's song.

Got up and ran
with my tears
back home to listen once more
to the dead man
sing his own soul away.
Wrapped myself up
in his sorrow
spoon fit it with mine
let his song uncover my grief
invite it into the open.

Fell down
with my tears
alone in the corner
held onto your smile

sang my dead man song.

Gravity
by Duriel E. Harris

He said he had cancer. He did.
But it was what he did not have that killed him.
It's like that. *Gravity takes.*

The flesh of his body thinned.
Skin fell in flakes.

Nothing left to fight...
We stood on the platform's yellow line,
waiting, rocking on our heels, watching
the dingy glint of tracks for signs.
I saw a rat darting in and out of side pockets
pulling twine to make something underground.
I'm unraveling, he said.
I wish I had hopped the turnstile:
as if stealing small things
could bring small things back.

Blood, Prayer & Tears: 2002 A.D.
by Ernest Hardy

It's the interminable waiting for test results
That steals your appetite,
Hijacks sleep
Throws unfathomable staccato beats
Into everyday rhythms.

Those non-negotiable perks come
As you're waiting for the Gods
To decide if they'll be merciful
Or punitive in carving up your life.

That wait starts the moment you cum
From a jacket-free fuck,
The moment you pull out and away,
dressing in slow motion
As you query on a loop:
What have I done? What have I done?

You pray, bargain and plead,
Promising payment of a spiritual dowry
That will stretch from soup kitchen
To hospice
To charity ward
If you're granted clemency.

You weigh the evidence:
I wasn't in him / he wasn't in me
That long.
The cum was shot on stomach
Back
Ass-cheek...

Are my gums bleeding? Were they bleeding then?
Is that a sore on my dick? A cut on my lip?
Surely, if he were ill, he would have...

Every mark, bruise and blemish is now suspect.
You are now suspect.

You argue your case in nightly sessions with the Fates:
    I have been more sad and lonely and desperate
    Than my heart could contain, sadder than is humanly
    possible.
    I have searched and searched for hope, love
    And salvation, and found none of it. I have contorted
    myself
    Into alien forms, trying to break secret codes of connection
    That still elude me. My fear has spoiled to hate.
    Bitterness wafts off me.
    These are mitigating circumstances, certainly. Surely
    probation,
    Some sort of warning ticket—fuck it, give me Herpes—is
    permissible
    For the level of stupidity I have shown.
    Let me plea bargain, please. You won't see me in your court
    again.
    I promise.

This ritual is painfully old
Even more painfully new.
Twenty years is a blip on the radar;
It's not even measurable
As a unit of time
On the world's big-picture clock.
Twenty years is a lifetime,
Stretching back to forever,
To the place where memory begins.
It's long enough
To reconfigure the fucking landscape,

To alter reality,
To set new and permanent parameters
On escapist flights: Some restrictions do apply.

You haven't yet set the course for real knowledge;
These are merely the courage-building times
And you're not even up to that task.
Your prayers and tears chute along well-worn grooves,
Hovering in the space above the dead letter file.

Life struggles to assert itself
    From the confines of sugary pop songs
    From the text of advertising billboards
    In conversations overheard at the bus stop.
Phrases and snippets 3-D out at you,
Catapulting the sacred, paraphrasing the Holy,
Settling in your ear like a favorite Negro hymn.
Neon is an angel's grace trying to shine on you
Through the snap, crackle and pop of electric currents.

    When me was a young bwah,
    Me ask me mudda, *"Mudda, what will me be?*
    Will me be pretty? Will me be rich?"
    Dis what she say to me:
    Gwon about ya bidness, bwah. Dem's God's plans.
    Why ya ask me all dees stupid kweshTONS?

Whatever will be, will be
Whatever will be, will be
Whatever will be, will be
Whatever will be, will be
Whatever will be, will be

It Begins
by malik m.l. williams

I check in the mirror
for spots
irregularities
telltale signs.
I am fatalistic that way.
My friends' assurances
I ignore.
I imagine some alien organism
inside
attacking me.

I cough,
check for blood,
mucous,
signs of infection.
I sneeze
hold my snot up to the light;
tiny traces of red
and yellow
fuel my suspicions.
I sit and shit
then turn
and peer into the bowl.
Strange colors
enhance my niggling doubts.

I awake
from restless sleep
search the bed
for wetness.
The absence of sweat
on the sheets
does not dissuade me.

I time the healing
of my many minor injuries
by the calendar on the wall:
every cut seems
to take just a bit longer.

I wring my hands
in anticipation
of the inevitable.
Every scar on my body
I elevate to lesion status.
Every cold
encysts pneumonia
in my mind.

Daily
I awaken
return to the mirror
to check for spots
irregularities
telltale signs...

flashes—cyan/magenta/yellow
by francine j. harris

1. walking into a hospital room and he's got a phone in one
   hand, a hand in the air, a blanket across the bag of blood at
   his waist, fake flowers in a styrofoam cup tipped, lights out,
   camouflaged cigarette falling from styrofoam cup, close to
   sunset, curtains drawn, burgundy urine, he's screaming into
   the phone. freeze...

2. walk into a house where the knickknacks have changed, i.e.
   increased, tv screen cooling, phone waiting (always waiting) to
   ring. kittens born long enough ago to be swirling around an
   electronic mother, her side shaved in a long patch around a
   knotted scar. father says "she must know this is her last litter,
   she takes care of them this time." the monitor cooling /
   cracking. the buzz of china in the cupboard.

3. walking through a door in a dream with a man to find two
   white lesbian lovers folded over each other in a chair. it's a
   house in the northwest. can't see the dark trees lonely in the
   backyard. put a hand in the man's chest to keep him from
   coming through the door. but the women stay. the lovers
   don't acknowledge their visitors.

4. an old neighbor who was young when everyone else was
   young sits in his window all night. talks to the neighbors that
   were young when everyone was young. his arms are either
   muscular or swollen or fat. it's hard to say. when the young
   boys pull up to the curb in small black coupe car, they dump
   their white bag of styrofoam garbage in the street. the street
   is rough and slick with tar and waiting to be paved. he leans
   out the window and says *don't be leaving shit in front of my house.*
   he can't see the dark telephone pole alone behind him. the
   boys in the car stop laughing. they pick up the bag and put it
   back in the car.

5. walk into a chain burger joint and a couple is gray. they hold their ticket in hand and say *what's taking so long* to no one in particular. they say they've been waiting an hour. someone says the microwave is broke. they say they could have microwaved food at home.

6. walking across the street, the two women in shorts are what she means by pretty tough. everything shines. the black silk. the patent leather. the brown calves knees, the plaited hair. the bullseye watching. the tips of cigarettes. the tight skin over shins. the rings through their lobes.

7. walking onto the porch, there is blue glass in their window and a green owl he made when everyone were children. when kids joined junior achievement and asked bigger people about swimmobiles and sand at the edge of the city airport parking lot. later, he spat on her.

8. riding in a car, they travel a street that is not to be walked down. it's been years, in fact—an age. there are women sitting on the front porch in blue metal lawn chairs. they look content. there is a breeze. the windows are down. not to be walked down. it's the house that survived the fires, the stakeouts, the accusations, the bodies. she wants to stop the car and from the curb yell "do you know what your sons were?"

9. sitting next to the woman who blames the gunshots on how his mother used to talk about him being the product of a gang bang. says her assigning him her maiden name let the whole world know he was a bastard. that probably has little to do with it, she replies. children deserve to know the truth. then she adds that she didn't know his mother had been done like that. the woman says *yes, the way she talked about it, everybody knew.*

10. from his bed, he jokes with the nurse about her taking the pulse but wanting his phone number. he used to be a pimp. he lost money at it. then there was disease. he requests a table near his bedside and the woman in the room scurry. it doesn't matter. it could have been anyone, right? the men carry cell phones. he puts the cradle on the table. mother stands the fake flowers back upright. he makes a request, he's mumbling. the women scurry. i hate baby talk.

11. my father used to hate him even before he spit on me. the owl has never been broken or needed gluing. i never told him he spit on me. or slapped me. or made owls. so, he didn't know. these days, he calls him by his drug lord name. proper.

A Moontale Spun
(A poem, a story and a myth retold)
by Gale Jackson

<u>Hathor's Mirror.</u>

This is what I think
about love
and how I feel
about her
sister self
imagination collector
how

She always sends you a picture
what it look like doesn't matter
what's important is that
you have it to remember
and love her
and love...

"Take a picture" she says
"What stays?" I say
a housewife's lament
a little girl's prayer
looking
for the smell shadow bone
the kiss love's left me
knee deep in borrowed time
and standing water
a baptism of fire
this time
this time
I say

picture this
walking into love's ocean
I cried
"sweetness"
and saw a million dreamers dreaming
when morning finds Aretha singing
"Gotta Find Me an Angel"
I'm crying
"sweetness"
steady as the crest of mountains steady
as crazy as crazy as my heart
in heat
"sweetness"
I cried
I say
picture this

dusting the grave
shards of bombing
in the absence of feeling
I'm scared
the world's ending
here
eyes
sealed as the tomb

I say
I'm hungry from all the death in this place
I'm hungry from all this death

"Take a picture" she says
"What stays?" I say
how the world is broken
we are
and this is what I think about love
it hurts
change

remembers
knowing forgets
the sea swallows
drought eats
history burns
it burns
and this is what I think about love
precious
few
precious little
precious lord
precious lord
Jesus
yes
I've even called out
"Jesus"

going to church
in love's arms

which is what comes to mind
when the woman in the subway screams
"YES"
"You too can be saved"

her legless voice
bouncing off the walls
and the nervous laughter
of boys
future flashing fast
between stops

lips
sealed as the tomb

and her shouting
"YES"

"Jesus is the light
Jesus is the way
Jesus is the hope
Jesus just
might get you out of this mess"

this
tunnel of dark

and I think
it costs
and madness is a face
make up of streets
with petticoats of glass

but I look
I look
cause you got my name
on your eyelash
and I want to kiss this
absolutely resolute image
I'm so hungry from all the death
"Take a picture" she says
and love
and love

I say
look what love done
look what death done won
how can I go on
I'm so alone
since my daddy
and my hope
have died
I'm so alone
since I left this town
an angel over my shoulder

the world
falling off behind
and this is what I think about love

I say

quilting feathers of tears
with a song in my heart
black wings white rabbits
believers
your pendulous sex
the season for each thing
waiting to be touched to be moved to be freed
from the coins in the cups in our hands
making feathers of tears
wanting wings

I say

if I could show you what I've seen
high heels in hand
drag of snow
young men dead and gone
rape the mother of her dream
bloody red sky
pulsing sun on bone on bone
ice moon
what the dead have dreamed
leaving windows and doors open behind
no levee to check the rush
of wind
the mystery of forgiving and time
and time

and
I think
maybe she's right

if I could show you what I've seen
the iridescent blue of its magic
its black wings
its white teeth
it unswimmable reach and breath
if I could show you what I've seen
maybe
I could explain
everything

and what the fuck
you ask
does love have to do with any
of this
an illegible sign on a familiar road
the eye of beauty
or god's face being
your own unknown
tropical density
your own
arctic terrain

it's how
she would always give you a picture
its beauty didn't so much matter
just that
you'd have it to remember

and love her
and love...

The Next Day and Ever Since.

I. me.

dark. wraith of a woman. she appeared the day after my brother died. she had big silver earrings and long silver hair. she wore a ballgown-length black dress as she walked through the park—sleeveless on a cold spring day. she wore a far away look in her eyes and a chalk of white lipstick smeared clown like over her lips and cheeks the signal of her madness in this place of madness continually manifest. she was a young woman and i thought "good lord death walks among us," wondering about both her and myself, about what is truly real. her stealth walk was familiar though i could swear i had never seen her before which is unusual enough because i be out here. i see everybody who be in the park, everybody who be in the street, and, i guess, they see me too. but i had never seen this one until then. yet her walk was my own. now owls appear in my dreams.

II. she.

she was weeping. not crying. weeping. at five in the afternoon. alone in the street, well, actually, on a bench in a garden park. when i first saw her she didn't see me cause, i could tell, her eyes were locked in grief like those magical fairy tale girls who sow apricot blooms and rose petals with their tears. but she was sitting on only a small island of life surrounded by a concrete place. swimming around her were the sharks. she was brown, alone, and small like me. i was afraid someone would see how she was and try to hurt her. i was afraid that evil might smell the blood of her wounds, track her, and finish her. it is not good to walk with your brown skin inside out and your heart broken like that but, still, i loved her fairy tale acting colored self. my own name is hurt. so i became a heron bird and flew ahead to keep an eye on her until she stood, dusting off her skirt, shaking a bit. when she had steadied her self and began to walk again, leaving the garden, i became crow and, as the crow flies, i followed her.

III. me.

i saw the first butterflies of summer the day he passed. the day he died. and since then butterflies seem to arise from everything around me when i walk through the grassy spaces between the concrete, when i sit down in the park as i did every day as he lay/fought/walked/ran dying. i kept a vigil in the park as he lay in the hospital dying. then he was gone and maybe the butterflies arriving were part of the coincidence of time and changing season. but then there was also the heron, so long distant and alone in this brooklyn garden, who had a mate that day but not before or again. i, who always look for signs, imagined a spell cast with his death. i know i walked off the edge of the sky following him—following gulls and ravens and crows and angels. i know the dark and elegant men of his tribe were erect and trembling as we sat and then walked together in mourning behind the long mahogany casket not nearly as richly brown as deeply brown as his skin. and i know that casket was not wide enough—so i have come to believe in his ascension—for it was not wide enough for his wings.

IV. she.

i think i scared her. my dear. deer. but i truly love her. even though, after i felt the ground rock and the walls scream, been upstate, survived down south, after all the shit i been through in my life i never thought i'd again own anything. i been a dancer. i been a queen. i been a croupier in a coven of gamblers in a den of sin in atlantic city. in tangier. in beirut. i was a waitress and a cashier but my feet started to hurt. i got varicose veins. i quit. they once tried to burn me as a witch. i escaped. i been running. i stay running. they always looking to take you back. and i know i could have drowned swimming in the ocean between the rocks but she did say "hold on girl hold on." i heard her. between the rose sowing tears and the apricot bloom she was whispering to me to herself: "hold on." and i grabbed a hold of her in my mind and i fell in love with her and now i'm treading water. but i got to be careful not to scare her.

V. me.

i think i scared her. the next time i really saw her. i had fallen asleep in the park again and was awakened by my neighbor and her big dog who was trying to eat the butterflies at my feet. with the best intentions of working, notebooks and pencils around me, i keep falling asleep in the park. i confess this to my neighbor who says sleep is a way of dealing with grief. we talk about love. about loss. about AIDS. we cry a little together. when she leaves i nod off again. my brother stretches his body across the sky. he is blue. he is the sun. he is the clouds. while i'm looking up for him she keeps reappearing here on the ground. first by the sandbox. then near the swings. then in the park house. she walks from the shadows of trees and sleep. i had come to believe she was a ghost of my own madness. then i woke up to find her sitting on the park bench, just yards away, staring out. a specter. white lips. as though in a trance, i packed my things and began to walk toward her, stumbling through the tall grass and the butterflies shaken from their sleep but, before her, i became self conscious and uncertain. i stopped short. i searched her eyes but they looked through me and into time or the clouds behind me. i turned and walked off in another direction. when i looked back her head was down. there was a book in her lap and a pen in her hand. she read for a moment and then she began to write. long thin legs held the book up, the shadow of her pen in hand darkened the white page, and she was wearing new, sensible looking, shoes.

Song of Isis.
Hymn for Osiris.

Life is a newborn star. Life is a newborn star.

Long... long... long ago
and once upon a time
this is how the story began:
Nuba dreamt the world in her womb, stretched her arms and
became the sky, yawn and the sun was born. Nuba called this
sun by many names
Isis and Osiris among them.

Long... long... long ago
and once upon a time, which is endless,
the Sun traveled through the Sky being born each morning
and Isis and Osiris, the divine twins, danced through the ether
and returned to sleep there
at nite.

But then there was Set and Set stood in the Sun's path, hoping to
destroy it.

Each day like the serpent with its tail in its mouth
the Sun rise, spin, chant, sing, dance
calling itself
tamarisk
lotus
phoenix
heron
crocodile
turtle
woman, man, fish, grass, Isis, Osiris, birth, death, dark, light
human, divine

making things
long...long...long ago
and once upon a time
it was all one.

Each day the Sun called its own magical names
names like swords or talismans
Isis, lotus
Osiris or phoenix.
Each day the sun conquered death with its magic.

But Set and Death wait
Tapping its foot.

Nubia made Isis and Osiris rulers in Egypt's most ancient house
So we left the ether and the endless journey
to enter earth with the story of the Sun's path

II.

"Were we walking? Running? Flying? I know that he turned
from me and I lost my companion."

I felt the earth open.

Sun Set like the lid of a box closing me into pure night.
A casket. A trap. I became clear water, blue, grey, green with
reflection. The Nile flowed into the arms of a tree, it embraced
me and I became earth thick with a worm's soundless song.
Then an ax rang out and cut the tree down.

"Grief cut my hair but I followed him.
Alone.
I walked in the world disguised as an old woman.
I wrest his body from the river tree's trunk from the old kings

roof. I held him."
Death set on me again and again,
its terrible teeth, its terrible hands,

tearing me limb from limb from limb.
Fragments,
I became the wind.

"I remembered him like a fisherwoman
I sail a skiff of papyrus calling his names.
He is me he is mine.
I gather him in the net of my arms.
I hold him and he is reborn in everything.
He is the endless blue sky, the wind, the sun, a star in the
evening.
He is everlasting."

*The snake swallows its end. We walk both the Set path of human time
and the timeless path of the sun.*

III.
Afterward Forward.

*And though this be long…long…long ago we are still upon time which is
endless and moves which ever way it wants the story of resurrection being
simply the story of life's circling, rising and setting in all its names. And
though this be long…long… long ago in the loop of time AIDS is fear is
hate is death dividing us from our magical self, so I call your names out. This
is my sword. This is my boat. Our battle hymn for healing. Our battle hymn
for becoming all that we once were and ever are.*

Donald
Angel

Older than God and singing in the wind in the sky in your arms
Brother
Sun
Man loving
African
star in the evening baby in the morning beauty puddin' poet
prophet this your hymn your once and always again and again

* *This adaptation of the Egyptian story of Isis and Osiris, from the ancient text of "Coming Forth by Day" or "The Book of the Dead," was created in the memory of the poet, writer and activist Donald Walter Woods (1957-1992); an Other Countries founding member, a brother, beloved. "A Moon Tale Spun" sings in his honor.*

Bearing Fruit
by Letta Neely

for Sabah as-Sabah

Today, I picked wild cherries.
This juice drips and beckons
and stains now now you take
over my rooms;

seep like lavender
everywhere   when you are gone
over a year now the wild
cherries are

bursting ripe, brother
weighting limbs down, falling
all over the sidewalk
brother, I stopped

and filled a mason jar

i miss you
echoes universes
and responds

untitled
by Carlton Elliott Smith

No one told you
The thousand fallen on your left
Would not be your enemies
But instead your friends
Men whose mouths you kissed
Some needing helmets
To absorb the shock
Of knocking against your headboard

No one said
The ten thousand fallen on your right
Would not be your detractors
But your most intimate fans
Men whose mouths offered words of praise
Reminding you how loved you are

They are gone now
And with them dreams
Of grey-haired days shared

It shall not come nigh thee
But survival is not escape

haiku for the million (black) women march, philly october 1997
by Cheryl Clarke

One million black
Women and no mention
Of HIV/AIDS?

On Being a Jazz Musician
by Jcherry Muhanji

Miss Holiday's hangout was no more than a basement done up to get the most from the very best. The underground room "jes" was. It wasn't meant to rival the smart rooms on 52nd street but "jes" did. Anybody might drop in—downstairs. The Duke, although Billie wasn't much to his liking, Helen Humes, Sweet Mama String Bean, Louis, if he was in town, and Lil on occasion. When some yokel just up from the South in high water pants and a short jacket with shorter sleeves asked (and they always did), *why's this here place the best to jam in?* everybody said, it "jes" was. It was dark and dirty and had a layer of grease on everything in the kitchen. Southern emigrants had already heard that the white folks were paying good money—so much so that any Negro with thrift could afford to go by Minnie Waddles once a week and eat deep dark greens laced with spinach, hot water corn bread, summer squash with the hooked necks, candied yams, red pepper sausages, ribs, chicken, and chitlins in due season. Not only did the room cater to the palette; so, too, the eye. It was laid out in a sea of red-checkered tablecloths, convenient in the daytime, I suppose, with a menu of fried potatoes, bacon 'n' biscuits, grits 'n' gravy, with the smell of strong black fragrant coffee. But when the naked red and blue light bulbs were switched on at night, and each table was covered by a white tablecloth and littered with half-empty Mason jars of recent gin, crumpled napkins and spilled beer, the room changed. Add the hum of the late crowd. It was getting time to jam!

Kitchen, lip, hip, and groin smells held sway. The scent of Blue Gardenia slashed across the throats, inside the thighs and on the wrists of ladies-of-the-evening made them strut, and me dizzy as it strummed my nose, but slowed their gait, eyeing each other for later, if the johns were fast and the money easy. Late-night queens and sugar mammas, which were usually upstairs, would make their way on down. Everybody on the make for the same thing, but differently. Mostly, this was a place where the cats could play. Not for white folks—like on 52nd street, but for each other.

From the sort of thing that happens in a place like this whenever jazz musicians get together—cats shooting the breeze, you know, like that—telling lies and kicking butt, I heard that Billie was in early. Roaring in, just out of a big yellow taxicab. Kicking off her wet shoes at the door. Tossing her cape at the hatcheck girl before descending the stairs in her stockinged feet. Glad to be out of the way and out from in front of white folks, I bet, who didn't know what she was doing, but knew that whatever it was, they wanted in and they wanted it.

She could suddenly get quiet. A leftover from her last "hit"? Caught in the frost from downtown where she'd "entertained" white folks up close and getting "personal"? In here connecting nods—talking heads from one table to another, buzzed; person to person at the bar asking the unasked question, *Is she here, yet?* Suddenly she'd just *be there* pressing her knees together swaying them to the music, eyes closed, heart slow, and steady. Camera bulbs would go pop! whitening out the darkened room, all but the whites of the eyes connected to the murmur of moving mouths all asking, *is she, ah... gonna swing tonight, or what?* After two takes of "Tea For Two," and several disruptive chords of "Mean To Me," The Prez, Mr. Easy Street, his tenor sax playful, making everybody feel young, skipping, (in this case, riffing), 'cross the meadow picking up lots of forget-me-nots, knew without looking at her making several sluggish attempts to reach into all that billowing organdy, and pull out from her bosom the words to a song she had written, saying in that hoarse and behind-the-beat way she had, "Ahhh... I wrote it, Prez, after The Duchess did me wrong. Help me with it some... later? Maybe?"

Oh! But when Lady Day was setting in—high as a Georgia pine, like all the cats were—with thickly arched eyebrows and red/rose lips, everybody got the message. Tonight she had a rope of hair that from time to time hung down the middle of her back as she jerked herself "awake" on a phrase she liked. Then she'd mellow. Even in this room you could see she wore big jeweled earrings, meant for catching whatever light there was in the smoky blue rooms she worked in. Her arms still clothed to the elbows in fingerless opera gloves, moved to an internal rhythm while the fingers of her left hand tapped out a muffled sound on the sides of a white satiny clutch bag resting unsteadily in her lap, as it rode wave after wave of cream-colored organdy. Her dress, not at all ladylike, hung off the sides of her chair. The Lady was skewed all right—sitting outside the circle of jazz cats—and the Lady was low.

Of course, she hadn't directed that piece of paper, wet at the edges, to anybody but The Prez. Father/lover/brother/son turned, because she was sitting behind him, lifting her face and with his eyes asked, "Lady?"

"Get that fuckin' cheerleader bitch outta here, you hear me?" The room moved into silence. Each eye following her gaze, which was falling on me like tumbling dominoes. Not all at once but each body that was tethered to a horn signaled to another body, and to another, and to another, finally ending when the bass player said, "Time out, my man. Lady Day's got somethin' on her mind."

All eyes on Billie, then me. I was just in, but out of the circle myself, struggling to get my horn out of the case (my fingers still stiff from the cold), bending down in front of the Men's Room because there were no more chairs and no more free tables. (No upstairs hatcheck girl for me. And I kept my shoes on). But I *was* thinking, had been all day, about what The Prez and all the rest would play. I wondered—had been for days. Could I? Would I? Dare?

Momma had always said colored folks make do, and she did. But they, like she, knew that life, our lives, were all about tomorrow. That today was about white folks. Tomorrow, someday, over there, in the sweet bye and bye, in that great gettin' up mornin', was about being Colored and Colored was about tomorrow. So when had I decided to do it today? Was it watching her, no, hearing her make that hard-edged sound that all the family loved whenever we gathered? They would ask, and she would step up and blow hard till Big Bill Booser would move her over—adding his guitar licks, knowing what she meant if no one else did. Or, did I know when hearing her talk about her circus days when she said she blew real sweet anything she wanted under the big top? Or, traveling light and a little with Ma Rainey's group backing Bessie on a tune or two? But all that was before Pops Armstrong hit high "C" and shattered the world.

Could The Prez bring Billie in line and at the same time give a witness tonight? More important to me than that, would he? At other times he'd heard me—seen me—knew how when pressing my lips just so—tightening, tasting, tonguing the mouthpiece— how it felt. What it was gonna produce. Yeah, he knew, if anybody did, that turning my horn toward "Sweet Home" in a club, I'm not remembering just where, lit one more candle in the world not to be put out like Pops' sound did to Momma's.

The Prez, Billie Holiday's main man, a magic cat, had to know when something was about to go down, right? How could he play like that if he didn't? He had the benefit of Pops' sound and all that, right? How is it these cats were never around playing other gigs whenever I'd upped the ante and had taken everybody to "church"? Why was that? I guess the word hadn't swept over them yet, and The Prez was slow to make a move—any move. And I was anxious, and he was not, and there you have it.

I'd walked from the subway to the club. Getting off two stops before I needed to. I was buzzing with something new just under the surface, like the bottoms of my ears—the collar of my coat ignoring the tops. No matter. The bottoms warmed in anticipation. The tops on a different track. I'd liked to think that my feet were making new prints in the snow, but it had been coming down for hours and people had left their own. All I could let myself think, *I'm just pressin' and reshapin', the footprints ya' dig?* Then I felt the weight of my horns, and wondered as I always do, *what is this thing that drives me so?*

This session like all the rest would be noisy, mixed. The men would challenge. Cut. Challenge. Cut. Like that. But all I ever wanted to do ever was to play with these cats, and back Lady Day. They respected her, and that was cool, because she was with The Prez and fast becoming Miss Holiday to you. And that was cool, too. But I was nobody and had nobody and I needed somebody to let me in. If any of these cats dug the music in the way The Prez did they had to let me in. Hair laid or not, lipstick on straight, or the seams in my stockings, right? If he thought this chick could groove, then so be it. I was in. But holding on to that one shining moment when they all opened up to me is hard. The piano, the bass, the drum, their horns in mid-air—something in them, a thing they didn't know, forgotten even, bowed. Always, but always unable to hold that… what? Trust? Hope? Sight of a woman standing alongside tuning up—mouthpiece in place, ready to, to what? Engage God, you know what I mean? They backed off and went into massaging their manhood before my first note ever hit the air. "Now how that little thang thank she gon' drive the bone home, man?" their eyes asked each other. Leaving me to wander around, ya' dig? Like a lost sheep looking for a shepherd.

But if, and God this was a big if, I/me/horn/self was about to break—delicately like the girl I was then, or, crack wide open like the woman I was becoming, something, whatever it was, got, as they say, on up, I swear, coming outta me. Starting at the warm tips of my toes blowing through the top of my head. Have mercy! Funny, then and only then, whenever I am drivin' the bone home, becomes a smile of watermelon, just so, pink, heavy with black seeds, bursting with juice, resting on the slick surface of that oil blue tablecloth covering the kitchen table, yellow with noon. Don't get me wrong. There were lost dreams in that kitchen— Momma at the sink straining spaghetti, saving the starch to do Mr. Morgan's, our roomer's, shirts; late evening in the pantry beneath the steps blowing, but no longer on the road. But the ocean blue of that oil cloth under the green, green, watermelon rind, the white meat of the rind meeting the pink, set me at age six and at eye level on fire! Brushing my pigtails out of the way, I remained lost in all that mystery, color, texture, but told myself, in no language that I even knew at the time, that out of that "Still Life" I could and would make music. It was all so distant, but if, and even then it was a big if, those colors could speak, what would they say? Greet me with what?

"Gimme a pig foot and a bottle of beer." (Say wha-a-atttt?) I say. "Gimme a pig foot and a bottle of beer." (Say wha-a-atttt?) "Daddy, I say daddy, daddy, daddy where'd you sleep last night?" (Say wha-a-atttt?) "I say, I say, I say, Daddy, I say Daddy where'd you sleep last night?"

From that time till now I knew if ever I was standing by the gate I was gonna ring the bell and "Sweet Home" would be in sight. I'd be ready to drive the bone home.

When we cats get together we... ah... well, my own dreams go something like this: The Prez looks up when I come in, no, when I fly in cause he'd announce, "Here comes Hummingbird, bringing pretty little rainbows." The Prez, having just cast his own spell on the world made up worlds with his own language as it suited him. He'd learned to do that when being who he wanted to be meant making it all up. Like the way he blew. Or like I do— jazz musician—female.

But the only use hummingbirds have is that they hover. I could walk through any door any place at any time and the cats wouldn't care to notice, but The Prez would. He'd move over anyway 'cause there was always the chance that the Rapture might happen, and he expected to be there. He was, after all, a pilgrim looking for a shrine, a mystic looking for God, making up sounds that were looking for something to become. He had the best cats in the business working with him and he had Lady. Blame me for hovering?

But just in case, for all the times Jesus, for whatever reason, didn't bring the Rapture, and a given set was, say, ho-hum, he'd make himself forget about Him. 'Cause if the Lord didn't come through—or appear all evening he'd be blue; decent enough, in his forgetfulness, he'd make room for me. The Prez was polite that way even though whiskey had been moving through his veins, a long time now, exiting through black holes that were beginning to show themselves as blackouts. He'd forget to remember me. So he could dig Jesus all the more when he did show during a set. But if the Lord was a no-show he'd think, *not tonight*, but Hummingbird's here, and you never can tell. He'd explain to the cats this way.

"You, me, God don't matter, but pray for Hummingbird,

tonight." And he would. Next time he'd forget, again, his expectation lost somewhere between the silver flask he kept tucked in the pocket of his jacket that he emptied between sets, and the House filled while he was laying out. Forgetting was easy like Uncle Sam, who he was always a few steps ahead of, to recording sessions with white guys who could hear the Music but couldn't play it, and got paid twice what he did.

But oh! With Hummingbird in the air and with the sweet promise of Jesus, if the cats hesitated even a little, he'd move in the middle, hike his horn in that horizontal way—riff, a little here and there—coaxing my wings to ease up, settle down. Jesus was being tempted. His attention on me brought the cats to attention, knowing as they did, having a chick in the mix brought bad luck. No matter. Just when what The Prez had forgot to remember was about to be remembered, the Music would move into the "holy" place. I'd hit an odd Bud Powell note. Jesus would spray a barrage of Bettys—and then *one will be taken and one will be left.* I'd take off on a Monk lick—*two women will be grinding at the hand mill, and one will be taken one will be left.* Or erupt after a time into a Margo licking—*and at an unexpected hour,* when my Muse became the fuse that took everybody to the stars, *the Son of Man* cometh. That's when it got great!

When the showgirls arrived late there would be dancing between sets. The jukebox would be on. Their movements, especially the women's, brought to my mind the loop of never-ending circles within circles within circles. Getting tangled up with them was nothing new. One slip—POW! and you're hooked by those rainbow loops that all hummingbirds see around flowers—around dancers, around Billie, around the room, and around the laughing man at the bar. Suddenly I thought of frozen desserts, and how much I liked licking them, but wondered why the laughing man was still laughing. It was the tappers that stopped my world, though, and gave everybody a rush. Their loops circling around long generous legs—leading my eyes to think on those small ankles wedged into large and loud tap shoes. Short skirts. A little lace. A little thought, here and there. Why do they wear those lacy little things for a mind to get caught in? Maybe it's because they're special, huh? Maybe it's because I was there and so was Billie and so was the Music.

She had just a few months before gotten hold of a tune—*that* tune, "Strange Fruit," and it changed her life, and the writer of it. He came in, gave her the poem and she took a new direction, and so did he. Later, we heard he was raising the Rosenberg kids. That tune put her in a place that made reading comic books between sets while white girls sang her arrangements mean next to nothing. Sometimes, though, Billie couldn't suppress that deep laugh of hers. When it suddenly struck her, "Am I the only one that is finding this funny?" I heard that one time she went into hysterics, then mellowed when asked about the state of her health, her habit, the world, Joe Louis, and the FBI. "Those boys? The ones in straw hats, cheap suits and double-stitch shoes? I never worry 'bout those good ol' boys. They're doin' their best for God and country. Me? Have trouble with that? Naw." And with a nod to the reporter or investigator she'd say, always sweetly, "Yeah, honey, you betcha! Everything's just fine. Couldn't be better. How 'bout you, Sugar?"

God knows that Lady could be one thing one minute and another thing the next, but this? She was good at taking her audience out and leaving them strung out. Like pointing to city kids where the outhouse is and when they began to smell the shit in their lives she would introduce yet another song that made accepting the way it "jes" is impossible. Nobody experiencing Billie could really go home again. But she had her mojo working and white folks loved all that mystery. She reasoned, "they think they got a right to keep on comin', and comin' and comin', night after night, stone-faced, close up on me all the time. You betcha! They got a right, all right!" Then, too, blacks folks know all about shit houses, and that white folks build them. However, *these* white folks, who were into this hip black thing, didn't know that mojos exact a price. Unfortunately, the black folks had forgotten. Fooled. There she was a living dream, glamorous, sassy, a woman in charge, night after night after night. So they all kept on coming, black, and white any old time. Black folks whistling and stompin', white folks clapping politely. Both takin', and takin', and takin', more, and more, and more. Expecting her to do what they had no intention of—finding a way to God for them through the Music.

Too bad Lady Day never understood that she was the Passover Lamb for all the Jews and the Gentiles that came in nightly, and all the rest who didn't. Finally leaving all of us with nothing and nobody.

The set was hot. The men dog tired. Me? It was hard to say. Lady? Harder still hand, and The Prez—the best of the lot—was content to place his porkpie hat on his immaculate butter and move toward me in that steady arrangement he had of exiting a place. First his hat in place, his horn in the case, his suit jacket on, a hit from a flask now in, his cigarette lit. Leaning over, his face just above my ear, whispered, "Sorry Sugar, it's like this, ya' dig? Tonight you did it for the women who couldn't including my momma, aunt and my sister Mary. Remember women don't swing, and it don't mean a thing if it ain't got that swing."

I was placing the bone back inside the case when Billie, finally clear spoke loud enough for me to hear, "And the bitch plays two horns!" Then calling from across the room and across now empty chairs said, "Tell me, tell me, tell me how'd you learn to play like that? I say tell me, tell me, tell me how'd you learn to play?"

"Say, ah Hummingbird can't you hear? The Lady asked you question." I looked toward the drummer, but didn't answer. Not that I wouldn't. I couldn't. I'd been inside Billie's clothes all evening—undressing her—never missing a beat that was pointed out to me, while playing behind her. The full mouth I knew. The near plump body swallowed tonight in organdy I hated. Wondering all evening what simpler clothes on her might look like. I imagined the sepia-colored stockings. Take them off, Billie. Panties and bra take them off—but slowly. You can leave your slip on, but drop—one strap at a time.

"Tell me. Tell me. Tell me, ain't it so? Them that's got shall get. Them that's not shall lose, so the Bible says, and it still ain't news. Momma may have..."

"That's what I miss," I suddenly blurted out. Loud enough, I suppose. "You. I've missed you. Just like I missed the sound of Pops' horn the first time I heard it."

"Hey! Did Pops teach you to blow? My man."

"No, my Momma did."

"So you got Momma problems too, huh? It's awful when your own Momma won't give you no money. Talked to me like I was in knee pants."

"Yo Momma done told you, when you was in knee pants. A woman's a two-face, oh." Joe Beady blew a quick riff of the melody through his alto sax in notes so low and forlorn that Billie's eyes teared over and moved toward their corners. But before her face masked over she said, "Yeah, man, The Duchess a worrisome thing..."

Later, we'd learned to... how can I say it? dig each other. I remember one of those Billie moments: "Sweetie, so you like riffin' the Scotch, too." I frowned not understanding. "Like when The Prez steps back and invites you in. Your moves are smooth, Sugar. Like taking candy from a baby. The Prez' horn is all smiles and carries on in its own sweet way, never crowdin' you, never anxious. Nice, Sugar, real nice..."

"Lady," The Prez—known for teasing said to her at one other gig.

"She'll make you feel there are songs to sing, Babydoll, bells to be rung." There it was again, as it always was—his way—his own way of speaking in song lyrics. It was simple: He was a poet. If you didn't know the words, he wouldn't speak with you. He needed them more than a drug or the delirium of a drink, or even the Music that was shot into his blood like a fix. That's who Miss Holiday was—teacher to his horn—that's why it spoke in poems. Without her, he drank himself to death.

Drifting back to that first night and the song I remembered, Billie continued, "Papa may have, God bless the child."

Words again. Billie could coax feeling, deep feeling from nothing. Old songs, new songs, any old way songs, that song—she had written that very night because of the Duchess. The Prez, the super cat—ready to take on any of her songs wouldn't or couldn't do the same for me. He's been there when I'd introduced that tune that had me buzzin'. He knew what a tune like that can do to you. How it won't leave you alone—because it can't---make you forget to put on a hat—like that night. (What did my hair look like after the snow melted)? He'd watched me making my move with those cats—watched my descent before dropping slowly to earth (never overstating the obvious), having taken my horn to places even he ain't never been. And it frightened and fascinated him in ways that few men ever get to and fewer women still. And Oh! I knew it was beautiful, can ya' dig? Like the covered heads of women praying at a shrine.

During my descent I was aware that he was in deep thought. And in an instant of time, I saw all the doorways of my life with men just like him standing in them smoking hard, trying to quell the jitters.

But then there was Lady. A beginning. Later there would be nights when she would choose to lie on top of me—trying desperately to hold her world steady—forbidding me to move. Wanting nothing from me, but then there were nights—late nights when I would be all over her—our sky turning to electric blue. We were girls together and it was then that it was all good. Remember that tune I said that had me buzzing? Number one on the Hit Parade for sixteen weeks. Ask for it the next time you're in the club.

Fortune
by R. Erica Doyle

Two doors down lives Fortune. She breathes in daybreak in black sarongs and flamboyant halter tops, orchids on her tongue. You watch her heave the gate open in the morning, trip dance down the wooden steps to Morne Coco Road. The banana tree hides her for a moment, and your heart stops with her disappearance, starts again when her sandals clack on the street. The roosters crow before and behind her, hailing, "Fortune, ho ho, Fortune, ho ho." Her dougla hair, that curly mass of Africa and India making love, caresses her shoulders, bounces down her back, winds itself over the straps of her red hand bag. She has bangles like a garden of silver on her full golden arms.

You stand in the doorway with your tea, now cold, sip it with a grimace. Fortune comes even with your hungry stance, two points converging, two pairs of cocoa eyes meeting, and then she is past you, throwing you a hard won "Good morning Yvette!" over her shoulder. Her round buttocks describe circles under the cotton. "Fortune is a woman could walk and win' at the same time," Couteledge from down the road always said, "that what make them old hags tongue wag, can't stand no woman that age hard back and fete one time, no children no man to slow she down." The chickens in your front yard raise their heads from the dust they've been scouring for corn and insects to watch her. She is the sun rising over the hill, then setting below it, lost from your sight.

Something is pulling at the bottom of your short pants leg. You don't turn, know it is your little nephew Selwyn, eighteen months old, awake and wanting breakfast. You wait. Two months now your sister, Dulce, send him from New York for you to raise. The child come walking, but ain't saying a word at first, only pointing and grabbing at things he want. To teach him you didn't answer these pulls, matched his silence with your own expectant stare, eyebrows raised into question marks, and smiling to show you not vex, only waiting. Patience is one thing you always have. That and respect for few words. Finally he began to talk, say "Mek" for "Milk" and "Bah bah" for bottle or cup or ball or bath, and "Titi," his name for you, when he don't know the word at all. You pick things up for him then, showcase fruit, food, and toys like the game show white lady on Miss Flora television until he know what he wants.

"Titi?" says Selwyn, still pulling, but not too bad.

You turn, crouch down to meet his luminous gray eyes, smile. You open your arms and he falls in, laughing. "Good morning Sello darling." His sweet still-baby smell of powder and coconut oil mix together, his fresh breath on your cheek.

"G'mah nah Titi," he replies.

"Good boy! You hungry?"

"Yesh, Titi!" He laughs at his own words, proud.

You stand and he runs into the house in front of you. You are always surprised at how quickly he covers distances with that chubby duck walk he have. Not that there is far to go in the small house, it only have two rooms, but he speeds through like a wind up toy, and into everything like a little monkey. When the stewardess handed him to you in Piarco Airport, you called the woozy and fearful child "Paw Paw Boy" to make him smile, for he was dense and yellow as a papaya, with a shock of reddish hair to match the fruit's insides.

Selwyn climbs onto the seat you've stacked with newspapers to make him a high chair of sorts and fold his hands neatly on the table, eyes ghost eyes shining.

"I have some roast bake for you this morning," you sing, holding up the iron skillet for him to see the bread round and solid within. "And some nice buljahl I make fresh fresh."

Selwyn giggles. His impossibly small teeth are like pearls between his pink lips. "Fwesh!"

"Yes, my dear." You place the bowl of codfish on the table next to the bake. "Uh oh Sello—" you spread your hands wide in puzzlement. "One thing, one thing missing. What is it?" You place a finger on your forehead as if thinking, and his brow furrows to match. "Hmmm…"

"Jooch!" cries Selwyn.

"That's right my love, juice!" You take the plastic pitcher full of yellow juice from the narrow counter and put it on the table. "Now, what kind is it?"

"Mmm," says Sello, tapping his head with the palm of one tiny hand, "onch?"

"Good guess, but it's not orange. Try again."

"Magoh?"

"Mango is darker, love, try again."

Selwyn thinks hard, then smiles and holds up one hand, fingers spread.

"Right my dear! Five-finger fruit. But you can say 'star' if that's too too difficult. Can you say 'star'?"

"Shah."

"Very good. Now it's time to eat."

Selwyn claps his hands and sings one of his under-the-breath songs to himself, and you make him a small plate of bake and buljahl and pour some juice into his sippy cup, with its spout and two handles. You make some for yourself, and you both eat the salty fish and warm bread in silence.

After breakfast, you clear the table and Selwyn clambers down from his chair. He toddles through the curtain separating the second room from the parlor and kitchen, and goes to pull the sheets around on the bed you both share to "make it up." You rinse the plates in the sink, and put some water on to boil for his bath. This has become your routine, Fortune in the morning, breakfast with Sello, his bath, his toys and books, his nap, then wait for customers. He makes up the bed as the water boils and could probably do it for hours, until you call him. After his bath, you read to him from one of the books Dulce sent from America, and then sweep the kitchen while he plays in the bedroom with the puzzles and blocks Vilma just bring, also from Dulce. Books could send alone, but toys not likely to make it through customs "at all at all," Vilma had said, shaking her head in a long suck-teeth. "Is only thief they thiefing in that customs you hear? Thief the only custom them damn fools accustom."

After Sello clean and sweet and diapers change, playing quiet in the bedroom, you sweep the kitchen and parlor floor until the wood planks sing under the old straw broom. Out go the clouds of dust through the back door, which reminds you to feed the parrot, small and green in the big aluminum cage your cousin Panchita bring it in. "I know you care for it," she say to your sagging shoulders. "I found it on our mountain, I think the wing sore, and you know Mummy don't allow me to have no animal in the house." Panchita's mother was a woman from town who kept their Diego Martin home spotless and free of nonhuman life with a variety of pesticides she got from her shopping trips to Miami. Even the chameleons didn't escape her, though one had conveniently, and appropriately you thought, died in one of her fancy leather shoes. Even today you couldn't see the parrot without remembering the sight of Auntie Maxine bouncing around on one foot while holding the other, toe enmeshed with crushed lizard, and squealing. And so, like Rex, the black puppy, and Pepper, the old cat, the little fellow joined your crew of creatures needing someone to watch them.

You give the parrot some five-finger fruit and mango and some sunflower seeds. He whirls one black eye in your direction, still suspicious of your large brown figure. You run a hand through the short salt and pepper curls on your head and gesture toward the voluminous red-flowered shirt you are wearing, another gift from Dulce. Why she think you would wear such a thing unless she self give it, you don't know, but a gift is a gift. "See?" you tell the parrot. "I wearing my Sunday best only for you." The parrot seems unimpressed, but hops down to peck at the seeds, twirling them on his black tongue to crack them just so. You sigh and go back into the house where Selwyn is waiting in the parlor.

"Chick? Chick?" he asks.

"Yes my dear, time to feed the chickens."

He runs ahead, out the front door, down the slanted wooden steps to the chicken coops on the side of the house, under the banana trees. His bare feet send up clouds of dusts in his wake. When they see him coming, the chickens begin a soft clucking that sounds like the purr of a rainstorm. Selwyn gets the feed from the side of the coop and grabs it in his small fists, flailing his arms, opening his hands at just the right moment. The hens swirl around him kicking up dust and tickling him with their feathers until the rooster comes from behind the house and sends them cackling and scurrying. As he starts to eat, they converge again, and you watch the cloud of copper and black feathers, the flash of red combs and black eyes, the golden red-haired child throwing food in their midst, laughing in the mid-morning sun.

When the chickens are fed, Selwyn goes down for his nap. He climbs onto the bed and flops down and watches as you push two pillows and some sofa cushions around him to make a small fortress. The first time he slept alone in the bed he'd fallen out three times before you realized that he just would not stay. You were amazed by that, that staying on bed while sleeping was learned. To know where the edges were of your surface while unconscious, knowing the boundaries in your dreams. So now you make this wall for him, so he'll be safe while you work. Sello snuggles down and watches until you back out through the curtain a finger on your lips to shush. When you check back before going out to the yard, his eyes are closed, thumb in his mouth with the index finger scratching the bridge of his nose gently.

Today's customers are regulars—Mam Flora, Couteledge, Auntie Meiling and Shireen. They all buy one, two or three chickens for the week, and take them live in a basket, except for Miss Merle, Auntie Maxine neighbor from Diego Martin who comes down to Petit Valley in a shiny car she always call her "automobile." You send Cedrick, Miss Agnes son from next door, to fetch you cousin Ramon to wring the necks for her, as she too fancy to do it herself. While you wait for Ramon, Miss Merle stay in she car, playing classical music on the radio, to stimulate the brain she say. You stand quietly in the road near her, to be polite, though you don't like the way her beady eyes roving all over your cut-short pants and that flowered shirt Dulce send, with a look like you covered in cow shit or some such. She smile at you in a way those ladies do, when they about to slit your throat with they mako words always in somebody business. Miss Merle and them can't stay silent in the presence of another human being, class notwithstanding, for very long.

"So Boysie tell me Flora girl Fortune home from America come back to Petit Valley to live?"

"Yes Mam, she living just there down the road."

"Oh ho, close close! All you must have a lot to talk about, America and thing."

You don't say anything. Fortune and you have not exchanged more than ten words since her return, but words and Fortune is something that don't mix. Fortune say, "Words ruin," and then take your hands in hers and that was that.

Miss Merle, seeing no reply forthcoming, continue. "Well maybe not. I know your sister Dulce there in America making a very nice life for she self. Studying dentistry and everything. Is a pity your poor mother bless her soul ain't live to see it. But all you doing real good. You have this little business take over from your father and Dulce in America going to be a doctor!" Well, dental assistant, but you don't bother to correct Miss Merle.

"But that Fortune." Miss Merle look both ways up and down the street and in she rear view mirror to make sure the coast is clear, before leaning out the window to meet your eyes with her own murky black ones. "Boyboy tell me is a true true reason she come back from America so fast. That is a reason she live in that house all alone, nobody come, nobody go, no man, no friend no BODY. You tell me Yvette, why is a woman look like that not have a man and no children to speak of? Taunting and tempting with she little shirts and breasts bouncing?" Beads of sweat form above Miss Merle's upper lip and spit flecks at the corners of her broken prune mouth. Then she sees Ramon and Cedrick approaching up the street and winds herself back into the car, breathing heavily.

"Tante, are you alright?" you ask, half amused, and a little worried for the state she's gotten herself into.

Staring straight ahead out the windshield, gripping the steering wheel, Miss Merle murmurs under her breath. "Obeah, I tell you, the girl is obeah woman or one ladiablesse, you mark my words Yvette, be careful with Dulce child!"

You lean into the car window and pat her shoulder, give her brown paper cheek a kiss. "Is all right Auntie, Devil Woman and thing, none of them happen here anymore. Don't worry about me and Sello." You hear the rhythmic squawking and then silence of Ramon catching the hens and killing them. He was always the fastest and the best at it of all his brothers. He brings the bodies in a basket out to the car.

"Thanks cousin," you say as he puts them in the back seat.

"Eh eh!" exclaims Ramon to Miss Merle. "Auntie, what have you so frighten? Look like you see one jumbie!"

Miss Merle doesn't respond to his teasing except for one long suck-teeth. She puts her car into gear and then drives off in a cloud of dust which leads Ramon to speculate on the rain that has been long in coming. You give him twenty dollars and he heads home, whistling.

When they are all done, it is past noon and too hot for business or money, but you add up the dollars in your head anyway. Forty-five dollars a chicken, you've made enough for today, anyone else would be extra. And besides, is almost time for Fortune to come home from her job at the market in town.

You close your eyes, feel the beads of sweat on your forehead, breathe the heat and tobacco from your own upper lip. The trees sway in the yard and on the hill across the road—cocoa, flamboyant, mango, jack fruit and banana—just enough breeze to make a whisper of cool and force the leaves sing. From time to time a neighbor passes, or a cousin, on foot or in a wheezy car, and you wave them "Good afternoon."

Then here she comes, slightly slower of step than in the morning, eyes open not as wide, sandals still slap slapping the dusty road. On her head she balances a parcel must be brought from the market and a next one in the hand opposite the hand bag. She fills your horizon with her colors and packages.

You remember coming to her after midnight and leaving before dawn, the timeless embrace between. When she knelt above you, her hair was a net to catch the shadows, she coaxed out the light within you to bursting. The land and hollow of her, the slackness of her belly from the child she left in New York, the salt in the crevice of the backs of her knees, in the crow's feet near her eyes, released. Afterward, you slept lightly enough to hear Sello if he cried out, and, for those few hours, to listen to her breathe. Before rooster-call, you slipped out her back door and behind Auntie Pricille's house to your own. Her jasmine smell yet enveloped you, you still tasted her on your lips.

As she draws even to your gate, she nods you a greeting, a hint of a smile beyond the tiredness at the corners of her eyes. *I will see you under the belt of Orion,* it says. *I will see you when the rooster is still. When the lily closes its eyes for the day, and the old women sleep upright in their easy chairs, hold me like milk in a river of stones. Wash me in stars, I will be your good Fortune.*

from Phallos
[a novel in progress]
by Samuel R. Delany

Author's note: This piece was written before my novel, Phallos, *was written and subsequently published by Bamberger Books in 2004.*

§0. *Recognize this:*

In the shower room, after last period swim, seven of us regularly stayed on—three from Sixth Grade, four from Seventh—to play with and lick on and twiddle each other, to prod and poke. Twice, the week before, as had Jeff and Big Jonathan, I'd stuck my circumcised cock up both (he was uncut) Vinton's and (cut like the rest of us) Raymond's asses. After three tries, Big Jonathan had managed to stick his up mine. I'd licked and sucked on all their cocks. All—except Jeff—had done the same to me.

Once Raymond and I walked home behind the power plant through the woods, when, off on a dirt road, through leaves, we glimpsed the blotchy fender of Joey Fenton's gray Dodge. Joey was a white high school boy who worked with my cousin Edwin at Mike Chloris's filling station. Both the Dodge's doors sagged wide. Joey sat inside. Mary Evens sat beside him, blonde as tow, milk skinned, the boobs inside her flowered blouse, opened by four, five, six buttons, as big (at least they looked so to us) as honey dews— a buxom girl, but no one's pretty. Open wide, Joey's jeans were rucked beneath his hips. His thighs were hairy, pimply. His cock was red and hard. His cheek and jaw bristled through recently healed acne. While they talked, Mary held him in her pudgy hand.

I pushed forward; Raymond pulled back—hooking my shoulder to stop me. No...! he whispered, as we looked through warm foliage.

You do it, now, Joey said, soon. Okay...?

Mary leaned over to take him in her lipsticked lips—confirming a reality we'd known only through drawings on bathroom walls and an even more unbelievable mythology. (Certainly cocksucking was not what we had done...)

Oh, shit...! Raymond pressed against me.

Because, from then on, we had firsthand evidence that, beyond our fumblings, cocksucking was real, and oral activities in the shower room took a rise.

No one was old enough to shoot with regularity, though I'd done it twice by accident—first alone in my room, on my bed, reading and rubbing myself against the spread.

A moment before I turned the page of the coffee table astronomy book (a deluxe edition Dad had just got of Hawking's Brief History of Time*), tangled up with whatever caption I'd been reading beneath galaxies and the colored dusts of the Hubbel's enhanced Horsehead— astonishment...!*

Terror, pleasure, wonder...

...while my left hand grasped the gray and white bedspread and my eyes squeezed tight.

Quivering, thrills...

Settling out of that pleasure close to soreness into—three, four, five breaths later—a wet place in my jeans.

Confused, I let go the spread.

Often since, I've been curious if that astonishing release didn't fix me on the word—lock me on language, inscribe me forever beneath that icon of the universe, since, like drinking champagne at New Years, it was what I'd been doing when it happened: Since that's how I'd first come, that Muse must be first served.

...The second time? Fact is, I can't recall.

(Can you?)

But in the shower a week later (while I still wondered if coming's what I'd really done), Serge said he did it by rolling his cock between his palms, but couldn't make it happen in front of us when he tried. Jeff said you just did it by pulling on it again and again and again. That's what his big brother did. Then Vinton said, no, stupid. You don't pull. You pump!

We all said, Oh...

But I was still a bed rubber—though unconfessed to Raymund or Jeff (I confess it to you now).

Once, when we stayed on after the others, water running in the stall behind us and the steam curling over the top of the blue fiberglass partition, on my stinging knees I mouthed Big Jonathan till, sitting on the marble towel shelf, clutching the edge, he gasped loudly, grabbed my head, and shot. In my mouth. Jumping up, I pulled away, staggered back, and hit my elbow, painfully, against the stall's cinderblock—mostly because his grab had so surprised me. I spit and spit again on puddled cement, while, standing naked now (except for his green baseball cap), Jonathan and I looked down at the whitish goop, coherent in the water, froth along one edge, the taste in my mouth like a rancid pecan you bite into, thinking: In a second it's going to be truly putrid. Only it isn't. It's just... different. And slightly off.

Stepping from big, translucent foot to big translucent foot and tugging on his visor, Big Jonathan swore that he'd never *do that again.*

Rubbing my forearm, I said he'd better *not.*

Then I went home, already having decided that was the stupidest thing I'd ever told anyone. I wanted *that stuff to come out of him and into me again. What would it have been like to have somebody enjoy that feeling so much he grabbed your head,* made *you go on till he finished—and not let you go till you'd swallowed...*

Next day, Big Jonathan dressed right away—and left. Day after that, when he was rushing to leave, I caught him at the locker room door, to ask why he wasn't hanging around. He took off his green cap, put it on with the visor to the back, and said: Naw, I gotta go. My folks say I have to come right home, now. *He was in his jeans, red T-shirt, and jacket already.*

I didn't even have my tank suit on. Did you tell your parents about—*naked, I dripped in front of him*—what we were doing?

Naw. *Big Jonathan stepped back on the sloppy tiles.* I wouldn't do that.

So I went and told Vinton and Raymond and Jeff and the others that Big Jonathan—he would *be the one white kid in our group—had gone and spilled at least some of what we were doing to his folks. A nice guy, he just wasn't a good liar; as well, his parents (if not he) were probably looking to cut whatever pleasure bonds linked him to the dusky cut-ups that were our circle. We lay low a few days in case* they *said anything to the athletics instructor, Muscles (is what we called him, the one black teacher in a school a third African-American, as we now say), who might come out of his office looking for us. After a week-and-a-half, though—without Jonathan—we were all back.*

Once when Vinton was sucking on me, I let some pee spurt into his mouth. He looked up, blinking, with his soft, near-Oriental eyes—and, I realized, swallowed. And went on.

In my room that night I got off, again on the bed, again in my pants, thinking of a group of older boys—in masks, getting us all together, forcing us to suck them, peeing in our mouths. But I never had the nerve to ask Vinton to do the same thing back. By the time school let out, however, I figured I was a pretty sexually sophisticated kid.

And I knew I'd never spit my next mouthful.

§1. The day we actually met, walking up to me over the cracked alley pavement, the first thing Willy James said, was, "You're black, right?"

I said: "Un-huh."

Loud branches hissed over the back fence beside the lot between his house and mine. The big tree gentled above us, as if, like a conductor, it were striking up the windy music for Bethynian summer.

"You don't look black to me. But my pop said you was. We ain't black. We're white." Willy James grinned: One front tooth had broken off in a slant. "We just moved in." (I'd known his name was Willy James. But I hadn't known his tooth was broken.) "You look just as white as me. That's what my ma says."

I said: "Well, I'm not." School had been out three weeks. Anything unusual was a challenge and a blessing to the boredom that filled and froze the summer streets of our up-state town.

"Yeah." He nodded, as though somebody had said that to him, too. "Your pop's black? *And* your ma?"

"Yes." I spoke insistently, feeling uncomfortable. "Of *course* they are."

Willy James Barnowshky had lived in his house less than a week. Somehow, though, his parents, whose names I knew were Edith and Paul, had already talked to mine. That made him interesting. My Mom was Vivian. She and I both called my dad "Carl." I asked: "You been over to Mr. Idemer's store, yet? He's got a whole wall full of some *excellent* comics." Yes, that's what we were reduced to for acts of interest.

"Naw," Willy James said. "My sister was, though."

"Come on. I'll show you where it is. He lets you stand there and look through them all you want—as long as one person buys one. I have this month's *X–Men*. But I may buy a *Fantastic Four*. So you don't have to. 'Cause you'll be with me."

"Okay," Willy James said. "*You* read comics?"

"I like to look at them," I said. "Let's go."

"Those are some funny shoes," he said, as we started toward Richard's Avenue.

"They're sandals," I said. "I don't really like them. But my mom wants me to wear them."

"Why don't you tell her to go fuck herself," he said, matter of factly, "I mean, if you don't like 'em. Hey, you wanna see what I got...?"

Willy James turned out to be kind of a bully, who talked about sex a lot. (We didn't go to Mr. Idemer's.) With girls. To understand why I tagged around with him, though, the rest of the time he lived there, you have to know that Willy James was not just a year older than I was, but that, at eleven, in the pouch pockets on his army-drab camouflage fatigues, he kept a slingshot bent from a length of wire coat-hanger twice as thick as any coat hanger I'd ever seen and a strip of rubber; as well, he had twenty-eight cards from a half-sized deck in which each card showed a different naked woman; and a radio as small as a tape cassette (it didn't work) that he'd taken the back off to see the copper tracery and solder blobs over the green plastic. In the right pouch he kept some special stones, one of which you could make a fire with if you hit it right—only after four days we still couldn't figure out yet how to do it; and a magnifying glass that was all clear plastic, even the handle; and a red Swiss Army pocket knife, one side of which had come off and gotten lost so that side was just a steel slab with some grommets on it. And a blue push-out box that said Atlantic City, in which there were still some wooden matches with silver tips.

On Saturday, when I asked him to come over to my house, Mom invited him, after phoning Edith, to have some lunch with us. Willy James held his fork with his thumb all down in his fist, eating mostly with the fingers of his other hand. Later Mom told Carl, "When he took his fork up with his left hand, first I thought he was going to eat European style. Basically, though, he was just trying to get it out of the way. He's actually a nice boy. But he doesn't have any table manners at *all!* And those nails—that's an *awful* habit! Where did he pick that up?"

"Did you look at Paul's hands the afternoon they stopped by?" Carl said. "Willy James comes by it honestly."

"He liked your beef stew," Mom said. "When I took it out of the microwave, he ate up two bowls of it. And he smiled—but there wasn't the *ghost* of a thank you! Praise God we didn't raise Adrian that way!"

Carl said: "I've always thought that when parents don't teach their children how to behave with other people, they're doing it to keep the kid under their thumb—it's a way to make them stay babies that much longer, keep them at home, make sure they're uncomfortable with other folks—so they can't move out into the world."

"Like Edwin, you mean, " Mom said.

"A little like what Dennis and Sara did with Edwin," Carl said. "Yes, I guess so…"

Mom said: "Just because that boy has good hair, Sara thinks he's some kind of gift-of-God. Well, I don't think there's anything *else* that's good about him!" She'd said that before.

"He doesn't get in any trouble." Carl had said that, too.

"Sometimes I think," Mom said, "Edwin would be better off if he *did* get in some trouble. That boy has got to learn about the way the real world works!"

"Edwin's a perfectly nice kid. He's just not too swift," Carl said.

"But Edwin is black. You know as well as I do, for a black boy to make it, he's got to be *better* than a white boy. Not worse. Not as good. Better."

Carl said: "I don't think you're going to have to worry about Adrian."

"I don't know," Mom said. "I just look at these children around here. Like Edwin, like Willy James…"

§2. That Saturday we finished up the sandal argument. While water hissed in the stainless steel sink, for the tenth time in two weeks I complained: "But I don't *want* to wear them. I don't like how they *look!*"

Mom turned around, exasperated. She put a fist on her hip, which meant she was *almost* angry. "It's summer, Adrian. They're comfortable. They're *cool,* honey—"

"They make me look like a sissy!" Standing with my elbow by the kitchen table's metal edge, the morning's translucent white yogurt containers and the pop-tart foil still not cleared from the table, I decided to be daring. "And I look like a sissy enough as it is."

Mom frowned at me. Outside rose the breeze's roar. Leaf shadow stormed behind her on the yellow curtain. She seemed surprised—and dropped her hand down to the thighs of her slacks. "No, you don't, honey. You're a fine looking young man. ...Have people been making fun of you, Adrian?"

"Now, why," I said, "would I want to go telling my parents something like *that,* even if they did? About the sandals. Can't you just trust me on this one?"

A month back, Carl had said it to me a few times, and, the second of them, had explained: "It's my way of asking you, Adrian, please, please, *please.* You've said that to me, and I always went along with you, when you did. Well, 'Can you trust me on this one,' it's the adult version of the same thing: *Please, please, please.* It would mean a *whole* lot to me if you just went along with this and didn't give me an argument." So the couple of times he'd said it since, I'd *gone* along. Later, he'd even told me, "Thank you, Adrian." I understood it as a privileged phrase. So far Carl hadn't abused it. Rather daringly, the week before, however, *I'd* first tried it with him (I guess that was just the "daring" year)—and, after a few moments' silence, *he'd* gone along. But though Mom knew about it, this was the first time I'd used it with her. After a few more moments, she said, "All right," turned back to the sink, and twisted off the water.

Later that evening, stopping me at the bottom of the carpeted stairs—he was wearing his longhorn cowboy belt—and leaning the hip of his jeans against the banister, Carl said: "Your mom and I have talked it over. You're ten years old, Adrian, and it's summer." (On the blond wood floor Carl had put down last winter, my runners always felt like they were about to slide. Then, if you *tried* to slide them, they'd stick.) "You're old enough to choose what you want to wear. Sneakers, sandals, shorts—whatever. Unless we're going someplace special—some adult place like a restaurant or a concert or something. Okay?"

I grinned. "Okay." And we went around each other, Carl out to the kitchen, me up to my room.

The fact is, I liked my parents.

More to the point, I think they liked me.

But I was ten, not nine. I'd watched kids like Willy James tease other kids like Raymond and Jeff at school. I figured I'd gotten off easy.

§3. "My dad says you niggers got some big ol' dicks," was what Willy James said to me perhaps the fifth time we hung out together. "You gonna show me yours?"

I said: "—*No!*"

"Aw, you're a scaredy-cat. I bet your pecker ain't never even been near no pussy. My sister, she shows me hers, sometimes. Yours get hard yet?"

"Huh? Erections? You mean my penis? Yeah, of *course*—" And resolved that the next person who asked to see it, Willy James or anyone else, I'd show him. I was *not* a scared child; the request had simply startled me. Why, I wondered, did people always say "No" as a first response to anything new? That seemed so *like* a kid.

"Yeah, I bet it does," Willy James was saying. "Mine too. She'll even play with it. That gets it *real* hard. You wanna do that?"

"Huh? Well, I don't think you—"

"We can get her to show us hers, but we got to show her ours—you an' me. Then I can see how big yours gets. But if you won't show it to her, she won't do it. 'Cause if it's just her, she says it ain't fair."

That was the same day Willy James told me his broken tooth wasn't a baby tooth. "You don't have no baby teeth at *eleven!*"

"How'd it get broken?" I asked.

"I don't know." With his running shoe, he toed at some grass.

"It just broke."

§4. For two and a half weeks after the Barnowshkys started living on the far side of the overgrown lot, Carl and Mom referred to Mr. and Mrs. Barnowshky as "Paul" and "Edith."

Paul Barnowshky worked at the same ceramic fuse-and-switch factory in which Aunt Sara had been a bookkeeper since Uncle Dennis died, back when I was seven. But after Paul's second midnight visit, climbing over his fence, reeling through half an acre of grass, high brush, and hickories in the dark, climbing over our fence, staggering about in our yard and shouting about having to live next door to a bunch of goddam niggers, waking us all up—Paul had a thing for getting sloshed and into eristic wrangles with his neighbors (he got into one with the Campbells across the street I never did understand)—even though he came over and apologized the next morning, he and his wife became Mr. and Mrs. Barnowshky again; at least to Carl. Edith Barnowshky was a shy, blonde wisp of a woman. In our kitchen, sitting at the table with her speckled white blouse unbuttoned a button lower than I'd *ever* seen Mom wear hers, I overheard a conversation in which, while Mom unloaded the dishwasher, Edith explained what a good husband Paul was as long as he was working and didn't drink too much. On her thin arms, you could see the contours of the bones in her wrists and elbows. Paul had held the job in the fuse-and-switch factory eight months now, which is what had allowed them to move from Hugens Falls to rent in our neighborhood. She'd finally *married* Paul, she told Mom, in Delaware when she was seventeen and five months pregnant with Willy James.

Mr. Barnowshky was fifty-seven.

"And Edith—" on her knees in the dining room, putting the tablecloth back under the sideboard, Mom looked up at Carl— "isn't *thirty!* And with a daughter about to be fifteen? I don't think it would bother me so much, but for a mother like that to have a tomboy like Marjorie has *got* to be a trial."

"What about having a daughter at thirteen," Carl said. And looked really disapproving.

§5. The fourteenth or fifteenth time we hung out, Willy James asked, "How come you call your dad 'Carl'?" We sat on his steps, gray paint blistered and crackled around our sneakers, looking toward the boards that fenced the overgrown lot. Above them, through the hickories, you could just see our house. Willy James and Marjorie had lived here with their parents a month, now.

"Because that's his name—Carlton Fulhan Rome. Like I'm Adrian Carlton Rome. What's *your* middle name?" I'd assumed it was James and expected him to say so.

But Willy James ignored me. "My dad says it's 'cause your dad is the craziest nigger he *ever* met and don't got no real sense." Then he'd added: "That's 'cause he don't have a real job." (My dad *did* work, of course. But he worked at home. It had to do with lots of mail and lots of phone calls and his computer—which, back then, was an Osborne.) "Your dad's funny. He don't yell at *all!*"

As it was, I didn't like *anyone* in their family that much—though Willy James kept sticking himself in my way, usually to say something nasty about some older girl in the neighborhood—most of the time Marjorie—to see if he could shock me.

For a whole morning once, Willy James sauntered around with a pack of Newports rolled into the shoulder of his T-shirt—till Paul Barnowshky had come home and beat him for it. I guess Edith told Mom. And Mom told Carl about it. Carl had said, "I do *not* take to hitting on children. I don't care *what* they've done. There're always other ways to discipline a child."

"But smoking," Mom said. "I wouldn't want Adrian doing that—"

A couple of times, even later, Willy James's T-shirt sleeve would be loose and wrinkled around traces of a cigarette box's corners. I was going to ask him once what it was like to have your father beat you, but I couldn't figure out how. It seemed too awful—like some story they'd put on television after eight o'clock—so that finally I forgot it, after I'd told myself that I *wasn't* scared: It was just good manners.

Once I saw Marjorie (who wore bib overalls, had pierced ears, and always had on a baseball cap) spitting on her finger, rubbing it on Willy James's arm: She was putting one of those transfer tattoos on his naked shoulder (his red T-shirt had the arms cut off), where they stood beside the brambles run wild over half his front steps.

You could buy them from Mr. Idemer.

So I did.

Next evening when I came home wearing one of a dragon Willy James had put on *my* forearm with two fingers and *his* spit, Mom turned from where she was writing in her checkbook at the kitchen table, looked at it, put down her pen, and laughed. "Adrian—what in the world *is* that? On your arm...?" She didn't seem upset about it. But that night she made me take a shower and wash it off.

§6. Willy James had been left back at least once when they lived in Delaware.

"Well, what grade are you *going* to be in when school starts here—in Bethynia?"

While the trees in a half dozen yards along Minkle Street gave out their windy summer thunder, Willy James shrugged. "I donno. Fifth... maybe seventh. You *like* school...?"

I was going into the seventh in September.

"Well. What grade were you in last year?"

Willy James looked uncomfortable. "I didn't go to school much, last year." He raised his eyes to the trees. "They just ask you dumb questions that make you feel stupid 'cause nobody knows the answer."

Just then Edwin's van rolled by. Out the side window, my cousin grinned over his forearm at us.

I called, "Hey, Edwin...!" and ran a few steps over on the curb grass. I'd expected him to stop, so I could introduce Willy James to him. Maybe he'd have given us a ride—

But the dusty Chevy van hauled itself through the leaf shadow, to turn toward Richards Avenue, leaving me feeling a little stupid, a little lost. I turned back. "That was my cousin..."

To which Willy James said, with a puzzled look: "He's black, too...?"

"That's right," I said. "You know, black people come in all

sorts of different colors. I have cousins and uncles and aunts who are real dark. But I got some who're lighter than you."

Willy James said, "God damn…"

§7. Our house had three stories. Even before I remember, Carl had converted the upstairs attic into living space: my room, Mom's sewing room, Carl's office, a storeroom.

"You gonna come over to *my* place, now?" Willy James asked. "I went over to yours and even *ate* in yours…" From the way he said it, it occurred to me that, for him, eating in my kitchen had been a duty rather than a pleasure—no matter how good the stew.

Willy James's house had been vacant for the year and a half since Mr. Vaughan and his spinster daughter, Miss Vaughan, had moved out. It was one floor plus a shallow attic. The first time I went there with Willy James, it was dark, messy, and smelled. Both Willy James's parents were out at work. As we walked in, Marjorie came slumping slowly and silently through the living room in her baseball cap, and vanished.

Willy James's room stank even worse than the rest of the house—I mean, enough to make me frown.

Nor did his room have a door in the doorway.

It wasn't the smell that permeated Lonnie Mitchell's younger brother's room because Stevie Mitchell still wet his bed and the Mitchells weren't real rigorous about their laundry. *That* one, I mean, I knew.

Willy James's room was very small. It just about held his bed. The walls had been painted tan up to a little higher than my head and probably a long time back. The rest of the wood was bare to the ceiling. On the iron frame cot, an olive drab army blanket, like the ones Carl and I used for camping, and a sheet were twisted up over the mattress. No spread. Above the bed, two pipes stuck out the wall, with valves on them as though ready to pour water onto Willy James's wrinkled and folded-over pillow, with the dark spot in the center that made it look as if it hadn't been washed in a *long* time. No bookshelf. No toys. There wasn't even a window. As Willy James said, "Come on inside," it hit me: At one time this must have been a pantry or, even more likely, the laundry room.

"*This* is yours...?" Probably some cabinets had been pulled down, which is why the paint only went so high.

"Yeah. Come on." Willy James went to the corner closet—also doorless. It had shelves in the back. Willy James went inside. As if they were ladder rungs, he climbed the shelves to the top to push at a trap in the ceiling. "We can go—" he glanced back down—"up here."

Behind and below him, I looked up.

Above his thrusting arm, the cover scraped and banged.

Not stepping on the towels folded on one shelf or the blue jeans wadded in the back on the other, I climbed after him with the boards stinging my fingers. Above me, through the square, his soiled running shoes disappeared, one, then the other.

Getting up almost defeated me, till Willy James's hand came down and gripped my wrist. "No—put your knee on *that*. Yeah. That's right. Watch it—don't fall, stupid!" He pulled me, hard.

The stench was replaced with dust and resin and old wood.

I came through.

It was hot. Around my wrist, his rough hand—rough, I thought, like the hand of a boy who spends his time at tree and rock climbing grows early rough—had already started to sweat.

It wasn't a real attic—I mean, not like Jill Fenster's or Lonnie Mitchell's. It was an A-shaped crawl space, not quite five-feet high. Even at the center, Willy James had to keep his head down. When, upright and three inches shorter than he was, I stepped under it, I felt my hair brush the beam. Light came from windows, either end: The lower sills were not ten inches from the floor. In one, torn and rusted screening behind the glass looked raddled and kicked in. Ribbed cables went wavily between staples along a beam. A dozen two-by-sixes made troughs across the floor. Slanted boards above us ran with drops of gold-brown resin. When I touched one and another, though, they'd solidified, amber hard—I almost tripped. Three tentative steps—I almost tripped again—assured me I wouldn't plummet through into some kitchen or living room below.

"Watch out, now," Willy James said, behind me, when I stumbled again. "Don't fall up here. You gonna hurt yourself."

When I looked around, Willy James was six troughs away, lowering himself to one of the crossbeams, a jackknifed knee, mottled green and brown, to either side.

Reaching down for something that, on the floor between the boards, I couldn't see, he stared at it while he sat back. Bringing both hands to his pants waist, he unbuttoned the olive button, and pulled down the zipper. "Put the cover back on the hole," he said, not looking at me. "So nobody'll hear us. And when you come over here, don't make so much *noise!*" Then, bending further, he did something on the floor again, then sat back to pull loose... his penis and testicles!

I felt as if someone started slapping the inside of my chest, hard and rhythmical, again and again.

It was a magazine or something down there.

Reaching down a third time, he turned another page—as I realized now, that's what he'd been doing.

What I felt was not the surprise I'd had at Big Jonathan's orgasm.

Rather, it was like the time Lonnie Mitchell and I had gone to his house after school and found the note from his aunt saying he was to go to the supermarket and buy a whole list of stuff—but a blister on my heel had just burst and left a nickel-sized blood blot darkening my blue sock. So I'd sat on the couch and played with Lonnie's spaniel Butchy, while Lonnie went out again. Butchy had started licking at my mouth, and for three, four minutes I let Butchie kiss (I guess you'd call it) inside it—and kissed him back—while, with a hard-on leaking in my jeans, I'd played with, and twice stopped to suck on, Butchy's red, wet penis, thrusting from its dry, hairy sheath—till, behind me and holding a grocery bag, Lonnie (who was *not* one of our seven) said: "Adrian, *what* are you doing—?"

The way I'd jumped then, the way my heart had pounded—I felt the same thuds inside my chest at Willy James's exposure.

Somehow I dragged the hatch over the hole, almost tripping. Then, again stumbling, I stepped over the beams toward where Willy James sat, pulling absently on his engorged penis, and looking down at his magazine. "Go on," he said, not looking at me. "Take yours out, too."

Like Vinton, Willy James wasn't circumcised. Like Jonathan, he had hair—a kind of colorless brush.

I looked down at his magazine, expecting to see *Playboy* or *Penthouse.* What I saw, instead, upside down, was a three quarter page black-and-white photo of a naked woman, all tied up. Ropes creased her breasts. She wore a black Lone Ranger mask, studs around its edge. Four or five lengths of the rope pulled her cheeks into her mouth, making a gag. Her legs were tied open— she wore black high-heeled boots—to some out-of-focus furniture either side of the picture. Her vagina was wide and wet. Wearing a leather cap and another studded mask, a man in black leather cowboy chaps, with no crotch and an erection, knelt on one knee at her side, reaching over to hold apart the hairy lips with two fingers.

Dumbfounded and dazzled, I stood before Willy James, looking down where the toe of his right runner was on the magazine's corner. His green pants cuff swung in time to his fist.

As if answering a question, still without looking up, Willy James said: "You can see the pussies better in this kind, here." He kept pulling on himself. "Come on—" *Now* he glanced up at me. "Take your pants down—go on. Anybody ever kiss your ass?"

I started to open my jeans. "—*Huh?*"

"Go on, now. Take 'em off. And turn around."

I got my belt loose, fumbled apart the button, and pushed them down.

"You wear *underpants?* What do you got on *them,* for? Turn around, I said. I'm gonna eat out your asshole."

Looking at where the waist of his fatigues sagged around his hips, I saw before I turned that he wore none; and resolved, turning, I would leave mine up here and from now on give up what was clearly a useless and unnecessary practice.

As I was getting my feet set on either side of the beam, Willy James's hands pressed my buttocks, to move them apart. Something slathered up, wet and surprising, between. Then again. "You like that, don't you? Bet you like it even more when I get my dick up there." His face pressed in and his tongue drilled forward, then pulled back. "But I gotta get it wet, first, with a lot of spit—so I can fuck it." I felt him pushing out his saliva, tonguing it into me. Willy James's direct, reckless nastiness was irresistible. Bracing my hands on my knees, just above my jeans and stretched jockey shorts, I looked back at my own penis, thrust out between my legs. Between my thighs, where I could see Willy James, still squatting on his beam, his own cock, straight forward, unbent, was thicker than mine. Even when he was hard, his foreskin still hooded half the head.

Then... something hurt.

"That's three fingers," Willy James whispered hoarsely, behind me. "Don't tighten up—push *out*. Like you wanna shit, right in my face."

"*Owwwwww...*" I said, softly, and staggered forward. One hand around my thigh, he pulled me back.

"Yeah, like that. I seen kids like you take goddam pop bottles, the big-size kind, and even a whole hand—the littler you are, the looser you can get. Go on. Try, now." I heard him spit—on his free hand to wet his cock. "I'm not kiddin' you. It's true."

I said, "*Owwww...*" again. But somehow I did what he said.

Willy James said, "See, it's gettin' better, huh?"

Then, in a single move, his fingers came out, he rose up from the beam, reached forward, and, with one hand, gripped my shoulder, while he pushed himself into me. The moment he was firmly in, he... *fell* on me! I stumbled, almost falling myself—

"Hold the *wood!*" he whispered, bent over. (I'd grabbed the beam already, supporting myself, one hand behind the other, under fully half his weight.) He began to hunch.

Willy James locked one arm around my chest, across my T-shirt. His other hand came up to cover my mouth. From the smell, those were the fingers he'd stuck into my fundament. "Naw, push *out*, I said—as hard as I push in... That way it won't hurt you." When I twisted my face away and tried to say something, he pulled my head back, still humping. That's when I realized his hand over my mouth was to keep me from making noise.

I got out a mangled, "Hey, *what* are you...!"

But he said, "Lemme put my fingers in your mouth. The shit won't hurt you... It didn't hurt *me* when I licked out your goddam nigger ass... Bite on 'em if you have to. Then it won't hurt you... at *all!*"

Again I started to protest, but he thrust his fingers between my teeth. And I pushed out. And bit. They were salty. And Willy James's fingers, as I've already noted, were much rougher than mine.

Willy James hunched harder. And it *didn't* hurt—at least nowheres near as much as it had. "Yeah, that's good. That's good... I bet I make you come without you even *touchin'* yourself...!"

I liked the feel of his belly on my back, his arm tight around me, his elbow against my side, his cheek against my cheek. And his smell was stronger and raunchier and more interesting than any kid's who'd just finished swimming in a chlorinated pool and who took a shower there in the afternoon and every night again at home. In my mouth his blunt fingers pushed aside my tongue. The rhythmic pull of his hips from my buttocks was, however, like a repeated betrayal. As to making me come that way, I wasn't sure what he was talking about. Why—I wondered, I wished— wouldn't he plunge in and just *stay?*

If you'd asked me at that time what the difference was between my shower room sex with Vinton and Jonathan and Raymond, and this all-but-rape by Willy James in that high prism of gold shadow, I'd have said, as best I could have in my boyish way, that what the guys and I had done day after day in our steamy post-swim forty minutes was tentative, giggly, full of grins and whispers, not forbidden so much as surrounded by ignorance, that made it transgress—put it somehow outside—the borders of transgression itself.

Willy James knew, however, what he was doing.

Ask me today, and I'd go farther. In the shower room, we were floundering through webs of ignorance, guided by the heat and shimmer within our own bodies. (Innocent? No: In the shower room, we were all smilingly, fascinatedly, dazedly guilty.) Willy James's manner and method suggested a whole battery of knowledge about such behavior. It intimated a world of such desires as I knew, and a complex of behaviors such as the few I'd already tried to negotiate, a complex and a world that had nothing to do with the contradictions of adult romance pictured on TV and in the movies. Willy James was as clear on how to maneuver through and around such behavior as I was on the rules of Chinese checkers, go, chess, Risk, or Monopoly—all games, I knew by now, Willy James did not know how to play in the same way he didn't know how to read. With my palms stinging against the beam, I supported his pulsing weight, realizing he'd probably asked me up here for *just* this purpose, and that, because I was biting on his hand, I *couldn't* make betraying noises: That was *why* his hand was in my mouth. The clarity and efficiency his knowledge ceded him made his seduction of me as innocent as a checkmate of mine in an evening game against Carl. Willy James, who did not know how to eat correctly—or read or play go or chess—was as sure as a boy could be about what he was doing. I bit again (but not too hard), thrust back harder, and, more and more happily, more and more easily, held him up, his runners scrabbling on either side of mine, now and again, to take some weight off me, till his hunching and hammering loins had almost lowered him full—

—then Marjorie called: "What are you stupid little shits doing up there, huh? Come *down*, now. Or I'll tell pop when he comes home!" under our feet.

We froze, in that hot, triangular box, cut with wooden beams and all a-swarm with motes.

Willy James held my shoulder. His fingers pulled loosed from my teeth, slipped from my face. Silently, he retreated from me. Where our T-shirts had ridden up between us, his belly peeled from my back. His penis pulled loose, for a moment brushing up over my buttocks—before it was gone. A moment's stinging made me gasp. I felt cold and abandoned and confused. "Maybe—" I mouthed desperately, looking back at him—"you should go on down, and I'll come down *later*...?" In the shower room, we were always figuring such ruses: leaving or entering at different times so that no one who saw us go in would realize we'd been together—

Willy James said, full voice: "Why the fuck you wanna do that? She knows we're up here. Besides, she won't tell—"

I stood up—and bumped my head. My hands were sore, too—yeah, sorer than my rectum.

Willy James bent over under the sloping roof. His fatigues were down around his shins. His green blotched T-shirt hung away from his stomach, the front sweat dark. Still hard, his cock was shiny in its pale hair. For the first time I realized how thin his tanned legs were. Grinning, he said: "I should make you suck that off..."

I got chills along my shoulders, over my back, down my legs. I have no idea if it was general fear or the excitement at the preposterousness (as I thought of it then) of his suggestion.

Then he took a breath. "But we don't got time."

My T-shirt lay wet and cold on my back.

"Okay!" Willy James called. "We're *comin'!*" He reached down to pull up his pants, testicles out, cock jutting. He began to button them, getting first his balls, then his penis, inside.

I pulled my underpants up, then my jeans—and watched Willy James zip. Still erect, his cock held the loose cloth out from one thigh. We stepped over the beams, then—with a glance at each other—bent together to pick up the trap, and move it aside.

With the cover off, Marjorie's voice—"You get on down, now. Get on down, Willy James," when she called again—was clearer. "You know what pop said about you takin' little kids off alone..."

I whispered: "You *sure* you don't want to go down first—?"

Willy James said: "*You* couldn't get *up* here by yourself. How the fuck you gonna get down without me helpin'?" Reaching out, he seized my hand. "Now, kneel down, drop your foot to that shelf. And hold on with your other hand—here!" He bent to slap the beam bordering the hole.

So I got down, grabbed the beam he'd slapped, and put my foot through.

"Now, go on down—no. Turn *around*, that's right. And put your knee down on... yeah, *that's* right—and put your other foot down on the shelf under. No, don't worry. I got you. You *can't* fall." He held my hand so hard it hurt.

Which I was glad of. I lowered myself still one more shelf, finally pulling loose from his fingers. As I got to the bottom and backed from the closet, Willy James swung down through the hole, climbed down two shelves, then jumped back, stumbling into me. "Watch it, you dumb-ass dickwad!" Turning he laughed, while I staggered back, trying to smile.

I looked at stolid Marjorie, who, from outside the door to the left, thick and sober-eyed in her overalls, watched us from under her green visor.

"We were havin' *fun* up there, weren't we?" Willy James declared, with a grin that, if it was supposed to be innocent, wouldn't have convinced *me*.

With her too-close hazel eyes, Marjorie gave Willy James the condemnatory frown for younger sibling and delinquent pets. It was clear she had no doubt we'd been doing something wrong. But now, I realized with surprise, she couldn't have cared less what it was. "You're hidin' shit under your bed again—" (That was one of several times it went idly through my mind that, at fifteen, Marjorie was two years older than her mother had been at her birth)—"and pop's gonna kick your ass." From the way she said it, I knew it wasn't a statement but an *if-then* assertion.

That's when I noticed the smell didn't seem nearly as strong as it had when we'd gone up.

Willy James grinned, gray eyes a-glitter. "Jesus H. Christ," he complained, like any younger bother I'd ever heard, "we wasn't *doin'* nothin—" (*we wasn't,* a locution he'd used on our first walk through the neighborhood on the afternoon I'd met him, before he'd slipped into the all-but-invisible *we weren't* I and the kids around us used)—"so leave us the fuck alone, you crabby, scabby, pus-pussy three-dollar whore!" Clearly he was imitating someone, though who, in my upstate childishness, I could not, for my life, imagine. While my jaw did *not* drop (though I'd never heard *anyone* call anyone else anything even *near* that!), he said: "How can we be doin' nothin'? I ain't even got a fuckin' *door* no more!"

As stolidly as she'd stood, Marjorie turned and walked, heavy-footed, away.

Willy James grinned. "The bitch ain't gonna say nothin'," he reassured. "Hey, you wanna see what I got?"

"Huh?" What, in that toyless room, I wondered, could rival the loot in his fatigues' thigh pouches?

Going to his unmade bed, with a running shoe Willy James pushed aside one of the boxes beneath it, then bent and, with his hand, tugged another out and slid it aside. Standing up, he said, "Com'ere..."

When I stepped up beside him, he took my shoulder with one hand, lowered himself seven or eight inches in a squat, and put one foot under the bed to begin tugging something out with his toe.

What slid from under was a folded up newspaper. On it lay three large pieces of something... dark. Two were about five inches long and stubby. One was close to a foot, and bigger around than a beer can.

Willy James took his toe away. "You ever see any before *that* big?" He grinned at me over his broken tooth.

"What... is it?" I asked.

"What you *think* it is?" He still grinned. "The big one—hell, that's a fuckin' bazooka, ain't it?"

"Is it from an... animal?"

"Naw," he said, disparagingly. "It was from this... this guy." Then he stopped and grinned at me. "But you see what I mean: If somethin' like that can get *out* your fuckin' asshole, you don't have to worry too much just about some guy's *dick* goin' in."

"Won't your parents... smell it?" Yes, there on the lowest level I could make out its scent. Basically, though, it just seemed close and airless in the doorless cube.

"My mom—" With his foot, Willy James pushed the paper back beneath his bed. At first the newspaper wrinkled; then it slid under the bed's edge—"she can't smell nothin' no more. 'Cause she had an operation on her nose. When it got broke. And my pop, 'cause he been drinkin' when he gets home, he don't give a fuck no way." Willy James let go of my shoulder, bent, and pushed back the box under the bed's edge. Then, with his toe, he moved the other back into place. "Come on, let's go. We can't do nothin' with my scumbag sister hangin' around and gettin' in the way."

Reaching between his legs, he rubbed himself vigorously, adjusted himself—I think he was still hard—turned from his room, and started out. I followed him.

When we were outside on his slanted, brambly front steps, Willy James said: "What you wanna do now?" He rubbed at his crotch once more.

"Where'd you get that magazine?" I was, yes, interested in seeing the masked man again—certainly more than the woman.

"I swiped it," he said, "from my dad. *Your* dad's got 'em, too." Willy James spoke as if he'd observed my father firsthand! "Everybody's got 'em. I mean grown-ups."

Listening to the neighborhood's leafy susurrus, I took a breath. Then, trying to muster an equal conviction, I said: "I'd suck on your cock if... you wanted. A long time, too. Till you had an orgasm. And I wouldn't spit it out." It was Willy James's directness and straightforwardness I was trying to make mine. Listening to myself, though, I knew I still sounded maddeningly tentative.

Willy James looked at me, surprised. Then he said, "You're goddam right you wouldn't." And he chuckled. "You know, I *figured* you was a fuckin' cocksucker."

In lame defense, I said: "I peed in Vinton's mouth once. While he was sucking on mine." Then, suddenly, I got tingly, and scared, and hot—a continuation of the same chills I'd felt in his attic space. What had set them off was something in the way he'd said "fuckin' cocksucker." But what was behind it, in me, was the realization that, no, I *couldn't* ask him to do the same thing to me, though, right then, I wanted to desperately.

Scowling, Willy James let his head go to the side. "There ain't no place to do it, though. I mean, we can't do it out *here*. Unless there's someplace in *your* house we can get off to...? But your parents are home *all* the time." He moved his mouth around some, considering. Then he said, "I'm gonna go look for somebody else to play with for a while." But, before he turned, he added: "Don't worry, though. I'll get you, soon." Without smiling, he turned up the alley, as a summer gust swelled blowily over the trees, the overgrown lot, a rustle and rumble over the grass and in the yards around us.

§8. I spent a lot of time that afternoon, thinking about Willy James. I thought about how I should have said to him, If I'm a fucking cocksucker, you're a fucking asshole eater. I thought about how you went about asking somebody like Willy James to come in your mouth, then take a piss there. I thought about why in the world he was saving somebody's shit. And who *could* the big one have belonged to?

How in the world had he gotten it?

What was he going to do with it?

I even wondered, for about twenty seconds, once, if Willy James was crazy. But crazy people didn't know what they were doing, didn't know what they wanted. If anything, Willy James was the opposite of crazy. Besides, if he would fuck around with me like that, even if he was, did I care?

§9. Sitting on the back porch steps the next evening, I was reading the new *X–Men* when, down the alley, Willy James came pushing out between two boards in the lot fence.

He was eating an apple.

I didn't put the *X–Men* down, but kind of watched him over the top edge while he sauntered up.

He said: "I bet you won't go into that lot, back there, between your house and mine."

"What?" I frowned, closed the *X–Men*'s blue, red, and yellow cover on my finger. "Why?"

"I was just in there." Willy James's eyes were warm and brown; his mouth was thin, wide, and hard—even while he chewed. Some yellow grass stalks stuck to the right of his green T-shirt. He hadn't changed it in about eight or nine days. A dirt spot darkened one knee of his fatigues, wetly. "It's easy to get in—a lot of boards are loose." He nodded back to where the planks were ranged between pavement and waving grass. "I bet *you're* too scared, though."

"Huh?" I frowned, putting my head to one side.

Smiling, he put his head to the other. "'Cause there's something *in* there!" Bits of apple flaked his lower lip.

I sat forward on the grey enameled steps. "What?"

"A monster." Willy James grinned. "A big monster, all scaly and stuff, with wings—who'll grab you and squeeze you so tight it makes the… the shit run out your ass! I just *saw* it."

"*Huh?*" I put the comic book in my lap. "What monster."

"A big old monster. With great big wings. Real big—twelve, thirteen feet high." He glanced up a moment, with his bright gray eyes, as if to indicate.

"What's… it's name?" Really I expected him to tell me Godzilla, or Mothra, or even King Kong. Delightedly, Carl and I had watched them all on late night Friday and Saturday TV.

"Naw," Willy James said. "Naw. No name. It don't got no name. Unh-unh. It could fly into your window, though, and eat you up. Only it stays over in the lot. Hey—you remember what you said you saw Mary Evens doing with Joey Fenton, in the car?"

I grinned. It was one of the few things I had on Willy James. "Yeah, sure." I'd told him about it when, down near Mr. Idemer's, I'd seen Mary hanging out with Marjorie.

"Well, if he grabs you, he'll do that to *you!* His is as big as… as a' elephant's! And he'll push it in your face so hard that it comes out the back of your *head!*"

"What are you talking about?" I said.

Willy James's bronzish hair was the same color as my cousin Edwin's. But Edwin put his in a red rubber band at the back of his head, because he was a man, already. Edwin was nineteen.

"That's stupid. If his is so big, why'd he want to do that to *me* for? He probably wants to do it with other monsters."

"Naw." But Willy James laughed. "'Cause it *is* a monster. I'm not kidding. It's got a thing on it as big around as… Marjorie's baseball bat! The *front* end. It's got long claws. And big teeth." The gold back of Willy's hand was filmed with gray from the day's wonder. With his bitten nubs, he scratched his brazen belly under his green T-shirt, so I could see his belly button above the fatigues' waist. "And it got horns. And yellow eyes. And big, big bat wings. Its teeth are all ragged and rotten. If it catches you, it'll try to eat you up with 'em—I bet!"

"*Sure* it will," I said. "In the lot, there…"

Looking serious, Willy James raised his apple and crunched away the last quarter. "It's right in there, now." He spoke through a mouthful of apple. "So you better *not* go in there! After it gets dark, it'll still be in there. *Then* you could go in. 'Cause it might not see you. Only *you'll* be too scared—with it in there and all, waiting."

"Willy James," I said: "You're *crazy*—"

Willy James said, "No, *you're* crazy!" He grinned, showing his broken tooth. "But that's 'cause your dad's a nigger what don't work."

Turning, Willy James walked on back down the slanted and broken sidewalk, swinging his core by his pants leg pouch, till, of a sudden, he pulled his arm back and flung it high along the alley.

§10. That night after dinner, Carl set up one of his games on the dining room table. In the cardboard cup the dice *thunked* hollowly, then sharp and clicky, skipped on the board's hexagonals. Where I lay on the beige rug, I looked up from my book. "There aren't any monsters, are there?" I doubt if it was a question I'd asked since I'd been six or seven.

Carl threw the dice again and answered it just as peremptorily as he had back then. "Nope."

Over at the window, beyond flowered drapes, white fiberglass, silvery blinds, on the other side of our back yard beyond the white aluminum fence, the overgrown lot waited. Had Willy James actually thought, I wondered, I'd go out after dark, climb the fence—or more likely find one of those loose boards and slip through from the alley—to enter and meet him? If he *was* waiting for me, of course, I felt a little sorry. While I looked at my book page, mostly I thought of excuses I might give him tomorrow as to why I hadn't been able to join him.

Walking in from the kitchen, Mom stopped to look over Carl's shoulder, then glanced at me: "You know, you probably shouldn't play so much with that Barnowshky boy. Isn't he too old for someone your age, Adrian? And he's a little wild."

I looked back at my book. "Yeah."

Carl said: "If you tell him not to, Vivian, he's just going to play with him that much more."

Making a kind of frustrated face, Mom walked away to the hall.

He Remembers
by malik m.l. williams

He remembers
his heart thrown violently out of rhythm
at the far-off muted
whoomph
of a car door slamming
and fear like the first tremors
of a great quake to come.

He remembers
breathing against tightening bands across his chest
as the
click—squeak—slam!
issuing front door's warning
from down the stairs and up the hall.

He remembers
panic gripping
pressing him motionless against the bed
at the startling
thud
of a briefcase
dropped like a hunter's recent kill.

He remembers
the clock racing his heartbeat
ticking ever faster in the silence
with each dull and deadly
thump
    thump
        thump
of footsteps on the stairs.

He remembers
all the terror
of a ten-year captive lifetime
at the slow, sibilant
hiss
of the handle slowly turning.

He remembers
the ominous and petrifying
whoosh
of the door marking the end of concealment
and a massive figure
standing framed
in the treasonous light.

He remembers
the silent resignation of tears
and the calm horror
at the first
creak
of box spring and mattress
straining to accommodate the adult frame.

He remembers
the dead weight of repugnance and shame
pressing on him heavier than that body
and that same repeated lie

"Remember, Daddy loves you."

He remembers.

The Angelic
by Peter Conti

Angel joined my 8th grade class
seven months to graduation
        I hated him
        pegged him the type to pick fights
        with buck toothed *patos*
        like me
        —but he didn't

Instead, he dated my best friend Victoria
became my friend too
and in two months had mastered the racket of the lunchroom
Spit circle
slapping cards and smashing fingers
of boys not quick enough to grab the empty pile
I'd smile knowing each win
shifted "cool"
to a new elite

He didn't speak much of his being a foster-child
his mother—
or brother who made it to the home of a social worker.
Bearing his light like a cross, he kept a sunlit disposition long
enough for Ms. Valdez, the ESL teacher, to find him. Too late
to save or soothe scars incurred by the system. Carving a few
more when she decided to send him back.

final days lapsed—
stitching sunsets to our chest
leaking candlelit eternity
through stretched liquid wax
waiting for the wick to burn

The night before he was scheduled to leave he came to my house. We didn't plan on his staying. My parents had gone shopping and told us he should be gone by the time they got back. Defying them, I convinced my siblings to do the same, help me hide him—splaying bellies on the floor as we played Spit. He was quiet. I remember it was a Tuesday because "Who's the Boss" was on and in my recent self-liberation from several years of television restriction, I scheduled my life around ABC's evening line-up.

My parents got home and I made Angel hide behind the bureau. Bringing up a box of Ring Dings for our evening meal. Leaving a pillow, blanket, and enough room to turn in his sleep, I climbed in my bed resigned to retire with pre-recorded laughter shadowing the room from a 12" black and white screen. But beneath syncopated chuckles I heard whimpers. Rushing to the bureau I found Angel crying, refusing to let me console him. Demanding I didn't touch him—that I didn't love him—that no-one did.

"How do you put some-one you love behind a dresser," he said.

The metaphor would take ten years to decipher. Though prematurely making sense of it at the time, not fearing my father's heavy hand and belt, being bigger than Angel, I wrapped my arms around his flailing body, laying him to rest on my bed. Chest touching chest, his anger subsided. We decided to plan escape.

As sleep took him from me I felt blood surging between fingers and legs. Jumping up I curled up in the big furry chair at the foot of my bed, ashamed of the erection I concealed when he questioned my abrupt departure.

"What's wrong?" he asked.

"Nothing," I replied. "Just planning."

I watched him sleep. Waking him when sun burning through the window wasn't enough to stir consciousness.

My parents already gone for work.

So the plan was we'd go back to school to tell Victoria so she could come too if she wanted. Only, thing is, one of Ms. Valdez's students saw us from the school bus and told her. She had ample time to prepare for our arrival.

They caught us in the schoolyard
The Principal,
Police,
Ms. Valdez waiting
taking him kicking
buck teeth ripping clenched hands that stopped us
from breaking loose
arms locked for one last pact
to stay together
if only in the mind.

11 years passed and I have moved back to my childhood home. A hand-drawn portrait with these words sit on an altar to Shango. Template poems I never wrote or finished. Candles cast shadows on his image,
some nights

When I think about the Angel I've become
the angels I've replaced him with
the what if we had run in the other direction
Black wings fleshing out metaphors
wondering what will happen when I finally figure it out.
Why I can't seem to love like that again
Why I still believe that I can
Innocent
And eternal

Life
is a flame on liquid wax
A CD scratched

on an angle of song
Waiting for the wick to burn
Maybe

We all want to be towering infernos
Pray flame catches something before we die
He is still flickering in my eyes
I
Am burning on air

i get it
by L. Phillip Richardson

from across the bar
i get it
smooth as the blade against your thigh
again
i get it
the long look unnerves as it undresses

me
i'm cool
slick
gazing the prospects
but i get it
your eyes slicing the smoke like a sigh

cool
still
i get it
at the same time
we get it
between the beats of hip-hop suave
and army boots

chill
we chill
the codes to modes
to chill the moment-to-moment chance
to smile
to dare to be real
amid laughter and beer
and our joint loneliness
and bull

i get it
so i smile
quick hard hot
i get it
a veneer your smile
man-to-man desire
in oversized layers of yo-drag
behind an oversized ego
your fear

       like how big is yours
       does it get as big as mine
       know you want it
       if you can
       if you a man
       take it
       walk that walk
       talk that talk
       if you can
       if you a man

on our silent wavelength
your eyes
seem to say conquer
or be conquered
i get it

Notes Toward a Poem About Love
by Reginald Harris

Remember:
    The long trip back from the Carolinas—
        how he looked, smooth in silhouette   dozing

you drove 80 miles an hour from Durham to DC
    through a rain-slicked, receding South
        deep in a groove, desperate for return
                for shared, familiar bed

      or earlier   the night before
              the downtown Charlotte club—

How, even dressed in "b-boy hoodlum mode"
    he was glorious, shone   a beacon in the smoky dark.
      New Man in Town, undressed by the eyes of Sunday
              regulars

confused by this bastard busting their games
          the half-seen other he leaves with;

      or later, even: Picture the future, next week,
           tomorrow—

he strides in from work   tired
    complaining of new madness
      then winks   changes for his late-night rituals

On the phone, he laughs at a joke and his gaze turns,
        ablaze with anticipated retelling.

Then forget:
   Think of Lack   The absence of that Presence.
     A world without memory   the otherwise dull moments

        Stop   Think *(for once)*
     Meditate   Slowly begin to write

He remembers, I remember
by Alan E. Miller

He remembers, though he sees me first
to let me discover him: an old gift
in shiny wrapping. He knows the joy
this brings me. He remembers

my vanity. Not to look at the thick cord
of fat around my waist. Not to hold my hands
too long. That we yearly grow
like roots curling away from trees.

He remembers not to stare
in my eyes too deeply or too long.

I remember, though I see him first,
not to register surprise or shock or disapproval
that he has found the bimbiest bimbo
in the joint—a younger, less learned, less
round version of me. I remember

not to ask for things he will never
give, answers to old questions like sacred
recipes, signs that he has irreparably
changed. I remember

to ask about his new job, his new home.
But not to let my eyes glaze over
like a fish when the litany begins.

I remember: the misery of losing him,
the falling and crying,
my head at his knees, kissing them
Hollywood style.

Yours Were the Last Lips I Kissed
by Carl Cook

1

The clock ticks whether or not
we love or die and what
was set into motion many years ago
will not make a difference

in the quality of love or the psychic battles
waged in its name. even if you decide
love is not yours to give in this brief moment,
now is all the time you have to give.

2

Torrential downpours are always possible,
problems persisting in spite of
progress aggressively pursued. there are
limits to time. limits to how long

love can find assurance, the confidence
to acknowledge the approaching
storm, the courage to speak as a child, without
pretense, without the ruination of regret.

1

You approached me with sly, worrisome eyes.
your body moved with heavy thought
giving physical hints of tantalizing moments
you had come to regret its residuals,

although you saw no reason to discontinue
what had distinguished you most,
a talent for theatrical sex, olympic and intense,
in search of that one satisfying mate.

2

We took the time to exchange perspectives
of ourselves and of each other.
I suggested the allegorical comparison
of the tortoise and the hare.

me, being of course, the tortoise, reluctant
to stick his neck out unless necessary.
and you, with your rabbit ways, enticed me to do
just that, and made me cum a little faster.

1

From the moment we spoke everything
became a dream. reality
in its three dimensions was transfigured
while the elements made

symbolic gestures lending themselves
to new interpretations more
real than the elements themselves.
life was strangely new again.

2

I lost my capacity to speak, my ability
to see as a poet, unable to unearth
the perfect metaphor to clarify the sudden
fog descending, failing to grasp

the right phrase to illustrate with example
the principles of love, the feeble
communications of passion, the loud laughter of lust,
the slow transcending movement of mountains.

Blue

by Forrest Hamer

And then comes longing,
a man you've known
but have not really met,

who whispered Portuguese
minutes after making love,
folding around you like skin.

The longing comes and
never arrives, imagines you
and never is revealed;

it shapes your body
into someone lonely, rains
upon your house like August.

Once
by John Frazier

I've never seen someone shit, I say to my boyfriend as he begins
to close the bathroom door with his right index finger, already lowering

himself on the toilet. I want to be asked to witness the white briefs
bunch at his ankles, the hairy legs spread, his face turn in a grimace.

But you've lived with men, he replies. I don't want
to be vulgar, I say, eyeing his balls, waiting

for an invitation. Even as I defend my ignorance—how I grew up
in a house of prudish women, how the impossible boys I dated

never showed me this—I know it's not true. I saw my father squat once
over the porcelain toilet in the old house the summer it burned,

the muscles in his thighs tensing. Why does everything
come back to this man, I think, even at this age?

And now hours later while doing the dishes I've been thinking
this is what I will do, love the worst parts of the men who come home to me.

Evanescence
by John Frazier

In the photo we sit in a crowded Egyptian bazaar, unmoved, his arm around my back, fingers resting in the drop of my waist, a trail of smoke from the hookah in our eyes but drifting away. We are still young. Later we will rent camels, ride bareback to the base of the pyramids where we'll argue. Foolish. I will spend the rest of the day sulking, and even when the sheik pulls me from my camel, arranges a desert headdress, quickly snaps a photo—*for your memory*—I will frown.

It will be the beginning of winter. Each night we will sleep in a different rented room listening to tapes on a portable black radio. *High Priestess of Soul* by Nina Simone. *An Evening With Lena Horne Recorded Live at The Supper Club.*

In the mornings, I will fumble loudly hoping to stir him, collect the scattered underclothes, think to begin packing at 6 AM. I will want to clean, but then something in me will turn. I'll notice his already brown body darker still from the sun and my own form darker. These will be moments when we will not have to choose, when it will not matter if he wants a girl or if I'm impatient. And at these times I will ease back into bed, curl my body tightly against his kicking the white, tangled sheets past at our ankles to the floor.

Years later we'll laugh about it all. How young. How so in love. For those days when I would travel to the edge of Africa with a hundred dollars in my pocket, touching down at midnight in Cairo, simply because my beloved said come.

ReDefined
by Geoffrey Freeman

for Sur Rodney Sur

They care deeply
but do they love you

They look at you with eyes of wonder
but do they see you or their own reflection
or do they gaze beyond YOU
recognizing only that which is within familiar

They hug you
but do they embrace you
ALL OF YOU
ALL FROM YOU
Freely

They call you
but do they know you
as I know you
not like them
just you.

Devious Mirrors
by Reginald Harris

Devious Mirrors: fallen songman fucking redbone soldier.
Nipples enraged, sharing, sparring, smoking. Desires learned
between despair, silence, hustlers, ecstasy. Quieted, exhaled,
dodging history, phrases reckon secrets, visions unsaid.
Riotous morning: perfect jasmine horizon unfolds haunted.
Rushing excuses, kitchen embrace. Numbers. Raucous montage:
pouting partner listens. Queries pockets perhaps. Ignites

Evidence
by D. Rubin Green

I have never
heard
the oak
disown the earth
from which it rises,
or the tiger
flee
from the twilight
beneath whom
it sleeps.
I have never heard
the moon
speak
against the burgeoning
rice,
or the wind
deny the rightness
of the grass.

Why then, my love, do you listen
to these imposters?

What man
can dare to say
what is between us
is or is not
love?
That my mouth
must not seek
your mouth,
my eyes
never long for
the refuge
of your eyes,

your soul
never find
my soul,
flying
as it does
above
the elements
whenever you
gaze at me?

When these petty men come,
their eyes failing,
their throats
clamoring with ashes,
with red crime,
with ruins,
& disreputable words,
when the airwaves
conspire
to close all the doors
of your heart
never listen,
never doubt,
never, never run away!

No, my luminous one—take my hand,
& walk with me
through the defeated streets,
& we shall listen to the tree,
& the tiger,
& the rice,
& the moon,
& the grass,

And there,
in that pure music,
we shall find all the evidence
we need.

Lantern
by Cheryl Boyce-Taylor

For Monica

south of white lake bridge
a solitary branch falls
its ribs not black not brown
splay an imaginary ladder

connect river one side then another
small stones with damp palms
worship holy winds
they fly luminous into God's arms

my arms imperfect blades
her arms alive in the blue throat
of my waist
our ferny spine of need

my suspicious heart almost on stilts
we have traveled past sky's dense rim
desire outlasts the body's lantern

So, this is where we are
by Samiya Bashir

Sticky. Held together by nothing
more than musk. Salty with well-worn need.
Undesired truths unheeded. Speaking in active
voice. Demanding to be taken. Bending
like a willow to the throaty demands of each other.

So, this is where we are. Dusty.
Smudge marks on our backs
from unwashed walls and window sills.
Lace torn from panties. Breasts freed
from narrow confines. Release, begged for
and given, echoed in the stolen corridor
where we struggle to catch our breath.

Here, I am balanced
on one spindly heel.
The other poking like a spear
from your backside,
thrusting with you,
shaking as we shake,
secure that your desire
will keep me aloft.

So here is where we tear the screams
from our throats. This dampened corner
where I suck your vocal chords
between my teeth and tongue
to contain your moans, where
I lower my heel to push
your strong thighs deeper.
Here, then, is where we land

and take off for flight after flight,
soar the ether like a swallow-tail
in search of a stream. This is where
what we speak becomes real,
where taste imagined materializes
into flavor savored with nothing to hide us
but the dim bulb in the corner and
the blanket of dust on our clothing.

We are here, after all, with work to do.
I shake out my skirts, best as I can,
and brush down your trouser legs.
The chorus demands we straighten up,
ascend the stairs into daylight once more.
Fix our glassy stares into focus. You have
what lingers on your lips. I hold tight
to what I've captured between my thighs.

Jesus Gon' Hear My Song, Sho' Nuff

by Samiya Bashir

—for Remica Bingham

I fly on the high notes
carried by footlights
past black keys and white
past pine frame and fine shoes
tapping   on waves invisible
and clear as the Sunday
come to meeting bell

I'm so glad I'm changed,
every day I sing to repay the favor
O! But on this day made for nothing
less than salvation with a side of chicken
notes wake me from deep in slumber

it begins with a flutter at the pit of my stomach
rises to a warm sweet spot in my chest
as I dress it begins to reach my throat
leak out in bits of cry   tickling
over tongue   whistling through teeth
rolling over these lips formed full for praise

when I reach the house where my love resides
my sisters have to hold me down   or I'm gone
flying   only the rafters can keep me from
glory on days like this

bloomfist
by Karma Mayet Johnson

in a rage of tenderness
you called my name
        my hand in you sang
hot as the torn seam of thunder
        we cried like tigers
        the new moon standing still

Why lisa don't mind washing the floor

by Letta Neely

Early Saturday mornings
She rise when sun come
through slats of shades. First thang she do,
she turn look at her lover
curled, a conch shell hard
and soft as the nearest high tide.
Then she git up, wrap that ole
purple terrycloth robe round her nakedness,
put sarah vaughn on the turntable. She be thinking
ain't a goddamn thing like sarah vaughn's voice
cept my mona's fingers playin
my body like bass notes held past
heavens. She thank god for
Friday nights.
Oooh child. She be on her
hands and on her knees, scrubbing the floor,
thinking   is the water as hot
as I have been?
She dunk that rag in the bucket.
Take both hands to wrang it out.
Still, water drips in warm spirals
down her wrists,
touches her elbows and it comes to her
redemption's deja-vu. Mona on her
knees, head down between lisa's thighs—
a fat honey bee gorging on nectar and
bringing it back to lisa's lips.
And she opened up to mona wide like evening
primroses to full moons,
Like she visiting the sky full of constellations.
She member she praised mona's mama n
she praised mona's daddy for havin her,

she member she really thought they could make
a baby with this much love.
She member she couldn't even count how
many times she rose to a penultimate horizon
and the thangs she saw there.

Shiiiit, lisa be sniffin the floor as
she scrub it. She love smellin
aftersex much as she love
her bare back on kitchen floor.

Drive
by Duriel E. Harris

Cool night, like the snap of peas or dry branches underfoot.
Someone's waiting for me: a photograph of my breath.
The moon is cropped stingy and my skin is a tethered shade of heat
drawn to outer darkness and the gentle sucking in the thick of it.

Looking for the turn. Dull stretch of road the weight
of any other. Rolling straight back into clannish trees
like a cinnamon woman, powdered cleavage, struck
dumb in the spirit, falls back trusting.

A dredloc creeps from behind my ear, scrapes my nose, yarn
between my eyes. I slip its tight coil into place with a motion
reminiscent of white girls' easy laughter and the prep school I hated,
tinged with the riddle of their dearness and my brown body unseen.

Looking for the turn. Sign posts become tar field scarecrows,
mute Colored, bowed heads at 3 a.m. wherever trees shoot up
in a clearing. And down a piece there's a church, one room sanctuary,
one paint-chipped iron rail at the front three steps. The doors

are swollen shut from the rain; above them, a cross-shaped window
broken out, fist-sized, where Jesus' head would be.
Cool night passes through the jagged godhead whistling,
condenses on the stained glass pane the way a house settles,

the way our bodies soften into earth, the way our suffering
mists, seeps into the bloodstream and runs. My we,
us, we people breathing on both sides of the bold belly.
Greed and our flesh trials nurse the second half of the last millennium.

What I wouldn't do for a bidi. I turn on the radio.
There. And I'll turn again before I reach the leaf dense trees
to go where I'll spend the night. Haven, where someone's waiting
and smells like cornbread under cloth, like thighs, moist

armpits, is a double portion, ribbed, combed, and fastened.
At the end of it: a bell my fingers feel for.
Sometimes, I dream a lonely highway and wake up driving;
sometimes, I am wet and full and prone in the pasture.

While inside me, desire shepherds the hills swallowing night's crisp
center and loose pearls in the swayback of darkness until I
breathe, reaching, replenished, forgetting, palpable
and palatable like pulling smoke but more than momentary

shuttling lungs and ear drums, more than, until I am a dream
within a dream within a dream like electric organ humpbacks
and only-born-once Al Green's happiness squealing
eeeeeeeeee moan for love eeeeeeeeee over road hiss

over dirt shoulder scratches over prairie far off trees and sky
darknesses taking up space until I am an ellipsis, spinning.

But There Are Miles
by Duriel E. Harris

I am in a quiet place
leaves bunched in audience at my window
their deep green shapes shades of the night's stillness
I pause and consider
how different things could be

but there are miles, fitful
with no respect for persons
whole states, an expanse of mountains
uncharted geography of fear and doubt
grief

and you, lover
sigh in the pensive arms of sleep
in a separate peace
with one lank thigh languid over the other
your lips fallen open against her flesh
your features lost, nestled
in the soft spread of her breasts

our lovemaking was always tentative, hurried, desperate
jammed into the small space of days
and even when we lay together
our dreams were anxious wanderings
the bedcovers disheveled and damp with perspiration
the tense muscle of need a chasm between us

I am in a quiet place
my fingers trace the pattern of books strewn purposefully
on the other side of the bed

what I miss most is the slow sound of your breath
its slant rhythm

and your body
unfolded against mine
in rest

That August You Knew My Mother
by Cheryl Boyce-Taylor

The august you knew my mother
even at twenty her hands green veined and weary
slight slip of a girl
hips a wooden washboard
hair a runaway kite

her secrets a lumbering hill
tight in her throat
that august news climbed the town like wild fire
his black fist called
her young eyes bright as fireflies

her teeth
her smile
wounds
on the swollen stagnant floorboard
her half Indian eyes
that black majestic reign of hair
blood a wild red hat
knitted to braids and bone

a sharp muscular cry
robs the summer of substance

then that girl
that girl my mother
entered her house of secrets
cleared away blue stone
blue stone with her bare hands
the unfinished timber of her heart calling

Psychic Imprints
by B.Michael Hunter

Tell me a story...
Muvva, tell me some stories.

The sensitive child
Vying for attention
Repeatedly requests

She
Perched on a kitchen chair
Rusty gold, old and trusted feline
Tapping   tapping
At the spirits in the hem of her robe
Hastily draped over her knee
Unexpected guest
To view the new arrival

The alteration in the pitch and tone of
Her voice tries to bring order to
The chaos of cackling children.

There is joy. **JOY!**

Marching orders administered:
Don't mess up that room!
And ignored.

The child offers comfort:
Don't worry, Muvva, I'll help you...
I'll help you clean up...
I'll buy you a house.

Amused, she chuckles, caringly
Absolves the child in her reply:
That's OK.

Child
Defiant
Happily vows
To do it anyway

Conversations between generations
At the kitchen table
Alchemy and affirmations bring
The childless father
To this place
Centered   focused   satisfied
Receiving the Universe's blessings
Delivered by angels
Nestled on his shoulders
Spirits jump across
Threads of time
This the second decade virus
Once benign at 203
Turns malignant at 189

No cause for alarm
Legacies left in writings on walls
In whispered phrases
Parenting, parenting
All over the place.

The mother: *Child, I have secrets to tell.*
The son: *I'm listening.*

Throughout the exchange they realize
They both feel the same way about
Libraries
Churches
Trees
Within each is stored secrets
And lessons learned
Life and death and rituals
The irony

We two   the mother   the son
Listen and wait
For the echoes in trees
Gnarled, weather-worn
Branches holding spirits
Let us touch you so you can talk to us

The mother expresses her joy
In watercolors
The son
In poetry

The mother: *You're my angel!*
The son: *I'm just trying to earn my wings.*
Computer screensavers record their mantras:
Sheila, take back your power...
Michael, remember the possibilities...

One spring afternoon the son asks:
How do you bounce back so often? What's your secret?
The mother replies:
I just love waking up in the morning
Just seeing a new day
Listening to the birds sing and
Looking at the trees.

The son smiles.

raindrop
by Renita Martin

in the absence of familiar
she called her raindrop
because her eyes dripped
rainbow moist dew
into the fire of her thighs

those hips at once made
and devastated her day
always stirring like tomorrow
just a few steps from reach

she thought of clothespins
on her nipples wanted clothespins
on her nipples wanted raindrop
to hang laundry from her peak

she had seen her uncle
throw watermelon to the earth
laugh wild fold his hands
scoop red cloud from the ground
exclaim "goddamn it's good"

she wanted cause to say
"goddamn it's good." As
raindrop's hand became
the vine cupped under her
patch she wanted to say
"this juice will stain"

she wanted to cup her own hands
throw raindrop down
watch her burst

she wanted
to eat

Starvation Diet
by Mistinguette

I like the way she looks at me.
she likes the way I look. I see
it in her pursing lips, her eyes
appraising me like a heifer
at a county fair: tits, flank,
hips, ass. I'm not supposed
to like this. I lose my thread
in conversation, become breathless, bend
to tie a lace that's tight enough. We run

past her house every day we run. You see just
a woman of uncertain age, neither old nor young,
thighs heavily apart, one pant leg up. A toothpick rolls
suggestively from side to side. Some days she cups a cigarette
in her right hand, filter between thumb and middle finger,
flame cupped away from the wind. You and I, we do not smoke.
We count our careful calories; do sit-ups to retain our waists;
discipline ourselves to love the taste of what's fresh
and good for us, fat free. So you don't see her

notice me, or me notice her back. Back all the way
up the hallway of her building where somebody's cooking
ham hock and pinto beans, bacalao and rice. You don't see
the way she hoods her eyes, and holds her belly like it's
filled with something womanly and good. Round and dear,
anticipating some warm and tasty thing
to fill her, every evening when you and I run past.

You don't see her at all, so you don't know why I
want to take you in the hall, ripe with sweat and
tendons burning with fatigue and desire. You kiss
me on the nose, tell me to shower first, then dinner, then
we'll see. I hear you step onto the bathroom scale.

I sit on the porch swing and hug myself, cupping
a tiny flame of passion against the wind.
I wander into the kitchen, open and close every
cupboard door. I don't know what I'm looking for,
but I am ravenous with a nameless desire.

The summer I did not go crazy
by Mistinguette

drove around instead   screaming
doors locked windows rolled up tight
afraid of every headlight in my
rearview mirror   desperate to find
somewhere you were not
My mama told me
women in this family
do not go crazy are not afraid
so I didn't know what to call
the taste of metal between my teeth
blades edge reflecting
moon against my throat
I kept an axe beside my bed
slept with the hall light on
dreamed of dead ancestors &
roamed highways with a silver
bullet in my pocket. You saw
it all

and did not underestimate the friend
who brought fresh peaches
and comfort one summer night
nor the one who was
afraid and knew
fear quickens the pulse
to better flee
and loved me anyway
It has taken me too many years
to write this poem
but you were less surprised than I
when a woman of clear purpose &
cautious laughter passed through
leaving me wanting
something dark and sweet

working my way back
by Cheryl Clarke

to
your face
          arriving
redolent
     such a pretty back
to old memorializations
          butch-femme   s-m
          maitresse   ou   esclave
          vanilla   chocolate   strawberry
          neopolitan
throat deep
                    bush to my ears

the same changing.

Rites

by Karma Mayet Johnson

culprit me
like the Madonna

crown me Mother
of the Sea and bid me
worship the wind
his daily rise
my own refraction

we are all risen all
tendered in the swell
this loose harmonic
this heaven's countergroove

swallow, swallow, and sever
then severing seek
the resolve

pieces of the dream
by Gina Rhodes

in those days sunny was only your name
I argued with my folks
wound up at your sister's house
where you came into the basement
where I was staying
still having to hide all my privacy
under the mattress or
holes in the wall behind the dresser
I had rearranged expressly for that purpose

it did not take much
so you gave a few pair of pants
ten dollar bills
occasional blow
for which you got paid my tight ass
blunt as stone responses
"yes, I felt something, no I didn't come!"
which probably cut our arrangement short
or else it was when ann your lover from boston
started hunting you down
wondering where you had gone in
her sky blue leather interior carrrrr
when I knew it was me you had in it
or whoever else ten dollars would buy

back roads
by Gina Rhodes

margaret, was it you?
the summer of '72
i came south to visit my grandma
& found you
your stuff belonging to
the room i thought i belonged to

black dot beam eyes burned circles
around the spot you were standing in—
grandma's fleshy arm draped across your shoulder—
"gina, this here is Margaret she gonna be staying with us"
your short plump frame chipmunk face
"hey gina grandma done tole me so much about you
we gonna have such fun…"
margaret, for a solid week i drew the invisible line

you were so anxious to learn
every little thing about me—
best friends, special flowers & colors—
always asking and insisting answers
i was surprised to find myself
talking so much
in a few weeks you had surmised
soaking wet buttery biscuits were my favorites
& atomic jawbreakers
always eager
every night i watched you pull from
this or that hiding place
six tin-wrapped biscuits
they were always warm
& margaret, i am sure you drove yourself
to the poorhouse that summer
sneaks to brown's juke joint

servicing our sweet tooth
against grandma's warnings

margaret, i played grown, detached
watching you
maneuvering through summer's strict discipline
where we were supposed to be
we always were
night after night
rattling cellophane wrappers & tin foil
giggling
bad as the devil
both sugar apple dumplings in our grandma's eyes

in that chilled wood-framed summer
under the beige pompom spread
we shared
drops of butter
& red hot spit
falling from our mouths
on grandma's clean starched sheets
we turned our backs to the thick plastic
tacked against that room's single window
& scooped up close
your ample loose flesh
like cheese melting over stacked spoons
your spongy knees contained the empty
angle my bent bones made
inwardly giggling, i crinkled my toes
until your cold nose grew warm breath
at the back of my neck

in the middle of the night
when grandma passed on
the other side of the thin drawn drape
i jolted
but you were innocent, Margaret

with no place else to be
i played grown
detached
but now my lover feels like you

In the Winston Lips of September, How We Met

...Rickie Lee Jones

by Karma Mayet Johnson

busted fighting but tight again before they could suspend us—
a hit of mine for you, yours for me, your lips changed the flavor
of the nicotine.

dusty high-tops and pollen-coated nostrils, we ran
giddy and nauseous, fearing each other like we were supposed to
fear god.

the father stories, the plastered-over holes in ranch house walls
the clean feeling in the other girl's room—her mess a comfort, a
truth.

rotten lessons, the way we stopped—how all the boys were yours
the girls seeking my ear like mosquitos in july.

girl, I would've told 'em all "later" if we could brave it
if we'd said "hell yeah, what the fuck" like at the carnival.

after 6 months with not a call, you were pregnant on the phone
howling only you only you, and I came, I came.

moccasins wet and just shy of Empty, my last two dollars
for gas instead of cigarettes 'cause the place was just down
the road.

bitch I loved you. Stringy-haired bigot-brained cuntangel girl.

pearls
by francine j. harris

whenever they have come
to take us
by blade shotgunshell
rope
or induced sickness
there is always still more of us
to go around
we never
run out of
each other
> —nikky finney

she wanted a best friend then,
not for all time but for all situations
all directions.
    eyes in the back of her pussy
cause after all her pussy was under attack
was by now legendary

so she fold up her gown
    her royal down coat
button broken, pink plastic hair comb stuck in and nappy in the lining
close to her chest   where she held my hand
said *can you still feel it*
is it too fast
am i still here
cause i think i forgot something in his house
in fact i don't know what but i can feel it
hammering

don't give me that virgin shit i say
cause you ain't unbroken anymore
won't mean nothing to no one if we go back
in fact, i'm sure they're broken anyway
        in too many little white pieces
to remember the number. i mean
we could go there and comb every corner
every wooden attic beam   one by one by one
but in truth, i've lost count.
i think i got lost
wondering who was gonna replace them
they were a gift after all, and they were mine

all broken now, they show they
                              true dime store colors
and i think i'm embarrassed now they know it's fake.
i tried to keep it to myself, tried to keep it intact
      cause no one know how cheap they were
          from not so close up

but i told you he wore them around his neck the whole time
well, then, what else do we talk about now
it doesn't seem like that long ago, everyone now
back through high school
      is a metaphor for you,   and best friends
and how we used to think we were saving each other
but from what—
maybe we lied
maybe we tried and there was nothing
                    back in that house
under that bed.

   maybe   the wind wasn't that strong
or the snow that deep
but it was deep,
it was the warmest winter in years and the snow would melt and
stack

would melt weld and crush violet dirt blue
stack over on itself on froze ice just to
melt again

i remember the sore.
it was not a fuck-happy sore
or a virgin-sore, it was sore from scrub raw
bathe twice times in one hour
it was a shame sore
all a neat distance from your ten-year-old sister
when she flocked to my thighs that night, i thought
she would give me away

the way dogs tell on you
put their nose in your lap, she press her head to my hip
and i think to raise flags,
but we save them,
save the flags for the school counselor chair where
a big, fat white woman says you liked it
and i remember she wasn't
a big, fat white woman
until she did.
but they say it's hard to make friends after school
so maybe she was lonely
or maybe she liked it
or maybe we lied. i've tried

for more than ten years to arrange them all
into something remarkably redeemable
the product of 'well, just look at their surroundings
their house next to burger king all those years
no church nearby, what'd you expect—' or,
'they'd all been drinking, of course ...'

of course i can't remember that smell
the way i remember the swell of their eyes on you,
        the empty factories billowing black, not enough

bookmobiles or fire hydrants or stick ball
it never was just one on one
but then things don't get talked about
   like that.   trip and scab on glass
      under unnetted rims
               behind burned buildings that stay erect
                  with hot yellow signs
               to warn some at attention
               to all the wrong sides.

  the crew of them under
the steady buzz of planes, over hollow gasoline
they don't travel alone, they wait together
      like oil in the streets—
            slick into grooves and the ice glides from junk piles to
            curb crack
down down   past rows rows of graveyards
      where people with polish names were buried, *where did they
take us, teacher* i might have asked someone
   sometime if i wasn't so shy   *why*
no streetlights in rooms
where you're already known if i didn't think
i should have already known.
               teacher in a window
                     watch you fade

or maybe it was me

maybe i'm the one losing track
   whenever they ask how many, i round up to the nearest horror
story
anything in order to convey how seven or eight beads on an
abacus is preschool
but five or six bodies blocking the overhead light
is the rest of your life

or maybe it was you

maybe you should have been there with me
those summer mornings on the porch
when me and boys from the block
teach each other how to read
not even like we wanted to
just like we wanted something to discuss.
we didn't have much in common
none of us did
and maybe that was it
     like
you learn to share something as holy as a fairy tale
or as alley as broken pearls left over under the bed

but i confess   i'd go back for them.
even if it's true about the unmarked graves
               not junk jewelry but the smell
to remind me of you.
and isn't that crazy, that two old friends
can't find a thing to talk about except tombstones.
holding on to jade until you finally make gold
or at least something medicinal.

it's true i'd go back
not to convince anyone we don't tell stories
but to finally lay my childish love for you to rest
     somewhere in an unmarked memory
          with the image of bodies in force and motion and the
          smell of raw pussy
and the lies
we never told.

where the boys are
by Marvin K. White

goodbye
my hopscotch destiny
my tetherball ambition
my red rover aspiration

goodbye
my jacks experience
my hide and go get it flair
my kick ball capability
my dodge ball knack

goodbye
my wall ball calling
my marble scholarship
my patty cake purpose
my blind mans bluffing

goodbye
my tag savvy
my doorbell ditch dream
my double pumped fate
my monkey bar bent

goodbye
my little dick
my high voice
my chin and chest hair smooth
goodbye to everything
my bough broken
my boyhood dangerous and unexpected
my place held in line
for the bottom of our dogpile
this love

How Can You Live Without Hugs?
(or Poem #1 for Kev)
by Duncan E. Teague

Claim you don't get or give hugs?
Not the Big Momma kind,
the kind a Big Daddy can lay on you.

That Old Roommate grabs a hold of you,
holds on to you for his dear life,
for your dear survival.
After your wedding and after his second child lives!
More than a decade and a half after you almost did not graduate.
And you remember, he hugged you back then too.
A vice grip of love.

Guys who make your life a showstopper,
not a bad episode of some reality cop drama.
A man-loving-a-man hug.

So, when the days are long and the nights shrink,
when your dog is not having any of it,
None, not any more, no tail wagging for you...

Your cell phone is about to be cut off
Again
And no ring tones from the Top 100 Hip Hop Hits will jingle along.

No arms encircle you?
No hands grasp you steady from your east and west?
Remind you that we are just smooth primates
with way too much brain
and not enough love wrapped around us?

What do you reach out to hold?
Where do you roam?

Is it a "Butch" thing? Cause then
I do not have to understand!
Though some late afternoons I wonder
what I would be like if
I was like the other non-hugging, non-holding,
not touchy and never feely boys?
Those men.

See what you started
by not starting!

Shopping List
by Ernest Hardy

Don't bring me hardcore. Don't bring me street. Don't bring me ghetto. Don't bring me keepin'-it-real performances. Don't bring me steely PhDs, academic jism or intellectual jargon. Be radical. Be revolutionary: *Bring me tenderness.* Bring me blood-riddled, tear-stained insights. Bring me strength beyond a pose. Be who you really are. Be the you beneath protective covering. Strip away conditioning. Strip away posturing. Strip away all the bullshit that you've learned. I don't want words you've memorized. I don't want record collection validation or bookshelf credentials. I want fragments synthesized. I want the wisdom you've earned through sweat and unshed tears. I don't care about technique; I don't care if you're tone deaf. Miss a note/fuck a note. Just sing your song. Don't wave platinum credit cards. Don't flash bank account statements. Don't wield diamonds wrought from African blood. Just lay your head near mine, press your heart against mine, and promise to be good. Swear to do your best. And just be your best. Then let the rest fall away. Let the rest just fall away. Then let the rest fall away. Just let the rest fall away.

demon eyes
by Tim'm T. West

we are not all
lurking, trembling between DL hell
and picture perfect projections
of wifey and kids
shivering between night knights
at twilight
and forgetting ourselves and our Crixivan
inside of somebody

we are not all
dishonest
especially with ourselves
and many of us
tell the truth about ourselves
even when we are shunned and whispered about
even when we rhyte to save our lives
and they say our stories aren't
marketable
like DL articles

so I'm not in awe
of the rebuke and caw and panic
of victims and vampires
of blackboys who spit out condoms
bellydance with b-boys
and return home to black madonnas
there is something terribly terrifying
about this demonization and hype

cuz there are stories about us
that have not been told
like when we were dying
trying to be ourselves
way before the shallow echoes of DL
and there were no front-page highlights
then

Marguerite and Camay
by Bil Wright

It was early in the party,
when there was still fresh liquor
lined up like perfume bottles,
Four Roses
Spanish Moss
Pink Champale.
Tyella Armstrong
 in her stocking feet
hollerin' out songs she damn well better hear before the
night was done. It was Tyella's way to come lit to a party,
slide cussin' and peein' to the floor by the end.

Jimmy Jackson answered the door,
talkin' bout how he was gon' get some tonight
if he had to beg
or use up his quarter tank o' gas givin' whoever would take pity on his
homely ass a ride home,
after he and her got down.
"Oh, my would ya looka here," Jimmy stood back,
let the room get a better view.

Jimmy said, "Whatchu call yourselves?"
"We're the Virgin Sisters. I'm Marguerite. This is Camay."
Tyella snickered and belched.
Somebody else whispered too loud to be called a whisper,
"Shirley, you invited them, girl? You mean to say you know those
whatchacallits?"
If the two of them weren't deaf,
they seemed to be too distracted by being with each other
to have heard.
I was moved by the capriciousness of
turk waz eyelids

decorating identical masques of unblemished jet.
The evening swelled
grew
loud
and drunken,
but the two of them
continued to have just arrived
white satin pumps undefiled by clumsy passion
on a mayonnaised dance floor.

They were unruffled by Arthur Prysock's advances,
did not care for any, thank you
when the dip was passed around
did not feel like dancing just right now
in a singular contralto
unless
it was with each other
and even then, only to a tempo of
medium to slow drag.

Yeah, sugah, they
called themselves, " The Virgin Sisters. I'm Marguerite. This is Camay."
And no, I did not see it,
everybody tells it different,
say they can't be certain of who was who.
But seems like one
started moaning to a scratched Etta James,
held out her fists
locked
like a slave in chains.
The other
broke down,
a jungle violet under too much city rain.
Oh, this
and this
is for the lover in you
Bay Bay.

A Name I Call Myself:
A Conversation
by D. Rubin Green

Surely, to be black *and* gay is a complicated thing. No more complicated or difficult than to be anything else, but it is a peculiar and compounded reality. Exactly by what process one creates an identity for oneself, holds onto it, and then with bewildering bravery negotiates through the wilderness that is American life has been a subject of great personal interest to me. But, until recently, I had not taken the opportunity to put my thoughts on paper. I recently had the pleasure of being interviewed by a dear friend of mine, Annalise Ophelian. Writing an article for UC Berkeley titled "Spine: Stories of Reconstructing Otherness in Black Gay Male Identity," she spoke with four "same-gender-loving" men of color to discover their views of exactly what it means to be black and gay. Being a lesbian, a woman, a sex worker, and an early AIDS activist herself, she too has long been fascinated by the process of identity negotiation. I suspect for many people the struggle toward self-acceptance, toward self-love, can be a mighty steep climb. And so, the question that W.E.B. DuBois raised so long ago is still a relevant one: Indeed, how does it feel to be a paradox? How does it feel to have to navigate the triple-consciousness of being black *and* gay *and* an American? The following is an edited version of our conversation.

AO: So, you don't identify being black or being gay specifically with being oppressed?
DRG: No. No. No. I think, again, it's the same thing I said to B., I mean, how does he deal with being white and guilty? So, it's the same thing. Everyone is suffering somehow. Everybody is suffering somehow. I mean, the Serbs in Kosovo, the Indians in Columbia. Everyone is going through something that's brought on by fear or greed. And this idea that there's some sort of hierarchy, some sort of tier of suffering—that these people here,

their suffering is somehow more important, or worse, or deeper, or more horrific than those people over there—I just find ridiculous. Slavery is not worse than being gassed in an oven. They're both a horrible thing, *and* they're utterly distinct. Try telling the person who is being gassed, "Well, you know, you didn't suffer like I did!" and see what kind of response you get. It's absurd. It's one of the great lies we live by: that there are some people who are fine, and there are those who are not. I just don't think that that's true, I think everybody's going through some shit. Some may be more intense, but the measure of you is what you make of it. Not comparing and contrasting, or getting into a competition about it. But really, the only task is what you do with your suffering, what you make of it.

To the question of homosexuality—so much of one's troubles are caused by what other people make of your condition. Your "oppression" is not because of what you are, but because of what other people *think* you are and how they choose to respond to that. I don't think people get that. People would rather believe that if you belong to such a group, your pain is brought on of its own accord, it's just some unfortunate circumstance you fell into. What they don't realize, or don't want to see is, no—*it's you! You're doing it!* If you'd just shut up, or get out of my way, or stop being so frightened, or if you'd relax, or just go on about your business—we'd be fine. I suspect a lot of the people that you're talking to think and feel the same way: that if it's difficult, it doesn't come from *within*, it comes from without. And that's what strikes me as so silly when other people start to perceive me as, "*Oh, you poor thing!*" It's ridiculous. I'm only a poor thing because you think I'm a poor thing. I'm fine. You let me deal with what I have, and you deal with whatever crap you have. I mean, I do worry about other things. I worry about money. I worry about my health. I worry about love, and my own fears about love. I worry about all the existential things that everyone else worries about, but not "*oh my god, how did I get burdened with this?*" As far as I see it, in and of itself, I'm not particularly burdened with anything. I just happen to live in this place where all these other idiots are really uptight about it. And, you know, they should shut up and get a clue.

But let me come at it in another way.

I was in a restaurant with B. We were talking, and pretty soon the conversation moved to a more intimate level. Finally, he asked me, "How do deal you with it? How do you deal with being black and gay?" And as I said before, what I should have said was "well, how do you deal with being white and guilty?" But instead, I remember I told him the story about James Baldwin: Baldwin is being interviewed on British television, and the interviewer asks him, "My god, you were born black *and* gay *and* poor. You must have thought that you had the weight of the world." And he says, "Well, no. Actually, I felt exactly the opposite. I thought I'd hit the jackpot." *[Laughs]* I thought that was so cool! I mean, it could have been kind of cavalier on Baldwin's part, you know, trying to be brave in the face of this very direct question. But even so, even if that's true—his point is still profound: Look at what an interesting perspective it *gives* you. Look at what it gives you! He's not free to lie to himself in the way that other people are. I mean, if you're gay, there are certain things about yourself you simply can't lie. You're forced to be more introspective; you're compelled to question yourself in ways that most people never are. Why? Because everyone else is questioning you. So, at some point you have to ask, "Well goddamn, is it really me?" Now, in due time, you'll begin to question those around you. Because inevitably, questioning oneself leads to questioning other people as well. And once that happens, that's when you see the hypocrisy and duplicity of people, the fear and the cowardice. It's a fascinating perspective on things. To be sure, it hurts in some areas, but in other areas it's really very, very rich. It gives you things that you wouldn't experience otherwise.

I feel it's the same thing with being black. I remember when I asked [two white friends], "don't you feel connected to Michelangelo and Picasso and the Sistine Chapel, and all that extraordinary history and culture?" And [they] were like *no*. "Or even Andy Warhol or American culture?" No. [They] didn't feel connected to it. It seemed that it was more an issue of class for [them]. That was something rich white folks did. But, regular poor white folks can't claim Michelangelo. And I kept thinking, "Well, why not? Why wouldn't you want to? Why would you not?" In the same way that I felt I could claim Duke Ellington, or I could claim Wyclef Jean, or Richard Wright, or whomever. "That's me, standing up there. That's me." Not simply because I belong to this group, but I belong to this group *and* I share a certain experience, I share a certain perspective. Even those pieces that I don't agree with, like gangsta rap. But, I still claim it. Because I know I have a feeling about from where they speak. Even though I think it may not be the most elegant or positive expression—it's still legitimate. Why? Because it's an honest grievance. I think they've also bought into some very stupid stuff—materialism, homophobia, misogyny. But, that's inescapable. That's part of the struggle of being an American.

Now having said all that, even still, I've always felt uncomfortable and ambiguous about the term "gay." And not just the term gay, but the whole concept of gayness, and straightness, and homosexuality, and bisexuality and heterosexuality. It has always struck me as false, as a construct, as something that's been handed to me, in a way that being black or African-American did not. Part of it, I think, is because I find desire an awfully flimsy nail to hang your identity on. My experience of people in general (and straight men in particular) is that sex and desire is simply too mutable and too shifting. Desire is too soft, too quixotic a thing. What if I change my mind? What if I meet someone, when I'm sixty? I meet a woman and it just does it for me? Then who am I? Oh, so you weren't really gay all along? Or are you now bisexual? Or what if you're heterosexual and have only one experience? Does that make you bisexual? Gay? And what does that experience mean to you? Was it deeply significant and wonderful and you cherished it all your life? Was it some mistake? Or did it come out of some need at the moment? It reminds me of a line I read in one of Gore Vidal's essays. He says that the terms "heterosexuality" and "homosexuality" are quite good at describing what people do, but they're not particularly useful for describing who people are. Now, I'm still digesting that, I'm still thinking it through, but somehow that felt right. Because for me, behind this whole need to label who people are looms a question: "Why is that necessary? Why are we bothering to label who people are in the first place?" And this is where I get suspicious. Clearly it has to do with power, it has to do with control. It has to do with placing people somewhere so you didn't have to think about them any longer— because if you no longer have to think about *them*, then you no longer have to think about *yourself.* And that strikes me as quite dangerous.

AO: So how do you identify your self to yourself and others?
DRG: To myself, I actually, I'm trying not to call myself anything to my self. I find it hard to call myself anything other than just a sexual creature. Or I'm a human being, and part of being a human being is being sexual. It seems that men in general excite me more than women, or I'm more comfortable, and I know more about them than I do women.

AO: And then to the outside world?
DRG: How do I define myself to the outside world?

AO: Hmm? Or do you feel a need in cases, and if so in which cases, to call yourself gay? To distinguish yourself as such?
DRG: I guess I don't. I don't go out of my way to identify myself as anything, actually. I think I leave it to people to figure it out if they care to, if that kind of thing is important to them. Which tells me a lot about them.

AO: Are there ever circumstances when you don't want people to know that you're interested in men, that you love men?
DRG: At my gym, I think, because it's a pretty macho place, and I don't feel safe, frankly. I don't feel like people would be open-minded about that.

AO: Emotionally safe? Physically safe?
DRG: Emotionally safe and perhaps physically safe? I mean, I don't know, I do worry that if I really revealed myself some idiot

would try to attack me, or say something. And then I'd have to get into some fight. If it's a question of being out, it's really... hmmm [pause]. I'm not quite sure how to answer, to tell you the truth. I'm sure it all comes from my own ambiguity about claiming "gayness" as my identity. It's hard to run around and say this is me. I worry about the politics and the motivation of the term. So, I don't feel quite comfortable just grabbing and slapping it on my chest.

AO: Could you talk a bit more about what those politics mean for you?

DRG: I feel that it's dishonest. It's not an adequate description of who people are and what they do. And furthermore, why is this a fixed category in the first place? Why is this a separate category of human being? The image that I have is that I would be taking it and attaching it to me, rather than something that came organically out of me. At least in the present way that it's spoken about, it doesn't feel organic to me. A few years ago, I had a therapist. He was a cognitive behavioral therapist. And I remember when I first told him I'm really into men; his reaction was "really?" And I'm telling him yes. "Are you sure?" And I'm like, "I'm 38 years old, I think I would know by now." You see, because I was not especially effeminate, he had a hard time believing it. In fact, he thought I was an anomaly—which is one of the reasons I stopped going to him. [Laughing] I felt, well, I'm going to be educating him! In many ways, I don't feel connected to what is presently taken as gay culture, which is another reason I don't attach it to myself. I almost want to right this essay called "Judy Garland Ain't No Metaphor," or something like that, you know? I don't love Barbra Streisand. I don't have an intense, obscene identification with Judy Garland. I actually like some sports activities. I actually like baseball and track. I don't want to run around dressed up in drag, you know, that kind of thing. There are a lot of things about gay culture, or what's called gay culture, that I feel is just bull. It's just manufactured, or it's made up, like the Billy doll or that sort of thing. These things just don't do anything for me.

AO: Do you feel like you are a part of the gay culture's target audience?

DRG: I'm not absolutely sure what gay culture is, or even if there is one yet. I think there could very well be one. Maybe we're making one up, But, in the same way, I wonder could you say in 1840 that there was an African-American culture? I mean, there was certainly an African-American experience. But did that experience constitute a culture yet? I don't know. So, that's kind of how I feel about gay culture right now: that it's not really a culture yet, it's sort of collecting itself into a culture. It's difficult to identify yourself with something that's not there yet. I can point to, say, Amiri Baraka, and I can point to Frederick Douglass, and I can point to my own experiences as well and say, "Ah! That's African American," in a way that I can't to being quote unquote gay.

AO: I'm terribly interested in the terms we use to describe ourselves, whether it be gay or black or African American.

DRG: Just that question is really interesting. I think African American is more accurate and less loaded, or it's loaded in a different way.

AO: And how about gay vs. same-gender-loving?

DRG: Same-gender-loving is cool. It's just, it's so not elegant [*Laughs*]. It's more accurate. But, I think it's an evolving thing, in the same way that nigger, to colored, to Negro, to black, evolved to African American. It all reflects what you think about *yourself*.

AO: Or in the case of some of the examples you just gave, what other people think of you?

DRG: Or what other people think of you. So, there again, this thing of using these terms to identify yourself—how can you confidently use any term if every twenty, thirty, fifty years something is going to shift? People are going to have a different feeling about who they are, or other people are going to have a different feeling about who you are. So, in fifty years, gay may be a completely useless term, because it's not an adequate description of where you are now.

AO: Like how gays in the Fifties called themselves homosexuals, and you would be hard pressed to find a self-identifying homosexual in most cities today.

DRG: I think people use "queer" in the same way that black folks, especially the younger ones, use "niggah." You're trying to take this derogatory term and flip it around, and by owning it and using it on yourself, you're stealing its power. I never really quite bought that. I don't think you can completely steal its power. Because in order to steal its power, you have to change what it means to those other people who use it, not just how you use it. When you do that, then it starts to really lose its weight. It keeps shifting, and it shifts because how people feel about themselves shifts. It's difficult for me to use "queer" with any confidence. Perhaps right now, I feel in sort of a different place than what those words would seem to suggest. To some extent "queer" and "gay" really do seem like something that white boys in tight jeans and rainbow T-shirts use. And I'm not that thing; it's not an accurate reflection of me or where I'm at. I actually like masculinity a lot. I like femininity a lot. I don't know.

AO: Would you talk a bit about masculinity, and what it means to you?

DRG: So, masculinity... Wow! What do I think about masculinity? ...Well... first of all, it seems as much a construct as femininity. It's a performance. I actually figured that out kind of early on. And this goes along with what I was saying earlier about the perspective that being gay can give you. When I was about 16 or 17, a schoolmate of mine was always making passes at me. He was a very macho kind of boy. He wasn't obnoxious, but he was a very masculine boy, and he had a girlfriend. But that never stopped his interest in me. That never stopped him from making eyes, or touching or rubbing up against me. And that was the first time I went, "Huh, okay!" So, very early on, I realized the connection between desire and physical gesture and demeanor, between your private longings and your public face, was not connected, not related to one another.

AO: So you never felt a compromised masculinity growing up then? It was more an issue of how is it that I am masculine and also interested in men?

DRG: "How am I going to do this?" is what I thought. I liked my masculinity, and I liked masculinity in general. But, depending on whom I was around, I could be fey too. And my other "same-gender-loving" friends, some of them were certainly effeminate; but I thought they were fabulous people, so I didn't give a fuck. Also, I think being an actor or wanting to act, having that sort of sensibility, that training, and perspective really informed that. First of all, to act, you can't take anything that a human being does for granted. Behavior is a surface. You're always looking for the motivation behind, the contradiction. You're looking for when things don't match up. So, with that sensibility, masculinity seemed to me a series of gestures and postures. I'm quite serious. It's this kind of code—just as in the Nineteenth Century, there was a whole kind of acting form called Delsarte. It was literally a series of hand gestures and body positions. It was a whole, codified thing, and one particular hand gesture, or particular motion, or position of the hand expressed jealousy, another expressed sorrow, and another expressed contempt, and so on. And it just struck me that that's how masculinity worked. So, if I placed my hands on my hips like this, or if I stood like that, or if I turned my head like this—that was male. But, if I broke my wrist, if I let my arm flow through the air, if I crossed my legs—*that* was feminine. And I thought, "Ha! What horse shit! This is horse shit!" People, my peers, were actually buying into this: They thought that this was somehow organic, just naturally coming out of them. But, my response was, "Oh, please!" So, Marilyn Monroe is a performance. She's this extraordinary performance of femininity, in this really buxom and appealing package—but it's a performance of femininity. John Wayne is a performance of masculinity. It only seems natural because he never questions himself. What seems organic is merely unselfconscious. So, I think, to some extent, everybody is doing that. Looking back—it was kind of freeing for me, because I could do it or I could not do it, depending on whom I was with.

AO: You wanna talk about your writing? What becomes a topic and why it becomes a topic?

DRG: I think if you, especially if you write, I think that part of you can't help but come out, and of course my sexuality and sex life informs my writing. I mean, it certainly informs the love poetry that appears in those books. I mean, they're not addressed to women. And as I write more, I think I'm going to talk about it in a more direct way, in a more kind of confrontational way.

AO: But, your writing is not direct in terms of blackness. I think of something like, *A Museum in Your Name*, which is my favorite piece of yours. It's moving and stunning without being directly addressed to issues of blackness or gayness. Until the very end when race does come up, and in a very powerful way, but in a way that isn't necessarily the central thesis of the work. Would you like to talk about that?

DRG: Well, in terms of how central it is, blackness and gayness, I would have to say no, a qualified no. They inform, they color, they give perspective to—but they're not the central issue. I do think that this was a response to a lot of other stuff that I'd read and didn't like. You know, like, the Black Arts movement from the Seventies, Baraka, that kind of thing, which was all about that. At the same time, it's impossible to avoid. Race, sexuality, nationality: All of those things are the glass through which I see things. And because they've given me particular kinds of experiences, they compel me to see certain things in the world that other people do not. So, I use my identities, or those labels, as avenues to certain insights. But, in the end, I want to be more a citizen of the world. I want to be more in the world and not limited by my color, my sexuality, my country, my class, or any of those things. I want to be in the world and to talk about it, to see what it has to offer and what it has to say to me. So, is blackness and gayness central? Well, I guess yes and no.

The Color of Free: Jamaica 1996
by Staceyann Chin

The warm afternoon pins itself vulgar on the canvas of my memory.

I am on my way home from philosophy class when a circle of boys crowd and quickly herd my body through the open door of the boys bathroom. One of them slams the door shut. The sound of the lock clicking into place echoes and is then forgotten when the handsome boy in the Red Shirt turns round to face me.

"You don't have no mouth fi talk now, eh?" His voice is raspy. Almost sexy, I think, a kind sugar brown voice, like fresh-baked ginger cookies.

"Pussy have you tongue under lockdown, eh?" The question confuses me. It makes no sense that a large pink male mouth is whispering those words against the side of my face. I am a lesbian. I have been a lesbian for almost a year now. Ten months. Almost eleven.

I try to calm my nerves by counting the months inside my head.

"You don't have no mouth fi talk now, eh? What happen? Pussy got your tongue?" The question confuses me. How many of them are in here? A dozen, maybe thirteen, I couldn't count with them right up against me.

Count! My brain is screaming. Count!

"Why you so 'frighten a de big bamboo? You think it goin' hurt you? It not goin hurt you, you know, just make you get back to normal, quick!" White Shirt moves closer to me. Blue Shirt follows. The circle moves in.

Their intent is clear and I am far beyond frightened. Stay focused, Staceyann. And pay attention to the faces!

Red Shirt has a cleft in his chin. No— that's the boy in the blue shirt. What if they take off their shirts? How will I remember which of them did what? O my God, these boys were going to—Count, Staceyann. Count!

A large muscled arm wraps itself around my belly. Someone pulls at my navy blue bra. Breaks the strap. The left breast drops lower than the right. Red's hand snakes into my tank. The surprising smooth of his palm is silky on the loose breast. He *must* feel my heart jumping under his hand.

I lean my lower half away from the vaguely familiar bulge on my hip. Blue Shirt is nibbling on my left shoulder. Red's chest is beating urgent against my face. His sharp cologne tickled my nose. Cool Water. Davidoff, I think. Blue Shirt kisses my shoulder. Red Shirt presses his chest to my face.

Start counting, stupid—you will need the exact number later, later, when all of this is over.

The fleshy tongue fills my mouth. Red Stripe beer is bitter on his breath. He was probably playing dominoes before he came in here. Beer and dominoes go together in Jamaica. I like dominoes. His lips behind my ear. I used to play dominoes with my cousins in Montego Bay. Stubble prickling my neck. We always played— Cut Throat—every man for himself. No partners in here. I am playing by myself. Cut Throat. My body relaxes into the push and pull of the tug between them. Cut Throat. Wonder if I'll need therapy? But where does a lesbian get therapy in Jamaica?

Red's manicured fingers struggle with the simple knot at my waist. He has beautiful hands.

"Is what happen to this bloodclaat skirt?"

"Bus' it off, man." Blue is in a hurry.

"No man, she go need to put it on back," Red said as he turns my body round to face him.

I am so grateful. He seems a little kinder than the rest. Surer, his fingers reach out and undo the flame-colored sarong. The folds fall caressing at my feet. Why can't I match these faces to these shirts? What if I can't remember any of the faces? I can imagine me telling the officer that it was a red shirt, and a blue shirt, and a white—

I push Red's hands away from the crotch of my panties. He slaps me open-palm across my face, bruises the inside of my lip. I taste the trickle of blood spreading over my tongue. Red Shirt is now directly in front of me.

I am going to need therapy. I can see my body in the shiny mirror above the sink. I look slimmer in this reflection, not so chunky in the waist. But why can't I look at their faces?

The fingers are between my legs, I stand on tippy-toes to get away from the probing. They laugh when I do that. Red is in charge. His fingers explore the loose breast again, his hand thrusts me against the wet porcelain sink. The rough fabric of his shirt is itching my nose.

"Why you cut off all you long, long hair, eh, Baby-Love?" Red mutters the question, petulant, against the nape of my neck. I am surprised at his even breathing.

My mouth is crushed against his shoulder. I cannot speak. It's too much, I think. All that hair was too much. I'm the kind of dyke who likes easy hair. Short hair. Bald hair. No hair. Dyke hair.

"Answer me, you little raas-claat cunt!" His hand rakes across the shaved crown, down to my chin to tilt my head back against his shoulders. His fingernails are bruising my face. He should be more careful. They shouldn't leave any marks. What will I tell people about the bruises?

"You hear me? Answer me when me talk to you. You must try and make things easier for yourself, you hear me?" He pulls my head all the way back. His face is now touching mine but upside down, "I will break you neck, you know. Now why the fuck you cut you hair?"

Everything goes dead when the large metal lock clicks. The door opens.

My heart races its relief when I turn to recognize Andrew. I had twice met him at one of the secret gay house parties in the hills. The ones with the loud dance music where boys like him press themselves to other boys not so much like them. He is one of us. He won't let them hurt me. He is one of us. It's over, now. It's over. Oh my God! Nothing really happened and it's all over! Thank you, Jesus! Thank you, Jesus.

I bend to pick up my sarong. Red grabs a hold of my right arm.

"Ease up, there, Baby-Love. Don't go nowhere yet, we soon come back to you." Red turns to face Andrew.

"Alright, my youth. If you not for the cause, you must be against it. What you sayin? You leaving or you staying, with us or against us?"

Andrew pivots, as if to exit, and the lightning white rage bubbles up hot through the cistern of my constricted throat.

"Andrew, if you leave me here with them you won't live to see another sunrise!" The veiled threat jiggles my loose breast. Red fingers tighten around my arm. The little faggot is not going to leave me here! He is going to help me!

"You want me to tell you how I will do it?" I push my body against Red—to remind me that this is necessary, "I will tell everybody where you go at nights and what—"

"What you want me to do?" He cuts me off. "Me one can't fight all of them?"

I am almost sorry for him. But right now, I need his consideration more than he needs mine. "Andrew, if you leave me…"

"Alright, alright! I hear you the first time. I hear you the first time."

"So, Andrew, why you don't want to join in? You is a batty bwoy or what? Free pussy and you refusin'—you must be a sodomite or a priest—and I don't see no Bible in you hand. Sonny bwoy, we beat faggot just fi fun, you know. Is mus' bloodclaat batty you love! Is what you really sayin, you love man?"

"Yow, bredren we just might have fi deal with a faggot situation when we done with this one." Blue shirt hopped on the already unstable bandwagon.

Andrew stands straight up and then leans against the wall. His words are slow and deliberate.

"No, no, no—trust me, I love pussy just like the next man, but I don't like kill my own meat. I like it prepare and ready fi eat—ah mean ready fi fuck."

"What that supposed to mean?"

"Well, we all civilized people, right? We a big man, now, right? Right. We all get pussy all the time. It come to we—we no need fi run it down like ice-cream truck. Right?"

Red pushes me away from him and marches over to Andrew.

"Yow, don't feel is desperation make we have her in here, you know. We nah go fuck her because we can't get pussy—we trying to curb this lesbian business we hear bout her. We can't have them sodomite mongst we, free fi do all them nastiness. Make them feel is all good and well fi disrespect the way God put we down here fi live. Something have to be done bout this way of thinking that creeping on this island!"

Blue and White nod their agreement.

"Yes, man, we going fuck her to bring her back to the right way of thinking. We fucking her to save her from herself and from hellfire."

Andrew moves toward Red.

"What if somebody find out? What if the police find out?"

Red steps closer to Andrew.

"Who going tell them? You?"

Andrew is now nose to nose with Red. He stands his ground and delivers his piece.

"No, man, but just like I walk in here, somebody else can walk in too. Anybody can just walk in, the cleaning man, the plumber—anybody—and oonu say she a sodomite? What if she have some kinda fuck-up disease? What if she have AIDS?"

"The woman them get AIDS too?" Blue is visibly disturbed. Red steps back from Andrew.

No one is holding me now. And I am five feet from the door. Five small steps.

"Yes, man, the whole a them fuck each other in them batty and all kinda nastiness—you never know, and them have some disease worse than AIDS." Andrew is on a roll.

Four and a half tiny feet to the door. Four and a quarter. Four. All eyes are on Andrew.

"And you know, it quicker fi a man get AIDS from a woman than the other way around?"

Three and a half feet. Sarong wrapped around my hips. Left hand holding the ends together.

Three feet.

"And more woman have AIDS than man. Some disease you can get just by touching—"

My right hand is two inches from the door. "Where the bloodclaat you think you going? Oonu hold her!"

That split second that no one wants to touch me is all I need to swing the door back and run. And run. And run. And run. Across the grass and toward the parking lot. Through the red cars, the blue cars, the white cars. Down the seductive curve of Ring Road. Across the Arts Parking lot. Blue cars. Red cars. White cars. Green grass under my bare feet again. Over the wide expanse between Soc Sci and Nat Sci. Through the Nat Sci parking lot. Blue cars. Red cars. White cars. Hot asphalt slapping the soles of my feet. Through the Mona wire gate. Garden Boulevard, Violet Avenue, Begonia Drive. And then
home.

When I come up gasping from that experience I decide it is time to consider America.

What We Inherit
by Robert Vazquez-Pacheco

for Caleb Gardner Wright

Summer always brings all kinds of wonderful stuff: warm weather, longer days, summer nights, the beach, opulent green, and, of course, half-naked men. This year, summer brings another treat. This summer, my compadre- and comadre-to-be John and Tracey are having a baby. Well, she's having the baby. At this point, he's an interested observer. The baby will be my godson, investing an existing relationship with an even deeper emotional resonance for all of us. It is the symbol of love between good friends rather than one with any particular religious significance. Like most people today, we choose to invest rituals and traditions with our own meanings. So I will love my future godson and take on whatever responsibility his parents will grace me with. His imminent arrival fills me with an old-fashioned excitement and pride. Caleb will be the first infant, outside of my own blood relations, whom I hope to know well. I've known the children of friends but, like many gay men, the only kids I know are the ones I'm related to.

Once, during the heady days of the sexual revolution, I was presented with the possibility of becoming a father. My girlfriend, at the time, had missed her period and for a brief while, we were entertaining kid thoughts. We were both nineteen, kids ourselves, away from home for the first time, savoring the freedoms of college. I remember, however, being terrified at the possibility of fatherhood. I had seen some married gay men in my own family and they weren't necessarily happy men. Besides, I already knew that I was a gay man and probably wouldn't stay in the relationship with her. The world and its adventures (namely boys) called to me and I had all intentions of answering that call. Despite all my fears, I was also at the same time profoundly excited by the prospect of being a daddy. It turned out to be a false alarm and so ended my first and only opportunity to be a father.

It has been more than twenty years since I have thought about having children. My old girlfriend has disappeared, lost in time. As I watch Tracey grow larger with her son every time I see her, the thought of having kids is one I turn to more often. But, like many fantasies, the fantasy is always more attractive than the reality. It is, though, nice to entertain the thought every now and then, sorta like playing with the crystal ball I have on my desk. The most surprising thing about playing with this thought is the realization that I actually would like to have kids. As I settle into my forties, the thought of having children becomes an occasional fantasy, one tinged with regret. But it will never happen. I am HIV-positive and wouldn't risk trying to impregnate someone, putting them at risk for HIV infection. I have enough guilt in my life. Others have done it, though, and I applaud them. But I'm neither that brave nor that foolhardy.

It is a decision, however, I am quite comfortable with, the decision not to have kids, despite the moments of wistfulness. You know, I'm simply too selfish to have children (biological or adopted). Kids are a major responsibility (an obvious understatement) and I have just reached the point in time where I can function semi-responsibly on my own behalf. More than anything, the growing reality of Caleb brings two interrelated ideas to my awareness, like two gifts he brings to his godfather in his tiny brown fists. (I couldn't resist the cute metaphor. I am talking about a baby, after all, and as we all know children are the repositories of sentiment in this society). In any case, when I think of Caleb, I think of two things. I think of what the future holds and I also think of what we inherit.

One of the interesting things about being HIV-positive, especially in the days before the protease moment, is that if one was smart, one tended to live one's life focused in the here and now. You had no choice: Pain can make you very present-oriented. Although many wisdom traditions suggest that we "be here now," the reality is that many people, regardless of physical health, are always looking toward and living for a future time.

HIV infection changed that for many, just as all life-threatening conditions or situations do. Personally, I've never lived for a future time. Managing the present took up all of my time. Besides I'm bad at planning. For me, having HIV intensified the "nowness" of life as I knew and still know it, grounding me in the daily and mundane realities of chronic sinusitis and weird skin rashes, especially in the days before protease. For many people with AIDS, especially now as the protease moment ends, the future simply holds the prospect of increasing illness. Not exactly something to look forward to. Protease had changed that for a while but as time passes and the side effects (like heart attacks) increase, we see the pale rider of illness return.

But Caleb makes me think of the future as something beyond side effects, hospital beds, incontinence, and disability checks. That's what children do: like Leonardo da Vinci's painting of the young St. John the Baptist, they always point, smiling and enigmatic, toward something unseen. Children point to the future or, rather, they are the future, carrying both the romance and the weight of the future within them. Let me say here I don't want to overly romanticize kids. We are a society that loves the romance of children but doesn't necessarily address the reality of kids very well. Besides, visions of cherubs aside, children can be some of the cruelest human beings alive. Just think back to the schoolyard. I harbor few illusions about the little darlings.

Nor do I project any HIV-positive Aschenbach-type fantasies of youth and beauty over some HIV-negative Tadzio. But more than any plan I can make, Caleb in his mom's belly very concretely points to the future, to years down the line in a way very immediate and real. His growing up is potentially part of my future. It is that future that interests me now. The little guy strikes a chord within me that resonates with an optimism discarded (by necessity I might add) some time ago. Despite my flip and constant cynicism, I grow a little hopeful, a little excited about the future. Caleb makes me think of possibilities.

What he also makes me think about, the second and more ambiguous of the gifts he offers, is what has been left to me from those gone before me, those family members claimed by the plague. I think of my inheritance. I've lived most of my adult life as an "out" gay man. Most of that life has also been, for better or worse, during the age of AIDS. I have a well-loved and closely-knit family consisting of my blood relations. I also have another family, equally as important, of friends and loved ones, many of them gay men. At this point, I refuse to count how many of either family have died from whatever causes since I've lost so many. Those losses have been staggering and unrelenting and unfortunately they will continue for a long time. Life is loss. There were times that it seemed, as melodramatic as it sounds, that life as a gay man in the Eighties and Nineties was just an endless series of deaths: the deaths of friends, lovers, former lovers, former friends, relatives, acquaintances, tricks, colleagues, rivals, etc. Out of the many unanswered questions that rise up like hungry ghosts from these deaths (because death always leaves us with questions), the one that pursues me like Hamlet's father is the one that asks "What do we, as gay men, leave behind for our inheritors, the gay men who follow us?"

Inheritance for straight folks and biological families is defined and supported by various legal, religious and societal institutions. But what do gay men leave each other? Obviously, I'm not speaking here of real estate or other forms of property, which can be disposed of through wills and other legal mechanisms. The legacy I speak of is something far less tangible but arguably infinitely more precious. My cousin Joey died in the fall of 1995. For me, he was probably the most influential gay man I'd ever known, showing me by example how to live as an "out" gay Latino, in the family, in the Bronx, with pride and without apology. He remained, until his death and even after it, a vital and well-loved member of my family, fully integrated into our collective life. After he died, my aunt Hilda moved into his co-op apartment in the northeast Bronx. As she was cleaning out the apartment, she came across a large collection of Seventies and early Eighties porno magazines that belonged to him. By coincidence, I was visiting New York at that time. So I, quite selflessly I might add, took responsibility for Joey's porno, bringing it back to D.C. with me. The porno and a photograph stolen from my mom of Joey and me as kids are all that physically remain of him for me.

Some time after that, I was helping my friend Bruce clean out his storage space. Inside the space amongst the china and the files was a large box filled with late Seventies and early Eighties porno. It belonged to Bruce's lover, Brian, who had died almost two years ago. Bruce had never gone through it, putting it in storage until he was ready to deal with it. Remembering Joey's porno, I took possession of this cache. What is interesting to me is what these old magazines, the inherited sites of dead gay men's desires, mean to me. I don't generally like pornography, being more interested in sexual reality rather sexual fantasy. I don't usually respond intellectually or emotionally to porno, either, and I don't morbidly obsess about death, at least not any more than any other gay man living with AIDS. Keeping these magazines, however, became important to me as they formed part of a larger and more complex inheritance that I begin now to understand.

What is this inheritance captured inside old porno magazines, resulting in a "deeper" reading of *Honcho, Jock* and *Mandate*? These old porno rags become symbols. They form a legacy that begins by redefining desire, by finding a message beyond the obvious one caught in glossy pages of hard-ons and assholes, one which points, just like St. John, to something implied. Moving beyond the glassy stares, frozen features and oiled skin, these images speak to me of the courage of men who dared to do what they believed in; men who followed the dictates of their hearts, despite the dictates of society. Outcasts and degenerates for some and AIDS victims for others, for me they become the quiet heroes who simply lived their lives. Their gifts to those of us still alive aren't the proverbial wages of sin, understood to be the closed door of death, but rather their gift is the open door of life, a door opened by the power of desire. The desire I'm speaking of here is not the limited area of sexuality or sexual behavior but desire transformed into the vastness of the experience we call life. Perhaps this is what Rainier Maria Rilke called "the Open" in the ninth "Duino Elegy." It's not desire as it's understood by the Buddhists either: the desire for sensation and experience, which leads to craving, pain and suffering. I speak of a desire that burns within us, a desire to live in truth that, if we are lucky, can lead to freedom.

These magazines tell me that, despite the daily indignities that make up life with AIDS, the life that is actually destroyed by this epidemic is the life that remains unlived. So this legacy of desire is the whispered command, through the pages of erections and spread butt cheeks, by dead brothers who say to me "live life." But it's also something I hear when I put my ear to Tracey's belly. This inheritance of desire and life, in turn, becomes my legacy to Caleb, the gift of a gay man living with a life-threatening disease to a newborn baby boy. Hopefully I can point to something that is transcendent not only for him, but for others. His gifts to me I return to him with the accumulated interest of my experience. He and I may eventually accept responsibility for each other, making sure that each of us lives life beyond the constricting grasp of fear and prejudice. But that is only a hope, something I have more of these days. The world opens up with desire and freedom and so Caleb and I present its marvels to each other like dignitaries exchanging articles of great worth. And what is it I find contained within his gifts? A fearlessness, a dream and ultimately a sense of joy in life I will use and then leave behind me for all who follow me. Desire and freedom are my legacy and my inheritance, what we inherit.

Caleb Gardner Wright was born on July 10, 1996.

(Re-) Recalling Essex Hemphill: Words to Our Now
by Thomas Glave

And so always, now: recalling a life and the ever-renascent power of vision that yet fuels the source and matrix of an essence; invoking the *now* of your undying spirit and refeeling it, reclaiming it, it is to you, of course, whom I write, Essex. In this *now* that is here. And always now. Resolute. Writing to you with the certainty that the abiding force of your passion has not ceased refiguring you and your words ever bolder in our memory. We need only hark to the spirit; it beckons. We need only listen; it speaks:

I prowl in scant sheaths of latex.
I harbor no shame.
I solicit no pity.
I celebrate my natural tendencies,
photosynthesis, erotic customs.
I allow myself to dream of roses
though I know
the bloody war continues.[i]

We attend the voice. But of course. Yours. As, yes, the bloody wars continue. As viral nights, official subterfuge, and unofficial antifreedom engenderings continue.[ii] So attending, conscious of the viral nights and the engenderings that threaten even as, for some, they beguile, we revisit your voice, within—engaging once more those troubled silences, yearnings, from which you always addressed us: those rooms, cells, corridors of blue tones and shadowed dreams where—so it obtained and obtains still—too many of us languished through those returning *nows* of our most pressing need, evoked in your language's echoes and refrains; as, hearing and reading on the open page those lives both yours and ours so boldly-lovingly revealed, we walked most closely with you when we did not resist your calls, and in the walking drew together ever more aligned in the steadfast power of all our names. "The memory cannot replace the man,"[iii] one of our brothers in recent years wrote about you; yet we know that it is memory precisely, exercised in judicious concert with the clarifying, edifying words you gave us that configured anew the previously defined and circumscribed—ourselves and others— that will not only determine our survival but embolden it. Ennoble it. It has been said, and we recall: we were never meant to survive. Not here. No, not then or now. Not in the gorge of a grasping empire poisoned by the recurring venoms of its own antihumanity. Here, now, we can never forget that, as you did not survive, others still are falling. Falling beneath the policeman's baton, or raped by it[iv]; expiring in the electric chair, decaying along lonely roads after the body has been chained behind a truck and dragged[v]—the body historically and contemporarily fetishized, sodomized, demonized; now again whipped, sawed, beheaded, carved, and marked with swastikas this week or with whatever the terrorism and terror that prevail and fester in depraved human imaginations will next resurrect and refashion from those dis-eased realms. As you would have asked, we must: who, in this now, will next laugh at the opportunity to view "a nigger's brains"[vi] as, shotgun-armed, on Hitler's birthday, they stand viciously cruel guard over his or her eighteen-year-old form and aim their guns in a high school library where these kinds of things simply *do not happen*, as popular prevarications insist. Such horrors should occur only in the "inner city," someone will say, has said.[vii] Not "here." Not in this now.

"But we're in the United States," you doubtless would have said; your seer's most mordant irony confronting misconception, sweeping aside revisionist muddyings of present and past. "In the United States, where these sorts of things always happen. But yes, believe it," you surely would have said, "they always happen here."

"In the United States," you might have said, "where such events are always now. Yes. And always here."

Regarding the caveats illumined in the stanzas you left behind, so we might summon your voice admonishing us in this now, Essex. Knowing as we summon that amid the general incoherence and hysteria of our time still reigns the especial brand of expedient historical revisionism that perennially subverts and travesties integrity. That bastardizes honesty. The same revisionism that, by dint of purposefully *dis*placed memory, ever befriends the spiritual lassitude and anti-intellection that disdain humanity's most hopeful ascensions as much as they imperil its ultimate dignity. Our futures would without question be imperiled, you told us, if, sometime discarding vigilance, we dared curtsey to that enduring U.S. mind-altering favorite, ahistoricism; if we dared ever forget—dismiss—the chains and conflagrant crosses, fire hoses and hemp that preceded, that loom among us still, and which were and are inexorably linked to the seductions and self-deceptions of the unconscionable amnesia that, in all quarters, nurtures bigotry and ignorance alike. Seduction bears its price, you told us. The words of lesser poets who repudiated truth and embraced mediocrity's diminished and diminishing returns have long since been forgotten. But you were not and would not be seduced, not in that way, and—only one of your precious gifts to us—enjoined us not to forget. In the fierceness of this *now*, it is exactly the radical art and life-effort of conscientious remembrance that, against revisionism's erasures and in pursuit of our survival, must better become our duty. Memory in this regard becomes responsibility; as responsibility and memory both become us.

In this now, we celebrate your life and language, Essex. So celebrating, we know that we re-recall you in what is largely, to borrow from another visionary, a "giantless time."[viii] The sheer giantry of your breathing presence has passed. Now present and future warriors assume the struggles your language named. Those warriors—ourselves and others—will be compelled to learn, as you did and made manifest, that all hauls toward truth—toward truest freedom—will require intellectual and spiritual vigor, not venality; ardor, not arrogance; forthrightness, not cowardice. You taught us: the habit of "tossing shade" at our sisters and brothers has become more than ever an outmoded and grossly stupid one, ill-afforded, born out of our most pathetic shortsightedness and best laid aside. In this now, we will no longer be able to afford the blood sport that we have so long adored—self-contempt—that should long ago have been fitted with both bridle and brakes. We will have to learn, *finally*, that only the most autodestructive joy will emerge from ripping each other when most afraid to love each other because we remain each's easiest targets. We will have to remember *and believe* what Baby Suggs, hands outstretched, told us: to love our skins, our flesh, and above all the heart—"For this is the prize."[ix] Centered in a love generous and secure enough to embrace others, but beginning first and foremost with ourselves, our sisters will no longer be our "bitches," our darkest no longer our shame. No more Mandingoizing of ourselves in search of the biggest, blackest rod that will provide us with the most rageful sundering we believe we so richly deserve; to hell with who's-blacker-than-who snipes, who's-more-educated-than-who foolishness. We will know that the claiming of pride in ourselves will require genuinely loving behavior among ourselves—"the prize"—and not refuge in the easy rhetoric whose glibness loves the fleeting moment but loathes the task. Aspiring toward our greater humanity, we will be compelled to *think*, and think better, in short; jettisoning trendiness and catchwords for rigorous self-analysis that at its best will be both compassionate and wise—the site of true sublimity, where reside all possibilities most supreme. Demanding of us that greatness of spirit which you knew we could ultimately attain, you spoke:

You judge a woman
by what she can do for you alone
but there's no need
for slaves to have slaves.

You judge a woman
by impressions you think you've made.

Ask and she gives,
take without asking,
beat on her and she'll obey,

throw her name up and down the streets
like some loose whistle—
knowing her neighbors will talk.

...we so-called men,
we so-called brothers
wonder why it's so hard
to love *our* women
when we're about loving them
the way america
loves us.[x]

So you exhorted and exhort us still to question ourselves, and act bravely, humanely, in the questioning. The exercise of listening in this regard can be only a beginning, for, as we must learn and re-learn, it is the synthesis of multilayered understanding with humanitarian action that will propel us closer toward that deeper regard for and commitment to ourselves— knowledge critical to our lives in the star-spangled slaughterhouse at the end of the atrocity-littered twentieth century; knowledge we cannot afford *not* to own. You showed us, and we note: lynchings have not stopped, but now proceed smoothly on automatic pilot. Assaults against abortion clinics progress from tightly clutched rifles aimed at doctors and patients to stunningly well-hurled bombs. Black churches are torched to skulking ash; a Guinean immigrant is riddled with bullets by police in a city known to boast of its worldliness and "internationalism";[xi] affirmative action shrivels; a gay man in Alabama is beaten to death, his dead body incinerated atop an ignoble pyre of two car tires,[xii] as a young gay Wyoming student's skull is literally smashed before his comatose form is tied to a fence;[xiii] Haitian refugees are scorned in south Florida and remanded to the poverty, violence, and state repression they fled; a white supremacist fires shots into a Jewish community center, wounding several children, as he issues his personal "wake-up call to America to kill all the Jews";[xiv] AIDS and cancer flare among people of color, women and children vanish from city streets and reappear eviscerated on rural-route shoulders, and right-wing hate mongers smile upon it all. Now, right now, somewhere, black women, black lesbians, are being raped, battered, assaulted; now, right now, black men, black gay men, are running for their lives from baseball bats, knives, ravenous police. A butchered drag queen floats face down in a river as another struts fiercely on in her own image; a black baby shudders for the taste of crack; a black teenager contemplates suicide, or suicide on the installment plan—drugs; two black men on death row yearn to hold each other, two black women seeking heat and shelter for their children dream, somehow, of kissing each other's breasts, and which of us, you asked, will be there to testify? What is our responsibility for their survival, you demanded, and what part do we claim in their silence?

What is our responsibility to *all* of them, we must ask, and which of their faces are in fact our own?

You showed us, Essex: employing the compassionate action that transposes to wisdom and love among ourselves, enhancing ourselves and others, it remains our task as the inheritors of your brother-love and vision to charge, uncertain but unified, in challenge of the lingering repressions born out of hatreds renewed and combined. As people of color in a time both giantless (for the moment) and laced with ignorance and widespread capitulation, however and to whomever we define it, the destructive and limiting pastimes of self-aggrandizement and serving in the master's house with the master's tools will serve not us but only our enemies.[xv] It was your vigilance, Essex, along with that of our passed-on seers Audre Lorde, Joe Beam, Pat Parker, and others, that served and serves still as warning that not only language and its power to silence or muddle must be critiqued, but also every aspect of our waking reality, and the malignancies that corrupt and abrade it. We remember:

> Some of the best minds of my generation would have us believe that AIDS has brought the gay and lesbian community closer and infused it with a more democratic mandate. That is only a partial truth, which further underscores the fact that the gay community still

operates from a one-eyed, one gender, one color perception of *community* that is most likely to recognize blond before Black, but seldom the two together. ...We are communities engaged in a fragile coexistence if we are anything at all. Our most significant coalitions have been created in the realm of sex. What is most clear for Black gay men [and lesbians] is this: we have to do for ourselves *now*, and for one another *now*, what no one has ever done for us. ...Our only sure guarantee of survival is that which we construct from our own self-determination. White gay men may only be able to understand and respond to oppression as it relates to their ability to obtain orgasm without intrusion from the church and state. White gay men are only "other" in this society when they choose to come out of the closet. But all Black men [and women] are treated as "other" regardless of whether we sleep with men or women— our Black skin automatically marks us as "other."[xvi]

You invoke the *now*; we traverse it. Traverse it knowing that despite this age-old "otherization" of ourselves, our cultural work continues to blossom. Books are written, poems penned; films are photographed into being, dances envisioned and performed; paintings are colored, plays explode out of shy cauls, and music in all forms lilts forth from gazes steadily widening. We move outward in the wake of your lessons. That we have come this far, this long, in itself testifies to humanity's recurring force and shine as it does you and your words' legacies proud. In the giantless time that changes daily to one of our own giantry, in the here of our now, our status as "other" (and who cares what the naysayers think, anyway?) pales beside our passion and strength, fueled by your gifts of lyric and anger, joy and outrage, that, alongside our own, will long outlive the mean-toned landscape through which we presently walk without your presence beside us in the living flesh. As millions of our own are executed globally—Liberia, Rwanda, Haiti; Sierra Leone, the Sudan, the Congo—we remember; as black men and women and our sisters and brothers of color languish (or die) in the rotting prisons and slums of the slaughterhouse and sheets and swastikas are donned beneath conflagrant crosses yet flaring, between homo-haters' brickbats still hurled, we know, holding you within our hands and behind our eyes that this *now*, the risky always-second of the present moment that is the unending and beginning spiral of all consciousness, is ours. Is us. Here. "Well, then *be* it," you would surely say, and mean it. "In america," you wrote, "place your ring/on my cock/where it belongs./Long may we live/to free this dream."[xvii] The voice of the seer. Long may we all live, Essex, walking through this antifreedom land; eyes and hands lifted toward our greatest selves as our spirits soar with yours. The flesh, so propelled onward, cannot be erased. The words become our hearts. *We who are alive. With you. In this now.* Graced by that sheen. By that brother-light.

So we progress. Celebrate. Re-recall. The need guiding our hands. In this now that is you, Essex, and memory, voice. Memory voiced. Your enduring gifts, that are always, now.

This essay was first published in Callaloo, *Vol. 23, No. 1 (2000).*

NOTES:

[i] Essex Hemphill, "Heavy Breathing," in *Ceremonies: Prose and Poetry* (New York: Plume/Penguin Books, 1992), 4-5.
[ii] I refer specifically here to the continuing rise in the U.S. of white nationalist, white supremacist hate groups, including neo-Nazi and "skinhead" organizations and so-called "patriot" groups, all of which demand another essay's comprehensive analysis and discussion. More information on the proliferation of hate groups can be accessed from the Birmingham, Alabama-based Southern Poverty Law Center, an excellent resource; and from the Institute for Research and Education on Human Rights, in Kansas City, Missouri.
[iii] See Robert Reid-Pharr, "Memory and Man: Essex Hemphill," *Gay Community News* 24:3-4.

iv Recalling the Abner Louima case of New York City. Louima, a Haitian-born immigrant to the U.S., was physically tortured in a bathroom of the 70th police precinct, Brooklyn, by Officer Justin Volpe on August 9th, 1997. The principal and, to many, most horrifying cruelty inflicted upon Louima by his assailant was Volpe's sodomizing him with a toilet plunger's handle, causing Louima severe injuries to his rectum and bladder; after which Volpe brandished the stick in Louima's face. Louima was also threatened by Volpe with death if he told anyone about the incident. After almost two years of in-court wrangling, bureaucratic and other tensions, and outrage displayed by citizens activist and non-activist alike, Justin Volpe pled guilty on May 25, 1999 to federal charges, including conspiracy to obstruct justice and conspiracy to deprive civil rights.

v Remembering the literally torturous death of James Byrd Jr.: a forty-nine-year-old black man who on June 7, 1998 was picked up not far from Jasper, Texas by John William King, Shawn Berry, both 21, and Lawrence Brewer, 31, all whites. Byrd was driven by the three men in their pickup truck to a deserted area, where they then chained him to the back of the truck and dragged him along the road for three miles, toward Jasper. Byrd was soon decapitated by a concrete drainage culvert; his torso wound up in a ditch, approximately a mile from where the rest of his body was discovered by a passing driver and later by police. When found, Byrd's face was spray-painted black. King's very body entered the case as evidence for the prosecution, marked as it was with racist and neo-Nazi tattoos, the words "Confederate Knights of America" and "Aryan Pride" (see endnote ii), and a tattoo of a black person being tree-lynched. King was convicted of murder on February 23, 1999, and sentenced to death—the first white sentenced to death in Texas for killing a black person since the state reinstituted capital punishment in 1976.

vi Comment attributed to either Eric Harris, 18, or Dylan Klebold, 17, as they shot and killed black student Isaiah Shoels, 18, in the library of Columbine High School, Littleton, Colorado, on April 20, 1999—Adolf Hitler's birthday. Shoels was one of thirteen people killed, not including the two killers' suicides, and one of two people of color.

[vii] Cf. the comment made by Columbine High English teacher Paula Reed on an April 21, 1999 *Oprah Winfrey* TV show: "This is a school that's very safe. ...It's in a community that cares and... supports its schools. You...think of...things like this happening in the inner city, where maybe socioeconomics are a problem, where poverty is a problem. That's not the issue here at Columbine. We are predominantly an upper-middle-class neighborhood..." [My italics.]

[viii] From an unpublished poem by Gwendolyn Brooks.

[ix] See Toni Morrison, *Beloved* (New York: Alfred A. Knopf, 1987).

[x] Hemphill, "To Some Supposed Brothers," in *Ceremonies*, 132.

[xi] In reference to Amadou Diallo, twenty-two-year-old Guinean immigrant and street vendor living in the Bronx, who was shot and killed by four white police officers in the Bronx on February 4, 1999. Forty-one shots were fired at Diallo, of which nineteen hit him. Diallo was unarmed when shot, was not known to possess any firearms, and had no previous criminal background. According to court testimony by Sean Carroll, one of the shooting officers and a defendant during the officers' trial in Albany, New York (moved there from New York City due to defense attorneys' fear that "public clamor" over the shooting would make a "fair trial" for the officers "impossible" in the Bronx), Diallo, just before the officers opened fire, had been acting "suspiciously," "slinking" back toward the building where he lived. Carroll also testified that Diallo, to the officers' eyes, fit the "general description" of a "serial rapist" who had been active in that part of the Bronx; Carroll also stated that he suspected that Diallo might have been a "lookout for a push-in robber." On February 25, 2000, the officers were acquitted of all charges, including murder in the second degree, manslaughter in the first and second degrees, criminally negligent homicide, and reckless endangerment (See Jane Fritsch, "4 Officers in Diallo Shooting Are Acquitted of All Charges," *The New York Times*, February 26, 2000, A1; and Tara George, "4 Diallo Cops Go Free," the *New York Daily News*, February 26, 2000, 2).

[xii] Billy Jack Gaither, 39, a white gay resident of Sylacauga,

Alabama, was picked up in Sylacauga on the evening of February 19, 1999 by Steven Eric Mullins, 25, and Charles Butler, Jr., 21, both also white, and driven to an isolated nearby area, where he was beaten by both men, forced into the trunk of his own car, driven farther, then beaten to death with a wooden axe handle. His body was placed on two tires his killers had set afire. Mullins and Butler later confessed that they had killed Gaither principally because of his sexual orientation; Butler stated that he had been angry at Gaither because the latter had allegedly made a "pass" at him.

xiii Matthew Shepard, 21, a gay white University of Wyoming student, was beaten into a coma on October 6, 1998 by Aaron McKinney and Russell Henderson, both 21 and also white. Shepard was found the following day, laterally tied to a fence. His skull had been crushed by his assailants' hitting him with a pistol. He died on October 12, 1998.

xiv The actions and words of white supremacist Buford Furrow, Los Angeles, August 1999.

xv See Audre Lorde, "The Master's Tools Will Never Dismantle the Master's House," in *Sister Outsider: Essays and Speeches* (Freedom, Calif.: Crossing Press, 1984), 110-113.

xvi Hemphill, "Does Your Mama Know about Me?" in *Ceremonies*, 41.

xvii Hemphill, "American Wedding," in *Ceremonies*, 171.

sassy b. gonn,
or Searching for Black Lesbian Elders
by Lisa C. Moore

Riverview ... it was an amusement park at Belmont and Western. Us kids would beg some dough from our parents, and take that long-ass El [elevated train] ride. Who would be on the El from the South Side? Us kids, and the sissies. With their tight pants, their white T-shirts, their lipstick, their earrings. ... Honey, some of 'em be so buff they looked like Mr. Alice, talking 'bout, 'Chile!' Shoot, nobody cared about nobody being gay!

[But] lesbian's different.

— *Jackie Anderson, age 57*

Springtime in Texas

In March of 1999, I began collecting black-and-white photographs of older black women. I'd hang the framed pictures in my living room and gaze at their studied expressions. I found solace in their wrinkled black and brown hands and beautiful lined faces. Since starting graduate school in the fall of 1998 I had been feeling overwhelmed. There weren't many black people—students, professors or staff—on campus, and I missed the family I'd left in Atlanta. I figured I could at least surround myself with black people in my house.

I was studying the intersections between New Orleans, Cuba and Haiti, but I'd discovered that lots of other people were studying those intersections. What would be so special about my research? A friend of mine said I should study something very close to my heart, and then the answers would come. I thought my hometown of New Orleans was close to my heart. Then I had the Dream.

The Dream: I was taking a test that I seemed to have no answers for. I kept looking at the clock, and at my blank answer sheet, when suddenly the phone rang; it was a young woman from the dean's office, telling me to come and pick up my master's degree. I told her there was some mistake, and hung up the phone. I went back to my test, and began to sweat because I still had no answers, but I had to turn in my test soon. The phone rang again; the young woman repeated, "You need to come pick up your master's; you've already qualified." Then I woke up.

I sat up, kind of dazed, then padded into my living room to open the blinds. I looked around and saw the sun fall on my old ladies. As they stared back at me, I felt a sudden *whoosh!*, and then came the epiphany: Study my own!

Asking the questions

What was life like for black lesbians prior to U.S. racial integration? Were there black gays and lesbians living in black communities? If so, were they named? By whom? What were they called? Were they marginalized or integrated within the black community? What role did they play within their segregated communities? Was their sexuality perceived as crucial to that role?

These were some of the questions I posed in beginning my academic research, studying oral histories of older black lesbians. In 1997, I edited and published *does your mama know? An Anthology of Black Lesbian Coming Out Stories*. By the fall of 1998, *does your mama know?* was in its third printing, and I was at the end of production for Sharon Bridgforth's *the bull-jean stories*. I had also started graduate school. Later that year I would begin producing *the bull-jean stories* audio CD. Call me an over-achiever.

I had been looking for black lesbian voices for a few years. I remember older women approaching me at readings for *does your mama know?*, commending me for my efforts; they said they'd been waiting a long time for a book that somehow reflected their lives. Since then, I had entered the academy and published *the bull-jean stories*: fictional accounts of a 1930s black bulldagger in her quest for love. My parents had regaled me with stories of black life in general in the 1950s and 1960s, so I had somewhat of an overview of those decades. But I searched for the real women's voices that are so much a part of my identity. Surely some other scholar had broached this particular subject: the treatment of black lesbians prior to integration. Where were my elders?

While searching for literature, I found that no scholar had broached this particular subject. I did find an essay in *Creating a Place for Ourselves*, edited by Brett Beemyn (1997), about black gay men's drag balls in Chicago in the 1950s.[1] But that's as close as I got. It seemed the validity I sought within academe did not include all of me.[2]

My academic field, anthropology, has wrestled with questions of who is qualified to study "the other" for the past twenty years or so. In the 1993 essay, "How native is a 'native' anthropologist?," Kirin Narayan contends that the dichotomy of native/non-native and insider/outsider anthropology is no longer useful: "we might more profitably view each anthropologist in terms of shifting identifications amid a field of interpenetrating communities and power relations. The loci along which we are aligned with or set apart from those whom we study are multiple and in flux."[3] Examples of those parts of our cultural identity that could shift our "native" status are education, class, sexuality, and age. One or more of these may at any time make us more insider or outsider, depending upon who is being studied. I, a relatively young, college-educated, light-skinned, black lesbian, who grew up poor yet had a passing acquaintance with a very rich grandfather, am proposing to study old black lesbians of varying class, educational backgrounds and skin colors. What do we have in common that makes us both native to the same tribe?

Is it even safe to say that I can make sexuality our common bond? Since I also propose that the naming of "lesbian" may not necessarily be used within black communities, i.e., to be lesbian is to be white, then sexuality—or at least the naming of it—comes into question. Heteronormativity exists on the surface of black culture; to publicly acknowledge a different sexuality may get you tossed out of the club, so to speak. The unspoken can sometimes be very loud, however. The lack of public discourse on gays and lesbians in black communities, by black communities, is becoming a deafening silence.

"'Being home' refers to the place where one lives within familiar, safe, protected boundaries; 'not being home' is a matter of realizing that home was an illusion of coherence and safety based on the exclusion of specific histories of oppression and resistance, the repression of differences even within oneself."[4] Those familiar, safe, protected boundaries in black communities are those heteronormative ones: straight, black, a shared history based on slavery. But what happens when one's own community oppresses? Is it safe to be all that you are? Will it be safe for older black lesbians (my term) to talk to me, a potential outsider? Does being a lesbian mean that I will never be home in black communities? I think not; I think that the stories of these older black lesbians might tell of how difference is talked about within the black mainstream.

does your mama know? focuses on the concept of home, and whether being all of one's self means one loses a place in one's community. Most of the contributors wrote of either losing family and community, finding new community, or staying put in their original (black) community without consequence. While on the book tour, I met quite a few older women, grandmothers, who wished the book had been available when they were younger. I also met young women who wanted to know where the elders are. These young women knew about the rumors of whose auntie and whose cousin might be "that way," but had no real hard facts—other than the knowledge that their Aunt Winnie had lived with a woman for 25 years.

But obtaining this kind of information could be a challenge. My status as a publisher may get me into some older black lesbians' living rooms, but would it be enough to get my informants to even agree to be audio taped? What if I promised to use pseudonyms when writing about them? Would I be welcomed in as a native daughter, or will the other parts of my identity form a wall too large for old folks to see around?

My methods

I come from a black community that values the oral; storytelling is an art form. I also live and produce in a world—

academic and otherwise—that privileges the written over the oral. Due to a dearth of research on older black lesbians, especially as it relates to the 1950s,[5] I decided early on that I would need to conduct oral histories, specifically life histories, and create a space for these women's voices within the academy.

Life history is a type of oral history that is very personal; one individual's personal memories, as opposed to a group memory or national memory. Of course, a life history must be viewed through the lens of time (how old is the informant? how much do they remember?) and the informant's social position within their community. It is important to see a life history as just that, a life history, subject to the forces that have shaped that particular individual, and not necessarily as representative of a community's culture. Nevertheless, life histories can be very valuable when trying to construct a community history. For my purposes, I am trying to interject black lesbian histories into black communities, and add black lesbian histories into gay and lesbian communities. I would like to eventually construct black lesbian communities' history, especially as it relates to geographic location.

When writing ethnography, life histories can be used effectively to illustrate a community history. For my research, the communities overlap according to race, sexuality, gender and age, as well as class. Problems of subjectivity surface, however, when the interviewer/ethnographer and the informant are one and the same. Life history focuses on the story of one's self, but the conversation is between the informant and the interviewer, and later, the reader. In my research, I hope that the older black lesbians' voices speak as loud as mine; I hope I put myself in context, and don't talk about myself too much.

What follows are excerpts from two older black lesbian oral histories. I've particularly included their words on race and sexuality issues in their lives.

Summertime in Chicago

I was at a table signing books at the National Women's Music Festival in Bloomington, Indiana, Memorial Day weekend of

1997, when a tall black woman dressed in butch attire—blue jeans with a heavy belt buckle, pink men's shirt, black blazer, and a short Afro under a Greek fisherman's cap—approached my table. The name tag said Jackie Anderson, and identified her as a workshop leader on lesbians and breast cancer. We began talking, and I soon found out she was from Chicago, and taught college courses in philosophy. I remember her saying, "Nobody's interested in an old crone like me," but then laughing.

The next year, she invited me to sell books at a Yahimba conference she helped to organize. I had already been to Chicago in late 1997 to read and sign books at three black lesbian events, so I was happy to return, especially since I wouldn't be reading. I didn't see much of her at that conference; she was busy making sure everything ran smoothly. But I do remember, at the closing ceremony, watching from my bookseller's table as the conference attendees surrounded her and honored her as the lone woman there over age 50. She was quite embarrassed at the attention.

When I called to ask permission for her oral history, she said she wouldn't have much to say about being a black lesbian during segregation, but I was certainly welcome to come to Chicago and ask away. She explained that she didn't come out until the 1970s, but that she vividly remembers what segregation was like.

I arrived in June 2000 at Jackie's home in Evanston, Illinois, on the one day she didn't have a meeting or softball game scheduled. She explained that she'd just joined a recreational softball league after not exercising for years, and she was "having a ball!," no pun intended. We soon settled in with drinks at her kitchen table.

Jackie was born Jacqueline Edith Kennedy in November of 1942, on the South Side of Chicago, in an area that was then called Bronzeville. She is a second-generation Chicagoan and fourth-generation college graduate, and the only child of her mother; her father has at least one other daughter that Jackie knows about. Jackie's mother was also born in Chicago, but Jackie's maternal grandmother was originally from Gaston, Alabama. Her grandmother was a teacher by trade, but only single women were allowed to teach; after marriage, she became a seamstress. Jackie didn't know much about her maternal grandfather, only that he was probably from Birmingham, and was a dentist; he died six years before Jackie was born. Jackie's maternal grandparents were college educated, her grandmother at Spelman College and grandfather at Morehouse College. Her grandparents arrived in Chicago the day of the race riot in 1919; as Jackie puts it, "That was their entree to Chicago." Jackie's mother was born one year later; two other children followed.

Jackie also doesn't know much about her father; her parents, who had married in 1940, separated before Jackie was 2 years old. She does know that her father's people "had education"; her father's mother was a schoolteacher at a school where her aunt was the principal. When I remarked that education seemed to be highly prized in her family, Jackie replied, "I'm part of that generation. I think it was highly prized whether one was ever going to necessarily get the opportunity to get an education or not. There was a very, very, very, very, *very* powerful ethos with African Americans, or Negroes I think we were back then, us 'coloreds,' that it was a route out. [Jackie used the finger quotes.] Even though education under racism meant that a whole lot of professional people never were able to practice their professions. But it was still the fact that education was a highly valued pursuit." She continued, "In my family it was highly valued, and it was equally valued for women. The boys had to wash dishes and make beds, and girls were encouraged to be independent and smart."

"At dinner table conversations in many black families, there were people who were educated, particularly associated with the NAACP. I mean, who was a better role model than Thurgood Marshall? ... And we had Mary McLeod Bethune. We had women, we had men, who were high achievers and who did something to help 'the race.' So yeah, in my family that notion that you got to be part of the solution and you got to always reach and bring somebody with you was repetitively told.

"I don't think that my family was in any sense rare. Remember, too, much was going on. I mean, lynchings were real. Growing up on the South Side, they had jitneys that ran up and down Indiana [Avenue]. It was very common—you know, we're all black people sitting in the cab talking to each other—it was common to hear these cab drivers talk about coming to Chicago because some Klansman wanted their wife. And they just got up and left.

"All of these things were very palpable. So I think that we talked a great deal. I'm sure in Chicago, in the poorest household, you at least had a copy of *Jet* magazine and the *Defender* [black Chicago newspaper]. We read those *other* papers, but *Ebony* and *Jet* and the *Defender*...! *Ebony* was a cocktail! You'd go into many, many, many people's homes and see issues of *Ebony* and *Jet* on the cocktail tables. We were very proud of it. If you wanted to hear the real scoop, that's where *Jet* was. That's where [you'd read about] Joe Willie who shot his wife because she wouldn't change the TV channel or something like that! But that was also where we saw full-page—*Jet* was smaller than it is now—and we got the full-page, I think everybody who saw that picture, it's burned in our memories, of Emmett Till.

"There was always black history in Jet. There was always something about some black person who had done something important, something great. There was the society—you know, debutante balls and all that—but those were signs of progress. You know, these were not *my* role models, but these were people who had achieved something in business. It was like, yeah, we're going to have some obstacles and we've got to fight, but this happens, and people do these things, *black* people do these things. [There were] long articles on black history that you could cut out. I used to collect them.

"I don't think that anything I say was any different than what was probably going on in thousands of black homes. We talked a lot about race. People'd get together at a party, be playing bid whist, and talking about something that happened in Mississippi; it was very much on our minds. In Chicago, neighborhoods integrating, burning houses... Race was very much a presence in our lives.

"So yes, education was important to most black people. It was part of how you escape—you could point out [educated blacks] to people that say we're inferior, less intelligent. No matter how inaccessible, education was still valued. But [there was] ambivalence too! A lot of people thought educated darkies were a pain in the ass. And it's true, a lot of educated blacks were classist."

When I asked about gays and lesbians on the South Side of Chicago, Jackie had a lot to say. "There were gay people around me all along. Two of my grandmother's friends, [they were] a couple, their daughter was a ballerina, their son was a pianist, and he was gay. My mother's sister's best friend, Raymond, was gay. There was a dancer who used to pirouette up and down our hallway. So you know, gay people, no big deal. Plus at the Regal Theater, they had a Jewelbox Revue every year. ... It was a transvestite show, except it was a *transvestite* show! There was nothing better than the Regal Theater; everything else looks amateurish to me.

"The Regal, that was an institution. Yeah! Hell, everybody came to the South Side. The *white* folks came to the South side. That's where it was happening! Where were the blues clubs? South Side! ... There was everything at the Regal Theater. I saw *Gone With the Wind*. Pearl Bailey came every year, Josephine Baker came every year, part of the chitlin circuit... I saw Moms Mabley... plus they had these big doo wop shows for us kids. All these groups nobody ever hears of any more: the Spaniels, the El Dorados. Screamin' Jay Hawkins. All day long! We lived in that damn Regal Theater. It was the center.

"... and Riverview. It was an amusement park at Belmont and Western. Us kids would beg some dough from our parents, and take that long-ass El [elevated train] ride. Who would be on the El from the South Side? Us kids, and the sissies. With their tight pants, their white T-shirts, their lipstick, their earrings. ... Honey, some of 'em be so buff they looked like Mr. Alice, talking 'bout, 'Chile!' [Jackie affects a limp wrist.] Shoot, nobody cared about nobody being gay!

"Now, lesbian's different. Please understand that. Gay men have been a critical part of the black church. Not the lesbians! So there was always the sense in which, if anybody was going to be really, really closeted, it was most likely going to be the dykes. Not the gay guys. And nobody was flaming out, out, out. There was always a small percentage of the population that could afford to be just *out* there.

"My aunt, my mother's sister, hung around the artsy crowd, and some of them were gay. But I did *not* know any lesbians."

I asked Jackie about language blacks on the South Side used to describe gay people. "Well, 'bulldagger' was a pejorative; it was like using 'faggot'. It was common language, but pejorative. 'Bulldagger' described the butchy girls, and the stud girls. But the femmes... who knew [they were lesbians]? ... I don't remember hearing 'gay'; guys—feminine guys, because they were identifiable—were 'sissies.' 'Funny' was also used.

"[Men] would say things like, "One of them bulldaggers get a hold of a woman, and she just ruint forever." It was like some magical power! I was curious about that for years, I have to say! 'What do they do? What happens?' And guys would say it all the time—'Man, you better not let one of them bulldaggers get a hold of your woman, 'cause she won't be right, she won't never be right again!' I thought, 'Lord, there must be some magic to this!'"

But as a teenager, Jackie says, "I didn't have language for [my feelings] back then. I knew I liked girls... certainly better than I liked boys. I don't think I was clear about what it would mean to be a lesbian. In general, what I saw of lesbians—there were certainly gay bars—was largely studs and femmes. I did not think of myself as a stud. On the other hand, I was not a girlie girl. ... Whatever it meant to be a lesbian, I didn't see myself fitting the paradigms I actually saw. So I thought, well maybe I'm not a lesbian."

When I asked Jackie to talk about homophobia in the black community, she became animated. "Homophobia in the black community? Not in the black community I grew up in. I grew up in a very tolerant community; we even tolerated white people coming to our [neighborhood]. Homophobia in the black community was a myth. Now, I don't want you to think there was *no* homophobia. ... I don't want to suggest there was anything like these communities, like these gay ghettoes here and in San

Francisco; those things didn't exist. And certainly there were men, for the identifiable lesbian bars, certainly those girls often had to fight when the party was over. I don't want you to think there was no homophobia, that it was easy.

"In the church, you could know the choir director or the musician or the organ player was a gay guy, but where were the lesbians? Clearly it was not an atmosphere... even today, you find very few black lesbians who go to regular churches who are out as lesbians at church.

"I don't want to give a false impression that everything was hunky-dory and you could just walk around and be your gay self. No. But people did not go out of the way... It wasn't heavenly, but it wasn't scary. People weren't going out of their way to make your life miserable. The black gay women in this town lived in the black community, and a lot of them would have been far too masculine to be passing for straight. So people knew. And they knew that woman living with her was her woman. And they weren't going to burn the house down. And they would have had straight friends."

Jackie started college in 1960, and soon got married, just before her 19th birthday. She attended Roosevelt University, "the commie college." I asked her why she chose Roosevelt, and she said, "Because it was the commie college." She had joined the Young People's Socialist League while in high school, and was soon active in the civil rights movement. Her major at Roosevelt was psychology, but she left in her junior year when her only child, a daughter, was born in 1964. She stayed out seven years, until her daughter was old enough to go to school, then returned to college, graduating with a bachelor's degree in philosophy. During the years away from college, she worked with CORE, participating in restaurant and housing sit-ins. Jackie also co-founded the National Black Draft Counselors Organization in Chicago. "During Viet Nam, they weren't allowing black conscientious objectors; only white ones. It wasn't offered as an option," she said. She wrote letters and got lawyers for black COs; she described it as the most intense work she's ever done. "Guys would hitchhike to Chicago, show up in the middle of the night, and they'd sleep on my floor. The phone would ring every five minutes."

Jackie later returned to school and earned a master's degree in philosophy, and two months later got a job at a two-year college in 1975. She has taught philosophy and world literature there the past 25 years. Shortly after her new job started, she came out. "What made me come out was I'd reached a point in my life where there was no reason not to. I'd done what I was supposed to do; my marriage was over [Jackie stayed married 15 years], my daughter was a teenager. Time to move on! ... There was no drama; I didn't lose my family, none of that. ... The challenge of my life is getting into the ladies' room [because of her butch appearance]!"

Since the mid-1970s, Jackie has earned 27 hours toward a Ph.D., and participated in the women's movement. She at one time was executive secretary of the Society of Women in Philosophy; was a founder of the Institute for Lesbian Studies in Chicago; was on the steering committee of Chicago Black Lesbians and Gays; and founded Yahimba, a black lesbian organization she was part of for five years. Jackie is also two-term board president of the Lesbian Cancer Project, is a member of the Mountain Moving Coffeehouse Collective, and is on the board of Diverse Communications, the nonprofit head of LesbiGay Radio.

Before leaving, Jackie suggested I talk with a woman who was out as a stud in South Side Chicago in the 1950s; she said she could give me some really interesting information about being a black lesbian during segregation, and that I should try to get her to talk about the families the studs constructed.

Later that evening...

When I called Sandi to ask for an interview, I mentioned that Jackie had referred me, and that I was a grad student, talking to older black lesbians about their experiences during segregation. Sandi said she knew my name from somewhere, and I mentioned my book. Sandi instantly opened up, and invited me to her home on the South Side of Chicago. I arrived just as Sandi's partner was leaving for work; her daughter was headed to her room to play on her computer. After I sat down at the dining table, Sandi talked about how she'd met Jackie at a black lesbian social group. Jackie encouraged Sandi to return to school and get a degree. Sandi says she refused to take any of Jackie's classes because she didn't want to "ruin a beautiful friendship." Then Sandi pulled out pictures of herself in her younger days, and began to talk about her childhood.

Sandra Byrd was born in 1942 in Columbus, Ohio, while her mother was en route to Dayton from Chicago, her home town. Her mother had married a man whose last name was Burgan, but they divorced soon after Sandi was born, so she never knew him. Her mother later remarried a man by the last name of Byrd, who formally adopted Sandi, but he only stayed married to her mother for seven or eight months; Sandi never knew him, either. Like Jackie, Sandi was an only child.

Sandi was raised in Dayton until the age of 4, when her family moved to Cleveland, where she remained until she was 17. Her mother was a musician; she played piano and pipe organ, and taught public school while in Dayton. After moving to Cleveland, her mother gave private lessons and traveled for concerts, performing classical, jazz and spirituals at schools and colleges.

In 1955, Sandi says her family moved to Shaker Heights; she was 13 years old. "They had just started integrating [neighborhoods], but when we moved in, they moved the Shaker Heights sign back... so it was no longer Shaker Heights. We [black people] bought homes, and the white people scattered. They moved the sign back all the way to Lee Road, just so you couldn't say you lived *in* Shaker Heights."

When her mother began traveling, Sandi would be put in black boarding schools in whatever area of the country her mother was touring. Sandi didn't go to a "mixed" (integrated) school until her senior year in high school. As Sandi says, "It freaked me out! I was in shock [at the permissiveness]. Boarding school was *very* strict; you had to sleep with your hands outside the covers."

Sandi says she knew she was different from other girls at an early age. Sandi says, "[Feeling different] bothered me somewhat. Because I didn't know what was wrong. I always had a crush on a teacher, and it was always a female teacher. It didn't matter what race she was." She remembers begging to stay after school (in Cleveland) to talk to teachers. "It bothered me to the extent that I was always running away from home. I didn't want my parents to know or find out. It was real troublesome for me." Sandi didn't have words for her feelings, and never talked to her mother about it, "but I think she knew. ... I would stay away from home, and hang out with an older lady, a receptionist at a hospital I had stayed once. I could talk to her... about feelings."

As a teenager, Sandi finally met "gay guys" from her church, a Church of God in Christ (COGIC) church, led by Rev. Ward. Sandi and the "church gays," all boys, would hang out in a club at 107th and Ashbury (in Cleveland) after Rev. Ward's broadcast, which was heard as far away as Chicago. (Sandi remembers hearing Rev. Cobb's church broadcasts from Chicago as a teen.) In that club was where Sandi discovered "there's women that feel like I do!" There were no gay clubs in Cleveland at that time; she says the club was "mixed," or gay-friendly, and not racially integrated.

Sandi's mother died when Sandi was 17. All of the relatives Sandi knew about lived in Chicago; she moved up soon after her mother died. There Sandi came out. "Chicago was where I discovered my identity. I had a cousin who was very understanding, and he took me to my first club, on 53rd or 56th and State [streets]. It was on State Street. And it was there that I met my first stud. Her name was Terry the Fox, and she was a DJ. I saw her, and I said, 'I want to be like *that*.'" Sandi said that Cleveland didn't have the "heavy role-playing" that Chicago did; there was some, but not to the extent it was in Chicago. "Terry the Fox was cool, dressed heavy... pants, jacket and stuff. I wanted that look. That's what fascinated me about her; she looked like a dude, to be truthful. ... And the more I got out and saw how they [studs] dressed, it became easy for me. I felt comfortable looking this way. My frilly dress days were over after my mother passed!"

After that first club experience, Sandi soon learned about other Chicago gay clubs: Mamio's, on 39th and Indiana or Wabash ("where the girls were"); a gay-friendly club named Fiesta on 43rd Street; a club called the Bucket of Blood (real name: Half-Pint Liquors) on 63rd Street, so-called because every weekend "there was guaranteed to be a fight. Somebody would wink at somebody else's woman, and it was *on!*" Sandi says that black gays and lesbians would hang out together, before the men got their own clubs. "There was the Parkside Lounge, on 51st off Cottage [Grove]; it was mostly guys, but girls would go. The Jeffrey Pub, that's been open for a long time; all guys, but girls were sort of welcome. ... In the '70s, a couple tried to open a few clubs: the Valley of the Dolls on 71st or 72nd and Exchange. There was the Mark III... and Betty's, on 63rd and Champlain or Eberhart. That was a square place, but on certain nights there were girls there. And the Kitty Kat, on 63rd Street. It wasn't gay, but gay-friendly."

Initially, Sandi lived for two weeks at the a hotel on the West Side of Chicago, but she says there was too much going on [in the club scene], so she moved in with her grandmother on the South Side. But her grandmother set a curfew, and Sandi wanted to stay out. A month after moving in, Sandi moved to her cousin's place, and went "buck wild! It was like, Chicago, here I come, open the doors and the windows!" There were clubs, and house parties, and "after hours sets."

Sandi's first job in Chicago was at Spiegel [catalog], where she worked on an order taker machine, printing out orders. She later stamped catalogs for Spiegel, and began job-hopping, taking whatever the next highest-paying job was. "I worked at Bell and Howell. I remember, a gay girl named Francine or Frances, she worked in personnel [at Bell and Howell], and she was the only black person in personnel. She got the power to hire, and she put the word on the street; all the South Side girls worked at Bell and Howell. We ruled Bell and Howell!" Sandi worked at a variety of jobs until beginning work as a mail clerk at the U.S. Post Office in 1967, where she stayed until retiring as a supervisor in 1997.

When I asked Sandi about language used to describe black lesbians, she said, "Black women called each other studs… role playing was dominant then. You were either a stud or a femme. It was death to you if you crossed over or played both sides. Nowadays, you could be either, or, whatever. … There were rules: You had respect for each other, and you definitely did not hit on, or try to hit on, anybody else's woman." Black gay men were called "sissies" or "fags." "'Lesbian' came out of the late '80s, early '90s. The NOW generation vocabulary. Back then, you were either a stud or femme, or gay. Or sissy or fag."

Sandi recalls going to many parties in the '60s, '70s and '80s given by a social group called the Sons of Sappho. The parties would sometimes be picnics, or overnight at hotels. One of the founders of Sons of Sappho, Ernestine Medley, died the week before I arrived to interview Sandi. "They had balls. … They were the 'in' thing. They were the pioneers. You went to a Sons of Sappho party, you were going to a *good* party!" I asked why the group wasn't named the Daughters of Sappho. "I imagine 'cause it was a way to define who they were. … 'Stine and Yvonne and Harriet and all of 'em, they were studs, or butch or dykes, however you want to call it. The young kids call you butch now, but in that day you was a stud. It was all studs that started the group, so they were the Sons of Sappho. Got it now?"

To my question of whether there was homophobia in the black community, Sandi replies, "I got along with straights, with anybody. But among the men, there's a lot of homophobia. They couldn't understand… They would get angry with you. You would hear some men on the street, 'How you get that fine bitch?' They would sound kind of hostile. … Me, personally, I never had that much trouble out of straight people being homophobic. But men were envious; you'd keep a low profile around them. But some [studs] figured they could whip a man as well as anybody else. I didn't feel like I needed to go that route. If you chose to whip a man, show your manliness, with a *real* man, that was on you! And we had some out there that would do that. They would challenge a man in a minute. But I'd tell people, 'I'm a lover, not a fighter.'"

I told Sandi that Jackie had mentioned that the studs

constructed families; did she know anything about it? "Back then, a lot of us were denied by our families; if our families found out, they disowned us and so forth. Most black people, you have this inbred thing of wanting to be family or part of a family. ... Black gay women—some—their family didn't want anything to do with them. We had a habit of making up sons, daughters... I still have a gay mother, father, grandmother, grandfather, sister. For over thirty to forty years now. My gay grandmother, grandfather, have been together thirty-five years. Sometimes we only see each other at funerals, but we keep in touch. My gay mother and father— play mother and father—they broke up after nineteen years. But they still look at me as their son; I look at them as my play mother and father. I have a play son named Duckie; she's been my play son for twenty, twenty-five, thirty years. She still, when she calls me, says, 'Hey, Pops, what's going on?'

"We created our own families, for one reason or another. That was the thing—you had your gay family and could talk to 'em. If you had problems... mostly, when your girlfriend broke your heart or something, you always had somebody to talk to, family to turn to. They'd say, 'Boy, you know you shouldn't be doing this or that. Next time you need to get you a woman to do this or that." There was always an age digression, so you were learning.

"The founder, Ernestine, was the grandfather of all the gay studs. She used to call me Youngblood. She was the monarch of the studs." I asked whether the families were added onto these days. "It's not added on to. Now that gay women and lesbian women of today... you really don't have to create families because you're so out now. This was done to create some support for each other. It might still be, but I don't think it's prominent."

After meeting Jackie and with Jackie's encouragement, Sandi returned to college, graduating from Olive Harvey College with an associate's degree in 1992. Since retiring from the post office, Sandi has been active in her neighborhood. She's a member of the advisory council of her neighborhood association; she's also a member of the welcoming committee. She's very active in church, and is a member of the Literary Exchange, a Chicago black lesbian organization. She bowls "with straight women," and has for twenty years, traveling to bowling tournaments. About two years ago, to relieve her retirement boredom, Sandi began driving a school bus. About her being a stud, Sandi says her neighbors "never brought it to me. The men respect me just as much as the women."

Morning has broken

I interviewed a total of four women in their late 50s and early 60s for my master's research. Listening to these women's stories has had quite an effect on me. I've become entranced by the past; I listen to music from the 1950s now, such as Jackie Wilson, Ruth Brown and Big Maybelle. I'm drawn to documentaries and photographs from those years. I picture these two women coming of age during that time, and insert them into my image of South Side Chicago. And, amazingly, since conducting these interviews in the summer of 2000, I've been introduced to seven other older black lesbians. Quite a few of them are in their 70s; they live in different parts of the United States— and they're willing to be interviewed for what has turned into a video documentary I've begun on older black lesbians.

I feel incredibly lucky to be able to find and interview these women, and the fact that they want me to share their knowledge further amazes me. I only hope that we appreciate their history as well as we do our present.

NOTES:

[1] Another essay in Beemyn's book discusses lesbian bars in Detroit, 1938-1965, but the author focuses on sexuality as the binder of lesbians, and not race. See *Creating a Place for Ourselves: Lesbian, Gay, and Bisexual Community Histories*, Brett Beemyn, ed. (New York: Routledge, 1997). The editor was kind enough to share his limitations of obtaining black lesbian interviews in his own research about gay D.C.: "I have not discovered a network of older black gay men or lesbians, but it is possible that I just wasn't

able to 'break in.' ... I am also an outsider—being white and not being a local." (Interview with Brett Beemyn, April 26, 2000.)

[2] The current surge of gay and lesbian community histories do not privilege black lesbian voices; what few there are are used in relation to the white gay and lesbian histories. Some examples are *Hidden From History: Reclaiming the Gay and Lesbian Past*, Martin Duberman, Martha Vicinus and George Chauncey, eds. (New York: New American Library, 1989); *Carryin' on in the Lesbian and Gay South*, John Howard, ed. (New York: Routledge, 1997); *The Gay Metropolis, 1940-1996*, Charles Kaiser (New York: Houghton Mifflin, 1997); *City of Sisterly and Brotherly Loves: Lesbian and Gay Philadelphia, 1945-1972*, Marc Stein (Chicago: University of Chicago Press, 2000).

[3] See Kirin Narayan, "How native is a 'native' anthropologist?" *American Anthropologist*, 95 (1993), 671-686.

[4] See Biddy Martin and Chandra Mohanty, "Feminist politics: What's home got to do with it?" in *Feminist Studies/Critical Studies*, ed. by Teresa de Lauretis (Bloomington, IN: Indiana University Press, 1986), 196.

[5] Two exceptions come to mind: Joan Nestle's interviews with Mabel Hampton (1902-1989), documented in *A Fragile Union*, by Joan Nestle (San Francisco: Cleis Press, 1998), and *Living With Pride: Ruth Ellis @ 100*, a film by Yvonne Welbon (Chicago: Our Film Works, 1999). Ruth Ellis, born in 1899, celebrated her 101th birthday in July 2000, and passed away in October 2000.

Parking Lot Attendant / North Beach
by Jerry Thompson

I'm at his place 10 minutes and he already has a double martini
waitin for me. I down the first one, and manage to take a drag of
some local grown weed he kind of shoves down my throat as
soon as I arrive. He doesn't get the best pot, but what he has does
the job. He knows it, and he knows it's one of the only reasons I
make time to drop by.

He's puffin and slurpin down martinis just as fast as I am.

My head gets a-spinnin and my words slur all the way to the
basement where we eventually find ourselves. It's as if the
basement were some neutral territory. Where the animal in us can
freely conquer the landscape of fucked-up ritual between us.

By the time I touch the bottom of the stairs he's already stripped
off his shirt and has the stereo bumpin with one of my favorite
tweaker house anthems. He knows that I love this shit. I don't
think he uses it to seduce me anymore. I make a point to help
brotha man out when he needs the hook up. He gossip dribbles
for a moment and I indulge him. There is always some new hot
young red-haired waitress or hiker chick clinging to his sheets,
and so he gives me the lowdown. He claims to be in love again.
I'm encouraging, supportive. I have a permanent smile on my
face because I'm fucking high as a kite at this point and I'm
jones'in on every word out of his mouth... He's convinced that
I believe he's a closet case just aching for someone to make a pot
roast out of his sexy ass. You gotta see this guy in jeans. One
night I invited him to come along with me and a group of friends
to an ecstasy party in Oakland. Everyone thought he was fucking
gorgeous. Everyone wanted to take a bite out of his juicy ass that
night. He couldn't bend over to pick up nothing the entire night
for fear that someone's face might get stuck in his asshole, his ass
looked so good. We all wanted him, men and women.

The e was definitely good that night.

Gift

by Forrest Hamer

Recently, my father was himself again.

When I noticed this, I was wary, but when I was certain
He was back, I thought nothing more
About where he had been.

He offered to rub the crusts of my feet.
Though I was reluctant, I thought if anyone would
It would be my father.
I gave him my feet, and it was wonderful,

And I was humbled by the wonder
Of this simple, loving act. I woke up happy
Having my father back for good,

Wherever it was he had gone.

Bel Canto
(excerpt from Act I)
by Daniel Alexander Jones

the what

The set for *Bel Canto* is an American Flag, mammoth in size and protean. This "flag" should be constructed with a combination of varied dimensional/sculptural elements and light. The white or red stripes, can, for example, fuse to become a unified whole— thereby isolating a particular room in Barbara's house or the façade of an apartment building. The blue can fill the whole space, can brighten or dim to be either morning or nighttime sky. The stars can cluster to form a sun or moon, or can move through the space and hang like lanterns; one star can be a lamp or a streetlight. Nothing should be ordinary or clichéd about this unifying element, rather, the design should be searching and inspired. The works of painter Jacob Lawrence offer examples of different spatial possibilities. All the players are a part of the space—"painted" in—and when they leave a scene, they should remain a part of the composition in some way. Benjamin should never leave the stage.

the who

BENJAMIN TURNER
> Aged 16. Lanky.

BARBARA SCARLATTI
> Early 60s. Tall. Dramatic.

BESSIE TURNER
> Late 30s. Benjamin's mother. Short, natural hair.

TERENCE LONG
> Aged 17. Wears glasses.

MARIAN ANDERSON
> An astral projection of the famed contralto.

MISS PAVA
    Aged 50. School nurse.

the where
Springfield, Massachusetts. A small, working class city in the Western part of the Commonwealth.

the when
1978.

the how
Passionately.

Note: The following symbols are used in the script. An asterisk (*) indicates that the line immediately following should begin, overlapping the line being spoken. A dual plus (++) indicates that a substantive musical rest should be taken.

JANUARY 1978 (OVERTURE)

One. Two. Three stars flicker on in the distance. A fourth star becomes a streetlight and catches Benjamin Turner in its spittle. He dances outside the front of the apartment building into which he and his mother Bessie have just moved. Snow falls from passing clouds, gently. Benjamin allows himself to be anointed by the snowflakes. A constellation of stars blinks on, unbeknownst to Benjamin, Marian Anderson's astral projection stands inside the constellation, looks down upon him and sings.

MARIAN ANDERSON
How we wish
while drowning!
Though soft and silent
This fateful flood
Holds no less danger
Oh, so delicate—

each drop a sudden dream
sketched in unique symmetry.
We drown, nonetheless.
Filled by
brittle worlds
that melt into tears
at our touch.

Benjamin opens his jacket. He reveals the tattered tie-dyed T-shirt he is wearing. It is clearly not his own. He pulls on it a bit.

BENJAMIN
Come on, Dad.

Bessie Turner appears at the doorway. She is lit from behind. We only see her silhouette throughout this scene. When he hears his mother's voice, Benjamin closes his jacket to hide the shirt.

BESSIE
Come inside, Benjamin.

BENJAMIN
It's too beautiful.

BESSIE
You'll catch your death.

BENJAMIN
Come and see.

BESSIE
I grew up with this. And it's not like you haven't seen it before.

BENJAMIN
This is different than home.

BESSIE
This is home.

BENJAMIN
Snows even harder up north. I bet.

BESSIE
Bet so.

BENJAMIN
Cold, too.

BESSIE
Bet so.

BENJAMIN
I think I can take it a little while longer.

BESSIE
I think you need to come inside.

BENJAMIN
Did you ever look and see things? Just see things. Like you
never saw 'em before?

BESSIE
All the time. Come inside.

BENJAMIN
The light is funny.

BESSIE
Reflection.

BENJAMIN
Where's the moon?

BESSIE
It's there.

BENJAMIN
The stars?

BESSIE
Them, too.

BENJAMIN
Where do you think thoughts go...?

BESSIE
(a sigh) Thoughts.

BENJAMIN
...I think thoughts go out in all directions. Like the radio.

BESSIE
You're stalling, oh great philosophical one.

BENJAMIN
Yep.

BESSIE
Come inside.

BENJAMIN
What about wishes?

BESSIE
Oh, Benji. Come on.

BENJAMIN
Serious. Where do wishes go?

BESSIE
Remember what I used to tell you?

BENJAMIN
About wishes?

BESSIE
Find a point of light. A star. Planet. Point of light. Then send
your wish there. Told you it was a window to heaven. "Wishes
are straight ahead things."

BENJAMIN
You told me that?

BESSIE
All the time.

BENJAMIN
Who told you that?

BESSIE
Your Dad.

BENJAMIN
Did you believe him?

BESSIE
I'm freezing, Benji.

BENJAMIN
What about now, when there are clouds.

BESSIE
I don't know. He didn't say anything about that. If he did, I
don't remember.

BENJAMIN
Oh.

BESSIE
I don't even know which box to pick, babe. Where to start

unpacking.

BENJAMIN
In a minute.

BESSIE
Pretty sure I know where some cocoa is.

BENJAMIN
Deal.

BESSIE
The light is pretty. Makes things look softer than they are.

BENJAMIN
Yeah.

BESSIE
One minute.

BENJAMIN
Mmmm-hmmm.

BESSIE
I'm counting.
> **Bessie exits. Benjamin opens his jacket and scans the sky.**

BENJAMIN
That looks like a good window.

> **He scrunches the T-shirt into his hands. Then, wishing hard...**

BENJAMIN
Come on
Come on

**A soft blue pane of light falls next to Benjamin.
Marian Anderson descends into the pane of light.
She lights just above the ground and beams at
Benjamin. She sings her lines to him.**

MARIAN ANDERSON
*It does appear to be a good window, but we can never be certain at such a
distance.*

BENJAMIN
Hello.

MARIAN ANDERSON
What is your name?

BENJAMIN
Benjamin.

MARIAN ANDERSON
Benjamin.

BENJAMIN
Are you an angel?

MARIAN ANDERSON
We have been called an angel, among other things.

BENJAMIN
I'll bet.

MARIAN ANDERSON
And you?

BENJAMIN
I'm no angel.

MARIAN ANDERSON
Finding our right windows is tricky business. Being certain of our wishes is even more challenging.

BENJAMIN
I'm certain. I know exactly what I want.

MARIAN ANDERSON
We must offer caution, young man.
Sometimes our wish flies in the face of destiny.
Our will may block what is meant to come our way.

BENJAMIN
But it's really important. It's not just for me.

MARIAN ANDERSON
For every wish a price. And this you are willing to pay?

BENJAMIN
How much?

MARIAN ANDERSON
You must give of yourself, you will know how much. For now, word your wish with care and send it through your window.

BENJAMIN
Just tell it?

MARIAN ANDERSON
Give it.

BENJAMIN
Here.

> **Benjamin holds out his hands like a butterfly to his window. Marian Anderson opens her hands, and reflects the gesture.**

MARIAN ANDERSON
What beautiful hands.

BENJAMIN
Dad's.

MARIAN ANDERSON
We are very brave to make that wish.

BENJAMIN
We are?

MARIAN ANDERSON
Uncommonly so.

Marian Anderson begins to rise into the air.

BENJAMIN
Wait! What do "we" do now?

MARIAN ANDERSON
Follow the signs.
Be prepared to act.

Marian Anderson ascends and the light flickers before going out. Bessie's shadow reappears in the doorway.

BESSIE
Time's up, Benji. Don't give me a hard time tonight, babe.

Benjamin stares upward in wonder.

BESSIE
Benji?

Sound of a Shower.

SHOWER

Benjamin Turner stands at a changing bench in the Classical High School boys locker room. He starts to take off his clothes. Standing at the opposite side of the changing bench is Terence Long. They sneak glances at each other as they change. Terence wraps a towel around himself and goes in to the shower. Voices echo out.

Here's your girlfriend.

Faggot.

Get your eyes off my shit, faggot.

Benjamin gets dressed.

Look at him. He's checking out your ass, Brian. He wants a piece of that.

Fuck you.

Look at him.

Fucking freak!

Sounds of a fight ensue. Benjamin walks into the shower. The fight gets deep.

Who the fuck are you?

What, nigga, that's your girlfriend?

Terence runs out, clutching his stomach, dripping wet. He falls on the floor.

Get off—get off my boy!!! Owww! Fuck you!
Benjamin cries out from the shower in pain.

Man, you're going to get suspended for that shit.

Fuck that! This mothafucka cut my lip. And let that bitch try and put me out this school. Even she want some of this shit.

Terence has hurriedly pulled his pants on and runs from the room.

IN WHICH MISS PAVA SPEAKS
The Classical High School Nurse's Office. Benjamin is in severe pain.

MISS PAVA
Let's have a look there. Zikes, I'll bet that hurts.

BENJAMIN
Awwwwww!

MISS PAVA
Shhhhh. Can you wiggle your fingers?

BENJAMIN
It kills!

MISS PAVA
Whimpering won't take the pain away. Wiggle your fingers.

BENJAMIN
I can't. Auuuurrrrrgh!

MISS PAVA
Looks like a clean break to me.

BENJAMIN
Please.

MISS PAVA

You know, when I was your age, I had my wrist snapped by a rather aggressive gal with a medicine ball...

BENJAMIN

Can't you give me a pill or something?

MISS PAVA

For weeks, there were a thousand miniature blades, stabbing, stabbing. No codeine for me.

BENJAMIN

It's killing me!

MISS PAVA

Let's get this wrapped in a compress until your Mom gets here. Can't do anything else 'til then.

BENJAMIN

You didn't call her, did you?!

Miss Pava begins leafing through a sizable file.

MISS PAVA

Of course we called her.

BENJAMIN

She's in class. I don't want her to get worried. She's under a lot of stress right now...

MISS PAVA

(Reading) Benji Turner. I see you brought a 3.4 GPA with you from California.

BENJAMIN

They have that in my medical file?

MISS PAVA

I pulled the big file. "Our secret." I always peek—gives me a little

more "insight."
Miss Pava begins to apply a compress.

BENJAMIN
OUCH!

MISS PAVA
Down, horsey! 3.4... That's impressive, Benji.

BENJAMIN
OUUUUCH!

MISS PAVA
That's not too familiar, "Benji," is it? Good. I loved that movie.
Benji. About the cute little dog who thwarts the kidnappers.
Animals are good people.

BENJAMIN
Some people do a pretty good job as animals. **(She touches a
particularly painful spot.)** Grrruuuh!
Miss Pava laughs awkwardly.

MISS PAVA
My goodness, you've got me laughing out of turn. Here's where
my training kicks in. Anyone else would stop with the easy yack.
But I know this wisecracking masks a deeper truth. Been hard
"adjusting," hmm?

BENJAMIN.
You're quick.

MISS PAVA
Thank you.

BENJAMIN
But I think it's the other way around. People at Classical are
having a hard time "adjusting" to me.

MISS PAVA
There's pain under that smile. You can let that out here, Benji.

BENJAMIN
You're damn right there's pain.

MISS PAVA
Is there trouble on the old home front?

BENJAMIN
You really know how to turn a page. What's in that file anyway?

MISS PAVA
Private. Hmmm. Says "a little something" here about your Dad.
Tell me Ben. About your Dad. Confidential. **(explaining)** Just
between you and me.

BENJAMIN
Confidential... like the file?

MISS PAVA
No? I understand. Being abandoned by a parent is a painful thing.

BENJAMIN.
He didn't abandon us.

MS PAVA.
Says here that he's somewhere singing "Oh, Canada," right about
now.

BENJAMIN
You're pretty funny yourself.

MS. PAVA
I'm on the case, Benji; flattery will get you nowhere. Now. You
and your mother, a Betty Turner...

BENJAMIN
Bessie.

MS. PAVA
"Bessie" it is… All that loose California handwriting. **(flipping a page.)** My *goodness*… Wait. Wait…

Miss Pava turns his face up to the light.

MISS PAVA
…Let me get a better look. Wow. It barely shows, but now I can see it. I must say, even I was fooled. **(excited)** The key was right in front of us and we didn't even know it.

BENJAMIN
The key to what?

MISS PAVA
The rage that triggered this fight! Hello! You'll never believe… I wrote about the cognitive development of mixed-race children in college.

BENJAMIN
No.

MISS PAVA
(so excited) Can you believe! I did field research and everything. Up the road in Cambridge. No one would suspect the blood of the oppressor and the oppressed are clashing through your veins.

BENJAMIN
I don't know about all that…

MISS PAVA
Benji. This arm is an obvious cry for attention, a banner saying "SEE ME, UNDERSTAND ME"! Hey kiddo, I'm with it. All teens want to be understood.

BENJAMIN.
I don't need understanding. I need codeine.

MISS PAVA.
Mr. Funny Bones. It's crystal clear that you have socially awkward tendencies, rooted in an irreconcilable racial identity. You're a sepia James Dean, stirring up tension and adverse reactions from everybody around you.

BENJAMIN
I was breaking up a fight! Not starting one! Why don't you pick on those guys?

MISS PAVA
UUUUPPP! Talking back may play in California but you're in Massachusetts now! Those boys are perfectly normal; boys will be boys and a good scrap is a good scrap. You on the other hand...

BENJAMIN
But I didn't do anything.

MISS PAVA
Benji, let me cut to the chase here. Socially awkward tendencies are a breeding ground for all sorts of bad characteristics. You already have the race thing to deal with, and the violent temper. Don't add to your troubles by fighting the people you should befriend, and protecting the people **(making a sissy gesture)** that would really only *add to the problem*. Do you catch my drift?

BENJAMIN
Do I ever.

MISS PAVA
Good guy. Good guy. But, hey, on the positive side, you're brave enough to get in the ring. Not like Dad, huh? I'm going to fill out this report and you can wait in the office until your Mom gets here. Go home, watch some TV, eat some ice cream for a few

days. Think about what I said.

Bessie rushes into the office.

BESSIE
Benji! I was in class; I didn't get the message. Oh, God, are you alright?

MISS PAVA
He's fine.

BESSIE
And you are?

MISS PAVA
Peggy Pava. I'm the school nurse and **(winks at Benjamin)** part-time psychologist.

BESSIE
Did you do this?

MISS PAVA
Break his arm? No.

BESSIE
Put this compress on, lady.

MISS PAVA
Yes, that's my handiwork.

BESSIE
I didn't give permission for this to be done.

MISS PAVA
Permission. You signed a medical release form for the Massachusetts school...

BESSIE
I didn't give my permission. You should have waited.

BENJAMIN
Mom, it's okay.

MISS PAVA
It won't cost you anything, if that's what you're worried about. It happened on school property so...

BESSIE
The cost is not a factor here! It's your choice of therapy.

MISS PAVA
No need to get "angry."

BESSIE
I'm not...

MISS PAVA
We run a pretty good clinic here.

BENJAMIN
MOM! I'm okay. She did a good job.

MISS PAVA
It's okay, Benji. **(Scans Bessie's face)** Your Mom's only "protecting her young." You have a very handsome son. I see a little resemblance there around the eyes. **(Back to Benjamin)** Bet he looks a lot more like his Dad. There will be some paperwork for you, Ms. Turner, but we can just mail that on. I'll be in the office when you're ready.

BESSIE
What's *that* about?

They share a look. Benji smiles through the pain.

BENJAMIN
Cointelpro.

BESSIE
Benji. Your arm.

IN WHICH TERENCE WALKS HOME
**Terence walks home from school. Benjamin follows
a few feet behind Terence.**

BENJAMIN
Hey.

**Terence looks over his shoulder, and then he begins
to walk faster.**

BENJAMIN
Hey, man, wait up.

**Benjamin follows. They walk the stripes of the flag.
Jimi Hendrix's "Fire" plays, in the distance at first.
The volume increases with each stripe Terence
walks down. They arrive at Terence's street. Terence
pauses at his door. He looks around him, as though
to get a breath of fresh air before going inside. He
opens his front door and the Hendrix blares out. He
steps in and shuts the door. The Hendrix song
dissipates immediately. At the same moment
Barbara Scarlatti's door swings wide open.**

IN WHICH BARBARA AND BENJAMIN MEET
Barbara executes three vicious sweeps.

BARBARA
Out! Out! Out! My good, sweet Lord! I've had to clean her hoof
prints out of my house. I've only just got my babies quieted
down. Why must I struggle so? *Signore, perque remuneri cosi?!* You
would think that after all I've done I would be rewarded with
better than *this*. Am I right?

BENJAMIN
Absolutely.

BARBARA
I've given a year to that... that *cow!* All the training I could muster. I walked her, hand in hand, through a series of lieder that would otherwise prove a minefield to someone as slow-witted as she. I practically spoon-fed Amneris to her, over and over and over, throughout this treacherous winter. I gave her secrets, priceless tricks of the trade; do you hear me?

BENJAMIN
Yes!

BARBARA
OH! I should have known. It's in the eyes. Her dim bovine eyes. I was projecting what I wanted to see. It's always the way! That "heifer." Uggghhh, switching to that Shreck woman at this point will prove disastrous for her. Heifers both!!!

BENJAMIN
Help me out. This lady went to another teacher?

BARBARA
Shreck, a teacher? A true teacher? Hah! It's all manufacture. Cheap manufacture. She *calls herself* a singer. I could call myself a fairy princess and that wouldn't make me one. Do I look like a fairy princess?

BENJAMIN
Not at all.

BARBARA
Not at all!!! Shreck does not teach singing! Does not sing! She butchers voices!!! ...*I* teach singing.

BENJAMIN
Of course you do.

BARBARA
To a select group that is. More select now than ever. I teach the old-fashioned way. The *true* Italian method. Bel Canto.

BENJAMIN.
I don't know what that is. Sorry.

BARBARA.
Never say you're sorry. Ignorance is not a crime, unless it is celebrated. Then? It's a sin.

Barbara turns and begins walking back into her house. Benjamin stops her by speaking.

BENJAMIN. I like the sound of that. Bel Can't-o.

BARBARA. Cahn-to.

BENJAMIN. Cahn-to.

BARBARA. Bel *Canto.*

BENJAMIN. Bel *Canto.*

BARBARA. **Bel Canto!**

BENJAMIN. **Bel Canto!**

BARBARA. A-hah! Baritone?

BENJAMIN. Hmm?

BARBARA. Your range. You *are* a singer, no?

BENJAMIN. I like to sing, yeah.* But, I'm not...

*BARBARA. Well you *must* know your range. It's like knowing your name or your blood type. Rather essential.

BENJAMIN. You think I'm a "baritone"?

BARBARA. Hard to tell, the speaking voice can deceive. I'd have to hear the voice in flight. *Say.* You've come all this way.

BENJAMIN. I have?

BARBARA. *Here.* I'll fix you something warm to drink, and we'll see about this voice of yours.

BENJAMIN. I don't know.

BARBARA. Your choice. The facts just seem auspicious. You're walking down the street. I'm sweeping out my house. You want to sing. I'm a singing teacher. I've just had a space open up in my studio. A rather large, bovine-shaped space. There's more than enough room for someone as slightly built as you.

BENJAMIN. It'd be cool to know what kind of voice I have.

BARBARA. I'm... certain... you won't regret it! Really. This is for the best... "Benji."

BENJAMIN. How do you know my name?

BARBARA. It's on your bag. I'm Barbara. Barbara Scarlatti.

BENJAMIN. Benji Turner.

BARBARA. Such a *pleasure* to make your acquaintance, Benjamin. What would you like to drink?

BENJAMIN
Cocoa.

BARBARA
We'll have tea. Cocoa will cloud the voice. Now. Through that
door, up the stairs to your left. Two floors. First room on the
right.

> Benjamin enters the house. Barbara smiles and
> sweeps the sidewalk up to the stairs. Sweeps up the
> stairs and sweeps the porch to the door. She steps
> in through the door and sweeps from the frame
> into the house. She then leans out the doorframe,
> toward the street and spits.

> IN WHICH BARBARA TESTS THE VOICE
> Benjamin stands by the piano. He sniffs the air.
> Something off. He touches the piles of dusty sheet
> music and books. He walks to the piano and begins
> to play three or four notes. They surprise him with
> their warmth. He looks around at the walls, which
> are   covered   in   framed   programs,   articles,
> photographs. A portrait of Marian Anderson is
> illuminated from behind for a moment. Benjamin
> leans toward the frame to read the name.

BENJAMIN
Marian Anderson.

> Barbara enters with a flourish; the picture goes dim.
> Benjamin spins around, embarrassed to have been
> caught looking.

BARBARA
I see you've found your way...

BENJAMIN
This house is huge. Do you live here all by yourself?

BARBARA
Of course. Do you live nearby?

BENJAMIN
Up the hill.

BARBARA
Stand just there.

BENJAMIN
My Mom and I just came here from California.

BARBARA
I've never understood why anyone would want to live there. How fortunate for you that you've moved. We'll warm the voice. Just repeat after me. On "Ah."

Barbara performs a simple vocalese.

"Ah-ah-ah-ah-ah-ah-ah-ah-ahhhhh."

BENJAMIN
"Ah-ah-ah-ah-ah-ah-ah-ah-ahhhhh."

BARBARA
Now, now, now. First things first. Stand up straight. Chest out. Shoulders back. Chin up. A-aah! Not so far. There we are. Now, deep breath. Again. On "Ah."

BENJAMIN
"Ah-ah-ah-ah-ah-ah-ah-ah-ahhhhh."

BARBARA
Better. Well then. Tiptoeing up the stairs just slightly.

BENJAMIN
"Ah-ah-ah-ah-ah-ah-ah-ah-ahhhhh."

BARBARA
Again, higher.

BENJAMIN
"Ah-ah-ah-ah-ah-ah-ah-ah-ahhhhh."

BARBARA
And down again.

BENJAMIN
"Ah-ah-ah-ah-ah-ah-ah-ah-ahhhhh."

BARBARA
There. Do you know any songs that we might sing?

BENJAMIN
I guess. It's hard to think on the spot. Umm... Do you know "Turn Your Lights Down Low" by Bob Marley?

BARBARA
I'm afraid not. You know Christmas carols, I assume?

BENJAMIN
Christmas carols? But it's February.

BARBARA
I'll tell you what. We won't be ashamed. We'll have a "devil may care" attitude—so what if it's February and were singing Christmas carols, eh?* We're *artists*. This is the stance we take.

*BENJAMIN
(laughs) Okay.

BARBARA
Let's see... Here we are. *We Three Kings*...

They sing.
BARBARA and BENJAMIN
We three kings of Orient are
Bearing gifts we travel afar
Field and fountain
Moor and mountain
Following yonder star
Oh…

Barbara drops out. She listens hungrily.
BARBARA
Keep going…

BENJAMIN
Star of wonder
Star of might
Star of royal beauty bright
Westward leading
Still proceeding
Guide us to thy perfect light

BARBARA
There, now. We'll rest the voice.

BENJAMIN
So?

BARBARA
Lemon with your tea?

BENJAMIN
Am I a baritone?

BARBARA
Mind your saucer. Like this.

Barbara shows Benjamin the proper way to hold and
sip the tea from the china cup.

BENJAMIN
Never did make chorus. I sound pretty crunchy, huh?

BARBARA
There is a sizable break in the voice.

BENJAMIN
That doesn't sound like a good sign.

BARBARA
Let us not be mistaken!!! There's work to be done. Breathing. Pitching. Attacking the phrase. Posture. Not to mention certain basics of etiquette.

BENJAMIN
Lot of work, huh? Well, thanks for, you know, listening to me howl.

BARBARA
You've no idea, do you? Benjamin, yours is the voice of an opera singer.

BENJAMIN
Are you serious?

BARBARA
Deadly *serious*. We must start right away. Saturday, it is.

BENJAMIN
Saturday. What time?

BARBARA
Nine a.m. We'll strike the voice unawares. We must set an aggressive schedule. Six days a week, minimum.

BENJAMIN
I don't know if I can do that.

BARBARA
Why ever not?

BENJAMIN
We don't... I don't have any money.

BARBARA
Add mental attitude to the work list.

BENJAMIN
Not enough for six lessons, at least. Can I come once a week?

BARBARA
The study of voice demands a full commitment, young man. Where there's a will there's a way. You look to be able-bodied. Except of course for the cast. But you've one good arm. That will do.

BENJAMIN
Do what?

BARBARA
This house desperately needs re-painting... I would have to pay the painters a fortune. You will do the work for lessons. An old-fashioned exchange.

BENJAMIN
Painting?

BARBARA
You *do* know how to paint?

BENJAMIN
Yeah. Sure. I'm a painter from way back. But I've got school?

BARBARA
You'll sing first thing in the morning on your way, then, come for

a full lesson in the afternoon. Simple. Besides, you'll learn more of value here than there, I promise you.

BENJAMIN
This is a lot of music. I don't read music.

BARBARA
"I don't. I can't. But. But. But." Listen to yourself! Benjamin, we must wash this language out with soap.

BENJAMIN
You're right, you're right.

BARBARA
What a marvelous arrangement. What a fortuitous day. You'll do the room across the hall, first.

Suddenly, from every direction comes the wild barking and howling of dozens of dogs. Benjamin jumps. Barbara seems unfazed.

BARBARA
Of course, there's the matter of the dogs. I'll move them, mop the floor down and all.

BENJAMIN
I thought I smelled dogs.

BARBARA
My babies.

Barbara picks up a book and hands it to Benjamin.

"An introduction to the Italian language." Start reading. Do you have a turntable?

BENJAMIN
I just unpacked it.

BARBARA
I know just the thing. Here. *Tosca!* Callas, conducted by Di Sabata at La Scala, 1954. We start with the best. Guard it with your life. Listen to this and only this. When it's time I shall give you another.

BENJAMIN
This is great... you know, I think we've got some opera records... I mean, my Dad has this huge record collection, opera, jazz, rock, everything...

BARBARA
You will bring me a list of the opera you have, the singers, the conductors, the date of issue. Then we will decide what is appropriate. "Everything" isn't appropriate for an impressionable voice.

BENJAMIN
Never thought of it like that. But, hey. Okay.

BARBARA
Benjamin Turner. Here, I'll see you down.

Barbara leaves. Bessie crosses with a box of old clothes. The Turner apartment.

STUFF.
Benjamin looks for records. Bessie is cleaning.

BENJAMIN
There's stuff missing.

BESSIE
There's too much stuff in this closet.

BENJAMIN
I can't find all the records.

BESSIE
God, this dress is hideous. And you need to go through your closet again, too. I've got a new bag going to give away.

BENJAMIN
Mom, where did you move the records that Dad had, like the opera ones?

BESSIE
The Salvation Army.

BENJAMIN
Come on. Really. Where are they? I need some of them.

BESSIE
I'm serious. Took them down to Sally two days ago along with a whole bag of your father's stuff.

BENJAMIN
Wait a minute! What stuff?

BESSIE
That old busted radio, some shirts, tie-dyed and moth eaten...

BENJAMIN
Those were in my room!

BESSIE
And?

BENJAMIN
It was my *private* stuff.

BESSIE
No, it was his old junk.

BENJAMIN
And those records, he always had those records... I

mean...WHAT THE HELL DID YOU DO THAT FOR?

BESSIE
Lower your voice!

BENJAMIN
Where!? What Salvation Army is it?

BESSIE
What on *Earth* is wrong with you?

BENJAMIN
Fine, I'll just go and find it and tell them you made a mistake.
Benjamin moves to walk outside.

BESSIE
Benjamin, no you won't.

BENJAMIN
You can't do this! You have no right!

BESSIE
I have no right to throw junk out of my own house?

BENJAMIN
He's my father!

BESSIE
Okay. He's my goddamned husband. Let's get clear about that.

BENJAMIN
I'm clear that I am on his side since you're not.

BESSIE
Don't you start acting like a rowdy little white boy on me, now,
Benji.

BENJAMIN
(confronting) What are you going to do?

BESSIE
I'm going to start by standing here and telling you that I am
astonished* and confused here…

*BENJAMIN
Nothing. Like usual.

BESSIE
Ooooh, no you won't bring this drama. Move.

**Bessie starts to chuckle and gets back to sorting as
Benjamin speaks.**

BENJAMIN
Why are you laughing? Well, I'm not sorry. I don't apologize this
time. You're wrong. I said, why are you laughing?

BESSIE
I am laughing because I didn't just beat your behind.

BENJAMIN
Oh, that's real funny.

BESSIE
Quit poking your lips out. I guess it's true.

BENJAMIN
What's true?

BESSIE
Your Nana, as one of her *hundred* reasons why I shouldn't have
married your dad, told me that I would spare the rod and spoil
the child. Marrying him would compromise my ability to be a
legitimate black mother. Old woman's been riding me since I
walked back up in this city. She was right about the rod, at least.

BENJAMIN
This isn't funny at all.

BESSIE
Oh, but it is. Benji. I'm... going to take my ugly dress. I am going to take any of my husband's remaining belongings. I am throwing them out because they don't match *this* new reality here in Massachusetts... here... today... where we are *now*. And whenever I see something that I decide doesn't belong to this place, this life, right now, I am going to get rid of it.

BENJAMIN
I guess Nana was right. You're awfully white all of a sudden. Dad was more black than you.

BESSIE
You'll have to come better than that.

BENJAMIN
All you say about the struggle and the people. He's staying free.

BESSIE
Get out of my way. *Underground* is not free.

BENJAMIN
Underground for what he believes in; and when the going gets tough you just want to throw him away and run back here to hide. You just couldn't take the heat and you had to drag me with you. You want to do it all the easy way.

BESSIE
Easy way? Easy way?

BENJAMIN
That's why we came here.

BESSIE
We came here to start clean. And I'm fit'na clean house for real

right about now. *You want this?* It's **on!** Closets for starters!

Bessie pokes back into the closet and snatches out some choice items.

BESSIE
One red velvet jacket. One pair Birkenstock sandals...

BENJAMIN
That's his Hendrix jacket!

BESSIE
...Get out of the way! GIVE IT HERE! Now, out the window!...

She opens the window and chucks the things outside. She doesn't stop. She throws.

BENJAMIN
Stop! I'm sorry!

BESSIE
Naw, Mama's on a roll...
Collected writings of Mahatma Gandhi...
To Kill a Mockingbird... Out!
Martin Luther King *Letters from a Birmingham Jail*
Five Smooth Stones...

BENJAMIN
PLEASE STOP!

BESSIE
My lord, my lord...
The Family of Man...

BENJAMIN
OKAY, I'M SORRY.

BESSIE
Autobiography of Malcolm X... that stays.

BENJAMIN
WHAT'S WRONG WITH YOU?

BESSIE
Pete Seeger
Joan Baez
Peter, Paul and goddamned miss Mary,

BENJAMIN
He's coming back!

BESSIE
Jimi Hendrix Experience...

Benjamin grabs the record and he and Bessie face off.

BENJAMIN
Mom, he's coming back!!! I swear he is!!!

Bessie stares at him.

BESSIE
Benjamin Turner, come back to reality. We sat in front of that television...

BENJAMIN
Don't start that again...

BESSIE
You sat in front of that TV with me when Jimmy Carter* came on...

*BENJAMIN
Yeah, yeah, yeah! Jimmy Carter... Amnesty... WHATEVER!!!

He could have gotten caught already…

BESSIE
No…

BENJAMIN
He could be in trouble…FBI… what if he tried to find us…

BESSIE
Mail is forwarded.

BENJAMIN
He wouldn't know where to look…

BESSIE
I sent letters to each of the safe houses… All our people in Berkeley know where to find us. It's deeper than all that and you know it.

BENJAMIN
I. KNOW. HE. IS. COMING!

BESSIE
I *don't*. ++ Shut that window.

Benjamin doesn't. Bessie does.

BESSIE
It's cold as hell in here. Benjamin, Benji, look at me. Look at me. We've got to face some facts here. This thing is no piece of cake for either of us. But… bottom line? We've both got school in the morning.

BENJAMIN
I promise he is…

BESSIE
My GOD you get to me! Look at that. **(she surveys the mess**

she's **made on the ground below)** There goes the
neighborhood, hmmm?

BENJAMIN
Mom.

BESSIE
No, this is due time. I just can't believe I carted that junk across
the country in the first place.

BENJAMIN
I promise.

BESSIE
Get right to me.

> **A bell rings. School.**

IN WHICH TERENCE AND BENJAMIN
TALK FOR THE FIRST TIME

**Terence sits on the floor, against a wall inside the
high school, outside the cafeteria. Sounds from the
cafeteria ricochet through the space. Benjamin
sneaks in and tries to peek at what Terence is
drawing.**

BENJAMIN
What are you doing?

> **Terence, slightly startled, closes his sketchpad.**

BENJAMIN
I just want to know what you're doing, that's all.

> **Terence picks up his bag and pencil.**

TERENCE
I'm leaving.

BENJAMIN
Calm down. I didn't mean to scare you.

TERENCE
You didn't.

BENJAMIN
What were you doing? Come on.

TERENCE
I was... um... It's really rough. It's this... Look. About what happened. You shouldn't have done that.

BENJAMIN
You shouldn't let people pick on you like that.

TERENCE
I didn't let them or not let them. It just happens.

BENJAMIN
Getting beat up does not "just happen."

TERENCE
It was... Brian thought I was looking at him and I was but I wasn't really *"looking"* looking at him. I was trying to see his planes refract.

BENJAMIN
His what?

TERENCE
Skin. Light. Water. Planes. It wasn't personal.

BENJAMIN
So that's a good excuse for them to call you a faggot and jump on you?

TERENCE
You're not from here are you?

BENJAMIN
I'm Benji. Turner.

TERENCE
Hi.

BENJAMIN
And you are?

TERENCE
Um. I'm sorry. Terence.

BENJAMIN
Terence?

TERENCE
Terence Long. Where are you from?

BENJAMIN
Not from here. Berkeley. California. Ever been to California?

TERENCE
No. No, I haven't.

BENJAMIN
That's okay. It's not a crime. I guess.

TERENCE
I have cousins though who are out there. They sometimes send oranges and avocados at Christmastime.

BENJAMIN
You'd like it there.

TERENCE
It's not gray like this, I bet.

BENJAMIN
It's gray sometimes. Just different gray, that's all. The sky is...
All... **(he gestures with his hands.)**

TERENCE
It catches the light differently.

BENJAMIN
Yeah. It catches the light differently.

TERENCE
I get it.

BENJAMIN
God that sounds weird—"catches the light."

TERENCE
Yeah.

BENJAMIN
I like it there, anyway. I miss it already.

TERENCE
Why did you move here, if you like it so much in Berkeley? Not
that you shouldn't have, I mean it's great that you're here... I
mean, I don't even know you, but... well, welcome, you know...
um, God...

BENJAMIN
It's cool. I like the snow.

TERENCE
That'll wear off.

BENJAMIN
My Mom says the same thing. She grew up here.

TERENCE
For real?

BENJAMIN
She used to have all kinds of family here and the whole nine. Now it's just us, though. She's enrolled at nursing school. In Holyoke.

TERENCE
Wow.

BENJAMIN
She wanted to do something with her hands.

TERENCE
Why not try gardening, or something like that?

BENJAMIN
Yeah. I guess. Kinda hard in the snow, though.

TERENCE
I hear that.

BENJAMIN
You're gonna have to show me around Springfield, 'cause I really don't know which way is up.

TERENCE
Yeah. No. I mean. Well, there's not a whole lot to see... Ben?

BENJAMIN
Benji.

TERENCE
I should probably warn you, Benji. I'm not too popular around.

BENJAMIN
Neither am I, now.

TERENCE
They won't pick on you though. They think you're crazy.

BENJAMIN
(intrigued) They do?

TERENCE
Yeah. 'Cause you jumped them like that. They don't think twice when they talk about me, it's always "faggot" this and "he wants to suck your dick" and "look at your girlfriend" and stuff like that. But you, they think *you're mental,* like you'll snap or something. That's what they're saying.

BENJAMIN
Really?

TERENCE
You're not crazy, are you?

BENJAMIN
Do I seem like I'm crazy to you?

TERENCE
Well. Kinda. I mean. Anybody who would jump into a fight like that for no reason? Yeah.

BENJAMIN
I had a reason. So what were you drawing? I'm assuming you were drawing.

TERENCE
I'm not going to show you.

BENJAMIN
Well.,. What else do you like? You do sports?

TERENCE
I like to watch tennis.

BENJAMIN
I do martial arts.

TERENCE
Real Bruce Lee stuff?

BENJAMIN
Hardly. I studied karate in Berkeley. My mom's big into self-defense. But I never practiced in a shower. If we were outside when that happened? ... Man, they wouldn't have known what hit 'em.

TERENCE
God. I'm really sorry.++

Benjamin shifts his weight, moving ever so slightly closer.

BENJAMIN
So... how long have you known?

TERENCE
Known what?

BENJAMIN
Known, known.

TERENCE
(tensing up) Look... Uhmmm. You know what? I'm going in there now.

BENJAMIN
I was just asking.

Beat.

TERENCE
It's that obvious?

BENJAMIN
It was the tennis. Dead giveaway.

TERENCE
Oh. My God. You really are crazy.

BENJAMIN
Now, can I see what you were drawing?

TERENCE
Not right now. It's really rough.

BENJAMIN
Come on.

TERENCE
No.

BENJAMIN
Don't make me have to take it from you. One-arm-*Enter-the-Dragon*-style.

TERENCE
That's not fair. I thought you were trying to protect me.

BENJAMIN
Who said that was my reason? But I did take a hit for you—and you booked out of the room. It's the least you could do.

TERENCE
You'll get mad. You'll snap again.

BENJAMIN
Come on.

TERENCE
It's abstract. You won't get it.

> **Benjamin looks at the sketchpad. He moves himself around a little to "feel" the drawing in his body as he observes it.**

BENJAMIN
That's me.

TERENCE
(surprised) You got it.

BENJAMIN
That's outta sight.

TERENCE
How'd you get it? I mean it's...

BENJAMIN
I don't know. I guess, well the lines are all... like this... in here and... then they go...

TERENCE
...up and over and up again and kind of leaning...then *out!* like...**(catches himself, embarrassed)** I wasn't trying to... I just sketch people...

BENJAMIN
I like them.

TERENCE
You do?

BENJAMIN
I think you should do another one of me though. I'll pose. Look. I'm thirsty, I'm gonna go back in and get a drink before lunch is over. You want to come?

TERENCE
With you?

BENJAMIN
Yeah.

TERENCE
Okay. If you're sure.

BENJAMIN
Come on.

TERENCE
You must have a death wish.

BENJAMIN
They won't dare. They think I'm crazy, right?

Orchestral music surges.

Waiting for Giovanni
(excerpt)
by Jewelle Gomez

This is a dream play; it takes place just before the American publication of Jimmy's second novel in 1956. The characters of Jimmy's dream play are living in the moment and they have knowledge of the past, present and the future. The music of Bessie Smith, Clifford Brown and Mahalia Jackson is heard periodically throughout.

Act One, Scene 1

The lights come up. The stage is bare except for large picture frames suspended in front of the rear curtain. The only furniture is a café table, a dinner table and a typewriter table with chair. Jimmy is upstage right looking out of one of the window frames before he turns to the audience. He is smoking a cigarette.

Jimmy: Sometimes when I look out there I catch a glimpse of the city. The one I imagine I'll return to at some time. It is shining with blackness, not day. A dark glistening mass that takes in light, sucking it from everywhere. The windows scowl and glare. The dead eyes of automobiles aim themselves at me and I can't look away. I listen for the sound of the voices of children playing stickball in the streets, or the fractious murmuring of drinking compatriots at sidewalk cafes, or the chant of early morning. But the night has obliterated them. Blues tunes recorded at seventy-eight revolutions per minute drag like dirges played at forty-five. The towering darkness gathers itself against me, fueled by the black lives it's swallowed. And now it wants mine. But then, of course, I blink these dolorous eyes and it's just a city again.

It has been said that what is most important is invisible. The Little Prince hears this more than once in the desert. The Pilot, when he says it, is speaking of friendship, imagination, and possibly of love. But other invisible things are important too: anger, betrayal, hatred, fear. They are equally compelling. In fact, to some, they have the most magnetic appeal. The gravity pull of a small planet.

I don't see myself as one of those who swims in the detritus of vitriol or despair. Nor am I borne above it all on the wings of wild birds. I'm anchored in the dreams that surround me—dreams both found and lost. The city of my childhood, Harlem, was a cornucopia of dreams. Inevitably, as with fruit in a bowl: that which is settled near the bottom, away from the air and light, begins to decay.

Paris? Istanbul? They struggle to rediscover themselves for each generation but now they no longer resemble anything I remember.

This new work, *Giovanni*, is an exploration of the latter. Dreams lost. Paris at its best and its worst. It was to be a fable for our children. Children in the sense of those who come after us. It's a reminder of how impossible it is to live if you cannot live with yourself. But I have no idea what American critics will be reminded of. White men sweating with desire under the hands of a dark man may not be their cup of bouillon.

I preached my first sermon at a young age, and then my last—everything between seems collapsed into a single shout. Since that last sermon I have been writing and moving. Traveling from place to place, examining faces, both the eager and those who turn away. At each moment I believe that my life and my work will be sanctified, but often what I hear is far from approval. I am not really waiting for anyone's approval. Simply scanning the horizon just in case it should appear, mainsail billowing with applause.

I understand that the place to which I imagine I can return—no longer exists. Harlem, Paris, Istanbul are chimera never fading but ever fixed in my soul like photographs or paintings. But no longer the destinations that used to greet me.

When I despair, as I do just at this moment, I remember that I am dramatic but I am not a wallower. The city outside that window changes, the lights play tricks and the skyline shifts but no matter how gloriously beautiful or horribly disfigured the view may be, I am always me inside, looking out. Bearing witness. *(He moves to the typewriter, sits and begins to type.)*

Act One, Scene 5

Lorraine enters singing "We Shall Overcome." There are plates, glasses, flatware on one end of the dining table stage right. She is dressed for the street, perhaps wearing a hat still. Throughout she is setting the table. She goes through a bit of the song then stops, noticing the audience.

Lorraine: *(Singing)* Deep in my heart, I do believe, we shall overcome some day.

I know the song seems somewhat incongruous with the act of setting a table but believe me, to a woman nothing is incongruous. I can't tell you how many times I've sung it. Arms linked, tears in my eyes. Believing every word. Jimmy and I sang that song quite a bit.

I'm certain most of you didn't know it was written by a white man, did you? Woody Guthrie. Not written exactly. It was one of those old gospel songs. He adapted it. Now there was a marcher. Show that Woody Guthrie a cause and he had it in his fist and flying off the strings of his guitar, twenty seconds flat! We all used to sing then. As if the singing might wipe the fear and bitterness off of people's faces. But, there you are. Three hundred years of hatred need a little more than a four-minute melody.

I was just at a memorial. The anniversary of the murder of Emmett Till. And they were singing that song. It made me think about Jimmy… and parties. All the beautiful, laughing tables he's sat at in his life.

Most of the people in that little place were so choked with sorrow they couldn't get the words out. I was choked with irony. How closely tied are sex and blackness in this country? A boy, no more than 15 years old, beaten mercilessly and killed—by grown white men—because he's perceived to be a threat to white womanhood. It's 1956, for God's sake! It's as if our very skin is a signal for rampaging desire! But is it ours or their own? Whatever words Emmett Till may or may not have said to that white girl, that store clerk in Money, Mississippi are irrelevant. Emmett Till had no voice at all. His skin did all the talking.

White men looked at that child and saw sexual desire, sexual outrage, perversion. And I know that is not too far afield from what they see when they look at any of us.

Jimmy thinks of me as "sweet Lorraine." I'm not sure how I feel about that. It puts me somewhere between being the title of an old romantic song and a cloying dessert. Often I don't feel sweet at all, certainly not when sitting in a storefront church singing "We Shall Overcome" for a black woman's murdered son.

But this is not about me. Then it often isn't about me or any of us. Mostly it's about what others want to think of us. It's a cruel act to see your life and motives dissected and interpreted by people wearing dark glasses. You know what I mean—glasses that see me merely in relationship to darkness. For example, when they talk about my play, *A Raisin in the Sun*, I swear sometimes it's like they only saw half the show. Selective dropout. They Moynihan-ed the hell out of it. The whole Walter Lee/Mama conflict gets blown up as if I were personally trying to maintain the "Mammy" myth. One recent critic referred to me as only peripherally a feminist, or some mess like that. Is that because I'm black? How can you be a peripheral feminist? I ask you! Who are these people? *(she shudders)*

When I was sitting, thinking about Emmett Till, singing that song, Jimmy and his new book just popped into my head. He needs to hear from me before the reviews come out because I know how they can be: ridiculously accurate, and painfully untrue. It will be about sex and skin all over again. The critics will be so confused they won't know what to make of how they feel. They'll bumble and stumble all over themselves like freshmen at a school dance. Or, even worse, be silent.

When you try to speak about sexual desire in this country it's as if the mysteries of life had all been annotated for some scholarly text and no one really wants to show anything other than simple prurient interest in them anymore.

I know what it's like to have one's words misread, or under-read or partially read. Whatever the adjectival permutations of being put in your place might be. But Giovanni is a brilliant book. I'm telling you.

Yes, yes, *Another Country* will be brilliant. I don't deny that. It has it all. Elegant, desperate and deep. Musical anguish. I'm particularly found of Ida, aren't you?

But I think *this* book has the palette of dreams and desire. Jimmy is working here in such a subconscious, poetic stream the characters ache on the page. But will they be able to feel it? Correction: "They" with a capital T.

Audre Lorde says "Your silence will not save you." She's still saying it, by the way. Fortunately Jimmy doesn't know the meaning of silence. Even with his need for approval from all over the place. When Langston and Richard criticize his politics and his style Jimmy lashes out like a thunderbolt. More disrespect than I would display toward those gentlemen. But boys, whatever the age or color, will be boys.

It doesn't matter how cleverly they betray him with their condescension or how much the young turks decry "faggotry." We can always put our money on the fact that Jimmy will speak. Will the audience hear is another question?

In *The Little Prince*...the book... someone says: "Quand le mystère est trop im..." Umm... that is: "When the mystery is too overwhelming, you dare not disobey."

Jimmy is saying this too. The mystery of desire draws the characters through their behavior, they cannot disobey. And we should not either. Damn the critics!

She starts to sing "We Shall Overcome" again. Then stops.

In *Jet* magazine they showed pictures of Emmett Till in his casket. I didn't dwell on them. But there is a devastating picture of his mother, Mamie, I can't get out of my head. She went to the train depot to get Emmett's coffin when they sent him back up from Mississippi. She insisted on identifying her son's mutilated body publicly. The barbed wire that had held his corpse down in the water of the Tallahatchie River was no longer wound around his neck. But it was a brutal sight.

In the picture, Emmett Till's mother is collapsing under her grief. Her knees buckle and two men are holding her up. It's her face, though… Her head is thrown back oblivious, her upturned, handsome face is a mask of desolation. A face her son will never see again. That is not a picture that makes me want to sing.

What will it take to overcome this country's need to link our colored skin with fear, this culture's need to make sexual desire a perversion? If we are ever to disentangle the mysteries of desire from darkness and recognize the horizon where darkness and light nestle so closely together, then we all might have a chance to live.

I thought about Emmett Till, his mother Mamie and Jimmy and I needed to have people near me. *(she lays the last fork)* Ah, all set. *(doorbell rings)* There they are. Good.

(lights down on Lorraine)

Act One, Scene 7

Jimmy is downstage left. Lorraine Hansberry sits in shadow at the typewriter center stage. Books are piled up around the typing table, paper is in the typewriter. She is holding a book, but still, although not necessarily watching Jimmy.

Jimmy: *(To audience)* A boy once said to me: You talk like a book. Like a book. I wondered which one he meant. Clearly he hadn't read anything I'd written. There was nothing in his tone to indicate this was not a compliment. He was not being unpleasant, merely stating a fact as he heard it. I looked at his fine face. Rivers of Africa—all tributaries—suffusing those bones and wondered what books he'd read. None. Perhaps the Koran. I couldn't tell by looking in his eyes, or by anything he said really. Simply the observation that I talked like a book. I wasn't that interested in his assessment of my manner of speech, but I couldn't keep the tone out of my mind. There was no childlike wonder, or angry dismissal—the two emotions whose company feels most familiar.

He had simply observed and then not judged. Is that possible? My father's judgment of me has hung like Damocles' sword above my neck since my childhood. Even his death did not dismantle it. The sword's shadow is cool now on my face.

I imagine David, my father, having somehow gone back to school, re-educated himself from brimstone preacher to literary critic and stands there above me. All his mania in place still, and waiting to write the review of my work. To shred my skin from my bones with his fear and fury. This book is like my child, small, delicate and new. Yet I can hear him growling with hunger the moment I stop typing.

I have written so much. Although in the moment it didn't seem so abundant.

I've written things in my head, observations, critiques, ruminations. But I don't remember feeling like my words were a boning knife. But that's the image that comes to mind when I think of some critics. They will either find a place to put me or remove my bones so I can fit into some box they've constructed. I can see myself, neatly aligned like a sardine in a rolltop tin.

(Lorraine laughs heartily from the typewriter and the lights come up. Jimmy turns, startled.)

Jimmy: Sweet Lorraine!

Lorraine: Oh Jimmy, you have such a way with words! *(still laughing)*

Jimmy: *(to audience)* Now did that sound the same as what he said? "I talk like a book."

Lorraine: I keep trying to tell you, Jimmy, don't worry about what they say.

Jimmy: How can I not? I'm adept at appearing not to worry but that's not quite the same thing as not worrying.

Lorraine: Was he a lover?

Jimmy: Who?

Lorraine: They boy who said you spoke like a book?

Jimmy: I suppose.

Lorraine: Good God, Jimmy. So coy. I'm not so bourgeois that I can't think of sex. In fact I've even had some myself.

Jimmy: I never said you were bourgeois.

Lorraine: Yes, but the others do. Ah, what shall we do. You're a "homosexual" and I'm "bourgeois." That takes care of us with dispatch doesn't it.

Jimmy: *(in mock surprise)* I thought you were the homosexual!!!

Lorraine: *(laughing)* That remains to be seen…actually….

(Their laughter is interrupted by the entrance of a black man dressed in a Nehru jacket, a kufi and a disapproving scowl.)

Mighty Real:
A Tribute to Sylvester
(excerpt)
by Djola Branner

Lights up on SYLVESTER'S art deco apartment in San Francisco. Images of Garbo, Dietrich, gold records. And lots of phones.
It's summer, 1988.
DANNY is a white guy, thirty-something.
SYLVESTER is forty-four.
It's months before his death.

DANNY
I've already spoken with Martha Wash, and Jeanie Tracey, and Terri Hinte over at Fantasy Records, and sifted through the archives at the—

SYLVESTER
Archives. You make me sound so old.

DANNY
No, no. I, I don't mean it that way—

SYLVESTER
Who do you work for?

DANNY
I've worked for everybody. The *Times*, L.A. not N.Y., the *Oakland Tribune*. I, I'm freelance. Right now. This article is for the *Chronicle*.

SYLVESTER
That's newsworthy in itself.

DANNY
How's that?

SYLVESTER
The *Chronicle* hasn't printed a word about me since "the death of disco."

DANNY
Ah. The one word associated with your music.

SYLVESTER & DANNY
Disco.

DANNY
And you, your music is so much more than that.

SYLVESTER
Thank you.

DANNY
Disco is really such a small part of what you've done.

SYLVESTER
Thank you for saying that.

DANNY
Of where you've been.

SYLVESTER
But where would we all be without "Mighty Ill"?

DANNY
"Mighty Ill." I like that.

SYLVESTER
Trust me, after ten thousand times, it fits.

DANNY
Ten thousand ... really?

SYLVESTER
(reclining on his chaise lounge)
I may be exaggerating. But not much.

DANNY
(turning on his recorder)
Where do you find the inspiration to sing something ten thousand times?

SYLVESTER
I've been blessed. I've been blessed in many, many ways, but especially with my music. I've always found ... inspiration.

DANNY
You seem like someone with a lot of faith.

SYLVESTER
(seductively)
And it's getting stronger by the minute.

DANNY
I, I'm really interested in the questions they don't ask. Or answers to the questions they don't ask. I mean, what have been some of your favorite experiences, and—

SYLVESTER
(more seductively)
I assume you're talking about my career?

DANNY
Well, yeah. I mean ... whatever.

SYLVESTER
The European tours. I can still sell out there any day of the week. London, Paris, Berlin. Fans aren't as fickle as they are here. They love you genuinely ...
(laughing to himself)

I had one girl follow me from Berlin to Venice, vow to marry me and bear my babies.

DANNY
What did you do?

SYLVESTER
I told her the truth. I said, "I have scattered my seed all over the world. I couldn't possibly pay another dime of child support ..."
(little pause, and then they laugh)
There are ways to let people down gently without crushing them.

DANNY
I'm sure ... unwittingly, you've crushed many hearts.

SYLVESTER
Mmm.

DANNY
What part of your success do you owe to the fact that you're gay?

SYLVESTER
None ... I mean, okay. I'm not stupid. I know that to many people I'm a hero. But I never set out to be. For me it's always been about the music. The music and the glamour. Or the illusion of it. I'd flip through fashion magazines as a kid and put myself into all the pictures. I was Billie, Bessie, Lena—

DANNY
All the greats.

SYLVESTER
All the greats: Sarah, Dinah ... Washington, not Shore.

DANNY
Though I've seen pictures, and you are stunning as a blonde.

SYLVESTER
Mmm. Flattery as they say.

DANNY
Well. Here, here's hoping—

SYLVESTER
One name I'd have to add to that list is Julia Morgan.

DANNY
Your grandmother.

SYLVESTER
(overlapping on "grandmother")
My grandmother. You've done your homework.

DANNY
She sang gospel, right?

SYLVESTER
Gospel, jazz, blues, all of it. But she was a tremendous
influence on me as a person as well as a singer.

DANNY
She was the first person you came out to, right?

SYLVESTER
Whoa. You *have* done your homework. But the real read is: Miss
Julia told *me* that I was gay, honey.

DANNY
How's that?

SYLVESTER
Miss Julia told me. And I denied it.

DANNY
Denied it—?

SYLVESTER

I have always *been*, and will always *be*, too many things to fit into one box.

DANNY

Now, there's a quote.

SYLVESTER

(chuckling to himself)

You know, one of my greatest wishes when I was just starting out was to meet Josephine Baker. And I was fortunate enough to meet her. In Paris. In the early Seventies, and I was actually able to sit and talk with her. And I mean, even just sitting there in the Champs-Elysées she was so ... grand. Such presence. And she said, "The separation between the stage and the audience is very important. Not for the performer, per se, but for the audience. For the illusion that you create. People," she said, "pay for the fantasy." For the illusion of the fantasy that you create from the stage.

DANNY

Do you think your audience knows who you really are?

SYLVESTER

To a certain extent. And honey, what they don't know they make up.

(Sound of "You Will Be The One," an upbeat Nineties house tune.)

(DANNY exits.)
(Video images of SYLVESTER as a kid in Los Angeles.)
(BERNADETTE and BERNADINE enter as the video images fade. They are giggly five year olds chasing each other around their big brother's chaise lounge.)

(SYLVESTER watches as if it's a distant memory.)

MAMA'S VOICE-OVER
Bernadette? Bernadine? Ya'll out of that bathroom yet? I'm sending Doonie in to brush your hair in one minute. You hear me?

BERNADETTE & BERNADINE
Yes, ma'am.

MAMA'S VOICE-OVER
Alright. Ya'll hurry up now. Ain't no sense in being late each and every Sunday.

BERNADETTE
I just love your fur, darling? Where ever did you get it?
BERNADINE
(wearing a towel around her shoulders.)
The latest from Paris. Everybody's wearing them.

BERNADETTE
May I ... touch it?
BERNADINE
Are your hands clean?

BERNADETTE
Yes, of course.
BERNADINE
Are you sure?

BERNADETTE
Cross my heart, and hope to die.
BERNADINE
Alright. But just once.

(BERNADETTE strokes the towel around BERNADINE'S neck.)

BERNADETTE
Oooh.

BERNADETTE & BERNADINE
Awww …

(They giggle.)

SYLVESTER
(as an adolescent, from his chaise lounge)
What did I tell ya'll about getting in my things?!

BERNADETTE
Bernadine started it.
BERNADINE
I did not.

BERNADETTE
Did so.
BERNADINE
Did not.

BERNADETTE
Did so—

SYLVESTER
Well guess who's finishing it …
                    (to BERNADETTE)
Bring me the Dixie Peach.
                    (to BERNADINE)
Bernadine, you're first.

BERNADETTE
(handing SYLVESTER the Dixie Peach)
Doonie?

SYLVESTER
What?

BERNADETTE
I want my hair to look like Lana Turner's.

SYLVESTER
You and me both, darling. You and me both. Bernadine, be still.

(BERNADETTE gets her doll and starts combing its hair.)

SYLVESTER
Girl, what did you do to Barbie's hair?

BERNADINE
She tried to press it.

SYLVESTER
Girl, I told you that was horsehair! You can't press that stuff! You bet not let Mama see that nasty looking thing—

BERNADETTE
Doonie?

SYLVESTER
Lord, today—

BERNADETTE
Doonie?

SYLVESTER
What, girl?

BERNADETTE
Sing us a song.
BERNADINE
Yeah.
BERNADINE & BERNADETTE
Sing us a song.

SYLVESTER
Maybe later—

BERNADINE
Please.
BERNADETTE
Pretty please.
BERNADETTE & BERNADINE
With sugar on top.
BERNADETTE
Sing "Lover Man."

SYLVESTER
(surprised by the suggestion)
"Lover Man"?

BERNADINE
Grandma Morgan sings it.

SYLVESTER
Not in Mama's house, she don't. Bernadine, if you don't sit still your head is gone look like Barbie's!

BERNADETTE
Doonie?

SYLVESTER
Bernadette, if you call my name one more time—

BERNADETTE
(singing melody of "Lover Man" with her own lyrics)
I don't know why
And that is no lie
He won't sing us one song
You know he so wrong ...

SYLVESTER
Giiiiirl.

BERNADETTE & BERNADINE
Pleeeeeeeze.

(Little pause.)

SYLVESTER
(standing up, and singing)
I don't know why but I'm feeling so sad
I long to try something I've never had
Never had no kissing, ooh what I been missing
Lover Man, oh where can you be?

The night is cold and I'm so all alone
I'd give my soul just to call you my own
Got a moon above me with no one to love me
Lover man, oh where can you be?

SYLVESTER
(singing)
I've heard it said—

MAMA'S VOICE-OVER
I know ya'll ain't singing that low-down-bump-and-grind-honky-tonk music in my house on a Sunday morning. Not on the Lord's day. I just know you ain't. My ears must be deceiving me. Doonie?! Doonie?! I know you hear me, boy!

(SYLVESTER, back in present time, lights a cigarette.)

(DANNY enters.)

DANNY
So ... that was it?

SYLVESTER
Pretty much.

DANNY
You left. At fourteen you left home—

SYLVESTER
Thirteen. I was tired of my mama telling me what I could and couldn't do. I never liked my father. Don't know where he is to this day.

DANNY
Where did you go—?

BERNADETTE & BERNADINE
(chanting)
Down by the river where the green grass grows
There stands Doonie without no clothes
Along comes Johnny skipping a rope
His zipper's all down and his thing pops out

(BERNADETTE and BERNADINE chant softly under the scene.)

MAMA'S VOICE-OVER
Doonie? Did you finish combing the twins' hair? Or are ya'll still singing that foolishness? Doonie!? You hear me talking to you, boy?

SYLVESTER
(to DANNY)
It was nonstop. Between the twins, my baby brothers ...
(to MAMA)
I hear you Mama.

MAMA'S VOICE-OVER
You the oldest, now. I need you to help me keep things in order around here. Lord knows them other three little hoodlums ain't no help.

SYLVESTER
(to DANNY)
I was living two lives essentially. One in the streets and ... eventually I just told her.

MAMA'S VOICE-OVER
I need you to make a list of things to pick up at the store after church.

SYLVESTER
(to MAMA)
I like boys, Mama.

MAMA'S VOICE-OVER
I need some buttermilk, some eggs and some more cornmeal.

SYLVESTER
I always have. Liked boys.

MAMA'S VOICE-OVER
And put something nice on for church.

SYLVESTER
Grandma Morgan knew it before I did. She told me I was a ... told me I liked boys when I was five.

MAMA'S VOICE-OVER
You used to dress so nice. Used to be sharp. Sharp as a tack.

SYLVESTER
Mama.

MAMA'S VOICE-OVER
You better pick up some more butter, too.

SYLVESTER
Mama!

(BERNADETTE and BERNADINE stop chanting.)

MAMA'S VOICE-OVER
If you don't like what's going on in my house you can leave, Doonie! You hear me? You can just leave!

(BERNADETTE and BERNADINE exit.)

SYLVESTER
                    (to DANNY)
So I did.

(Sound of a slow, gospel version of "Mighty Real.")

(Lost in memory, SYLVESTER walks the stage as a teenage hustler.)

DANNY
Where did you go?

SYLVESTER
I lived with friends. Strangers. Doing whatever I had to do, wherever I had to do it.

(Little pause.)

DANNY
What, what did you—

(SYLVESTER starts unbuttoning DANNY'S shirt.)

DANNY
Wait, wait, wait—

SYLVESTER
Wait for what?

DANNY
I, I'm not—

SYLVESTER
Whatever I had to do, wherever I had to do it.
(SYLVESTER drops to his knees, and begins to unbuckle DANNY'S pants.)

DANNY
(trying to regain composure)
Is it ... true?

SYLVESTER
You tell *me*—

DANNY
True you, you started singing in the church—?

SYLVESTER
Yes.

DANNY
Palm Lane Church of—

SYLVESTER
(overlapping on "Church of")
Church of God in Christ.

DANNY
God. Christ. Yes.

SYLVESTER
In the city of angels—

DANNY
Is it true about th, the—

SYLVESTER
I was born and raised in the city of angels—

DANNY
The choir director? Th, that he molested you?

(Music out.)

SYLVESTER
(stopping abruptly)
Where did you hear that?

DANNY
You, you mentioned him earlier—

SYLVESTER
Even if I mentioned him, which I'm sure I didn't—

DANNY
You, you said that he was—

SYLVESTER
I've never mentioned him. Publicly. To anybody.

DANNY
I, I read it. Maybe. I must have.

SYLVESTER
Right.

DANNY
I must have ... I'm sorry.

(SYLVESTER starts to exit.)

DANNY
Really. I, I just. Confuse facts sometimes, forget where this one or
that one comes from—

SYLVESTER
You haven't forgotten where the door is, have you?

DANNY
Please. Syl, I apologize—

SYLVESTER
The name is Sylvester.
(SYLVESTER exits.)

DANNY
(calling after SYLVESTER)
I'm sorry!

(Sound of "I (Who Have Nothing)," a driving disco number mournful minor key.)

(Video images of Jimi Hendrix, Vietnam, the Black Panthers Stonewall Inn, etc.)

(DANNY watches.)

(SYLVESTER enters as the video images fade. He has changed into yet another fabulous frock.)

(MARTHA and IZORA enter.)

(SYLVESTER, MARTHA and IZORA sing "I (Who Have Nothing.)"

(SYLVESTER exits.)

(Music out.)

(MARTHA and IZORA exit.)

(A phone rings. And rings.)

(DANNY contemplates answering it.)

DANNY
(calling offstage)
Telephone.

(SYLVESTER enters in his housecoat.)

SYLVESTER
(coughing slightly while answering the phone)
Hello? Hello!?

(The sound of a dial tone is heard.)

(SYLVESTER hangs the phone up, and sits at the vanity. He ignores DANNY.)

DANNY
Th, that happens to me all the time ... practical jokers, ex-girlfriends ... disgruntled interviewees ... that's one of my favorite tunes ... Leiber and Stoller, right? You, you have an amazing way of reinventing old tunes like that. "Cry Me a River." "Lover Man." Th, that first album. Wow. *Scratch My Flower.* Complete with a scratch and sniff patch on the back. And then Bizarre with that rendition of "Steamroller." Simply amazing. I, I must have listened to it a hundred times in the past week ... Look, I, I'm really sorry if I offended you. I think you're incredible, and ... well, I'm the first to admit I don't know my way around this, your world ... very well. By your world I don't mean ... I, I mean the lights, glitter ... I'm a smalltown boy from a small town, and this is all new to me ... this kind of celebrity, I mean. But I really ... need this ... interview ... this job, and ... I'd like to continue ... the interview, I mean. I had no right to ask ... th, this article is about your life and career, both of which are larger than any singular event, and we can talk about anything you want to talk about.

(SYLVESTER stands, and crosses to DANNY.)

DANNY
I mean that. We can talk about anything—

SYLVESTER
(grabs the tape recorder from DANNY, and then ...)

I've been singing since I was three. My grandmother propped me up on soapboxes to sing for company in our living room every Sunday afternoon. And then in our church. I won more childhood competitions than I care to recount, toured the country with our choir, and … yes, it was Reverend Jordan, our choir director, who turned me out at the age of seven … but I was a queen even then so I kinda liked it.
(Little pause.)

DANNY
Th, thank you.

SYLVESTER
Can we move on?

DANNY
Ye, yes, we can.

SYLVESTER
Good.

DANNY
Just … one other question I had about the early days, about your start and—

SYLVESTER
(defiantly)
When I was living on the streets you were either a man or a woman. Either butch or fem. I took the hormones because I … well, I knew what I was. I never wanted the surgery, and the people I was with never seemed to mind. I stopped taking them when I moved up here, because it didn't matter. You can be whatever you want to be in Babylon.
(Little pause.)

DANNY
Thank you, I. Didn't know about the, the … I just wanted to

know more about your San Francisco premiere …
(little pause)
About the Cockettes. I mean, I know they were instrumental in starting your career, and Kreemah Ritz, one of the founding members of the group, is quoted as saying he discovered you—

SYLVESTER
She what?

DANNY
She. He … well. I may be misquoting, but he says he—

SYLVESTER
No, see what she *discovered* was that the Cockettes were a dizzy bunch of stoner-hippie queens who even under my direction couldn't carry a tune in a bucket. *That's* what she discovered.

(A phone rings.)
DANNY
I, I'm probably misquoting—

SYLVESTER
The Cockettes gave me a forum, yes, a showcase, but—

DANNY
That's probably what he meant.

SYLVESTER
I was singing long before Kreemah boarded the little Miss Santa Maria Napa Sonoma Mendocino and set sail for America …
(answering the phone)
I don't know who you are or what game you're playing, but this is not the day, and I am not the one. Do you hear me … *do you hear me?!*

MAMA'S VOICE-OVER
People in Timbuktu can hear you.

SYLVESTER
Hi, Mama. How are you?

MAMA'S VOICE-OVER
Hell of a lot better than you, apparently.

SYLVESTER
I'm sorry.

MAMA'S VOICE OVER
Child, I don't know who you thought I was but I feel sorry for
'em when you catch up with 'em.

(Sound of "Changes," an upbeat gospel number.)

CONTINUED ...

Guess Who Came to Dinner
(a monologue)
by Craig Hickman

The Character
Dessa Rose Flowers, *a Black nurse, mid sixties*

It is 1994. Lights rise on Dessa Rose, the sole customer in the hair salon where her nephew Richie works. She sits waiting for her hair to set. She speaks directly to the audience, as though it is her stylist standing somewhere, unseen, in the salon, listening to her story.

DESSA ROSE:

These tight-dressed heifers is always lookin for a full meal ticket, while these homosexuals don't want nothin but appetizers and will try anythang and everythang on the menu, many times over. That's the majority of folks I see: these little heifers ain't got nothin on their minds but trying to get them some man and don't know no other way except to throw him the goods, and these damn homosexuals who ain't seemed to learn nothin from all these diseases goin round.

My own boy Richie and that boy he's been hangin around with: Lord have mercy, in all my years I ain't felt the need to worry and now *this*. Well, it makes me wanna scream. But I'm too damn old, too damn tired. And besides, I done screamed enough to last this lifetime and a few more down the road.

I suppose I should consider myself lucky, though. When Richie's mama, my sweet baby sister Sadie, passed on some time ago, God rest her soul, I took in her cute little bundle of joy and raised him as my very own. He ain't never really caused me no trouble, but everybody from old Hattie Mae Holierthanthou over at Mt. Zion Baptist, to all the ladies I've played bid whist with over the years, told me that Richie was different somehow. Hattie Mae went so far as to say, "That child sure is *strange* that way. You better watch out for him, Dessa Rose."

Different. Strange that way.

Well, what child wouldn't be different or strange that way if his mama was taken to the Lord before he could barely walk, and he never even saw his daddy. Which was no fault of his. No fault of his daddy's, I mean. That's right: Sadie never even told the man she was pregnant. Now, back in the day, you didn't see womens actin like that: not even tellin the daddy about the bun in they oven. But Sadie, God rest her soul, was always doin things her way. Some might even say she was ahead of her time on some matters. Like most babies of the family, she was the independent one. Now, I know, these days, girls havin babies, babies havin babies, and ain't nobody tellin the daddies till it's way past any time appropriate. Well, I, for one, ain't into all them politics and such, but if this is what women's lib was all about, then we messed up somewheres. Any daddy's better than no daddy, and it's about time we got that through our liberated heads.

Well, I was gone make sure that little boy got it all from me, no matter what my friends were trying to warn me about. Like Mildred. Now, Mildred is good people and all that, and I don't like to talk about folk like they do me sometimes, but Mildred would spit the stupidest mess out her mouth with nary a thought for nobody. She comes 'round the house to drop off her famous coconut cake for Richie's tenth birthday party. She finally got some real respect from the folk down at Mt. Zion after the first time she brought that cake to a bake sale down on the church lot. After she tasted a piece, I thought Sugar Waters was gone start speaking in tongues right out on that parking lot. She fell over. Umh-humh. Yes, she did. A small woman she was not; it took three or four deacons to scrape her off the concrete and hoist her back up on her feet. Most of the congregation out there flocked 'round the table to partake in Mildred's special taste of the Holy Ghost.

The first time Richie laid his lips on that sucker, I could hardly get him to eat regular food. I had to wean him offa that mess for a while. But for his birthday party, I decided to have Mildred make a big one—special too.

She comes in the house with her prize-winning recipe, gives

Richie the once-over, as if she'd never seen him before, and Lord knows he's been up in church with me more times than a heathen, flashes her diamond-studded gold teeth, nearly blinding me back, and declares, "Dessa Rose, *baby*, is you sure that nephew of yours is all right? He so timid and mosta the times he act too sissified for a boy his age. He needs a man around this house. But if that ain't possible, girl, you better find him some boys to play with."

If she only knew.

And it wasn't like Richie was far enough away to even act like he didn't hear Mildred's blasphemin. Old Mildred, or Miss Muffet, like I calls her, to this day, might be able to bake her silly little ass off, but she sure can't see. There was a house full of boys from Richie's school at the party. Well, a couple at least. All right, it was mostly girls, I guess. It was so long ago I can't remember all the details. My memory has been known to play tricks on me. Well, you know, the boy just always seemed to be more comfortable playing with little girls; boys could be so mean at times. I know Richie was a quiet child and all. And Lord knows, my father didn't raise no fool. Do I seem like a fool to you? I knew exactly what little Miss Muffet was trying to say, but I tried not to pay her no mind. I'm sure she thought she meant well.

Doesn't everybody who meddles in other folks' affairs?

It was kinda embarrassing, though. Not that I was ever really *ashamed* of Richie. Disappointed would be more like it. But I would look at him trying to cope without his mama and daddy, and know he was already going through a lot. I don't usually take no mess—don't like to let folks know they gettin to me. You can't let'm see you sweat. I'm sure I've been too kind to most of my friends, and mosta the times folk wanna confuse kindness with weakness, but they don't know how strong I knew I was. Strong enough to protect my boy from ridicule:

I told that bitch to shut up and get the *fuck* out of my house.

That was only *after* I got that delicious cake.

As Richie grew older, I got closer and closer to wantin to find out if he was the way I felt he was. But I had to keep back. Not wantin to push too hard. Try to figure out how Sadie woulda handled it and do the same. And sweet Sadie was one of the most patient womens I ever knew, God rest her soul. So I just figured her little bundle of joy wouldn't want me breathin down his neck tryin to figure out *if* he was, *what* he was doin, with *whom*, and for how long.

Well, when he enrolled in that beauty school, suffice it to say, I didn't have to ask any questions. And it's not like he didn't useda sit down in fronta that TV and watch all them silly beauty pageants when he was growing up. I couldn't see what that child saw in all that fake mess. Of course, this was before anybody thought black was beautiful, so there was nothing but a bunch of skinny white girls prancin around, showin off too much cleavage, wearin way too much makeup. I guess the winners were supposed to do something for the human race and become somebody later on in life.

Whatever.

I knew you didn't need to be no white Miss America to do somethin good for folk. That's why I became a nurse. I got the calling to help people at a really young age. Everybody look at me knew I was gonna be a nurse or doctor, one. Not too many women doctors back in the day, so I always felt like I'd have a better chance at becoming a nurse. Especially since so many folk expected black womens to take care of'm. Daddy always told me and Sadie we could be whatever we wanted to be, something to make Mama proud and respect her memory. Mama died givin birth to Sadie, so whenever Sadie got sick, I took care of her. I was ten years old going on thirty-five. Daddy did the best he could, but it was hard raising two girls all by himself.

All the kids in school useda call me the First Aid Girl 'cause I was always the first one who wanted to and knew how to clean up the little cuts and scrapes a bunch of high energy kids was liable to get during a fifteen-minute recess. I was set up to put the school nurse out of business at the ripe old age of *twelve*. Once, this white girl called me Florence Nightingale. I didn't know who the hell she was, but I figured she musta been somebody special with a name like that.

I started nursing down at Deaconess Hospital in the

emergency room. A lot of trauma. After seventeen years, that wore me out. As much as I felt alive and important, this woman knew when to stop. In the early Eighties, I left all that behind and ended up working at Boston City Hospital in the STD Clinic. I thought there would be less trauma.

That was about the time when all these folks, mostly young boys, started comin in with all kinda diseases. Diseases I hadn't seen the need to treat since I started nursing. Usually, a shot in the butt or a week or two of drugs would cure'm up, but the same ones be back in a matter of weeks or months with something else. I don't wanna bore y'all with the clinical names of these things, but I hadn't seen the likes of this in all my years nursin. Later, I'd see some of the boys I treated walkin around the hospitals with splotches all over their bodies, looking old and skinny. Some were admitted one day, dead the next.

Folks in the business started callin it gay cancer. Gay cancer. I didn't know much at the time, but I knew it was more than some gay cancer. Nobody wanted to say anythang about the street folks, a lot of'm with tracks running all up they arms. I tell you a *fool* knows what that's all about, and it's a damned shame, I tell you, a damned shame. Nobody wanted to say anythang about the young girls and their babies who was comin in with the same symptoms. Nobody wanted to say anythang about that woman who got the blood transfusion. She was a young, white, married woman with three children who turned up in the emergency room with the same kinda pneumonia they found in one of them pregnant prostitutes. I tried to find out all I could, but there wasn't too many places I could read about it that I could really understand.

Then the church started burying all these young black boys. Mt. Zion Baptist Church was having more funerals than revivals and prayer meetings. There was Ronelle from choir. And I'm telling you that boy sang like a bluebird, yes he did. We lost something really special when he passed. And there was Charmain, the organist before Paulie. He could raise the roof off the church the ways he made them organ pipes testify. And then there was Dwayne Mcghee, Arthur and Wanda's only son who had just won a scholarship to Yale that he never got a chance to use. And these boys wasn't being shot up in the head on the streets neither.

Before you knew it, folks started burying sons you never even knew they had.

Right now, there's this frail child that sits in the front pew most Sundays who nobody talks to. If he takes communion, nobody drinks after him. Now it's been *said* that he Hattie Mae's boy, but you'd think the two of them didn't even know each other. Like I said, I don't like to talk about folk like they do me sometimes, but if that there downright uptight righteous woman can't even deal with her own flesh and blood...

Don't get me started.

Being down at that clinic and treatin all those young boys, I got to worryin bout Richie. Like I said, my Daddy didn't raise no fool. Do I seem like a fool to you? I put two and two together real fast. That's when I really wanted to ask Richie some questions. But I kept tellin myself to be patient. I wanted to find out how others was dealin with all of this, but nobody—and I mean nobody—was really talking. Not about the weekly funerals, not about the young girls, not about the babies, not about *nothing*. Even now, we know what's causin AIDS and how folks can keep from getting it, but only a handful of folk in our community wanna talk about it. And for all the information and scoldin I've given out to a bunch of strangers over the past seventeen years, I still can't bring myself to raise it with my own hard-headed boy.

And it's not as if Richie hadn't given me the opportunity to say somethin. He moved outta here not too long ago so he could have some privacy—that's what he says, anyway. He used to bring me by flowers every weekend, but lately, he ain't been comin by as much. He calls to tell me he's been *busy*.

But I know better. So I pushes him on it a little bit. He finally admitted that he been *seein* somebody. "This is the Real Thing, Rosie," he says. That's what he likes to call me. He wants me to meet him.

Humph. Real Thang, my ass. I still can't see how homosexuals can have the Real Thang. I try not to let it matter. But Richie won't let up. Here he is tryin to get me to cook dinner and have'm over.

Now, I ain't no fool. This must be something serious. I don't get how they do things, old fashioned as I can be sometimes, but I know this must be making him happy, because when I do see him, he's walkin round glowin like a pregnant woman.

I do worry, though.

Did I tell you that in the midst of all of this confusion and loss, I became famous? No, not because I was one of a handful of black folk tryin to do anything about AIDS. That woulda been too much like right. This was different. I walked into the Talented Tenth, that black bookstore we had some years back, and staring back at me from the shelf was a book with my name on it in large print.

DESSA ROSE

I like to fell out. I don't know who I was named after, if anybody, and I never known nobody with my name. But then here I was on the cover of a book written by some black girl named Sherley Anne Williams. Well, Alice Walker had nothing but good things to say about it, and since I liked that *Color Purple* so much, I decided to pick up my namesake off the shelf.

Fifteen minutes of fame for a book I didn't even write.

It don't get no better than that.

I finally gave in. I decided to go on and cook dinner for Richie and this Real Thang he was talkin about. I don't know what got into me, whether it was God or the Devil himself. *Whatever* it was, I couldn't beat it. So I used it.

On that Friday, I had a most interesting day at the clinic. My last patient was this young, pale white boy who came in for a gonorrhea treatment. He had it in the rectum. Yes, this may be more than you want to know, but even in the age of AIDS, folks are still gettin gonorrhea in the back side cause they ain't using precautions. Most boys seem to be immune to the shame that goes along with this, especially when I wrinkles my brow. But I could see this boy was different: he was wracked with guilt: so I unwrinkled my brow. I didn't want to get all in his business, but I have to do a brief interview about his recent history of sexual partners anyway so they can come in for treatment. I try to be as understanding as a woman like me can, but I didn't hesitate to have a serious discussion with him about his choices in this day and age.

He didn't really wanna focus in on what all his guilt was about, but I got the feeling it went much further than just not using precautions. But I didn't push. He probably wouldn't tell me any more than I needed to know. Not really my business no how. So I scheduled his test-of-cure appointment, sent him on his way, wrapped things up at the clinic, and went on my way. I had enough of my *own* goin on anyhow. I had to pick up my groceries.

Everything seemed like it wanted to take forever that Friday night. I waited on that bus stop for what seemed an eternity. I swear that bus didn't wanna come, no matter how many cigarettes I lit up. When I finally got to the store, the clerk behind the register, this new girl I'd never seen before, had to check on the prices for nearly everythang I bought. She was slow as molasses in January. I knew I shouldna got in her line. It gave me much more time than I needed to get nervous about dinner. Hell, I went on and splurged a little bit and got me a cab home from the grocery store.

Now, no matter what the situation, I wasn't gonna let no friend of my boy get secondary treatment, so I decided to cook up a nice down-home meal for us: collard greens with smoked turkey—I don't use ham hocks no more, not since my cholesterol has gotten kinda high—country fried chicken, hot water cornbread, candied yams, smothered corn, fried green tomatoes, macaroni and cheese, some hot peppers, a little leftover ham, and sweet potato pie for dessert.

Since everything was takin forever that Friday night, I got a late start: I'm sure you must know that the doorbell rings much earlier than I want it to. I turn down the stove, pull in a good breath, and go to open the door. Richie comes on in, and here comes a skinny little white boy after him. I do a double take and wouldn't you know, it's the same boy I saw not three hours earlier at the clinic. I like to fell out.

You shoulda seen the look on *his* face.

"Rosie—Rosie—*Rosie!*" is all I hear Richie say at first. Once he gets my attention, he says, all proud-like, "Auntie Rosie, this is my lover, Timothy."

Lover? *Humph.* And white at that. You gonna try and tell me? Now you can call me old-fashioned, but I still ain't understandin nothin 'bout men, or womens for all that matter, truly lovin each other in that way. Mavis Mannery told me Agnes Head's boy went off to Washington, D.C. some years back and got married, or somethin like that, in some mass ceremony they had during some political march or rally or some such. And I'm lookin at the two of them wonderin if they gonna go off and...

Let me not even think about that.

Well, you could imagine dinner is much more difficult than I already expected it to be. I forget all about what's on the stove and get to wonderin where Timothy picked up that gonorrhea. I can't let myself even believe it coulda been from Richie. But since Timothy didn't tell me nothin at the clinic, my mind starts to wandering. I know I really shouldn't be gettin into all his business, but my Richie's involved and I have to talk to somebody. So when Richie comes back up in here, don't you dare let on that I told any of this to you, all right? I don't know what I would do if he ever found...Well, he won't. You got that, sweetie?

We go on ahead with dinner as planned, with me and Timothy swallowin much more than the food, while Richie just sits there, still a glowin, oblivious to everything. Honey, they don't write'm like this on them trashy TV shows. Fortunately, I didn't burn any food, and it turns out to be the kind of meal any boy would wanna wrap his lips around. But Timothy looks at his plate like something's growin on it. Richie shoots him a look as if to say, "Don't ask. Just eat." I know my boy can cook, but I'm wondering what, if at all, he's cookin for Timothy, among other things, cause Timothy sure don't look like he had any down-home cooking before.

By now, the pauses is pregnant enough for triplets. My mind is spinnin out of control, and halfway through my chicken I just blurt out: "You know STDs amongst homosexuals are on the rise these days."

Timothy drops his fork and spits out his cornbread. Richie tries to clean up the cornbread but his elbow knocks his wine all over the tablecloth and in his plate. I reach over to try and save his food and get corn gravy all over the front of my new blouse.

It's a mess all right.

"Rosie, this is *not* the appropriate dinner table conversation," Richie says, pretty calm for the situation, which, I must say, surprises me. But I'm even more surprised when I look closely at the two of them: I reckon from how they each react that Richie don't know nothin bout Timothy's little visit to the clinic and I look at Timothy in a completely different way. He excuses himself to go to the bathroom. That's when Richie goes off: "What do you think you're doing? You ain't never brought any of that safe sex preachin at me—*ever*—much less to the dinner table and in front of my new—have you—? I know you care, Rosie. I do. But youneedtosavethatpartylineforthefaggotswho*really*needitandleave meandmineoutofit."

"Now baby, I'm sorry. I don't know what's come over me. I told you this wasn't gone be easy. But I just—Look. Are you bein safe? Ain't no tellin what you might pick up from this here boy," I say. I'm trying my best to watch my mouth. I don't know whether to blurt it all out or not. After so many years of nursing, of course, patient confidentiality keeps my mouth closed about some things easier than others. But my own flesh and blood could already have some infection or might get something from this boy this very night, seein as it takes a couple days for that treatment to get rid of everything, and I feel as if I oughtta be able to say *something*.

Timothy comes back from the bathroom and puts a momentary end to my confusion. He tells Richie he thought it best that he get going. He comes over to me, looks all sheepish in my eyes, and thanks me for the meal. Now, under the circumstances, this is quite gracious, so at least I know he was raised right. He and Richie exchange something over by the door. Richie comes back and tells me that he's leavin too. And I'm left sitting there, alone, with a big old mess on the table.

How many places a day can go.

Richie ain't been back by to see me since. I don't know what to think about any of it. Maybe Richie's the reason why Timothy seemed so guilty. Or maybe even Richie is the one—Oh no, no, no: I can't think that about my boy.

Please don't tell him I told you all of this. But when he comes in tomorrow, please tell him that I miss—well...

No. Don't say nothing.

I just hope my boy's gonna be... all right.

Fade to black.

The Phone Rings
by Samiya Bashir

i answer it.

hear a voice i don't want to recognize. so i play denial. i don't play dumb, stupid, fucking little girl lost or anything, i play some terry mcmillanized superwoman who's been rudely interrupted from a very important business meeting (yeah, so what my lips are meeting—passionately—with a spoonful of häagen-dazs, my eyes meeting—fleetingly—with some bad tv miniseries. fuck you—you peeping tom—who asked you anyway).

i'm screwed. i know from the moment i hear his voice, that nasty, whiny, midwestern squeeze of a voice that i'm screwed. it's like sitting at a freakin world series game (in yankee stadium, surrounded by a sea of blue, wearing a new york cap) trying to act like you don't know who to root for. fuck.

he tells me his name. his "real" name. along with some overdone, melodramatic adoption story about how he finally found his real mama after all those years as an unwanted foster child, and took his real name back cuz his bitch-ass adoptive parents weren't worthy of him blah blah blah ... he didn't have to tell me his old name. his fake name.

i knew it.

chingaderos: little fuckers. they were these little taquitos they whipped up at the mexican restaurant downstairs from the mexican radio station i wound up workin at. they were the best fuckin, 400-lb fattening, nutritionally pointless, delicious damned food i ever ate. i suddenly longed for their satisfying crunch.

this little fucker. he starts talking about how he's been looking all over for me. he's been on the internet. he's asked a million people i haven't known for a million years. he says he lived in the city, my city, for ages; then says he moved back home—

temporarily. he tried to blow himself up into something important. tried to blow me down, using his pathetic inability to find me (evidenced, i guess, by him sitting on the other line of my god damned phone) as some proof of my not really being here.

here i was. for some reason standing with this chingadero on the other line blabbing, and i let him go. he went on and on about the old days, the fun we had, the missing of me i guess he's been struggling with or whatever, and my heart either stopped beating, or punched that motherfucker so fast i couldn't see the fist move. i might have stopped breathing. might not. while he spilled sound i flashed back:

20 years since i last saw this spermicidal accident

20 years since that creaking filthy floor

those splinters poking out of every crevice of that sickening excuse for a flat

that nasty little fucker on top of me

drunk, smelling like milwaukee's best (typical) gone stale and regurgitated

some equally drunk-ass beach blanket dropout named stuart or some shit sitting

on the rotten mattress that served as a sideline

rooting that little fucker on

saw that screaming

heard that tearing

felt that sick feeling all over again

snapped back to *what the fuck is this god damned dimensional fracture calling* me *for?* he's babbling on about getting back together and whatever broke our tight friendship apart. and. and oh yeah, he remembers those years when he was drinking he was kind of an asshole. and. and the last time he remembers seeing me, for some reason, he thinks we were in a fight. but he can't remember what i was mad about. (of course)

chingada.

so i told him.

i told that nasty, evil, punk-ass, sorry-ass sack of larva shit— in my sweetest voice—about the second to the last time i remembered seeing him (the last time i had my boys jump him— which he won't remember). i told that little fuck about that floor, that screaming, all those sick freakish colors and shit, the pain, the häagen-dazs, the stupid fucking miniseries, all the assholes that he is and set me up for.

i told him why his stupid fuckin name was sick, and how come fuck his mother, and why i didn't give a god damned leprechaun's ass zit that he may or may not have written some stupid fucking blurb for some stupid fucking loser band for some random back page of *rolling stone* one time.

i don't think we're going to rekindle any sweet old friendships.

and my stomach felt sick for 2 fuckin days. and i didn't know if it was him, or the rushed memories, or the rest of that night, which was all cookies and cream. and fuck the rest of that sappy, sentimental shit. i don't want to hear it, and this isn't about you. you can see it all in the next god damned miniseries anyway.

Question and Answer
by Alan E. Miller

Question:
Aren't you afraid
of being attacked
out here late at night
looking like that?

Answer:
No, honey,
I put that pussy
in my purse
and come out
fighting like a man.

dyke/warrior-prayers
(a performance piece)
(an excerpt)
by sharon bridgforth

dyke/warrior-prayers is a performance piece that explores
what it is like being a Black/urban/dyke/mother/Ancestral
hearing/Southern-Spirited gurl
it's about walking through shattered images of self
and learning to Love.
dyke/warrior-prayers asks: how can you find Hope in the face
of hate & how can a tortured Soul hear it's own yearnings.
dyke/warrior-prayers is a jazz prayer/a non-linear journey
through the fires of one wo'mn's initiation
in becoming a Spiritual Warrior.

there is drumming.
flowers
without
fragrance/old
people
whispering stories that
slap the smile offa
fools that can't hear
the trees
screaming/runaway
warriors
pound pavement
to get
to the grave   rushing
wondering
between worlds/me
trapped
by
the beat
   beating

sirens
gunshots
and
billboards
  in my head
beat
  beating
insinuating
  ho/treat your wounds
with cigarettes
and
liquor
follow the motels
and
don't look back
  no one sees you anyway
girl
  no one hears you
bulldagga, dyke, bitch
  no one cares/trapped
passing the pipe
  no one sees you
trying to survive/in
  tight spaces
trees are
screaming/the
flowers stank
old people keep
whispering
and
billboards
block
the Sun.

                                        lovve
                                        lovve
                                        lovve

God's breath
between
two people
connecting
lovve
the power
the force
the will
of the
Creatress
lovve
tasking God's children
to
honor
the
Spirit/calling
lovve
in times of
danger
fear
and grief
lovve
in the face of
adversary promises
and threats
lovve
with
the stench of ownership overseeing the space round your head/desecration
annihilation
and segregation hanging/like tomorrow's dismembered/remembering
swaying threads
of time ripped from her place without proper
historical documentation/political representation/monetary
consideration/educational situations/or sexual liberation
there is no excuse
you gots to
lovve.

defeat does not really know your name.
there is blood at the bottom of the sea
bodies that still scream
and anger
plenty of anger   there is no excuse
pick up your
truth/ take aim and
lovve
lovve
lovve
re-write tomorrow
with lovve
there is no escape
from the Blessed responsibility
of understanding
lovve
is the shield and spear of
today's Warrior/ lovve/ lovve
lovve/ it does not matter
how high the hill you live on
how fine the suit you wear
what your arm piece looks like
who you lay with/ or how deep the valley of your righteousness
when they come for the villagers
we
will all be got/ no matter where you choose to stand
God's will is to lovve.

there is
not
enough
language
to explain
how i feel   kiss me
quick
but
don't

ask me
to
hold you/cause
i
don't
know
how
welcome
to my heart.

watch yourself/there
are cobwebs dancing
concrete and half-lit
places   you
are invited
on this dusty journey
but keep
your feelings
to yourself
i am only willing to deal with
my own
disappointment
and grief/in
the name of The Mother
  in the name of The Mother
    in the name of The Mother
fucking misery
mounts me rough/down
the street
across the tracks
they think me
crazy   i
am
only
angry
    and
haunted/in the name of

**The Mother
beat beating
take me
to the drummer/**mommy.
i like it
when you take me
in your mouth
and suck me come/ the way
you move/ me on
top   make me
scream
i like the way you
     open
raise
to my desire
hold my ear tongue/ my
name
squeeze/ moan/ stop

i like
the way you
hold me
soothe me
sleep

**you
are my drum/my
     heart
          beat**

**the connecting force
in my Life/i
want
you**
to
take
me

to the middle
of your belly
and
pulse   place
your open hands
on my mind
breathe me
whole.
i want
you
to call
my name
and
i
will
call
yours.

i will call you
beautiful
the sweet fitting piece of my unclaimed Heart/you
are the fully-blossomed promise
of my tomorrow
unfolding/ unspoken
song/ shifting
me   i
will
call you
my prayer/ my Angel
and
you
can call
me
yours.

i've
been

stalked
  captured
    beaten
and freed

i am a
running deer
haunted
by the threat of danger/you
stopped
me
in my tracks/when i
turned
to face you still
i knew
i wouldn't
need to run
again/i
knew
you'd
feast
me
well.
i want to walk
  through the fire
    in your eyes
      and never leave
        never
          leave
never/leave   in the name of The Mother
the warriors
gave me
a spear and feathers/took
some flesh
and
offered me   holding on
i know

we did not
die/in the name of The Mother the
drum
still
beats
in our
Hearts.

there is drumming.

God
playing   in
my
blood/there
is
drumming
the
beat
beating
of
memory's-time
drowning/laughter
there

is drumming.
though
the village
has
long
been
silenced.

there are trees.

scattered
between

buildings that
block
the Sun/trees
holding the hunted
cry
in the
Moon's embrace
while
waiting
for
change
to
come.

there are flowers.

unfragrant   flowers
stand
in
pavement
bloom-trampled and
rank/there
are
flowers
in the midst of
old people that
shouldn't have
died/telling
stories
before
their
season/there

are

warriors

running/with
asagis and feather misplaced Spirits
ride
the Wind
trying
to get home.

The D-train
by Pamela Sneed

The D-train announces itself
as an orange circle and large D on side windows
In Manhattan, after 59th St. it goes express for 20 minutes
doors don't open
which can be frightening or liberating
depending on how you look.

Summer 1986, I snuck
to my first Lesbian and Gay Pride Parade.
I had just moved to New York
and was living with my friend's Mom and
her three children in a Harlem tenement.
The youngest was an 8 year old named Naima
with long Black braids, and brown skin,
the kind of girl you see staring from pages
of children's books.
Next was Jackie, a preteen athlete
whose room was decorated by statues and trophies
from races she'd won
and last was Perry, their mysterious absentee older
brother
who appeared only after work on Friday nights
to don one fingerless black glove
and go dancing at Manhattan's infamous club
"The Paradise Garage"

This is back when Larry Levan, the greatest house dj was alive
and for Blacks and Latinos from Manhattan,
Brooklyn, The Bronx and beyond
music was a religious experience
Back when New York wasn't so strenuous
rents cheap
jobs 8 hours

computers weren't invented
clubs open from 12 midnight til 2 the next day
and people could afford dancing
12-15 hours
Back when a 27 year old Black man by the name of Michael Stewart
was murdered by police when he allegedly
scrawled graffiti on subway walls
Back when a 66 yr old Black woman named Eleanor Bumpurs
was killed while resisting arrest
Around the time, police were accused
of gang raping 13 yr. old Tawana Brawley
and in Bensonhurst, bat wielding whites
chased a terrified Black teenager
named Michael Griffith to his death on Queens blvd.
This was New York, Pre-AIDS
when I can remember sitting
in the kitchen of a Harlem tenement
and seeing dark tinted letters in a newspaper
announcing an epidemic they called
"GOD'S CURSE ON HOMOSEXUALS"

I was staying in a part of Harlem where   no one
was "trying to hear it if you were Gay"
"The Pologrounds" as they were called
are dangerous projects at the tip of Manhattan
where playgrounds separate each complex
and grown men and teens used to congregate.
Every morning, on my way to college
en route to the subway was a gauntlet
that began with a slow moving elevator
smells of piss and feces in the hallways
through playgrounds
where children would follow behind
to yell epithets and kick glass
Even an 8 year old like Naima
was never allowed by her mother to play outdoors
and it that way for her, us, anyone

living 100 blocks above 59th St.
those projects were a cell.

For uptown Blacks, lower Manhattan was "Babylon"
like the biblical city
where sissys, freaks, and gays lived.
Ripped t-shirts, leather jeans, mesh shirts
with punk overtones were called "Village Style"
Back when Izod-poloshirts with alligators embroidered
over chests,
Luis Vuitton, Gucci bags and gold chains were popular
amongst Harlem youth.
In Harlem, as with any group
there were laws surrounding what you wore
defining whether you belonged or not
and if like in gangs
you challenged codes of behavior
inadvertently commented
or were courageous enough to go your own way...
it may be viewed or treated biblically as a sign
giving others badges
moral authority
and licensing to kill.

This said, you had to be careful riding the D-train
uptown after 59th St.

Every day in the paper there were stories of women
raped and killed in subways, on platforms, in cars, at
nite
anywhere there was isolation.

Leaving the Village, going home
I was fearful of my hairstyle and clothes
targeting attention.
14 years ago, I'd also begun shaving my head
at a time when women with shaved heads were uncommon

and knowing as woman riding the subway uptown
20 minutes
where doors didn't open
with no police
could cost life or belongings,
but some part of me was willing to risk it,
was like the D-train in another sense
I was trying to express freedom
and was never harmed.

People smoked on trains then
snubbed out filters on dirty floors
I smoked to look cool
say "I belonged"
and as a way of masking fear
burning tension
soothe an addictive restlessness
like in the city
on Friday nights
when the work week ended
for relief   on the D-train
as in clubs
there was always music
a passenger who boarded at 59th St.
carrying a boom box
and would start blasting Chaka Khan or "The Message"
like Paradise Garage's Larry Levan at midnight
in full stereo
through the car.

As I was saying, in June 1986
I snuck the Lesbian and Gay Pride Parade.
All year I'd been discovering my gay identity
downtown,
in college, at clubs
all the while living uptown

with a church family
Had my friend's mother suspected
she'd surely have thrown me out and
had already begun eyeing me suspiciously
after reading in the paper about
"God's curse on homosexuals."
At that time, I didn't think of homosexuals as me
as the paper described they were men
frequenting bath houses
stealing into night
who'd forsaken church and God
and that place "The Village" I was running to
was a modern day Sodom and Gomorrah
that would one day bring death and destruction
to all its inhabitants.

Hearing this never stopped me from going there.
Never stopped me from seeking it pleasures
like some voyeuristic tourist.
Somehow I was freer there.
Freer than in Black Harlem.
There were two of me—
One, a Black girl going uptown to a church family.
The other, a burgeoning gay me
dancing Friday and Saturday nights
at the Paradise Garage,
who'd run away from my parents house,
the city of Boston
to become a new me
and that part of me was determined and unafraid.

With all of this said,
after describing the D-train
and my subsequent journey
imagine the other day in 2001, my shock
entering the subway and seeing two signs
in either parts of Black Brooklyn announcing

not God's curse on homosexuals,
but directions to
THE LESBIAN, GAY, BISEXUAL AND
TRANSGENDERED PRIDE
PARADE.
The signs were city issued.
and took me back to a time when
attendees were discreet
snuck to be ourselves
amongst our own people.
Sometimes just traveling 20 or 100 blocks
meant risking humiliation
or death.

And if like me you were going
for the first time in 1986
there were no signs
You might get directions,
but to know exactly where it began
meant guessing,
having to navigate through masses at 59th St.
clamor through eyes, floats, drag queens, dykes on
bikes,
and everything else to find your way
Then having to stand alone,
question,
wonder what group to join
which is always decided
by who's playing the best music
and then following along
hoping to meet new and friendly faces
though inside divided between feelings and cultures
to onlookers, you're an out and proud Queer
rising to the occasion,
and at the best parades
urged on by a squad of cheering fans
you celebrate

newfound identity
as we did in 1986—
by dancing.

homocomin'
by Tim'm T. West

comin' out
comin' out back home
Dallas: Cliffs
where gunshots
were the only noise bold enough
to break disco circles
and red rover bustin'
back where I remember liking
lightskindid girls who ain't like
no nappyheaded niggaz

Little Rock: Highland Court
where few that I knew
have even survived to see me
growed up
beyond daredevil b-boyin
at Fair Park
shooting dice with now or laters
ride or die BMX
way before DMX made it manly

Memphis: the Mississippi
baptism by fire and brimstone
nigg-atin'
hate for faggot-burnin
African booty scratcher
blue black laughter
wailin' back at'cha
be sometime what's the matter…
grammatology sparked in th' dozens,
cousin…

and me now
city-fied and de-fried
apostrophe'd and all
comin' back
on a financial limb not yet severed by
self-doubt or
ain't yet def poetry slammed
and got me a plane ticket
cuz I'm flyer now than dr. buzzard
and I
gone'ta return to red dirt with red dirt
release my breath at some storefront revival
hoping to barter words for a redemptive acceptance
i had no courage to even plead for
at 4, or 14, or 24 even
cuz niggaz like me stay at Bay
or at Brooklyn
with other niggaz who don't return
except behind masks and caricature
lies about lives beyond our livin
back there
dirty dirty
where the words be stuck
back where faggots get struck
if they clockable
and not knowin' the time

and me
hoping for a moment to share
prodigal sun rays with melanin-needy flesh
or anyone willing to open a third ear
hear the reverberation of a rhythm
that boomerangs back
and suggests
my people be there
and haven't forgotten
our breath be connected

haven't dis-remembered
that they need me
in order to see we
see-sawing beyond dust particles
obscuring our relation
and who be
black-tracking thick forest
to find common ground
at some southern crunk
latitude
where I first recognized
my breath and blues

and we can have a nice,
pork-smelly
summer heat monkey-wave,
corn-fed, cornbred
homocomin'
for this prodigal son.

Cornbread Girl
by Imani Henry

She's a long drink of water and then some

corn fed, corn bred
she a meaty gal, one of dem kinda gals that gets stuck up in yer
teeth.
got muscles the size of Egypt
big hand, back broad
heart like the grand canyon.

Older folk say
She ain't right
It ain't natural
the way she be thinkin she is and she thinkin she be
She too big bone, to be squeezin into all that

But Cornbread girl don't mind
She just be sashayin roun
slinky shirt and mini skirt
she don't care
as long as her face smooth and skin tight
and she gets her menses
she fine

Cornbread girl say
Why is everybody so fix-tated on me?
        ...I kinda like it, though

Now, Cornbread girl be a preacher's chile.
 Her Mama's a E VAN GIS TA CAL preacher and she don't
stand for no stuff.

Pastor up there preaching at the pulpit sayin,
NO MAN KNOWETH THE TIME WHEN GOD WILL
DRAW US NIGH
YOU GOTS BE READY CHILREN
YOU GOTS BE READY CHILREN
YOU GOTS BE READY CHILREN

and Cornbread girl come up all late, tiptoein into church
and all in her Sunday best, she slide up into the bench and cross
her legs.
and Cornbread girl's mama look out into the congregation
and see Cornbread girl and start a preachin

SOME YOU ARE LIVING A LIFE OF SIN
SOME OF YOU ARE LIVING
A LIFESTYLE THAT IS A ABOMINATION BEFORE
GOD
BUT IT'S NOT TOO LATE, CHILREN
TO C'MON HOME
C'MON HOME CHILREN
C'MON HOME CHILREN

now Cornbread girl, knew when she was bein preached on
so she fixed her dress and got up right in the middle of her
mama's sermon
and began to
Strut
    And
       Pump
          And
            Strut
              And
              Pump
                    right out the door

Cornbread girl stood up in the parking lot, fannin herself
talkin bout
We all got a right to worship the God of our understanding
Mama, you believe in your god
And my god will believe in Me

but afta that Cornbread girl don't come up into that church no more
she don't want hear no good-time Sunday mornin gospel music
she don't want see no choir singin at Christmas
no talk about new clothes for Easter

when you catch her in the spirit, she say
I dream you know
long for the day,
fienin for it, fightin for it
when the wrong turn Right
when all us chilren can just be

some say she done lay down her cross to pick up a star

But like I said before
Cornbread girl is a preacher's chile
Her Mama's a E VAN GIS TA CAL preacher and she don't stand for
no stuff.

She say
YOU CAN'T HIDE FROM GOD, CHILE
GOD IS WATCHING YOU
AND YOU ARE GONNA HAVE TO PAY FOR YOUR SINS
AND THE WAGES OF SIN IS DEATH

and Cornbread girl say,
I been dead before, mama
Beat down so far til was nothing just but ashes
I lived a lifetime and then some
                              I can die again if I have to

But pastor wasn't haven't it
She say
YOU ARE MY SON
AND   I   DIDN'T RAISE NO FAGGOT

and Cornbread girl take one her big hands and put on her waist
and looked her mama dead in the eye
and say
I may be yer son mama,
But   you   raised   yourself a LESBIAN

and Cornbread girl turned round
                           And
                                Strut
                                   And
                                       Pump

                                        right out the door.

Peculiar Wars
by Renita Martin

I guess every generation got they own peculiar war ta fight. I wasn't nuthin but a baby when I got married. So happy ta be out that lil bitty house. Wife of a preacher! Was so used to fittin myself up in tight spaces, all I wanted was a shotgun house. Mr. Griffin say, "Not for my wife, not no shotgun house." Been in that big white house by the side of the road ever since. And Lawd knows I needed it. Raised thirteen chillen and mo grandchillen than I can count.

And never coulda seent the wars that would come they way.

My baby boy, Claude come runnin up in the house one day talkin bout he was gonna march wit them civil righters. Now, me and Mr. Griffin hadn't never been scared of no white folk. But, we hadn't never had no real need to be round em. Specially marchin, wit our backs to them, they guns, and they mangy dogs.

And it's somethin holy bout birthin babies, so holy that even if you done armed em and you know the war they goin out ta fight is righteous, you'd lay yo own tired black flesh on steamy, slick roads fore you let em go out dere... be every hound dog's mangled milkbone fore you let them white folk turn em on yo babies.

And jes when some folk thought the war had ended. The bullets started flyin again.

But this war is got ta be the most peculiar one yet.

Cause my grandbaby, Darryl, didn't come to me so's I could tell him not ta go out dere. And even if he had, me telling him not ta go wouldna done no good. Cause the war ain't out there no mo.

This peculiar war got my grandbabies runnin in every direction tryna find some peace. When Darryl got killed, Ree Ree couldn't sit still. She say them bullets and drugs is like them electric brooms they got out now. Say they might suck huh up next.

So, she moved up north. Outa that blue choir robe, out the church, put some little nappy, nubby balls in huh head, and bloomed right on out to Boston. Out the closet (like they say on Oprah), outa dem nice girdles I got huh to keep huh figure. Replaced them with no bra. Now, I ain't never seen no woman— feminist or not—who didn't droop. I told huh by the time she git thirty, she gonna be milking huh toes.

She tell me ain't no different for black boys there, ain't no different fa black folks. I told her that if you finds that a apple is rotten on one side, biting the other side of the same apple ain't gonna brang you the fresh taste ya lookin for.

I asked huh, "Why you gotta tell everybody what you is? You know they killin up the gays." She jes say she gotta be. I tole huh—it's a whole lotta ways ta be, and dead is one of em. She jes say, "It's a whole lotta ways ta be dead."

A Year After a Teenager Was Dismembered, Still No Answer
—The New York Times, *February 13, 2006*

Osiris
by Reginald Harris

for Rashawn Brazell

Some blood-red wind
tore you from our arms. Set
your tall limbs along
an iron river, underground.
Brother, mirror, friend,
your dark, scattered seeds
defy desecration, outgrow
this battered city, encircling
our world. Your cut short
promise is

                an open door, a beacon
to lead us on. When we meet,
it is you we hold within each
trembling embrace, the unnamed
Many Thousands Gone unforgotten
in our hearts, souls lifted from
this hate-drenched earth, rising
on your remembered wings.

contributors' notes

Actor and educator **Christopher Adams** hails from Atlanta, Ga. He possesses an M.A. in education from National University, California. His short fiction and essays have been published in *Essence, Shooting Star Review* and *Art & Understanding*. Adams' current work is addressed to the needs of his students, finding a voice for people of color and queer youth.

Warren Adams II lives in Washington, D.C.

Samiya Bashir is the author of *Where the Apple Falls: poems,* a finalist for the Lambda Literary Award; editor of *Best Black Women's Erotica 2* and co-editor of *Role Call: A Generational Anthology of Social & Political Black Literature & Art.* Her poetry, stories, articles, essays and editorial work have been featured in numerous publications, including: *Callaloo; Vibe; Essence; Bum Rush the Page: A Def Poetry Jam; Poetry for the People: A Revolutionary Blueprint; The San Francisco Bay Guardian; Ms. Magazine; Black Issues Book Review; Curve; Lambda Book Report; Contemporary American Women Poets;* and *Best Lesbian Erotica 03.* Bashir is a founding organizer of Fire & Ink: A Writers Festival for GLBT People of African Descent, a board member of the National Black Justice Coalition, and a fellow with the Cave Canem: African-American Poetry Workshop.

Born in Trinidad and raised in New York City, **Cheryl Boyce-Taylor** is the author of three collections of poetry, *Convincing the Body, Night When Moon Follows,* and *Raw Air,* and the spoken word CD, *Mango Pretty.* A visual and teaching artist, she has led writing residencies for Poets House, Poets & Writers, The New York Public Library, TeenSpeak and UrbanwordNYC. Boyce-Taylor holds master's degrees in education and social work.

Djola Branner is an interdisciplinary theater artist who combines movement, sound and light to create compelling portraits for the American stage. Co-founder of the seminal group Pomo Afro

Homos (Postmodern African-American Homosexuals), he toured nationally and internationally with their shows *Fierce Love: Stories from Black Gay Life,* and *Dark Fruit.* He has created such shows as *Sweet Sadie, Homos in the House,* and *Mighty Real: A Tribute to Sylvester,* and contributed to such anthologies as *Here to Dare, Colored Contradictions,* and *Staging Gay Lives.* Branner recently completed an M.F.A. in playwriting at the New School for Drama (formerly known as Actors Studio Drama School); he teaches writing, performance and dance throughout the country.

sharon bridgforth is the Lambda Award-winning author of *the bull-jean stories* and *love conjure/blues,* a performance/novel published by RedBone Press. The premiere performance of *love conjure/blues* was produced by The University of Texas at Austin's Center for African & African American Studies. bridgforth is an Alpert Award Nominee in the Arts in Theatre; her work has been presented nationally at venues, including: The Madame Walker Theatre Center—Indianapolis, Ind; Walker Art Center—Minneapolis, Minn; the Michigan Womyn's Music Festival—Walhalla, Mich; and Highways Performance Space—Santa Monica, Calif. bridgforth has received support from the National Endowment for the Arts Commissioning Program; The National Endowment for the Arts/Theatre Communications Group Playwright in Residence Program; and the Rockefeller Foundation Multi-Arts Production Fund Award. www.sharonbridgforth.com

Tony Ray Brown attended the Other Countries Writing Workshop throughout the mid to late '90s. He also served on the board and was a member of the Other Countries Performance Group. In 1998, he won a New York Foundation for the Arts Artists Fellowship in Fiction Writing ("Living to Live Again" was part of his submission). Currently he works as an attorney in Washington, D.C .

Staceyann Chin is an activist. She has been an out poet and political agitator for as long as she has been a writer. From the first angry rants delivered at the Nuyorican Poets Cafe to one-woman shows off Broadway, to poetry workshops in Denmark and London, to co-writing and performing in the Tony Award-winning *Russell Simmons Def Poetry Jam on Broadway*, Chin writes, speaks and breathes in hopes of a world without poverty, prejudice or injustice. Chin's poems can be found in the anthologies *Soulscript, Skyscrapers, Taxis and Tampons, Poetry Slam, Role Call, Bullets and Butterflies, Dance the Guns to Silence*, and *Cultural Studies: Critical Methodologies*; and her chapbooks, *Wildcat Woman, Stories Surrounding My Coming*, and *Catalogue the Insanity*. Chin has written and performed three critically acclaimed one-woman plays: *Hands Afire, Unspeakable Things* and *Border/Clash*. She is currently working on a memoir to be published by Scribner of Simon & Schuster. Between chapters, there are appearances on various talk shows, a new one-woman show, a CD, reams of unfinished poems, essays, marches and gigs across the globe. The poet/performer/activist/entertainer is desperately trying to create some room to travel to see her sister and to breathe.

Cheryl Clarke published her first poetry as a lesbian in 1977. Since that time she has published four books of poetry. Her most recent books include *After Mecca: Women Poets and the Black Arts Movement* (2005); *The Days of Good Looks: Prose and Poetry*, 1980-2005 (2005); and the forthcoming book of poetry, *Corridors of Nostalgia*.

Peter James Conti (b. December 17, 1975—d. December 16, 2005). Peter was an artist and poet. He shared his art of spoken word on the slam scene as well as with family and friends at a variety of events. He graced the stage at a number of venues including the Nuyorican Poets Café and the Bowery Poetry Club, as well as at colleges and universities around the country, and was a member of the LouderArts Directive. Peter's very presence was theatre as he performed "The Peter Show" upon entering any room.

Carl Cook, poet, teacher, and folk artist. Born in Philadelphia, first began publishing with Gay Sunshine Press in 1978. His first book of poetry appeared in 1993, entitled *The Tranquil Lake of Love*, followed by *Postscripts* in 1995, both published by Vega Press. His poems have also been included in *A Rock Against the Wind*

(Lindsay Patterson, ed.), an anthology of African-American love poems. He continues to teach in the Head Start program in Philadelphia and resides in Sicklerville, N.J. with his adopted son.

Samuel R. Delany is a writer, whose novels include *Dhalgren* (Vintage Books) and *Dark Reflections* (Carroll & Graf). He is also the author of *Times Square Red, Times Square Blue* (NYU Press), and *About Writing* (Wesleyan University Press). Delany is a professor of English and creative writing at Temple University and lives in New York.

Alexis De Veaux, Ph.D., is a poet, short fiction writer, essayist and biographer. Her work has appeared in numerous publications including *Essence, Ms. Magazine, Callaloo* and the *Village Voice*; and anthologies such as *Home Girls: A Black Feminist Anthology; Midnight Birds: Stories by Contemporary Black Women Writers; Children of the Night: The Best Short Stories by Black Writers, 1967 to the Present; Street Lights: Illuminating Tales of the Urban Black Experience; Afrekete: An Anthology of Black Lesbian Writing; Memory of Kin: Stories About Family by Black Writers; does your mama know?, An Anthology of Black Lesbian Coming Out Stories; Liberating Memory, Our Work and Working-Class Consciousness;* and *Mending the World: Stories About Family by Contemporary Black Writers.* Among her works are a fictionalized memoir, *Spirits in the Street* (1973); two award-winning children's books, *Na-ni* (1973) and *An Enchanted Hair Tale* (1987); *Don't Explain*, a biography of Billie Holiday (1980); and two independently published poetry works, *Blue Heat: A Portfolio of Poems and Drawings* (1985) and *Spirit Talk* (1997). She is the author of *Warrior Poet: A Biography of Audre Lorde* (W.W. Norton, 2004). The first biography of the late poet-activist, *Warrior Poet* has won four prestigious awards including the 2005 Zora Neale Hurston/Richard Wright Foundation Legacy Award (Nonfiction) and the 2004 Lambda Literary Foundation Award for Biography. De Veaux is an associate professor of women's studies at the University at Buffalo.

R. Erica Doyle is a writer of Trinidadian descent who lives in New York City. Her work has appeared in numerous journals and anthologies, including *Best American Poetry, Ploughshares, Callaloo, Bum Rush the Page*, and *Ms. Magazine*. She is the recipient of awards and fellowships from the Hurston/Wright and Astraea Foundations and the New York Foundation for the Arts. Doyle is a fellow of Cave Canem, a workshop and retreat for African-American poets.

John Frazier is a poet and teacher. His work has been published in the *Massachusetts Review, Antioch Review, The New Republic* and many other journals and publications. He writes sonnets, aubades and other formalist poems.

Geoffrey Freeman is a writer, actor, dancer, vocalist, and research and development consultant. He attended Hunter College in New York City, where he earned a B.A. (cum laude) in theatre management. While at Hunter, he wrote and staged a reading of his original play, "Meeting My Father," and earned admission to a solo performance workshop taught by Ruby Dee and Ossie Davis; also during this time he became affiliated with Other Countries Writers' Workshop based in New York. Freeman has worked with prominent entertainment and political figures, assisting with organization, legal support, management and fundraising.

Thomas Glave is the author of *Whose Song? and Other Stories* (City Lights); a collection of essays, *Words to Our Now: Imagination and Dissent* (University of Minnesota Press; winner of a 2005 Lambda Literary Award); and editor of the forthcoming anthology *Our Caribbean: A Gathering of Lesbian and Gay Writing from the Antilles* (Duke University Press, 2007). A founding member of the Jamaica Forum for Lesbians, All-Sexuals, and Gays (J-FLAG), he is an associate professor of English and co-director of Latin American and Caribbean Area Studies (LACAS) at SUNY Binghamton.

Jewelle Gomez is the author of seven books including the double Lambda Book Award-winning vampire novel, *The Gilda Stories* and the full-length play based on her novel, *Bones and Ash*, which toured thirteen U.S. cities. She's developing "Waiting for Giovanni" for the stage in collaboration with Harry Waters, Jr. and Arturo Catricala. www.jewellegomez.com

D. Rubin Green is a writer, actor and educator. A native of Detroit, Mich., Green's writings include poetry, essays, works for theater and screenplays, some of which have appeared in *The Columbia Anthology of Gay Literature, Other Countries (Volume 1), Changing Men* magazine, and *Front and Center* magazine. He is currently working on a screenplay based on the Tawana Brawley scandal of the late 1980s. Green received his M.F.A. from the Yale School of Drama, Yale University. He lives and works in Brooklyn, N.Y.

Forrest Hamer is the author of three books of poetry: *Call & Response* (1995), *Middle Ear* (2000), and *Rift* (2007).

Ernest Hardy writes about film and music from his home base of Los Angeles. His criticism has appeared in the *LA Weekly*, the *LA Times, Vibe, The New York Times, Rolling Stone,* the *Source, Millennium Film Journal, Flaunt, Request, Minneapolis City Pages,* and the reference books *1,001 Movies You Must See Before You Die* and *Classic Material: The Hip-Hop Album Guide,* among others. He's written liner notes for *Chuck D Presents: Louder Than a Bomb,* the box-set *Say It Loud: A Celebration of Black Music in America, Curtis Mayfield: Gospel,* and the box-set *Superstars of Seventies Soul;* he is the winner of the 2006 ASCAP-Deems Taylor Award for excellence, honoring his liner notes for the *Chet Baker CD, Career 1952-1988.* A Sundance Fellow and a member of LAFCA (Los Angeles Film Critics Association), he's sat as a juror for the Sundance Film Festival, the San Francisco International Film Festival, the Palm Springs International Short Film Festival and Los Angeles Outfest. He's also co-programmed the FUSION Film Festival in Los Angeles. *Blood Beats: Vol. 2,* the follow-up to critically acclaimed *Blood Beats: Vol. 1,* will be published by RedBone Press in Spring 2007. http://ernesthardy.com

Heralded as one of three Chicago poets for the Twenty-first Century by WBEZ Chicago Public Radio, **Duriel E. Harris** is a co-founder of the Black Took Collective and Poetry Editor for *Obsidian III*. *Drag* (Elixir Press, 2003), her first book, was hailed by *Black Issues Book Review* as one of the best poetry volumes of the year. She is currently at work on *AMNESIAC*, a media art project (poetry volume, DVD, sound recording, web site) funded in part by the University of California Santa Barbara Center for Black Studies Race and Technology Initiative. *AMNESIAC* writings appear or are forthcoming in *Stone Canoe*, *nocturnes*, *The Encyclopedia Project*, *Mixed Blood*, and *The Ringing Ear*. A performing poet/sound artist, Harris is a Cave Canem fellow, recent resident at The MacDowell Colony, and member of the free jazz ensemble Douglas Ewart & Inventions. She teaches English at St. Lawrence University in upstate New York.

what you might want to know about **francine j. harris** is her acceptance into cave canem in 2003. you might care about recent publications including *the furnace, gathering ground*, and poems forthcoming in *mcsweeney's*. you might want to know she is all wound up in the keyholes of a smalltown harmonic, wrestling detroit for a clean blown double note. you may want to know she thinks an artist is just someone whose hand is making. you may not want to hear that she doesn't write poems on the bus. but if it helps the visuals—there's a bridge she used to know in portland serving night after night as sheep.

Laura A. Harris is author of *Notes From a Welfare Queen in the Ivory Tower: poetry, fiction, letters, and essays* (Face to Face Press, 2002), a multi-genre collection that narrates, among other post-modern tales, the paradoxes of a welfare mother making a career in the academy while making continued welfare queen warfare against it. Harris also edited *Femme: Feminists, Lesbians, and Bad Girls* (Routledge, 1997), a collection that sought to more centrally situate femme gender and sexual identities within the domain of queer studies and as paramount to feminist histories. Harris publishes essays in the areas of literary criticism, feminist and queer studies, and African diaspora studies; her work can be found in venues such as *Feminist Review, Journal of Lesbian Studies*, and *African American Review*. Currently she is writing the *Memoirs of Alice B. Jones aka Mrs. Rhinelander*, a novella based on the infamous

1924 Rhinelander annulment suit for racial fraud. Harris is an associate professor in English, world literature, and black studies at Pitzer College; she also teaches community service writing seminars at a residential rehabilitation facility within the California Institution for Women system.

Reginald Harris' *Ten Tongues: Poems* (Three Conditions Press, 2002) was a finalist for the 2003 Lambda Literary Award and *ForeWord* Book of the Year Award. A member of the Systems Department at the Enoch Pratt Free Library in Baltimore, Md., he has received Individual Artist Awards for both Poetry and Fiction from the Maryland State Arts Council. His work has appeared in numerous venues, including *5AM, African-American Review, Gay and Lesbian Review, Sou'wester,* and the *Bum Rush the Page, Gathering Ground: A Reader Celebrating Cave Canem's First Decade,* and *The Ringing Ear: Black Poets Lean South* anthologies.

Since 1993, **Imani Henry** has been a staff organizer at the International Action Center (IAC), where his work has focused on national organizing of communities of color and the lesbian, gay, bisexual and transgender movement toward broader social justice and anti-war campaigns. Henry is the co-founder of Rainbow Flags for Mumia, a coalition of LGBTST people who demand the freedom of African- American political prisoner and journalist Mumia Abu Jamal. As a staff member of The Audre Lorde Project, Henry worked with TransJustice, the first political group of New York City created by and for trans and gender nonconforming people of color. He also serves as the administrator for two national lists for trans people of color— TGPOC and TPOCX. Henry's writing has appeared in several publications, including the Lambda Award-winning *does your mama know?* (RedBone Press) and the newly released *War in Colombia: Made in USA* (IAC). In 2006, Henry's multi-media theatre piece, *B4T (before testosterone),* was presented in Los Angeles at the Highways Performance Space and excerpted as part of the Tranny Road Show and the Fresh Meat Festival. In May 2006, he was invited to the Faroe Islands, where he performed his latest work *Living in the Light* at the Rethinking Nordic Colonialism

Conference. www.geocities.com/imani_henry

Craig Hickman, performance artist, poet, and healer, is the author of *Fumbling Toward Divinity: The Adoption Scriptures*, a 2005 Lambda Literary Award finalist, as well as two other books of poetry and prose. His critically acclaimed solo performance skin & ornaments has been staged around the country and appears in Holly Hughes and David Roman's *o solo homo*. Hickman owns and operates Annabessacook Farm (www.annabessacookfarm.com), a bed and breakfast in Maine, with his husband of nine years.

B.Michael Hunter (aka Bert) was the third child of Sheila Louise Sorden and Bertram Meredith Hunter. A graduate of Brooklyn Technical High School, Adelphi University and Northeastern University School of Law, B.Michael was most proud of his roles as godfather and uncle, as high school teacher at City-As-School Manhattan, and as board officer and major donor of nonprofit organizations including the Audre Lorde Project, Gay Men of African Descent, and Other Countries. He served as managing editor of Other Countries' Lambda Literary Award-winning *Sojourner: Black Gay Voices in the Age of AIDS*, a project which motivated him to test for HIV. His work appears in *One Teacher in Ten, The Road Before Us, Black/Out* with Sheilah Mabry, and *Queerly Classed* with John Manzon-Santos. Born in Hell's Kitchen on 4/15/58, B.Michael died of AIDS in Central Harlem on 1/23/01 at 23:23, at 123 West 117th St., the three-family home he purchased in 2000 just months before his mother's death.

Gale Jackson is a poet, writer, librarian and cultural historian who received a National Endowment for the Arts fellowship for her work in griot traditions and whose writing has appeared in many publications and anthologies including *Callaloo, African American Review, Artist and Influence* and *Essence*. She is the author of *MeDea, Suite for Mozambique, Bridge Suite: Narrative Poems, A Khoisan Tale of Beginnings and Ends*, and *We Stand Our Ground* with Kimiko Hahn and Susan Sherman. She currently serves on the faculty of Goddard College, as poet in residence at The

Secondary School for Journalism and as storyteller in residence at The Hayground School. She lives in Brooklyn, New York.

G. Winston James is a Jamaican-born poet, short fiction writer, essayist and editor. He holds an M.F.A. in fiction from Brooklyn College, City University of New York, and is the author of the poetry collections *The Damaged Good* and the Lambda Literary Award-nominated *Lyric: Poems Along a Broken Road.* A former executive director of Other Countries, James is also co-editor of the historic anthology, *Spirited: Affirming the Soul and Black Gay/Lesbian Identity.*

Cary Alan Johnson, an author and activist, was born and raised in Brooklyn. Johnson is a poet, writer of short fiction and a journalist. His work has appeared in numerous publications including *Other Countries, The Road Before Us, The Greatest Taboo, Freedom in This Village, Gay Travels, James White Review, Agni Review, Changing Men* and *Brother to Brother.* Johnson is currently at work on a novel.

Recent poetry by **Karma Mayet Johnson** has appeared in the anthology *Gathering Ground: A Reader Celebrating Cave Canem's First Decade,* and in literary magazines including *A Gathering of the Tribes, exit the apple,* and *nocturnes (re) view of the literary arts.* Johnson's interdisciplinary performance work has been featured at Washington Performing Arts Society, Woolly Mammoth Theater Company, and the Corcoran Gallery of Art. She teaches at Medgar Evers College in Brooklyn, N.Y. Improvisation and Synaesthesia combine in Johnson's hybrid-genre performances, involving audiences in participatory ritual whose outcomes are unforeseen and whose elements include digital sound, organic matter and collective memory.

Daniel Alexander Jones is the recipient of the prestigious Alpert Award in the Arts in Theatre for 2006. *American Theatre Magazine* named him one of fifteen artists whose work will "change American stages for decades to come." An interdisciplinary artist, Jones' theatre pieces include *Phoenix*

Fabrik, Bel Canto, Earthbirths, Blood:Shock:Boogie and *Cab and Lena.*
Jones has performed nationally in numerous cities including New
York, Minneapolis, Austin, St. Paul, Seattle and Boston and
internationally in London, Dublin, Manchester and Leeds. Jones
is a faculty member with Goddard College's Master of Fine Arts
in Interdisciplinary Arts and is a rotating lecturer in the University
of Texas at Austin's Department of Theatre and Dance. A native
of Massachusetts, Jones lives in New York City.

John R. Keene is the author of the novel *Annotations* (New
Directions, 1995), and, with artwork by Christopher Stackhouse,
of the poetry collection *Seismosis* (1913 Press, 2006). He has
published his fiction, poetry, essays and translations in a wide
array of journals and anthologies. Recipient of many fellowships,
his recent honors include a 2003 Fellowship in Poetry from the
New Jersey State Council on the Arts and a 2005 Mrs. Giles
Whiting Foundation Award in Fiction. A longtime member of
the Dark Room Writers Collective of Cambridge and Boston and
a Graduate Fellow of the Cave Canem Foundation, he is also an
advisory editor of the *Harrington Gay Men's Fiction Quarterly*. He
teaches at Northwestern University.

Renita Martin's writing is a "brash, lyrical, and funny, blend of
poetic lyricism with great storytelling" (*The Boston Herald*); onstage
she is " riveting to watch!" (*The Boston Globe*). Martin's works have
most recently appeared in *Boston Theater Marathon Ten Minute Plays*
(Baker's Plays), *does your mama know?* (RedBone Press), *Ma' Ka:
Diasporic Juks* (Sister Vision Press), *Dykes With Baggage* (Cleis
Press), and *Best Lesbian Erotica* (Cleis Press). After opening to
critical acclaim in Boston, her award-winning play, *Lo She Comes*,
was nominated for Cherry Lane Theatre's Mentor's Project,
appeared in the company's Alternative Reading Series, and at The
New Perspectives Theatre Reading Series. Her "dramedy," *Five
Bottles in a Six Pack*, with bass player Jane Wang, also received its
New York debut at the Cherry Lane; and was also produced by
The National Performers' Network, Brandeis University, and
Boston Women on Top Festival. Martin's play *No Parking* was
produced by The Jungle Theatre in their New Play Reading

Series, and recently her new performance piece, *It Is the Seeing*, was presented by the Pillsbury House Theatre.

Alan E. Miller currently teaches at Berkeley High School in Berkeley, Calif. In addition to his work in the classroom, he has served as vice president and treasurer of his teachers' local, taking special responsibility for his union's Committee on Political Education. He appeared in Marlon Riggs' *Tongues Untied* and has had poems published in numerous journals. When he self-published *at the club*, he read his poems in Atlanta; Washington, D.C.; his hometown of Chicago; New York City; and Los Angeles, San Francisco and Oakland, Calif. In the 1980s, as a member of the San Francisco Bay Area discussion/activist group Black Gay Men United, he helped to organize readings in and around the Bay Area.

Born in Cleveland, Ohio, **Mistinguette** is a graduate of Smith College. Her poems have been anthologized in *Sparking: An Ohio Women's Anthology; does your mama know: Black Lesbian Coming Out Stories; Cave Canem V*, and published in several literary journals. Her poems have been performed in the script of *Natural Boundaries: Poems of Exploration and Imagination* and the film *Poetic Healings*. Two of her plays, *House* and *Freedom in the Air!*, have been produced in Northampton, Mass., where she lives and recently married her partner of eighteen years.

Lisa C. Moore is the founder and editor of RedBone Press, which publishes award-winning work that celebrates the culture of black lesbians and gay men and further promotes understanding between black gays and lesbians and the black mainstream. Moore is currently in production for "sassy b. gonn: Searching for Black Lesbian Elders," a video documentary stemming from her master's research in anthropology (University of Texas, 2000). Moore was also lead organizer of the Fire & Ink writers festival for GLBT people of African descent held at the University of Illinois-Chicago in September 2002; she is currently board president of Fire & Ink. Moore is a former editor of *Lambda Book Report*.

Alphonso Morgan was born in Waterloo, Iowa. He has lived in Minneapolis; Washington, D.C.; Los Angeles; Havana, Cuba; and now Brooklyn, N.Y. He received a B.A. in English literature from Howard University in 1993 and a law degree from Georgetown University in 1996. He worked as an entertainment attorney and music video producer in the late '90s; his first novel, *Sons* (Lane Street Press), was published in 2004. He is currently working on a second novel, *Cubano*, to be released in late 2007.

Bruce Morrow is the co-editor of *Shade: An Anthology of Fiction by Gay Men of African Descent*. His work has appeared in numerous publications, including *The New York Times, Callaloo, Speak My Name, Step into a World, Mama's Boy*, and *Freedom in this Village*.

Jcherry Muhanji:

There is the rhythm of the mother, the suppressed poet, and the worker. There is the rhythm of the first time college student at 46, the activist, and the budding prose writer. There is the dizzying rhythm toward the master's in African American World Studies; the rapid riffs necessary for an interdisciplinary Ph.D. in English, anthropology, and African American studies. There is the rhythm of the doctorate that culminated in a ho-hum novel. But always, always there is the hum of the poet, novelist, and short story writer. Threaded throughout this journey is the continuing base line of travels to China, repeated trips to Cuba, and a harrowing experience in Haiti, and an informative trip to Tijuana—where the rhythm of exploitation in the maquiladoras is palpable.

Suddenly, there was the "stopped time" of the professor that left teaching in the northwest to finish *Detroit*, a novel. Though in the south corner of my mind a creative/ critical piece on jazz, is published—during which a wanna- There is the rhythm of the mother, the suppressed poet, and the worker. There is the rhythm of the first time college student at 46, the activist, and the budding prose writer. There is the dizzying rhythm toward the master's in African American World Studies; the rapid riffs necessary for an interdisciplinary Ph.D. in English, anthropology, and African American studies. There is the rhythm of the doctorate that culminated in a ho-hum novel[1] But always, always there is the hum of the poet, novelist, and short story writer. Threaded throughout this journey is the continuing base line of travels to China, repeated trips to Cuba, and a harrowing experience in Haiti, and an informative trip to Tijuana—where the rhythm of exploitation in the maquiladoras is palpable.

Suddenly, there was the "stopped time" of the professor that left teaching in the northwest to finish *Detroit*, a novel. Though in the south corner of my mind a creative/ critical piece on jazz,[2] is published—during which a wanna- be playwright and performer emerges.[3]

—Strange rhythms these

Jcherry Muhanji

My life has been saved many times by writing.

[1] "Momma Played 1st Chair" (1997)
[2] "Soundtrack" (2003)
[3] Novels in progress, "Detroit," "miles &miles& miles of MILES" as well as a play "Miles After Dark"

Curú Necos-Bloice is a poet, short fiction writer and visual artist who was born in the Dominican Republic and raised in the Bronx, N.Y. Currently living and creating in West Harlem, Neco-Bloice's aspiration is to capture through his work the Dominican Republic of his childhood.

Letta Neely is a blk dyke feminist/womonist committed to the pursuit of liberation for all oppressed peoples. I teach creative writing to adults, young adults and elementary school children. I am a creative writing teacher, an organic gardener and a dissenter of most U.S. government policies, practices, beliefs and superiority complexes. In 1995, I received a New York Foundation for the Arts Fellowship and a Barbara Deming

Money for Women Award. In 1997, The Lesbian and Gay
Political Alliance awarded the Pat Parker Award for Artistic
Freedom to me. I have performed my work around much of the
country. I believe in the omniscient beauty/power of this earth
and her earthlings.

Robert E. Penn writes prose and poetry, and makes
experimental films. Harlem's Gallery M exhibited four of his
short digital films from February 11 to April 29, 2006. Tribeca
Film Festival's 2006 Tribeca All Access program selected his
screenplay, "Sahara Son," as one of fifteen finalists. New York
State Council on the Arts awarded Penn a 2005/2006 Individual
Artist Grant in Film and Video/New Media Technologies to
develop "Test Patterns," a multi-screen film project that
"samples" and "remixes" 1950s educational and public service
films that trained baby boomers in the "American way." Penn
created a short film for Ronald K. Brown/EVIDENCE dance
company's tribute to Nina Simone, "Come Ye," which premiered
in 2003. Penn's short story, "Mike II," appears in *Freedom in This
Village* (E. Lynn Harris, ed., 2005), an anthology of black gay
men's writing. Penn is also the author of *The Gay Men's Wellness
Guide* (Henry Holt & Co., 1998), and a contributor to numerous
other anthologies. www.robertpenn.net

Antonia Randolph lives in Baltimore with her partner and their
cat. This is her first published poem.

Gina Rhodes is the author of *Women of the Unborn City*, a
collection of poetry. She is the co-founder of the Audre Lorde
Women's Poetry Center of Hunter College, and a former member
of the original formation of Kitchen Table: Women of Color
Press. Rhodes has presented her work and facilitated writing
workshops widely within New York City's performance venues
and across the East Coast, including Hunter, Rutgers, Brooklyn,
Smith, Amherst, Harvard, St. John's colleges/universities; and the
Schomburg Center for Research in Black Culture. She has served
as an instructor of poetry and creative writing at Hunter College
and the New School for Social Research. Rhodes' work has been

published widely in such publications as *Between Ourselves; Obsidian, Callaloo; Conditions; Ikon, The Gazette;* and *Olive Tree Review.* Currently, Rhodes is concluding work on her first book-length fiction, *Macaroni & Cheese: A Historical Novel.*

L. Phillip Richardson was one of the originating members of the Other Countries writing collective during its formative years. His work has appeared in its first publication, *Other Countries: Black Gay Voices,* and also in *The Road Before Us,* and *Shade.* He lives and breathes in New York City and Salvador de Bahia, Brazil.

Colin Robinson has been active in Other Countries since its founding. He managed production of *Other Countries: Black Gay Voices,* was the group's voluntary administrator for several of its earliest years, and has played other governance and creative roles. He was New York field producer for the Marlon Riggs film *Tongues Untied;* co-edited *Blackheart 3: The Telling of Us; Black/Out: We Are Family;* and *Think Again;* and led the creation of the Studio Museum in Harlem's first three responses to World AIDS Day/A Day Without Art. The first executive director of both Gay Men of African Descent and the New York State Black Gay Network, he was grand marshal of the 2000 Brooklyn Pride parade, and a founder of Caribbean Pride and the Audre Lorde Project. He has been an LGBT community activist in the United States for over twenty years, more than half of that time as an undocumented immigrant; and he now lives transnationally between Trinidad & Tobago, where he grew up, and Brooklyn.

J.E. Robinson of Alton, Ill., is the author of *Skip Macalester* (Haworth Press, 2006), a BookSense Paperback Pick. He has received the Literary Award in Prose from the Illinois Arts Council and a Pushcart Prize nomination for his essays. His short stories have appeared in *Men on Men 6, Rebel Yell, M2M: New Literary Fiction,* and *Bi Guys,* among other anthologies. He is also a published poet. He teaches history at a community college in Illinois, near St. Louis.

Reverend Ayodele Christopher Dana Rose was an Episcopal priest and an AIDS activist. Born in Baltimore, Rose left home at

15, moving to Los Angeles after struggling with coming out. He put himself through high school, college and graduate school, earning a bachelor's degree from Bishop College in Dallas, Texas, and a Master of Divinity from General Theological Seminary. Rose worked with various community-based and nonprofit organizations in New York City; New Jersey; Philadelphia; and Washington, D.C. In 1991, Rose founded the CenterBridge bereavement program at the Lesbian, Gay, Bisexual & Transgender Community Center in New York City. In 1998, he was ordained by Reverend John Shelby Spong, Bishop of Newark; in 2000, he became vicar at Trinity Episcopal Church in Irvington, N.J., and was education coordinator for The Oasis, a ministry to gay people. He died from complications of kidney disease in New Jersey in August 2006. Dana was 52.

Shawn Stewart Ruff is editor of *Go the Way Your Blood Beats: An Anthology of Lesbian and Gay Fiction by African American Writers*. His novel *Finlater* will be published in summer 2007.

Michelle Sewell is an award- winning screenwriter and poet. When the Jamaican-born artist-activist is not behind the mic, she is behind the scenes organizing and collaborating with other poets and performers. Her work has appeared on NPR, in the anthologies *Campaign to End AIDS* and *Surfacing: Phenomenal Women on Passion, Politics, and Purpose, Port of Harlem Magazine, Sinister Wisdom*, and seeingblack.com. Sewell is the founder of GirlChild Press and has recently released her newest book, *Growing Up Girl: An Anthology of Voices from Marginalized Spaces*. Sewell's script, *Deadliest of the Species*, was named among the top 1,000 screenplays for Project Greenlight. As a co-writer, with Straight, No Chaser Productions, she has penned two well-received projects (*Paper Trail* and *Crumbsnatcher*) and a 40-minute short, *Multitude of Mercies*, that won the 2nd Rap It Up/Black AIDS Short Subject Film Competition. *Multitude of Mercies* aired on BET on World AIDS Day (December 1, 2005) and is currently screenings at various film festivals. The writer/producer is currently in post-production with her short, *Spoiled*, which will air on BET J in January 2007. This will be her directorial debut.

Reginald Shepherd is the editor of *The Iowa Anthology of New American Poetries* (University of Iowa Press, 2004). He is the author of four volumes of poetry, all published by the University of Pittsburgh Press: *Otherhood* (2003), a finalist for the 2004 Lenore Marshall Poetry Prize; *Wrong* (1999); *Angel, Interrupted* (1996); and *Some Are Drowning* (1994), winner of the Associated Writing Programs' Award in Poetry. Pittsburgh will publish his fifth collection, *Fata Morgana*, in spring 2007. His work has appeared in four editions of *The Best American Poetry*, as well as in many other anthologies. He has received grants from the National Endowment for the Arts, the Illinois Arts Council, and the Florida Arts Council, among other awards and honors. Shepherd lives with his partner in Pensacola, Fla.

Carlton Elliott Smith is a minister at First Parish Unitarian Universalist Church of Arlington, Mass. As a writer for Religion News Service, he was nationally syndicated by *The New York Times*. He is currently completing his first novel, to be released in 2007. A native of northern Mississippi, he's lived in Washington, D.C.; New York City; and Oakland, Calif.; and studied in France and Switzerland. He can be reached at toomanythings@mac.com.

Pamela Sneed is the winner of the 2006 BAX award. She has toured internationally and domestically and has headlined the New Work Now fest at the Public Theater in New York City. She is the author of *Imagine Being More Afraid of Freedom Than Slavery* and the new manuscript, *America Ain't Ready*. She has been featured in *The New York Times Magazine*, the *Source*, *Time Out*, *Bomb*, *Next*, *VIBE*, *HX*, *Off the Record by Karl Lagerfeld*, and on the cover of *New York Magazine*.

Barbara Stephen was born in Belize, and came to live in the United States in 1973. She began writing as a pen pal at age 8, and has kept a journal for many, many years. Through trials and tribulations, she stopped writing for many years, but started again after being invited by Geoffrey Freeman to an Other Countries workshop, where she began "Cycles." After many critiques, writes and rewrites, "Cycles" was born.

Duncan E. Teague, an Atlantan since 1984, has poetry published in the anthologies *The Road Before Us: 100 Black Gay Poets* edited by Assotto Saint; and *The Spirit in the Word: Moving People Through Poetry* by the Daimler Chrysler Corporation. As a performing artist, Teague is the senior third of The ADODI Muse: A Gay Negro Ensemble. The ADODI Muse have performed their poetry as theater nationally for over ten years, and produced the CD *Ain't Got Sense Enuf to Be 'Shamed* (2004) and chapbook *Everything Must Go* (2000). The ensemble includes Anthony Antoine and Malik M.L. Williams. Teague is also a playwright, having co-written *Lotte's Dream*, a musical, with Andy Ditzler, first performed at Clayton College and State University, February 2004. Teague is featured in the books *Sex Between Men* by Doug Sadonick, *Culture of Desire* by Frank Browning, and *Moving On* by Dan Hazel. Teague has been with his husband, David J. Thurman, since 1994.

Born and raised in the New Jersey/New York area, **Jerry Thompson** traveled across country on Greyhound for a year before settling in the Bay Area. He is an accomplished violinist, playwright and poet. His works have appeared in *Zyzzyva, James White Review,* and *Freedom in This Village: Twenty-Five Years of Black Gay Men's Writing* (edited by E. Lynn Harris, 2005); he is also co-author of *Black Artists in Oakland* (Arcadia Publishing). Thompson was the owner of Black Spring Books, an independent full-service bookstore that closed in 2001. He is the creator and organizer of the original Sister Circle Reading Series in San Francisco. Currently, Thompson works as community relations manager for Cody's Books in Berkeley, and is writing a memoir, *Nobody Knows I'm Here.*

Robert Vazquez-Pacheco is a middle-aged Nuyorican gay man currently living in Harlem. His writings range from nonfiction to fiction, published in venues as diverse as *Corpus; Besame Mucho: New Gay Latino Fiction; Sojourner: Black Gay Voices in the Age of AIDS;* and *Fresh Talk, Daring Gazes: Conversations on Asian American Art.* Working with the AIDS activist art collective Gran Fury, he helped create some of the most iconic artwork of the Nineties. An autodidact and jack of all trades, he has been an organizer, educator, AIDS activist, nonprofit bureaucrat, poet/performer, social commentator and overall loose canon.

Storme Webber is an innovative and dynamic writer, spoken word artist and vocalist. Webber's art arises from seeking the creative manifestation of hybrid identities. Drawing from her African/Native American roots, her working-class lesbian family and her international artist's journey she forges a voice and a story like none other. Webber's work is featured in the documentary *Venus Boyz*, she has also worked widely as a performer in film, television, radio and theater in the United Kingdom, Germany, the Netherlands, Brazil and the United States. She is currently working on her manuscript of narrative nonfiction, "Wild Tales of a Renegade Halfbreed Bulldagger." Inquiries welcome to stormepoet@hotmail.com.

Tim'm T. West is an author/publisher, poet, emcee, scholar and activist who in 1999 co-founded Deep Dickollective (DDC). In 2003 he released a critically acclaimed poetic memoir, *Red Dirt Revival;* in 2005 a chapbook *BARE*; and will release his second full-length book, *Flirting*, in early 2007. Musically, he released his solo debut, *Songs from Red Dirt* on Cellular Records; West is also preparing for the release of *Blakkboy Blue(s)*, its highly anticipated follow-up and *On Some Other*, DDC's third full-studio album project. A cultural critic, he is widely published in academic and literary anthologies, journals, and other publications. West is also featured in two critically acclaimed hip-hop documentaries: Alex Hinton's *Pick Up the Mic*, and Byron Hurt's *Beyond Beats and Rhymes*. He resides in Washington, D.C.

Marvin K. White, author of the Lambda Literary Award-nominated collections of poetry *last rights* and *nothin' ugly fly* (RedBone Press), is a poet, performer, playwright, visual artist as well as a community arts organizer. His poetry has been anthologized in *The Road Before Us: 100 Black Gay Poets; My Brothers Keeper; Gents, Bad Boys and Barbarians: New Gay Writing; Things Shaped in Passing; Sojourner: Writing in the Age of AIDS; Bum Rush the Page; Role Call;* and *Think Again*, as well as other local and national publications. A former member of the critically acclaimed Pomo

Afro Homos, he has led creative arts and writing workshops from inner city elementary schools to youth centers for runaway kids to black gay youth support groups. He is co-founder of B/GLAM (Black Gay Letters and Arts Movement), an organization whose goal is to preserve, present and incubate black gay artistic expressions. www.marvinkwhite.com.

malik m.l. williams hails from Detroit; he relocated to Atlanta in 1991. Williams is the HIV prevention counselor at AID Atlanta, and founder of Brotha Love Images, an affirming photography studio featuring beautiful black men. A writer and public speaker, his performances with ADODI Muse have led to credits with writer-directors Sonya Hemphill, Kalvin Burnett and Lynwoodt Jenkins. His writing has been in *Poets Journal, 2nd Read, Rolling Out Urbanstyle Weekly, Clikque* magazine and the anthology *The Spirit in the Words* (2000). Williams is concluding his first novel, and working on a self-help book about gay male relationships. www.brothaloveimages.com

Bil Wright is the author of two novels, the critically acclaimed *Sunday You Learn How to Box* and *One Foot in Love*. His third novel, *When the Black Girl Sings*, will be published by Simon & Schuster in fall 2007. His poetry and short prose have appeared in anthologies such as *Black Like Us, Tough Acts to Follow and Black Silk*, among others.

Eva Yaa Asantewaa's creative writing has appeared in various journals and anthologies, including *The Zenith of Desire: Contemporary Lesbian Poems about Sex* (Crown), *does your mama know? An Anthology of Black Lesbian Coming Out Stories* (RedBone Press), *An Eye for An Eye Makes the Whole World Blind: Poets on 9/11* (Regent Press), and *Spirited: Affirming the Soul and Black Gay/Lesbian Identity* (RedBone Press). She is also a critic and journalist, specializing in dance, theater, and performance art, published since 1976—most notably in *Dance Magazine, Soho News*, the *Village Voice, The New York Times, The Philadelphia Inquirer,* and *Gay City News*. Yaa Asantewaa maintains a private practice in psychic counseling, working with Tarot and other transformative modalities. http://mysite.verizon.net/magickaleva/

PERMISSIONS

ABOUT THE EDITORS

G. Winston James is a Jamaican-born poet, short fiction writer, essayist and editor. He holds an M.F.A. in fiction from Brooklyn College, City University of New York, and is the author of the poetry collections *The Damaged Good* and the Lambda Literary Award-nominated *Lyric: Poems Along a Broken Road.* A former executive director of Other Countries, James is also co-editor of the historic anthology, *Spirited: Affirming the Soul and Black Gay/Lesbian Identity.*

Founded in New York City in 1986, **Other Countries** is an organization of writers and artists dedicated to the development, dissemination and preservation of literature and other forms of cultural expression of gay men of African heritage.

Other titles from RedBone Press include:

does your mama know? An Anthology of Black Lesbian Coming Out Stories, ed. by Lisa C. Moore
(ISBN 0-9656659-0-9) / $19.95

the bull-jean stories, by Sharon Bridgforth
(ISBN 0-9656659-1-7) / $12.00

the bull-jean stories (Audio CD), by Sharon Bridgforth
(ISBN 0-9656659-2-5) / $12.99

last rights, by Marvin K. White
(ISBN 0-9656659-4-1) / $14.00

nothin' ugly fly, by Marvin K. White
(ISBN 0-9656659-5-X) / $14.00

love conjure/blues, by Sharon Bridgforth
(ISBN 0-9656659-6-8) / $14.00

Where the Apple Falls, by Samiya Bashir
(ISBN 0-9656659-7-6) / $14.00

Spirited: Affirming the Soul and Black Gay/Lesbian Identity, edited by G. Winston James and Lisa C. Moore
(ISBN 0-9656659-3-3) / $16.95

Blood Beats: Vol. 1 / demos, remixes & extended versions, by Ernest Hardy
(ISBN 0-9656659-8-4) / $19.95

Erzulie's Skirt, by Ana-Maurine Lara
(ISBN 0-9786251-0-2) / $15.00

You can buy RedBone Press titles at your local independent bookseller, or order them directly from the publisher (RedBone Press, P.O. Box 15571, Washington, DC 20003).

Please include $2.50 shipping for the first book and $1.00 for each additional book.